W9-BAX-107

• Journey into Revolution

JOURNEY INTO REVOLUTION

Petrograd, 1917-1918

by
ALBERT RHYS WILLIAMS

Edited by
LUCITA WILLIAMS

Foreword by
JOSEPHINE HERBST

QUADRANGLE BOOKS
Chicago · 1969

Dedicated to the memory of
Mary E. Dreier

Library of Congress Catalog Card Number: 68-26450

Editor's Note

Albert Rhys Williams was born in Greenwich, Ohio, September 28, 1883. He was the son of a Congregational minister who served churches in rural sections of Ohio, New York, and Pennsylvania. After graduating from high school in Hancock, New York, at the age of fourteen, too young for college, he worked in a sawmill and lumber yard in Apex, New York, and in a haberdashery in Ohio.

At seventeen he entered Marietta College in Ohio, where he became the outstanding speaker and debater of his class, one of the editors of the college newspaper, captain of the basketball team, and president of the Athletic Organization. While in Marietta he helped organize the first retail clerks' union in the country under the auspices of the American Federation of Labor. His valedictory address upon his graduation in 1904 was entitled "Altruism and Egotism in Politics."

Rhys, as he was called in later years, was twenty-one when he entered Hartford Theological Seminary in Connecticut. While there he persuaded the editor of the *Hartford Evening Post* to let him write and edit a regular column on labor affairs. He received his "license" for preaching in 1907, graduating with high honors and a fellowship to Cambridge University, England, and the University of Marburg, Germany, for 1907–1908. That summer, before leaving for Europe, he served at the Spring Street Presbyterian Church settlement in New York City, where, assisted by Norman Thomas, he organized debates in the Men's League.

Returning from Europe, Williams campaigned for Eugene Debs, the Socialist presidential candidate, in 1908. For the next seven years he served as minister of Maverick Congregational Church in east Boston's working-class district. He was in Europe on leave of absence when the First World War broke out, and became a correspondent for *The Outlook* magazine.

He was nearly shot when arrested and falsely accused by the Germans of being a British spy.

Williams lectured on the Chautauqua circuit upon his return to America, and in 1917 he published *In the Claws of the German Eagle* about his experiences in the war. The book's favorable reception influenced him to become a writer instead of returning to Maverick Church. After the overthrow of the Tsar's regime in Russia, he went to Petrograd in June 1917 as a correspondent for the *New York Evening Post*.

When he returned to San Francisco from Vladivostok in September 1918, he wrote and spoke throughout the country against American intervention in the Soviet Union. The next year he published two pamphlets, *76 Questions and Answers on the Bolsheviks and the Soviets* and *Soviet Russia and Siberia,* which sold in the millions of copies, and a book, *Lenin: The Man and His Work,* which was the first personal biography to be published in America. Williams' *Through the Russian Revolution,* his memoir of events in 1917–1918, appeared in 1921.

He returned to Russia in 1922 and the next year we were married. I had met Rhys in 1919 in New York City, and had come to Moscow to do a film sponsored by the Quakers to raise funds for famine relief. Until 1928 Williams traveled from Archangel to the Caucasus, into countless "dark" villages in the hinterland, gathering material for a book about the peasants and observing the impact of the Revolution on age-old mores and customs. The stories that grew out of his journey were published in *The Atlantic Monthly, Asia, The New Republic, The Nation,* and other magazines, and eventuated in the book *The Russian Land,* published in 1928, which many consider his best work.

In 1929, a son, Rhys, was born. The family moved to Cedar, Vancouver Island, Canada, then to Carmel, California, in 1932. Throughout the thirties Williams continued to lecture and write about the Soviet Union, and made two trips there in 1930 and 1937. In the forties and during the later years of the Stalin era, he lived and wrote at Cedar, or in Ossining, New York.

He paid a final visit to Moscow in 1959, having been invited by the Soviet leaders after writing an article of congratulation upon the launching of Sputnik in 1957. Back in Ossining he assembled his wealth of notes and manuscripts and enthusiastically began to write this present book. He was now the only living American eyewitness and participant in the October Revolution. He had known Lenin and the second-echelon Bolsheviks (whom he called Russian-Americans) who had escaped to the United States during the Tsar's regime and had returned to Russia in 1917.

When Rhys died in February 1962, he left his book incomplete. Having lived and worked with him for forty years, and having helped him with this manuscript, I naturally dedicated myself to completing it. I made three trips to the Soviet Union to consult friends and libraries. I am grateful to many friends and scholars for their encouragement and invaluable help in preparing the manuscript, and in particular to Rhys and Eleanor Williams of Boston; Ivan R. Dee of Quadrangle Books; Charles A. Pearce; William Appleman Williams; Margaret I. Lamont and Corliss Lamont; Frances Adams Gumberg; Bernard Koten of the New York University Libraries; Savva Dangoulov and Svetlana Litvinov of Foreign Literature, Moscow; B. P. Kanevsky of the Lenin Library, Moscow; and most of all to Virginia Marberry.

In this final tribute, Rhys did not spare himself. Because of his dream for a new world with freedom and peace, I hope the spirit of the people in the Russian Revolution will come alive in this book.

LUCITA WILLIAMS

Boston, Massachusetts
February 1969

Foreword

by Josephine Herbst

Journey into Revolution is the story of a young American's confrontation with the great revolution of the twentieth century, the Revolution in Russia in 1917. One may ask why such a work is so timely *now*, when the event is more than fifty years in the distance. Rhys Williams might say that Revolution set the pace for all the revolutionary movements to follow, but, whether you agree with him or not, this is the voice of a thoughtful man who often sounds closer to the dissenting voices of militant students from around the world in the late sixties than the voices of their living and often censorious elder kin.

Though this book was pulled together from voluminous beginnings and multiple notes after Williams' death in 1962, the voice is the same voice that spoke in his eyewitness account of the turbulent days of 1917–1918, when he had come from Russia across Siberia to Vladivostok; had taken ship to America when young American soldiers were landing for the Allied Interventionist war against the new regime; had been confiscated of his papers and the first draft of *Through the Russian Revolution* in Honolulu and San Francisco; and had met, head on, the interrogators for Washington officialdom who wanted to know about himself, the Bolsheviks, and his role as an activist in the October Revolution.

It is the same clear, confident, hot voice that sounded from the pages of *Through the Russian Revolution,* talking about the time, the events of those days, but with many insights added—the thoughtful adumbrations growing out of memory; the bits from his old notes that add a substantial detail, a color, a characterization skipped in the earlier work; and many citations from research libraries to back up his original findings or to correct others. But the new account really takes on full body with the excerpts from his journals of his dialogues with John Reed, his compatriot and fellow revolutionary in Petrograd, and where the language becomes the excited, nervous, idiomatic debate between two very American young men, both ardent and questioning, both open to doubt and conviction, and at the very center of what was to be for each the great authentic experience of a lifetime.

For Williams, the lifetime was to be a long one. For John Reed, Russia was to be the end of the road; he was to write *Ten Days That Shook the World,* to proclaim himself a communist, to die of typhus in Moscow, and to be buried under the Kremlin Wall. Different as the two men were in background and styles of life, they were alike in interpreting the events of their activist days during the October Revolution. In a deeper sense, their bottom views were not of the made-in-Russia type at all, but had been shaped in a pre-war America where, as international socialists, each, in his own way, had engaged in the struggles of a submerged working class for decent hours and decent pay, and in the course of which the major goal had been no less than a thoroughgoing social transformation.

It may be news to some of the young campus rebels to learn that demands for fundamental structural changes in American society were sounded so long ago. Or that, before the First World War, the radical movement had laid down deep roots in the United States, in spite of many obstacles from within and from without. In 1912 the Socialist press claimed 323 English- and foreign-language publications in the United States with a total circulation of more than two million. The largest of these newspapers, *The Appeal to Reason,* was so well distributed across the country that it was possible, before the war, for a librarian in my home town in Iowa to hand to me, a school kid and avid reader, copies of *The Masses* and *The Appeal to Reason,* and the literary magazine *The Little Review,* which, in promoting the aesthetics of modern art and literature, was by no means alienated from its more politicized counterparts.

Now, in the sixties, historians have begun to unravel some of the buried complexities, the diversities, of the egalitarian society of those pre-war days, when the early years of the century produced not only "new history" and brilliant theorists like Thorstein Veblen, but artistic awakenings in Greenwich Village and Harlem. The socialists, the trade unionists, the pragmatists, the muckrakers, the new generation of sociologists seemed to be converging and even uniting in their criticism of American society, and their accents were repeated and confirmed by novelists and poets—by Dreiser and Sherwood Anderson, by Frank Norris and Henry Fuller, the early Carl Sandburg, and many others.

In the historic textile workers' strike at Lawrence, Massachusetts, in 1912, led by Bill Haywood, leader of the IWW, it was possible for Socialists and AFL trade unionists to throw their weight behind a cause that transcended Haywood's militant tactics of direct action, sabotage, and the general strike.

And for all the factional strife that divided the IWW, even before our entry into World War I, their refusal to identify with wartime industrial capitalism made them brothers in jail with the intransigent Socialists when the War for Democracy was finally proclaimed.

When news of the overthrow of tsarism in Russia was followed by reports of the emergence in Petrograd of a uniquely revolutionary parliament called the Soviet of Workers', Soldiers', and Peasants' Deputies, Rhys Williams resolved to go to Russia to see for himself. It was in February 1917. President Wilson had been maneuvering to enter the war, but a despotic Tsar as an ally in a War for Democracy was an embarrassment. The February Revolution took Wilson off the hook; the United States entered the war in April. By May, Williams had picked up a journalist's assignment from the *New York Evening Post;* had interviewed and been briefed by representatives of the various political parties active in the Revolution; and had collected dozens of letters to members of the Provisional Government and the Soviet—Miliukov, Kerensky, Rodzianko. More important, he had letters of recommendation from the editors of *Novy Mir,* a Russian socialist paper in New York which had once counted among its contributors Trotsky and Bukharin, the Bolsheviks.

You might say that Williams' preparations were those any professional journalist might undertake to equip himself for a competent, "objective" survey of a notable world event. But Williams was no neophyte to politics, economics, and social history, or to war. By the time he embarked on his mission to Russia he had accumulated through the years a peculiarly rich bag of assorted experiences—personal involvements with industrial strife and infinitely varied relationships with people in every walk of life. He had lived abroad in England and Germany; had marched with the German Army into Belgium as an accredited correspondent of the American *Outlook* magazine; had been arrested and very nearly shot as a British spy; had been minister of the Congregational Maverick Church in East Boston, a working-class district; had become a Chautauqua lecturer; but *mostly* he had studied, studied hard, and had observed the way people lived and the way events operated upon their lives—and how people's actions could alter the press of events.

In a way, his total experience up to the time of the Revolutionary days in Russia was no more, no less than the pre-history to the major event of his time, no more than a prelude to his own entry into that history. But preparations are important and may be so prejudicial as to alienate one from the major event. In Williams' case he had accumulated, fortuitously, the right baggage for his role.

As the son of a father who came of a long line of Welsh miners and who, as a young boy from Wales, had begun to work in the mines before he qualified for the ministry, Rhys Williams had seen not only the raw edges of human existence but had partaken of rural delights in the little towns where his father was a minister to often needy congregations. His mother had also been born in Wales and had come to the United States as a young girl; she was to marry a minister and to be a mother to four sons, all of whom followed the ministry. Her own forebears had followed that calling in Wales, and the Welsh heritage was bred in the bone. There was a wild Welsh strain in the Williams clan, a fierce love of independence, an instinctive rebelliousness, a love of learning and of the arts, a passion for song and stories, all of which were to color indelibly the personality of the man who set out on his expedition to Russia in 1917.

Like John Reed at Harvard, Rhys Williams had been a brilliant student at Marietta College in Ohio, and so outstanding later as a student at the Hartford Theological Seminary that he had won a coveted scholarship for study in Europe. In London he had met an alert crew of young socialists from English universities, had mixed with members of the young Labour party, and, above all, had haunted the reading rooms, the clubs, the streets where the working men and women of the London slums congregated. He was no sentimentalist; in his journals he could berate the workers for their inertia, their infuriating acceptance of their hard lot, their sometime servility in the presence of "their betters." What he wanted was not to uplift them or even to save their souls but to shake them alive, to rouse them to struggle against the inevitability of an otherwise bleak fate. Their pale faces, busted shoes, broken noses; their hearty gusts of wild laughter; the hopelessness of drowning so much misery in the pothouses aroused him to a fighting sense of his own potential powers. If he returned to enter the ministerial ranks, it was as a very special kind of gospel preacher; the Eternal for Williams was to be the Now of this mortal life. If he had not already made an identification on the side of the oppressed against their oppressors, he did so then in London, and for all time.

Reed and Williams had met and mingled in the radical social centers of New York before their venturing collided in Russia. Both were already authors and lecturers. Reed had become famous as the young reporter who rode with Villa's forces in the Mexican Revolution, and had already snagged into trouble in the Middle East as a foreign correspondent of the World War. Williams had been a fund-raiser and orator for the strikers at Lawrence; Reed had made the front pages of New York papers as the organizer of a spectacular pageant in Madison Square Garden for the benefit of the striking textile workers in Paterson, New Jersey. The young Reed had been the intimate associate of Mabel Dodge, the rich bohemian patron of arts and letters in Greenwich Village; he was to marry Louise Bryant, who would go with him to Russia. Williams was an intransigent bachelor; he had not "settled down," in a domestic sense, and at that point did not propose to. Reed had rich parents in Portland, Oregon; Williams' parents never had more than a modest living.

But, significantly, the differences in background, styles of life, personal choices did not count when they came to confront the October Revolution in its actuality. Both declared themselves partisan. Reed joined the Communist party, but Williams did not join, then or ever.

If you want to get to the hot core of a revolutionary situation, only the partisan will be able to give you the essential raw reality. Do you want to discover the subterranean sources for the riots in Detroit and Newark? Don't consult a white policeman but go after an intelligent black. Are you interested in why students are rebelling against the Establishment? Don't interview the university president, but buttonhole a rebellious student. You can talk to the president afterward; what's more, should. In any event, you won't be handed a respectable blueprint for revolutionary action. Revolutions aren't made that way; the boiler bursts when the pressure of the steam becomes unbearable.

The vanguard action is always accomplished, moreover, by minorities, and the fear of alienating the majority is the fear of action itself. This patent truth, confirmed by all historians of significant political struggle and forward development, carries with it the evidence that, at best, under favorable conditions, the inchoate majority can be neutralized, but only in an extremely desperate situation can it be drawn into strenuous campaigns of resistance to official policies.

Whether today or in 1918, the American electorate knows little about the world outside the United States and has been conditioned to imagine it in Manichean terms. The public had been peculiarly vulnerable to the propaganda of the First World War: Germans became the faceless hordes of Huns; the Kaiser, the Beast of Berlin. With passions whipped up, once the Armistice took the enemy from the field the people were ready to supplant the Hun with the equally frightful Bolshevik.

Williams had left for Russia in the amiable glow of the February Revolution, which had been agreeable not only to Wilson but to the majority of citizens, for even schoolchildren had been told of the tyranny of the Tsar. But the amiability had been conditioned on the assumption that the Revolution had been made in the right-minded spirit of capitalistic enterprise; that the Russians, freed of the tsarist yoke, would knuckle down as a fighting ally and battle on, side by side, with the other good fellows in the War to End War. In *Journey into Revolution* Williams will tell you why this dream was no less than a grand illusion. With war-weary soldiers fleeing the front, industry completely busted up, and crops neglected by peasants needed for war, anger spilled over; only a militant, determined minority could come to the rescue. The fighting militants took means that were initially not so different from the tactics any backward people will be obliged to employ. The official United States policy toward Guatemala, Cuba, Santo Domingo, Vietnam is no more than the extended arm of its policy in 1918 when the Cold War actually began.

By the time Williams returned to America in September 1918, the social and political patterns of the pre-war era had been shattered; a new somber age had begun. But it is not so easy to atomize recalcitrant stalwarts. Jails might be filled with impenitents, conscientious objectors, and irreconcilables, but as late as the fall of 1918 Socialists succeeded in electing thirty-two state legislators. By the spring of 1919 the duly elected Socialist legislators to the New York State Assembly had been expelled as "traitors." The war was over, but the heat was on.

The Palmer raids, attacks on Socialists and pacifists—or any dissidents —gave public approval to misguided citizens who rioted at the doors of meetings suspected of Bolshevik leanings. Wobblies were murdered in Montana and Washington, or rounded up in a nationwide manhunt to crowd the jail cells at Leavenworth and to fill new graves. But Williams had not been a preacher for nothing. Now he became an impassioned educator, launching a barnstorming lecture tour of the United States, writing a pamphlet, published by the Socialist Rand School to sell for ten cents, 76 *Questions and Answers on the Bolsheviks and the Soviets.* It sold in the millions. You didn't have to agree with Williams, but his findings opened the door. A mind so informed could go on exploring and not get stuck on the official propaganda. It might criticize, object, revise, as indeed the unfolding history of the Soviet Union would require it to do, but it wouldn't flounder in the swamp of abject ignorance and pathetic illusion.

The Allied Interventionist war in Russia failed; the intervention in Vietnam has not succeeded. But already within the university world there is a sizable body of opinion, mainly of young people, which rejects the mythology of political Manicheanism and consequently rejects America's counter-revolutionary role, of which the war in Vietnam is the present, scandalous symbol. New voices have spoken up to interpret the profound malaise. The sources of this malaise are historical, social, economic, but more than ever the need arises for criticism to combat the grosser forms of deception, which incapacitate their victims and can carry a society to self-destruction.

Journey into Revolution will not take you past the early Leninist days. There's nothing in it about the Stalinist purges, the concentration camps, the bureaucratization of a young mobile revolutionary force which was obliged to take on the mighty of the world. It is a personal account, with the highly charged personal colorings of a man who wasn't afraid to stick his neck out for an unpopular cause. You can read it without identifying

with the particular slogans of the time or the factional disputes which rang
out, even in the early days. Basically this is a book about the human spirit
in action in a beleaguered outpost of the world. But then, as now, "feeling
human is a useful form of political subversion."

Nor can the value of *Journey into Revolution* be judged by its bias, or
its ideology, its world view—rather by its rendering of felt experience, the
intensity of its existential commitment, and, above all, by the force of its
concrete enactment. It's not a blueprint, though it could be a handbook for
a pilgrim. It may even read like a warning to some of the youth today
whose battle cries include the names of Che Guevara, Mao, Malcolm X,
and, in Berlin, Rosa Luxemburg—but are not so certain to ring with calls
for Lenin. For the revolutionary process as a whole, as it is evolving in the
Western world and even modifying some of the rigid patterns in the East,
behind what the Cold Warriors called the Iron Curtain, there is a common
groundwork, a human predicament, an enduring identification on the side
of the oppressed against their oppressors that is the living heritage of Karl
Marx—in Prague, in Moscow, and even in the United States.

I do not know what Williams would have thought of the Soviet occupation of Czechoslovakia, but he would have reminded me that the United
States was continuing its wholesale devastation of Vietnam. Would he have
sided, as I do, with the students of Prague and with Ivy Litvinov's grandson
who stood up for them? A long friendship does not give me the right to
interpret the mind of a dead man.

It was in 1921 when, as a student from Berkeley, recently graduated
from the University of California, I met Williams in a shabby apartment
on Charles Street in New York. All that spring he would rise up from behind a desk cluttered with page proofs of *Through the Russian Revolution*
to greet me. He was handsome, witty, and filled with ironic comments
about other people and about himself. We used to go for long walks, that
spring, along the aqueduct trail leading from Yonkers to Ossining, and
what I remember about him is the way he would pluck a leaf from a tree
and bite it, or how we loved to lounge on the grass looking over the Hudson, and between munches of bread and cheese spout poetry at one another,
and what fun it was to invade the big estates which the two paths traversed.
I remember especially the estate of Helen Gould, her great somber house
with the towering laurel bushes in full bloom, and how Rhys Williams, in the
voice of a Welsh bard, declaimed from Nietzsche: "Man is a perilous
arriving, a perilous traveling, a perilous looking backward, a perilous
trembling and standing still. . . . What is great in man is that he is a bridge,
and no goal." I don't think we ever talked politics on those long walks,
though everything Rhys said was related in diverse ways to his central
themes. There was a kind of unifying principle in him that seemed to have

evolved from an instinctual temperament, and which his findings as a socialist explorer had only reinforced. If I was antipathetic in later years to his "long view of history," which attempted to jump past the Stalinist tyrannies to a brighter day, he was tolerant of my oppositionist views; more, encouraged them, repeated his own opinions without rancor, and allowed us to remain friends. He could temper some of his views, less congenial to me than others, with an irony that evoked laughter. Or, as in his last years, he could make ironic sideswipes at the very subjects for which he had deepest respect, as the time I saw him at Ossining, when devout pilgrims of the early Bolshevik-Leninist type had arrived, and he told me in a whisper to "shake the hand that shook the hand of Lenin."

He has said what he wanted to say, and after a great deal of contradictory, devastating history has rolled over us all.

(This is the last piece written by Miss Herbst before her death on January 28, 1969.—THE PUBLISHERS)

Contents

• Journey into Revolution

• 1 • John Reed and I
Make Up Our Minds

Looking back at the golden September days of 1917 in Petrograd, I can well believe that such old hands at the American Embassy as Sam Harper[1] considered John Reed and me very brash young men. I am sure we were. We were insufferably decisive and opinionated about things that were very perplexing indeed to other Americans. What infuriated them—events such as the Bolsheviks' winning a majority in the Petrograd Soviet—seemed logical and right to us. What filled them with foreboding—the mushrooming growth of the Bolshevik party so soon after its forced retreat in the repression of the "July days"[2]—was to us a matter for rejoicing.

Lenin was still in hiding when Reed, after a long and eventful journey from home, arrived by train from Stockholm. I saw Reed a few days later, about September 2,[3] and it was a welcome reunion. I had first seen him

---

1. Samuel N. Harper, son of President William Rainey Harper of the University of Chicago, traveled and studied widely in tsarist Russia at his father's urging, became Professor of Russian Language at the University and probably the most influential adviser on Russia at the State Department during the Wilson administration. He accompanied Ambassador David R. Francis to Russia in 1917 to advise both Francis and the Root Commission.

2. The rising of July 3 lasted four days. It was initiated by the First Machine Gun Regiment in late afternoon and joined that evening by two other regiments of the Petrograd garrison. The next day thousands of workers also took to the streets. Chief cause of the unrest apparently was the order for a large-scale military offensive in Galicia despite the fiasco of the June 18 mobilization. After some vacillation the Bolsheviks, having failed to prevent the rising which Lenin felt premature, decided to put themselves at the head of the demonstrations to give them direction and purpose. By then it was too late. A bloodletting ensued, a period of reaction set in, the Bolshevik party was virtually proscribed, and orders were issued for the arrest of Bolshevik leaders.

3. A note here is necessary to explain the unfortunate complexity in calendars. Throughout this volume I shall use the dates in use in Russia at the time of the events: the Julian calendar for happenings within Russia prior to February 1918; the Gregorian calendar for those after February 1, which became February 14 as the Western calendar, adopted in

during the Lawrence, Massachusetts, strike in 1912. Then we met when Reed spoke in Tremont Temple in Boston in 1915, and later we met occasionally in New York's Greenwich Village. As far as I was concerned, Reed's arrival in Petrograd was fortunate. I had begun to feel pretty thoroughly alienated from most of the other foreign correspondents, with important exceptions such as Arthur Ransome and, later, M. Philips Price,[4] and from most of the old American Embassy crowd, and I was only just beginning to get acquainted with Boyce Thompson, head of the American Red Cross, and his colorful assistant, Raymond Robins. The friends I had made among the English-speaking émigré revolutionaries who were streaming back to Russia now, since the amnesty following the February Revolution, had less time to give me than they used to have. I welcomed Reed in addition as a kindred spirit and as a more experienced reporter than I.

Jack Reed, on the other hand, viewed me as almost a veteran on the scene, and he immediately proceeded, like the good reporter he was, to sound me out on all I had seen and heard and much that I had not. I had been in Russia only three months, quite long enough to outlast one Provisional Government, that of Prince Lvov, and it was now plain that Kerensky's was on the skids.

Reed bombarded me with questions. What about Lenin? Trotsky? Could I take him to some of the workers' meetings on the Viborg side of Petrograd? What were the chances of visiting the front before it crumbled away entirely? He wanted to see everything at once. He was furious at having arrived days after the revolt of General Lavr Kornilov. I told him I too had arrived back in Petrograd too late for it; I had been in the villages of Vladimir province interviewing peasants in July, and had gone again to the hinterlands in August, this time to the Ukraine.

He had just come from the embassy, as I recall, where acquaintances had been explaining that they saw increased strength for the Provisional Government in the failure of the march on Petrograd by Kornilov's chosen "Wild Division" Cossack troops. "Is there anything to it?" Reed asked. On the contrary, I said; the revolt had disintegrated without any real fighting, without a shot being fired, for one reason: the overwhelming response of the Red Guards, and the masses in general, when summoned to the defense of the Revolution by the Bolsheviks. Why did Kerensky appeal to the Bol-

January, was put into effect. For events outside Russia, I shall use the Western calendar; and for those so often referred to by both dates, as October 25/November 7, I shall use the two-date system.

4. British writers and journalists. Price, whom I met in 1918 in Moscow, was the correspondent of the *Manchester Guardian*. Ransome was correspondent of the *Manchester Guardian* and, in 1918, of the *Daily News* of London; many of his dispatches from Russia were carried in the *New York Times*.

shevik party for defense?[5] Only because he needed them. Reed, I promised, would see the Red Guards, their guns stacked in committee rooms at the big plants. He would see their increasing friendliness with units of the army, the Petrograd garrison. It was to the Bolsheviks, at this time, that the factory workers looked with whatever hope they had salvaged from six months of betrayal by the Dual Power of the Provisional Government and the Soviet, or, as Trotsky had dubbed it, the Dual Powerlessness.

This government, which was a bourgeois government but was backed by the moderate socialist parties, the Mensheviks and Socialist Revolutionaries, as well as the Kadets (Constitutional Democrats) until the tactical withdrawal of the Kadets just prior to the Kornilov crisis, was more in disrepute than ever. It was not love for Kerensky that prompted the workers' quick response to the Bolsheviks' energetic rallying of forces at the approach of Kornilov's Wild Division; it was simply that they refused to give up their revolution to the man on horseback, General Kornilov. As for Kerensky, he would be taken care of later. Lenin had given the cue, so I had heard: neither support of Kerensky nor attack at this point. Only one thing had mattered, defense of Petrograd and the Revolution. But the entire affair, whatever Reed heard at the embassy, had *not* helped Kerensky. It only underlined the growing power of the Bolsheviks. The American, British, and French embassies did not look at it this way.

"And Thompson, it seems, has just sunk a million dollars of his own money in a harebrained scheme to persuade the peasants that Kerensky is their man after all. Robins sold him on it. Robins didn't do it to hoodwink the peasants. He really believed he could persuade Kerensky to begin giving out land. He figured that was the only way to keep Russia in the war. Thompson and Robins tried to get the American government to give three million dollars a month to the scheme, but meanwhile, not to lose time, Thompson cabled the J. Pierpont Morgan banking firm to send him a million of his own money."

"You mean a copper magnate's million can't keep the Bolsheviks from coming to power?" Reed laughed. The story had all the fantastic elements I knew would appeal to him. "But seriously, how in the world did they *expect* to mesmerize the peasants? Or what *did* they think they could do?"

---

5. All the moderate Socialist parties stood ready to defend the revolution as they fancied it, and certainly wanted to rally their forces in any defense of Petrograd against Kornilov's picked Cossacks advancing under the command of General Krymov when Kornilov was detained. But Kerensky was well enough aware that they represented at this moment of history almost no one. He knew that the workers and most of the garrison were by this time listening largely to the Bolsheviks; so, in the name of saving the revolution against the general he branded traitor, Kerensky appealed to Smolny and opened the jails (where many arrested in the "July days" still were incarcerated) so that the Bolsheviks were able to send their most skillful agitators to the front to parley with the Cossacks. With words, not bullets, aimed at the Cossacks, the Kornilov counterrevolution collapsed.

I told him the little I knew. All the missions and commissions that came over, some quasi-governmental, all of them political, beginning with the Root commission, came with one idea: to keep Russia in the war. The American Red Cross was no exception. Robins was worried over the increasing hunger. He saw the cooperation of peasants as a key factor. Kerensky was still a Socialist Revolutionary, and Robins knew the SR's were the party of the peasants, that their program called for land distribution. A week after he arrived, in August, Robins was sold a bill of goods by "Babushka," Madame Ekaterina Breshkovskaya, "Grandmother of the Revolution," an old-time SR and member of one of their early groups of terrorists. Knowing she had been imprisoned and exiled under the tsars was enough to make Robins romanticize her. What he didn't know was that, although she had been revered, she was now hopelessly out of step with the Revolution and with the peasants for whose demands she had suffered exile. Nor was it illogical in Robins' mind to believe that the government supported by the SR's and Mensheviks should begin to do something for the peasants other than say, "Wait. Wait until the Constituent Assembly and *legislation,* and then you can have your land *legally.*" Breshkovskaya had persuaded Robins to form a committee of women whose names she would provide to help distribute food. He thought it a wonderful idea. The Breshkovskaya committee was in fact a political and intelligence ring through which Thompson's million was going to set up newspapers and news bureaus and organize soldiers' clubs to send speakers to barracks and villages urging the Kerensky line—patriotic defense of the fatherland, support for the Provisional Government.[6] The forthcoming Democratic Conference, I told Reed, would contain many of the well-to-do peasants who were SR delegates from the provinces, and Robins would be sure to be there, hoping it would strengthen Kerensky.

"At least he wasn't for Kornilov, whom our ambassador so greatly admired," I said.

"But who has the bayonets?" Reed asked. "Where is the army in all this?"

I couldn't answer all his questions at once. I assured him I did not think Kerensky had them—or enough of them. Workers—the Red Guards—had

---

6. Cf. Hermann Hagedorn, *The Magnate: William Boyce Thompson and His Time, 1869–1930,* New York, 1935, pp. 205, 207. The Committee on Civic Education in Free Russia, with the grandmother (Breshkovskaya) as titular head, Kerensky's private secretary David Soskice as executive, and General Neuslakonsky in charge of propaganda for the Army, established "a hundred or more newspapers," financed news bureaus, and purchased a printing plant. Speakers were sent to barracks and villages, and "Everywhere the appeal was the same. *'Fight the Kaiser and save the revolution.'* " When Thompson said to Robins, "Major, do you know what this means? . . . If we fail, you get shot," Robins' reply was: "That's all right. Better men, younger men and men with more to lose are getting shot every day on the western front. But, Colonel, if I get shot, you'll get hung." Thompson reflected: "I shouldn't be surprised if you were damned right."

their own. Of course, as soon as the Kornilov affair was over, Kerensky was issuing orders for the workers' militia to disband, to turn in their arms. Not a chance!

Reed and I went from the City Duma to the Smolny Institute, where in the labyrinth of halls and former schoolrooms for the daughters of the nobility the Bolsheviks now had their headquarters, and from Smolny in the evenings to Viborg, and to many other spots those first few days after we joined forces. At times he and I were alone in our wanderings. At other times we went with Louise Bryant, Jack Reed's wife, and Bessie Beatty. Reed had credentials from the radical *Masses* and the New York *Call*. Mine were from the *New York Post*. Miss Bryant, as she was called (for in those days no respectable woman radical was known by her husband's name), wrote for women's magazines, and Bessie Beatty represented the *San Francisco Bulletin*.

Everywhere a curious tension was in the air. By the side of the restless, probing Reed, the tension was not lessened. There were moments when we forgot that history was breathing down our necks, but they were not many. Reed and I walked by the spot where Aleksandr II, who had signed the edict of emancipation for the serfs, only to place so many conditions to their freedom that their oppression seemed all the greater, met his death when a nitroglycerin bomb was hurled against his carriage. We walked through the square in front of the Winter Palace, where thousands had been shot down on Bloody Sunday in 1905 as they marched in peaceful procession to present a petition to their tsar, Nikolai II. How much history had been enacted over the centuries in this proud city! What more suitable place could be found the world over for a workers' revolution than this city, which by fiat of Peter had risen out of the swamps on the labor of serfs? Thus we mused, and thought of the man in hiding not far from Petrograd who was to place his name upon this city.

I described to Reed the thrill of seeing the great demonstration of June 18, and the confused scenes of the later demonstrations which the Bolsheviks tried to prevent, then, seeing they could not, tried in vain to control—and the bloody repression that followed. It was then, in the final days of the Prince Lvov cabinet, that orders for the arrest of the three principal Bolshevik leaders were issued. Leo B. Kamenev had been taken. Lenin had decided to give himself up at one point, but was dissuaded, and with Grigory Zinoviev had slipped out. Lenin had later worn a wig and carried a worker's passport to cross the border into Finland. Mass arrests had followed, including those of Leon Trotsky, Anatole Lunacharsky, and the intrepid Aleksandra Kollontai. Little more than two months had passed since Lenin was indicted for treason and falsely charged with taking gold from the

German high command. Now, in September, no name shone as brightly in the workers' eyes; as their illusions waned in regard to the moderate socialist parties, their respect for Lenin and the Bolsheviks grew.

Together Reed and I discussed the course of the Revolution to date, especially as we crossed the Liteiny or the other bridges from Petrograd and entered another world—the slums, the tenements, the cramped, crowded settlements of the workers around the huge armament plants and smoky mills. Reed, sniffing the air, surveyed the scene and said, "I thought this was 'feudal Russia.' Smells more like Pittsburgh to me. You talk to these Mensheviks and Social Revolutionaries and you get the idea that capitalism hasn't touched Russia. How come?"

What an anomaly the whole political scene was! Except for the few monarchists and other almost nonexistent groups, every party except the Kadets (led by the able and hated Miliukov, whose regime had fallen before I arrived in Petrograd) professed to believe in some sort of socialism. All had had an honorable role in preparing this smoky, throbbing heart of the Revolution, the Viborg section, for the change now taking place. Crowded together, the workers were accessible to their education and propaganda over the years. "Expropriate the expropriators!" was everyone's proud watchword. After the Social Democrats had split into Mensheviks (minority) and Bolsheviks (majority) over methods of organization, the slogan "Unite, you have nothing to lose but your chains," remained the slogan of both factions. Over the years, now openly, now covertly, zealous teachers had brought the message of socialism to this fertile seed bed. (Among them was Nadezhda Konstantinovna Krupskaya, Lenin's wife, who again was teaching adult education classes in the evening at Viborg.) Low wages, long hours, squalid warrens to live in, the badgering and harassing of police spies, the disciplines of organization forced upon them in their factory work, and their growing hatred of the war had done the rest.

Yes, in backward Russia the conglomeration of factories representing Russian and foreign capital had incubated the forces for the destruction of imperial Russia. The February Revolution had taken everyone by surprise, apparently; it had been the child of no party. It was of spontaneous origin, at least. Householders, women in bread lines who after waiting for hours learned the supply was gone, rioted here and there. Workers joined them, girls from the mills as well as men, in sporadic demonstrations. These grew until they turned into huge mass demonstrations that continued for days on end. Soldiers, even the Cossacks, ordered to attack, held their fire when workers—and here again the women were effective—persuaded them not to mow down their brothers.

Again, almost spontaneously, the old forms of representation that had come into being with the 1905 revolution came to life again, in Moscow,

Petrograd, and countless other cities, even in some villages. These were the Soviets, or Councils, of Workers' and Soldiers' Deputies. There were also Peasants' Soviets. Under the old regime the State Duma, the City Duma, the various organs that did not govern but sent representations to the Winter Palace—all these at best were isolated from the masses. The provincial delegates, if peasants, invariably were kulaks. And when the Duma was not to Nikolai II's liking in 1906, he dissolved it and stationed troops before the entrance.

Power was lying in the streets, according to a remark attributed to Lenin. It was anyone's to take. But the moderate socialist parties, of which the Socialist Revolutionary was by far the largest, had handed the power to the bourgeoisie. The Provisional Government was not elected, and existed by consent of the soviets that the socialists controlled. The first provisional government—in which Miliukov and Guchkov were the strong men, Lvov the nominal head—contained one socialist, Kerensky. The coalition governments that followed also were committed to wage the war for the glory of the Allies and the Russian landlords and capitalists. Now there were six socialist ministers in Kerensky's cabinet. So there were almost as many socialists protecting the bourgeoisie as Kadets! And out of the despair that gripped so much of Russia, this Viborg held within its womb the black-bloused garrison of the coming revolution. And, I reminded Reed, all over the country—in Moscow, in textile-weaving Ivanovo-Voznesensk in Vladimir, in the coal-digging basin of the Don, in Nizhni Novgorod—wherever workers were congregated, there was a similar hardening of purpose.

Just talking about the textile-weaving district and the workers made us nostalgic about the United States textile strikes. We spoke of our friend Eugene V. Debs. He was no longer young, but he would hold out till the end against the war, we knew. I asked Reed how the other Socialist leaders were doing. The St. Louis program of the Socialist party had stoutly opposed the war, he said, but many were beginning to weaken. We agreed that Alfred Wagenknecht, C. E. Ruthenberg, and many others would go to jail before they would go along with an imperialist war. Alexander Berkman was already doing time in Atlanta. Berkman was an anarchist; Wagenknecht and Ruthenberg, as it later turned out, would, along with Reed and other radicals, lead the left wing out of the Socialist party into the Communist Labor party or its rival, the Communist party, forerunners of the united Communist party.

"So you think Kerensky's days are numbered?" Reed asked on one of our sorties.

"Obviously," I said. "What's wrong? You look so dubious."

"Nothing's wrong. I'm simply trying to find out what *happened*. In the spring the party was miniscule. How did it *reach* this point?"

"Seems like no one really wants the job but the Bolsheviks, and that's the way it's been all summer," I said.

"Now, come on." He was affable, but those green eyes that could light up with that wild, seemingly Celtic humor (though I believe his ancestors were all of British or German descent) could also be cold and detached, and they were now. Figuring I was not in earnest, he went on relentlessly: "Kornilov wants the job. Kerensky wants the job. The Mensheviks and Social Revolutionaries must want it or they'd have agreed to the compromise that Lenin offered them.[7] I just heard about that."

As it happened, I had been entirely in earnest. "Kornilov, yes. He wants to be the man on horseback. As Robins said, he didn't even have a horse. The railroad workers tore up the tracks, so he never even got out of army headquarters at Moghiliev. Without him, the Cossacks at the city's gates were talked out of attacking. The guns in the hands of workers who'd never used them were less of a force than the agitators' words. So there was this farce of a delegation of Cossacks appearing before the P.G. with hangdog faces saying they'd been wild about the Soviets all the time. Kornilov was a brave general, but he's a political innocent. He doesn't have the understanding the others do. The reason I say Kerensky and the compromisers, the Mensheviks and SR's, don't want the job is that they know what goes along with it now. They don't want the responsibility of offering serious and legitimate peace terms to all the imperialist armies. Nor do they want to say to the peasants, 'The land is yours now!' They know that any government that's going to last *has* to do both."

"You make it too simple. And what about the rejection of Lenin's compromise?" Reed asked.

"It's the same thing. All the way from Lenin's 'April Theses' to today,

7. This largely forgotten offer of compromise is contained in a modest, almost diffident letter Lenin wrote September 1/14 from his Finland hiding place. He did not claim to be speaking officially for his party; but the Bolsheviks "can and must agree to this compromise only for the sake of the revolution's peaceful development—an opportunity that is *extremely* rare in history and *extremely* valuable." The Bolsheviks, which Lenin notes casually were at the time in the majority in the Soviets, out of principle could not take part in any government less than a dictatorship of the workers and poor peasants. But, he proposed, they would support a government of Mensheviks and SR's responsible to the Soviets if the two parties would break with all bourgeois parties (meaning the Kadets). And he proposed this occur *now*. "Now, and only now, it may be *only for a few days* or for a week or two, this government could be created and consolidated in a perfectly peaceful way. In all probability it could secure a peaceful *advance* of the whole Russian revolution, and exceptionally good chances for a big step forward in the world movement towards peace and the victory of socialism." His party would forego revolutionary methods of struggle and immediate demands for transfer of power to the proletariat and poor peasants, in return for full freedom of propaganda and the speedy calling of the Constituent Assembly. His letter was published in *Robochy Put* September 6/19.

when Lenin has told the masses that they alone, without the bourgeoisie, can rule themselves and the economy, all these parties have sung the same theme song: evolution through capitalism. We can't have a socialist revolution until the bourgeois revolution is complete—in other words, capitalism more advanced. In the meantime, the Menshevik and SR leaders are caught. They sided with the bourgeoisie in pushing the war, so now their 'revolutionary principles' balk at teaming up with the Bolsheviks. Their principles say the revolution has gone far enough at this time. A bunch of pedants!"

"And so they prevented the rare opportunity, as I hear Lenin called it, of bringing about a bloodless revolution. Well, what the hell?" Reed said, hugging his trench coat closer against the fine mist that had turned to rain. "He said the chance existed for only two or three days, then it would be too late. Then that sad little postscript to his letter offering the compromise, saying he thought it was already too late. Maybe it never would have worked, anyway."

I have often thought of this letter, of which we had heard reports prior to its publication; it has curiously been lost sight of or neglected by most historians.

"No leader who wasn't supremely confident would have made such an offer," Reed said. "Of course, you didn't catch him making it before he had a majority in the Petrograd Soviet. How stupid of the moderates to reject the compromise out of hand! At least you'd think they'd go ahead and distribute land and put an end to the war and steal the Bolsheviks' thunder. Fantastic!"

We were at the Duma later in the day. Jack had tired of the speeches, which seemed to have little relation to the realities of the times. "These Mensheviks make Morris Hillquit sound like a revolutionary."[8] As we went out we found ourselves alongside a roughly clad worker who apparently had also had enough of the speeches. "Ask him if you're right, if no one but the Bolsheviks wants the job now," Reed said. It was characteristic; he liked to test all he heard against what workers said.

I tried my halting Russian. The impassive face regarded us steadily, looking us up and down. Reed added a word or two of his own brand of Russian. He had picked up a bit of the language when he was in Russia with the artist Boardman Robinson in 1915; they had got sort of sidetracked in an assignment to cover the front of the European war and landed in Russia, bent on covering the Russians' retreat. At one point the tsarist police decided they should remain, and indeed they had quite a time getting out of Russia. His pronunciation was, if anything, more atrocious than mine.

---

8. Morris Hillquit was a leader in the Socialist Party of America and long its representative to the International Socialist Bureau in Brussels. When the party split in the thirties the old guard remained loyal to Hillquit as national chairman.

The worker looked again at these two strange young men, spat out a sun-flower seed or two, shook his head, and said slowly, "I don't know why you ask. This is not my government. This may be *your* war, but it's not mine. You are bourgeois"—he called it *burzhuy*—"and I am a worker." And he stalked away.

Reed was delighted. That last sentence alone, he said, would have been enough. All the intellectual SR's and all the platitudinous Mensheviks we had just heard vaporizing, insisting that Russia must fight on in a defensive war, would be forgotten, passed over by history. "You are burzhuy, I am a worker!" Reed's voice boomed with his enthusiasm and echoed in the corri-dors, startling one of the uniformed old attendants at the exit. Then, ex-ultantly: "Well, one kidney is enough to fight in a class war!" That one kidney of Reed's, result of a nephrectomy, had got him exempted from military service by a draft board just before he sailed. It became a favorite saying of Jack's.

It was not surprising that the worker had looked upon us as ordinary bourgeois specimens. We were Americans, for one thing. We were coming out of the press section, for another. And, of course, we *were* bourgeois. "Possibly even ruling class, in your case," I said mildly. We liked to taunt each other.

"Yes, and you're a generation or two away from your coal-miner Welsh forebears, too," he reminded me. I replied by saying a few unkind things about the Harvard Socialist Club. (He had not been a member, but he had attended some lectures, and the club, headed by his friend and critic Walter Lippmann, had had an influence on him.) All he'd have to do, Jack count-ered, was to tell them I was a preacher; that would make a big hit at Smolny! By this time we were in fine fettle. I agreed to suppress Harvard, Socialist Club and all, and he agreed not to mention the Boston church where I had been a minister.

Reed wanted to know who was the most impressive speaker, Lenin or Trotsky. He would hear Trotsky himself any day now, as Trotsky, Kol-lontai, and Lunacharsky had been freed from jail September 4. Then I dropped my bombshell. I had not only attended the First All-Russian Con-gress of Deputies a few days after my arrival in June; I had spoken there. What, he asked, had I been on the same platform with Lenin? Then came my second bombshell. I had long since got over being chagrined about it. And, I said pointedly, now that I was confronting an American Socialist just as green as I had been at the time, I minded not at all admitting that I had missed Lenin's speech!

What? How could I do such a thing? Perfectly easy, I responded. Had *he* known in June who Lenin was? No, the U.S. press was just beginning to play him up in July. As for Trotsky, he was an orator, a firebrand. Dramatic.

"But I'll tell you an incident more dramatic than anything that happened at the Congress. Mind you, it lasted three weeks. This was on the second day. I hadn't arrived yet, but I got it from 'unimpeachable sources,' as you professional reporters say."

Then I told him the now famous story of how Heracles Tsereteli, the Menshevik Minister of Posts and Telegraphs, had been making a speech. Tsereteli was noted for the high theoretical level on which he made his apologies for the government's indecisiveness. I described Tsereteli—suave, handsome, urbane, his voice almost silky as he spoke frankly of Russia's plight. Assume he had covered the worst features—a transportation system old, out of repair, falling apart; supplies for the front piled up on a siding somewhere; trains overburdened with soldiers taking off on their own to plant their crops; speculators grabbing wheat from the provinces while bread lines in cities grew longer, and peasants seizing stores belonging to the landlords. But what could be done? "At the present moment there is no political party," Tsereteli's voice continued soothingly, "which would say: 'Give the power into our hands, go away, we will take your place.' There is no such party in Russia."

And as the minister waited, tall, self-confident to the point of arrogance, for the response he expected—the sad head-shakings signifying agreement that all was hopeless and the P.G. was to be forgiven—a sort of growl came from a bench in the Bolshevik section. It was, I explained, a rather small group that occupied those benches, mostly men in caps, workers in black blouses, though all the Bolshevik leadership was out in full force; of 822 voting delegates at the Congress, only 105 were Bolsheviks. And then, as it was told to me, and as the official minutes would confirm, the growl was followed by one word, uttered in a low voice: "Yest!"

The meaning of that Russian word is "There is." That was Lenin's warning to the Provisional Government, to the moderates. It was a manifesto in one word. In that dry, raspy voice, flung without any bravura from a back bench, that one-syllable word struck fear into many; it was a battle cry. Later in the Congress Lenin got his allotted fifteen minutes, all that any speaker was given. There was derisive laughter when he said then, "You are afraid of power? Our party is ready to seize it any time." Only the Bolsheviks clapped when his fifteen minutes were up. His speech was enough, however, to send Kerensky to bed for twenty-four hours, my friend Mikhail Petrovich Yanishev heard by way of the grapevine. At any rate, it was an anticlimax after that "Yest!"

Reed threw back his head and roared. That was a story after his own heart. Then as usual his questioning began. I had to describe the place in which the First Congress met—the Military School on the First Line, on Vasilievsky Island, where the classrooms were used as sleeping quarters by delegates from the provinces and Moscow, and to get to the hall we walked down a long, poorly lit corridor. What had I told the delegates? Oh, I didn't recall what I really said. It never matters, I added, because the interpreter always says what he thinks you should have said, anyway.

Why can't preachers just stick to the truth and give accurate reports? Reed asked plaintively. No, I said, I was giving it to him straight. "I don't recall what I said, but I hardly think I was bold enough to say what *Izvestia* reported that my translator said I said." Since I foresaw that from now on Jack and I would be speaking together at many meetings, he might as well know what to expect.

"So what the devil did *Izvestia* say you said?"

"Only that now they had made their political revolution, they should get on with their social revolution. And this, mind you, after a modest first remark which I think I really said, to the effect that I brought greetings from the Socialists of America but that we had no need to tell them what to do, we would not presume to, and that Socialists abroad had, we felt, only gratitude for their heroic revolutionary deeds of February."

Understanding no Russian at all then, I had been of course blissfully unconscious that my interpreter had slipped in a pure and simple call for a proletarian revolution as prescribed by Lenin's April Theses. I vaguely wondered why the president of the Congress, Nikolai S. Chkheidze, the Georgian Menshevik who had so enthusiastically invited me to speak, sounded a bit cool in his reply to what I thought were my simple fraternal greetings. At the time I had no idea as to the significance of the terms "political revolution" and "social revolution," even if I had understood the Russian of my interpreter. Now, telling Reed about it and not being at all sure that he was more aware than I had been of all it meant, I described my own naïveté at the time of the Congress. I had been in Petrograd only about ten days when I spoke at the Congress, and naturally found the various parties and creeds a bit bewildering.

Facing this great crowd at the First Congress, seeing the workers, the khaki-clad delegates from the front, the Poles, Letts, Lithuanians, Tatars, Cossacks, I felt only a great thrill, and assumed that they were all pretty much united, that they all believed in socialism, period. To me, the audience was one happy socialist family. I couldn't have been further from the truth. True, this same Chkheidze, as president of the Petrograd Soviet, had officially welcomed Lenin when he arrived at the Finland Station from Switzerland along with twenty-nine other political exiles in April, in a German train (just as Martov and many others traveled, before and after that date, as the only way they could make it home). In his welcoming speech Chkheidze spoke of the need of closing ranks to defend "our revolution." But the revolution Lenin spoke of in his answering speech then and there, clutching a bouquet of flowers someone had presented to him and looking past Chkheidze at the soldiers and sailors and crowds of working people outside the Tsar's waiting room who awaited him—that revolution was definitely not Chkheidze's bourgeois democratic revolution.

Up to that moment such a revolution was all that even the Bolsheviks, either in speech or in their organ, *Pravda*, edited by Kamenev and Stalin, allowed could take place. The Russian workers had overthrown the Romanov dynasty in February and that was quite enough. Not for Lenin, however. No, although he was not urging the overthrow of the Provisional Government *then*, the revolution he projected was the socialist revolution —the real thing, stipulated by Marx *et al.* as one that would put the forces of production and the government into the hands of the workers, and one that could only follow the other kind. Now I was a long time in figuring all of this out, let alone realizing that I had eloquently pleaded—at least, so my interpreter said, his message finally trickling down to me days later— for the overthrow of their provisional government!

Now that Jack had the full story, he burst out laughing, and made me repeat what Chkheidze had replied when he seemed "a bit cool" to my impassioned plea. This was the sort of situation that Reed reveled in, and I began to enjoy myself—needless to say, for the first time. "Oh, Chkheidze?" I replied. "He said nothing much . . . only that they were waiting for their 'comrade socialists' from other countries to force their governments to conclude peace on such principles as I had proclaimed. I had, he pointed out, said the learned did not need to be taught, but still, they would like to be taught, and waited impatiently for that lesson—because they themselves had given the start for that lesson."

By now Reed was wiping his eyes, weak with laughter. "No wonder," he said, "you're such a prize package at the embassy!"

"How about you?" I countered. "I understand the dear old ambassador has made a close study of that speech you made before a congressional committee on the conscription bill not long before you left the States—you know, when you dared them to shoot you or try to draft you to fight, and refused to say that religious views prompted your sentiments. You must have known all along you had that bad kidney."

"But they were home folks, Albert. I didn't come over here and call 'em a bunch of fakers for not finishing their job. After all, we got rid of King George in our revolution but we still have Henry Ford and J. Pierpont Morgan. Elihu Root comes over and tells them what to do with their revolution,[9] followed by Albert Rhys Williams. Oh, well, one cancels out the other.

"And then there's Robins and Thompson with their cure-all." On the trolley, heading back from Smolny, we forgot our laughter, looking out at the dimly lit streets and gray figures bent against the rain. I remembered I had not answered Reed's question as to who was the better speaker, Lenin or Trotsky.

By now I had studied all Lenin's speeches since April as they were reported in the press—part of my studies in the Russian language. Lenin's figures of speech were not dramatic. Trotsky I had heard; his speeches were more inflammatory, it seemed to me, but that might have been his delivery. Lenin's were plain, unvarnished. But then a phrase, a sentence hits you, I told Reed. Maybe it's days later when you're mulling it over. *That's* it, you say, that's *it!* He is always saying, "Get on with the Revolution," and showing how it can be done.

"You sound like a full-blown Bolshevik," Reed said, half in jest.

Actually neither Reed nor I had come to Russia as Bolsheviks, full-blown or merely budding. I was to be attacked in later days—in 1919, by a pamphleteer, Henry L. Slobodin, whose onslaught was rushed to press as a supposed refutation of my little pamphlet, 76 *Questions and Answers on the Bolsheviks and the Soviets*— as one who had arrived in Russia innocent of "any knowledge of Bolshevism, Socialism, Russian language," or Russian history. Undoubtedly there was a certain measure of truth in that indictment.

To come up with an estimate of the Revolution was not an easy thing to do in those days. Ideally it called for vision, understanding, a good deal of political sophistication, some experience of the class struggle, knowledge of socialist parties in their various shadings, and a grasp of Russian history. Needless to say, none of the Americans who had been sent to Russia either as out-and-out diplomats or on various missions, and none of those now in Petrograd and Moscow, was properly equipped for the task. Among those who had some socialist background, John Reed and I alone had no official

---

9. Root, a former Secretary of State, a corporation lawyer, and withal about as provincial as Ambassador Francis in his outlook toward the Russians, was a curiously dour and frigid man to be chosen head of a mission calculated to spread sunshine and subtly lure the Russians back into the war.

Root's worst blunder was his speech before the Council of Ministers in Petrograd June 2/15, in which he seemed intent only on urging them to go out and fight the Germans and keep the Tsar's commitments. It was not the blunt Root but the smooth Tereshchenko who spoke on that occasion of America's Declaration of Independence and of the "oldest, strongest and purest democracy." Cf. Max M. Laserson, *The American Impact on Russia, 1784–1917*, New York, 1950, pp. 417–18; he calls it "perhaps the last pro-American declaration by a democratic Russian minister."

or quasi-official government task to carry out, and we alone put socialism before "patriotism"—that is, before a commitment to judge everything by whether the new government was going to prosecute the war, which America formally had entered in April 1917. Compared to Sam Harper of the University of Chicago, with whom I had arrived in Petrograd in June, our ignorance of Russian history and language was vast indeed. Yet we knew things that were perhaps more useful in arriving at an estimate that would approximate history's.

Both of us had—imperfectly, it is true—identified ourselves with the working class. We had firsthand experience with mass movements, trade unions, strikes. We knew Bill Haywood, the great miners' leader and IWW organizer, and Jim Larkin, organizer of the Transport and General Workers Union in Dublin and leader of the 1913 Dublin strike. Larkin had come to the United States to raise funds when the strike was defeated, and was to be imprisoned when it seemed his return might coincide with a possible Irish revolution. I had campaigned for Eugene V. Debs when he ran on the Socialist ticket for President in 1912 and gained 800,000 votes. Reed had covered the Mexican Revolution and traveled with Villa. I had been a war correspondent in Europe for *Outlook* magazine for three months. In Reed's stories on the Ludlow, Colorado, strike and the mowing down of workers, women, and children by militia and deputies with machine guns —stories carried in *Metropolitan* magazine—he had given a foretaste of the kind of reporting he would do in *Ten Days That Shook the World*. Reed had been deeply involved earlier in the Paterson, New Jersey, silk strike, and I in the bloody textile strike at Lawrence, Massachusetts, in 1912. Reed had joined the IWW during the Lawrence strike.

Now, in reply to his quip about my sounding like a professional Bolshevik, I cut through the customary banter and got down to brass tacks, figuring that was what he wanted. I don't pretend to recall the exact words I used, but I said that in the three months I had been in Russia I had come of age. The Revolution was not something you could play around with. You could not take it up and then drop it. It was something that seized hold of you, shook you, and possessed you. No, I was not a Bolshevik, I said, if he wanted to be literal about it.

And then, before I knew it, I had made a decision and found myself saying, almost belligerently, for some reason: "I expect to be working with them, just the same, when they find something for me to do, because as I see it, the Bolsheviks want the sort of social justice you and I want. They want it more passionately than any other group here. They want it *now*. They want it enough to give their lives for it—and many of them doubtless will. I want what they want—that every man shall have the full product of his labor, that no one shall eat cake until everyone has bread, and therefore I intend to work with them. If you can find any better way to help along the Revolution, let me know."

Why I had to get so huffy about it with Reed, who was regarding me with that clear intensity his green eyes acquired when he was at his most serious, I do not know. I suspect that at the time I did not take Reed altogether seriously, and assumed he would make some flippant rejoinder. I could not have been more wrong. Liking a person does not necessarily give one great insight. I liked Reed, had liked him in New York, without knowing him too well—and I liked him for the very qualities that his pettifogging critics considered his faults, as well as for his accepted virtues. They were very engaging faults, if faults they were, and I responded to the very things in him that the humorless Walter Lippmann failed to understand. To the ham actor in him, to his ebullient pranks and antics and humor, I responded wholeheartedly; to Mr. Lippmann, the future authoritative apologist for the Republican party, they made him a playboy. Like him I did. Which is not to suggest that I had the remotest idea that John Reed would return home to help form a Communist party, or would die within a few years, in Russia, as a Revolutionary martyr, and be buried beside the Kremlin wall.

In the same vein I told Reed, at the risk of sounding self-righteous, that this was not like being a militant at home. What had either of us been, when you came right down to it? "A couple of dilettantes. Well, that's impossible here. Either you're on the side of Lenin and his party, or you become an apologist for the war, like Sam Harper and Bullard, who tell the boys in Washington what they want to hear—that Kerensky will stay in power and the peasants will start fighting any day now." Arthur Bullard, a novelist, was now writing reports to the State Department from Moscow, as Harper, until his recent departure, had done from Petrograd, and while their reports were more erudite than Ambassador Francis', I felt sure, they were probably no more illuminating.

Reed was if anything a reporter, and had no intention now of being put off with a generalization or a speech. When had I got my political bearings and how? How long did I wander around in this maze of political parties with their complicated theoretical differences, and in this fluid, rapidly shifting milieu, where the relationship of forces changed almost overnight, before I formed any special convictions? To answer him I found myself analyzing what had impressed me most about Lenin and the Bolsheviks. My progress had not been smooth and orderly, nor my conclusions arrived at without much backtracking and many doubts. It was not that I had witnessed certain events and, in a blaze of understanding, seen the light.

We went back to Lenin's April Theses. Their significance had become clearer to me after various sessions with some of my Russian-American friends. A funny thing, I said, was that the second- and third-string Bolsheviks, including the actives among the returned émigrés, in contrast to the top leaders in the party, welcomed the April Theses from the beginning. At least they told me so in June, and they were scrupulously accurate. Actually Lenin had depended on them to help persuade the leaders.

Whether Lenin was right in his April Theses, I went on, became for me the great test. From July 12 to July 28 I had gone with Mikhail Yanishev, a Bolshevik and one of my closest Russian-American friends, to Spasskoye and surrounding villages, and I had plenty of time to argue the Lenin proposals with him.

What Lenin said was that the Bolsheviks must explain, patiently and persistently, to the "only just awakened masses" that the Councils of Workers' Deputies were the *only possible* form of revolutionary government, and urge the transfer of all power to the Councils, or Soviets. No support must be given the Provisional Government, then headed by Prince Lvov, and the mendacity of all its pledges must be pointed out. He called for "not a parliamentary republic—a return to it from the Councils of Workers' Deputies would be a step backward—but a republic of Councils of Workmen's, Laborers', and Peasants' Deputies throughout the country and from top to bottom."

Confiscation of all landowners' estates and nationalization of *all* lands were called for by Lenin. Disposal of the land was to be in the hands of the local Soviets of Agricultural Laborers' and Peasants' Deputies. Separate Soviets of Deputies of Poor Peasants were urged. And he envisioned setting up model farms on each of the large estates (from 100 to 300 dessiatines— each dessiatine equal to about two and two-thirds acres—by decision of local institutions) under the control of the Soviets of Agricultural Laborers' Deputies. (These poor peasants, called by Lenin the semiproletarians, were not organized as such then, or even after the October Revolution, so manifold were the Bolsheviks' problems, until the specter of hunger in the cities compelled them to organize the working peasants against the kulaks.)

He called for the abolition of the police, the army, and the bureaucracy, the army to be replaced by universal arming of the people. All banks were to be amalgamated into one national bank. As for the war, it could become a "revolutionary national defense" only with (1) power transferred to the proletariat and the poorest sections of the peasantry, allied to the workers, (2) renunciation of all annexations, and (3) a complete break with all capitalistic interests.

It was quite a stiff program, in its implications, as these conditions could not be accomplished without overthrowing capitalism. And while

Lenin admitted that of all the warring countries, Russia under the P.G. was the freest, it remained a capitalist government, and the war a predatory war of imperialism.

Why had these proposals been received in April with shock and consternation by the leaders of his own Bolshevik party? Reed wanted to know. This led to a long discussion at the end of which we congratulated each other that, neither of us really knowing Marx and Engels, let alone how Marxism was interpreted by the Mensheviks, the Social Revolutionaries, and the purists among the Bolsheviks, we did not have our minds made up as to just what the next step in the Revolution had to be. (At the time neither of us knew that Marx in 1887 had believed that "this time the revolution will begin in the East . . ."; that is, in Russia.)[10]

In those seemingly modest, carefully worded proposals, in which Lenin nowhere called directly for overthrowing the Provisional Government, he had caught his own party as well as other horrified "Marxists" off base. For all of them were jogging along rather comfortably, including even the Bolsheviks, under the Dual Power of the Provisional Government and the Soviet of Workers' Deputies, with the notion that nothing more could be obtained at this time than the political democracy achieved in February. Along comes this "madman," as he was termed in the press next day—this contender for the crown of Bakunin, as a Menshevik scornfully called him when Lenin addressed both Mensheviks and Bolsheviks on the Theses —and says, "What are we waiting for?" So, I said, Lenin was flying in the face of all the socialist tradition that said there must be a bourgeois revolution before there could be a trained proletariat capable of making a revolution and a productive plant equal to sustaining it.

"Then those who hack away at Lenin claim that the bourgeois political revolution of February isn't complete, is that it?" Reed said.

"Lenin didn't say it was complete, either, as I get it," I said. "It's all very complicated. Nor did Lenin say at what moment the transition to a socialist government should be made—only that these first steps must be made, including the bringing of production and distribution under the immediate control of the Soviets of Workers' Deputies."

---

10. Marx explained in a letter to Friedrich Albert Sorge, German Communist who emigrated to the United States and became General Secretary of the First International in New York: "This crisis [the Russo-Turkish war and Near East crisis] is a *new turning point* in European history. Russia has long been standing on the threshold of an upheaval, all the elements of it are prepared—I have studied conditions there from the original *Russian* sources, unofficial and official (the latter only available to a few people but got for me through friends in Petersburg). . . . All sections of Russian society are in complete disintegration economically, morally, and intellectually.

"This time the revolution will begin in the East, hitherto the unbroken bulwark and reserve army of counterrevolution." *Karl Marx and Friedrich Engels, Correspondence 1846–1895*, New York, 1935, pp. 348–349.

"When? That's the important point." Reed always came to grips with the meanest part of the problem; I always saw the glowing overall picture. Thus we made a good team.

"Presumably, if you have to corner me, when his party can win a majority. He doesn't say so, but he spends a lot of time in the April Theses warning they do *not* have anything like a majority. So, all power to the Soviets, he says—but not as they were constituted in April."

"And now?" Jack persisted. This must have been after September 9 when we had this talk, for he pointed out the Bolsheviks now had a majority in the Moscow Soviet as well as Petrograd, and that Trotsky had been made president of the Petrograd Soviet. Both Soviets had voted by a large majority in favor of a government of Soviets, moreover, and against a vote of confidence in the Provisional Government. In Kiev and Finland, the same thing.

"That's right. You must be a good omen, Reed. It can't be long now!"

"Wonder what it must feel like," mused Reed, "to be in the shoes of a Lieber, or Dan, or even old Martov, let alone Georgi Plekhanov. Practically any one of the leaders, anarchist, Menshevik, Socialist Revolutionary, left or right, as well as Bolshevik—for years they were all hunted, shipped off to Siberia, or flogged with the knout in lousy Russian prisons. Besides fighting the class enemy, they had to fight each other—each group thinking it was right, each with its interpretation of Marx, or the anarchists fighting with the SR's over Bakunin or Kropotkin. How out of step the proud old stubborn ones must feel, how virtuous, as they see their comrades switching to Lenin! Martyrs, saints in their way, in their day; and now they're dated. One minute they admit that only Lenin can bring peace, bread, and land. But that's what they can't forgive him; so they furiously try to prop up Kerensky."

Then, just as suddenly, Reed became the skeptical reporter: How could I be sure Lenin wasn't going too fast for the masses? Granted that the other Bolshevik leaders—Kamenev, Rykov, Bukharin, for example (Trotsky, Riazanov, Lunacharsky, and the other members of the Inter-District Committee had formally joined only after their arrest July 23) had underestimated the temper of the people in April; did that prove that Lenin didn't overestimate now?

It was a good question, and we took it slowly. By the end of April Lenin had won over, by persuasion, the leaders who in the beginning, with the one exception of the gentle, stubborn Aleksandra Kollontai, had been horrified at his April Theses. The Bolsheviks were proclaiming the only program that the masses could support: peace, land, and bread, and all power to the Soviets. But would the masses move? That was the question. Either Lenin was a genius who knew then how the Russian masses would be feeling a few months hence, in which case his April Theses would be a standard to which the wise would repair, or he was courting disaster. For a time, with the terrible repressions of the July days, I had my doubts.

In effect the Bolsheviks had been left leaderless, with Lenin in hiding and Trotsky in prison. Although Trotsky had not joined the Communist party until August, there was no question that he was, next to Lenin, the most powerful and active revolutionary figure, and that, from the time of his return in May, Trotsky had recognized in Lenin the protagonist and propagandist around whom the coming revolution would focus.

Besides this, the indictment of Lenin, the publication in the bourgeois press in Petrograd of the affidavit, false and shoddy as it was known to be in every embassy and by every political leader, charging him with accepting German gold, had had its effect. In the factories for a while there were those who believed it. Membership fell off.

From his hideaway in Finland, however, Lenin continued to lead the party. Trusted visitors made their way to him; his wife, Krupskaya, visited him, picking her way through fields in the dark; and he sent letters to comrades, to newspapers. He kept drumming away with his unpopular ideas. And all of a sudden they became popular, or others noticed that they were. And he himself never lost his popularity. Now in September the Bolsheviks were the recognized voice of the giant steel mill, the big Putilov works, and the factories in general.

Reed was indefatigable, and by the end of this particular evening in Viborg, he seemed ignited. On our return trip his enthusiasm over the Red Guards he had seen was boundless; he kindled from the Bolshevik speaker's plain, direct language. A Menshevik speaker at the Duma had said scornfully that Lenin promised the workers "paradise." This did not jibe with the speech we had heard from Lenin's disciple that evening, Reed commented. No, I said, the Bolsheviks generally, and Lenin especially, did not sail off into the wild blue yonder. They speculated little on the future, and avoided like the plague any flowery language. I could not recall ever hearing any talk of paradise in the speeches of the Revolution. When I first pored over Lenin's words, their meaning seemed harsh and uncompromising to me. "Lenin can be harsh. But it's his basic humanism, his deep *concern* that men must be born anew, and direct their own fate so they may be, that makes him harsh."

Reed joshed me about being so carried away. "Remember, comrade, Marxists don't make heroes of their leaders," he said with a wicked gleam in his eye. He got what I meant, anyway. He spoke of the German Karl Liebknecht, who voted no when the 110 other Socialist deputies in the Reichstag voted yes on the war budget. "What you are impressed with is

Lenin's honesty in contrast to the smell of hypocrisy from the Menshevik and the Right SR leaders," he said.

Exactly, I said. And his assessment of reality. And I quoted from the April speech that under Yanishev's guidance I had almost committed to memory: how the majority was not yet with the Bolsheviks; "in this case, our motto should be: caution, caution, caution. To base our proletarian policy on overconfidence means to condemn it to failure."

That was interesting, said Jack, because Lenin now was preaching boldness. Yes, I said, he was like that; be bold, be bold—but not too bold. Flexible. Conditions change; no rule was immutable. My Marxist friends here, I said, informed me that was the soul of Marxism—not to be bound by any preconceived idea, even a Marxist idea!

At this Reed burst into a guffaw, slapped me on the back, and wanted to know: "Do you think we'll ever make the grade? Or are we tagged for life—the humanitarians, the dilettantes?"

Then, as he frequently did, he suddenly lapsed into another mood; this time it was on the surface a sullen mood. It was the first of many such I was to see in him. Others have described them as depressed moods, but they were much more complex than that.

"What counts is what we do when we go home," he said somberly. "It's easy to be fired by things here. We'll wind up thinking we're great revolutionaries. And at home?" He laughed bitterly. "Oh, I can always put on another pageant!"

I learned to recognize these self-recriminatory moods as part of a personality that, like all around us, was in flux. He knew and I knew that the pageant he had initiated and written and directed for the Paterson silk strikers in Madison Square Garden was a perfectly valid, even remarkable thing, both artistically and as agitation, with its effect on the men and women strikers who performed in it and helped in its creation not to be dismissed lightly. But we knew, too, that Reed had run away from the strike after the pageant; this accounted for his self-taunting. In working on the strike pageant he and Mabel Dodge had fallen in love. Mabel Dodge was a wealthy woman, a Bohemian in Greenwich Village life who lionized anarchists, labor leaders, and leftist writers—and in those days nearly every creative person in New York was more or less radical. And at the very period when the strike foundered, when demoralization set in for strikers and for Reed as well (in covering the strike he had identified with the strikers even to the point of getting himself arrested and jailed), Mabel Dodge succeeded in carrying away her prize. Reed and another favorite at Mabel's soirees, Robert Edmond Jones, who had done the scenery for the Paterson strike pageant, were carted off bodily to Mabel's villa in Florence,

Italy. Reed eventually broke away from her possessive love, fled homeward, became attached to Louise Bryant, and felt that she was a kindred spirit. (They were married secretly in Poughkeepsie, New York, early in November 1916, before Reed entered Johns Hopkins Hospital in Baltimore for the kidney operation.)

It was Reed's curse to have this contradiction in his personality—a buoyant, lighthearted spirit, a creative talent, and at the same time a mocking self-judge within him. It had driven him into many unexplored channels in which he found success too easily; the judge was not satisfied. What he now struggled with—his own relation to the events seething in Petrograd, where his sense of history told him mankind had reached a turning point—would challenge all his forces. Would he find himself wanting? The moods were but the natural waverings of a very human young American before he set himself a goal more difficult than any he had yet picked.

Of course I had not been altogether fair either to Reed or to myself in saying that up to now we had been little more than dilettantes. I had exaggerated deliberately; we did this with each other. The game was to try to keep from reacting to the other except in kind. It was a form of raillery which, however, concealed in each of us a jabbing, deadly serious questioning—of ourselves, of the other, of the people we met and our old ways of thinking, anything that might throw us off the track or give us comfortable illusions. When we finally recognized this quality in each other, a sort of moral urgency, then we could let the bars down. Then we could admit that we were both in this revolution with both feet. We had made up our minds.

• 2 • The Russian-Americans

From the beginning my Russian American friends took John Reed to their hearts.

Up to now Reed had been a restless, searching young man with a burning sense of justice, a thirst for adventure in ideas and action. His identification with strikers and working people had been ardent but fitful. He was a rebel, but in no sense a revolutionary. The October Revolution made him a revolutionary. Poet, dramatist, and satirist, he saw the Revolution in all its spectacular aspects. His integrity demanded more, however: nothing less than an explanation of the seemingly blind forces at work—a quest that ended only with his death and martyrdom, making of him a legendary figure the world over, forever young and forever passionate, the twentieth century's Western creative man with a commitment.[1]

---

1. Traveling on false passports in lieu of a legal one refused him, Reed undertook his perilous return to Russia after the Revolution, in 1919, when the blockade against the Soviets still held, to seek credentials for the Communist Labor party from the executive committee of the Communist International, established that March. Louis Fraina headed the delegation claiming recognition for the rival Communist party. (The two groups were told to unite.) While in Russia Reed learned of raids against headquarters of both Communist party groups in New York in November, and his own indictment with that of others. He prepared to return, but not before he had amassed considerable material in his dual role—for Reed was at all times the reporter, and was planning not only a second but a third book, making with *Ten Days* a trilogy. (Manuscripts, fragments, and notebooks of material attest to his industry.)

After one or two failures, he did cross the border en route home but got only as far as Abo, Finland, when he was arrested on a charge of "smuggling" and was held for thirteen weeks in solitary confinement in the Abo jail. Learning that arrangements were being made by Soviet authorities to exchange him for Finnish prisoners, he informed his Finnish representative, Mme. Malmberg, on May 25, 1920, that he wished to withdraw his request for an American passport. In a postscript he said: "You can use your own judgement about informing Magruder [of the U.S. Consulate] of my decision. It is very probable that he will not grant the passport, or even answer my request.

"The reason for my action in this matter is that the Finnish Govt. has allowed the

In this quest the Russian-Americans—most of whom arrived before I did, others continuing to arrive before and even after October—were helpful to Reed. I must say he returned their trust and affection wholeheartedly.

Many, but not all, of the Russian-Americans who acted as translators, mentors, and friends to Reed and to me were Bolsheviks. These Bolsheviks, and the Russian-American Bolsheviks I was to meet later in Vladivostok, came to have a special place in my heart. Besides Mikhail Petrovich Yanishev, there were V. Volodarsky, or Moisei Markovich Goldstein, the most prominent; Jakov (Jake) Peters, a Russian political exile from England; and Samuel Voskov (the few historians who mention him do so as Waskov, Woskoff, or Woskov).

And then there was Aleksandr Krasnoschekov, who alone among the émigrés left America with middle-class status, under the name of Tobinson. Arriving in Vladivostok in July 1917, he at once joined the Bolshevik party and was sent to Nikolsk-Ussurisk, where he was elected chairman of the Council of People's Commissars of the Far East. A local bourgeois paper promptly termed him an "immigrant roustabout" and urged its readers to "feel the shame of being ruled by a porter, a window cleaner from Chicago." None of the other Bolsheviks I knew would have reacted as Krasnoschekov did. But none had been a man of distinction in Chicago, an educator and lawyer, as Krasnoschekov had been, and as he reminded the editor in a letter he dashed off in a huff. Krasnoschekov was a politician, however, and bethought himself to drop by the local Soviet on his way to the newspaper office. The minute he entered the meeting hall men rose to their feet, cheered him as *"Nash! Nash!"* ("Ours! Ours!") and told him how happy it had made them to see the newspaper story. "We thought you were a bourgeois. Now we find out you are one of us, a real workingman!" The letter remained in his pocket until he could tear it up in secret. After being captured by the Whites and imprisoned in Irkutsk, and liberated during a local uprising in January 1920, he was elected President of the Far Eastern Republic.

Yanishev, a mechanic, had worked in numerous cities—on the docks of Hamburg, in coal mines in Austria, in Tokyo and Marseilles, among others; and in Boston, Detroit, and elsewhere in America. Volodarsky, a revolutionary since the age of fourteen, had lived in the United States from 1913

American authorities access to my papers." (John Reed Collection, Houghton Library, Harvard University)

Reed, emaciated, sores all over his body from malnutrition, arrived in Moscow in June and threw himself into preparations for the Second Congress of the Communist International. With the end of the Congress he set out with other members of the Executive Committee for Baku, to attend the Congress of Oriental Nations. Traveling through country where the typhus epidemic raged, he caught typhus and died in Moscow October 17, 1920. He would have been thirty-three years old on October 20.

to 1917 and was a member of the American Socialist party. He was among the secondary Bolshevik leaders, a member of the Petrograd Soviet even in the July days, a great favorite as a speaker in the smoky factory district on the Viborg side. Since July he had been a major force in swinging the 40,000 workers in the Putilov steel mill from the SR's to the Bolsheviks.

Voskov had been a union organizer in New York for the Carpenters' and Joiners' Union No. 1008. Prior to that he had gone through strikes in the Midwest and knew firsthand that police beatings of labor agitators in the United States were not uncommon in times of trouble.

Besides these Bolsheviks who were in Petrograd in September, and of course the émigrés from America with whom we had only a speaking acquaintance at the time, Leon Trotsky and Nikolai I. Bukharin, there was my friend and comrade who arrived somewhat later, Arnold Yakovich Neibut. Neibut had been a leader of the Chicago section of the American Socialist party, had been working in California in 1916 when I lectured there, and later had worked in New York's Greenwich Village. I may have met him in any of the three places, but one occasion remains vivid in my memory. This was an unforgettable day in March 1917. At the Christopher Street subway station, near my room in the Village, I saw a man standing by the newsstand, staring at a newspaper he held close to his bespectacled nose. The crowd swirled about him, but he stood unmindful, his eyes on the huge headline: TSAR ABDICATES—FALL OF ROMANOVS. I watched the tears rolling down his cheeks, then came to with a shock. It was Neibut. But before I could get to him, he shoved the newspaper into his coat pocket and ran down the subway stairs. I joined the crowd buying papers, and thought, "It has come!" Almost at once I knew I was going to Russia. . . .

Neibut, like Jake Peters a Latvian—and no more militant revolutionaries existed than the Letts—returned in April 1917 by way of Vladivostok, remaining there long enough to be sent as a delegate to the Constituent Assembly and the Third All-Russian Congress of Soviets. Urbane, versatile, he acted as correspondent for a Bolshevik paper in Vladivostok—sending in a too glowing account of my speech—and served later as a courageous and resourceful Red Guard commander.

Peters, a slight, curly-haired young man who liked poetry, tried without success during these September days to induce Jack to quote some of his own poetry. This pudgy-nosed, short little fellow was lifted out of obscurity a few months later into headlines all over the world. As top assistant to Feliks Dzerzhinsky, the first head of the Cheka, Peters became known to the Western world as "bloody Jake Peters."

Bessie Beatty describes Peters as typical of the radical and intense revolutionists bred by the oppression in the Baltic provinces.

Jacob Peters was thirty-two years old, and looked even younger. He was a Lett—an intense, quick, nervous little chap with a shock of curly black hair brushed back from his forehead, an upturned nose that gave to his face the suggestion of a question mark, and a pair of blue eyes full of human tenderness. He spoke English with a London accent, and referred to his English wife as the "missis," and to his little girl in the language of all adoring fathers.

Peters had left the English wife and the daughter in England when he returned to Russia after the February Revolution. He was sentimental about them, and about his rose garden, but he never returned to them so far as I know, and eventually acquired a Russian wife.

Behind that ordinary face lurked imagination and dreams and great capability and ruthlessness. He outsmarted the old-guard intelligence officers of the Whites in the counterrevolution because he was not limited by rules and codes and previous ways of catching criminals. He accomplished the big jobs entrusted to him. He could be absolutely ruthless as a revolutionary. He was not interested in myth. But he wanted to get out of the Cheka, and he did.

There were other émigrés with whom I worked in Vladivostok on the newspaper *Peasant and Worker,* especially Jerome Lifshitz, who had been sent to the United States by his parents after the 1905–1906 pogroms, and Lev Vaks, an American émigré and professor of English, and his wife, Elizaveta Dymzen.

The Petrograd group of émigrés who spoke English was not, however, composed of Bolsheviks alone. The group was far from united politically. It included anarchists such as Agursky and Petrovsky, neither of them well known in the labor movement at home in the sense that Bill Shatov was. (Bill and his wife, Anna, had come from New York.) Anarchist or not, Petrovsky was a member of the Military Revolutionary Committee, which shows the international character of that key unit which carried out the seizure of power. After returning from America he worked in the Obukhovsky munitions plant and was a member of its shop committee. A man of slight physique, serious, without that wild exuberance that marked Bill Shatov, Petrovsky greatly impressed Reed. Also included in the group was at least one Internationalist (Left) Menshevik, Nagel. There were also Alex Gumberg, whom I had met the day after my arrival, and the first returned exile whom I introduced Reed to; and Boris Reinstein, who had spent some years in Buffalo, which had the largest concentration of heavy industry in New York State.

It was always interesting to see evidence of certain aspects of American thinking that these political exiles had brought back to the Revolution. In

the prewar years there was in America a growing, healthy socialist movement, and all who had landed on our shores seemed to have had some contact with it. Reinstein typified this. He was a mine of information on
Eugene Debs, knew Wobbly and other workers' songs, and, like the others,
had experienced personally the ills of agrarian Russia with its famines and
of industrial, capitalist America with its depressions. His ambivalence about
America too was typical: his passion for its techniques, yet his shock at
learning that in the country where the machine had developed such vast
productive powers there was such waste of resources and of men. Like the
others, he saw socialism as the only way of delivering mankind from the
scourges of spiritual and physical poverty, unemployment, waste.

At the time I met him he was a follower of Daniel De Leon, an early
exponent of Marxism and advocate of industry-wide as opposed to craft
trade unionism in the United States who joined the Socialist Labor party,
then largely a German-language group, in 1890. Under De Leon's leadership it grew but became little more than a sect after a split in the party.
Reed used to twit Reinstein about the SLP, asking if there were three and a
half members, or four. Once when Reinstein was introduced as a leader of
"the powerful Socialist Labor party in America," Reed rocked with laughter.
But Reinstein knew Marx and Engels and did not let us forget that that
was more than Reed and I did. And he could boast, and did, of Lenin's
decided interest in De Leon, whose plan was that society should be organized as an industrial state with representatives in the government chosen by
industries, not regions, and responsible to the workers in those industries.[2]

Party distinctions were not very important in the fall of 1917. Droves of
Right Mensheviks and Right Socialist Revolutionaries were joining their
parties' internationalist or left factions, and many in the internationalist or
left groupings were joining the Bolsheviks. Reinstein became a Bolshevik,
as did certain anarchists. Not so Alex Gumberg, who functioned as an intermediary between the American Embassy crowd and the Bolsheviks. Dili-
gently preserving his lone-wolf status, he was trusted by both. Later he
returned to America, where he was an important behind-the-scenes figure on
Wall Street.

Shatov remained a disciple of Prince Peter Kropotkin, whose readable
books he loved to hand out, but that did not prevent him from being mili-

2. Born in Curaçao, De Leon (1852–1914) studied in Germany, Amsterdam, and New
York, lectured in Latin American diplomacy for six years at Columbia University, retiring in
1878, joined the Socialist Labor party in 1890, and won strength in it by his years-long
editorship of its organ, *The People,* dating from 1892. His opponents failed to unseat him
despite their attack on him as "dictator" and "doctrinaire." They formed a separate party
which became the Socialist Party of America. De Leon was one of the founders of the Industrial Workers of the World in 1905 in Chicago, but three years later an IWW convention refused him a seat.

tantly partisan in regard to Lenin. For one thing, Bill was convinced that some of Lenin's elder brother's anarchism had rubbed off on Lenin, and you could not argue him out of this conviction. Lenin's brother Aleksandr (Sasha) Ulianov, when he was twenty-one years old, was involved in a student plot to kill the Tsar, Aleksandr III, and was hanged. Lenin at the time was seventeen.

For another thing, Shatov always was for the underdog, and after all, the Bolsheviks *had* been the persecuted, small and have-not party until recently. Nevertheless, Bill explained later, he was able to maintain his loyalty to them because soon after October the international situation made their continuance problematical. (In 1919, after performing the miracle of making the Moscow-Petrograd railway run on schedule, Shatov, then commandant of Petrograd, told Ransome that the minute other nations stopped attacking them he would be the first to pull down the Bolsheviks.)[3]

To both John Reed and me the anarchists were a more familiar type than any other on the Russian political scene, resembling in some ways our Wobblies, the members of the IWW (Industrial Workers of the World). Not only had both of us known Big Bill Haywood; Reed had seen Mother Jones at work in the Ludlow miners' strike, and I had known Elizabeth Gurley Flynn in the Lawrence textile strike.

We also knew less noted Wobblies who were active workers, George Andreychin for one, among the 101 who were to go on trial in Chicago in 1918. I mention Andreychin because Reed and I knew him well, and because he managed to get to Russia, and later, after World War II, became a high official in the party and government of his native Bulgaria. To the IWW

3. In the late 1920's Shatov was placed by the Soviet government in charge of constructing the Turksib railway, an important line connecting Turkestan and Siberia. Between his stints as banker and railway builder Shatov, with several hundred other Americans, including engineers, scientists, and organizers, was enrolled in an undertaking dear to Lenin's heart: the reactivation of factories and mines in the Kuznetsk coal basin. Cf. *New York Times,* November 1, 1967, p. 26, "Americans Played Role in Early Economic Development of the Soviet Union." In this Shatov was once more associated, as he had been in the U.S., with William (Big Bill) Haywood, who went to Russia to escape the twenty-year prison sentence received by him and several other IWW leaders in 1918 (all 101 of the defendants were found guilty). Most of the Americans who took part in the Soviet venture, which was known as the Autonomous Industrial Colony of Kuzbas, in Siberia, and which was in progress from 1921 to 1927, were former Wobblies. Haywood was deputy to the leader of the colony, S. J. Rutgers, a Dutch-American Communist. Shatov represented the Soviet government in the colony after the work got under way. The agreement giving the Americans an iron and steel plant at Nadezhdinsk, now Serov, in the northern Urals, was signed by Lenin for the Soviets. The colony project was conceived as a large and vigorous industrial empire in which men of international sympathies, with trade-union experience in modern Western enterprises, would train Russian workers and get idle plants operating again. The Soviets, in their anxiety to lure conscientious experts with American know-how, threw in such items as coal mines at Kemerovo, brick plants at Tomsk, leather and shoe factories, chemical plants, and timber tracts. In the same period they offered land in exchange for a model machine-operated farm. This was operated by Harold Ware, another American and son of "Mother" Ella Reeve Bloor, veteran labor organizer and Communist.

boys from America, Andreychin, Lifshitz, and later Haywood, the Revolution was a historical confirmation of their famous phrase, "the new government growing up within the shell of the old."

Not fitting into any group, yet at home with all, was another Russian-American émigré who managed to turn up on the day before the October Revolution, Charles Kuntz, intellectual and New Jersey chicken farmer.

I said that all the Russian-Americans took Reed to their hearts. There was one exception: Alex Gumberg. Reed and Gumberg never cottoned to each other, and as time went on there was bad blood between them. With the others, Reed soon was at home. These friends were now working furiously and had little time for their old love, a game of chess. But we tagged along with them, riding on the clattering old steam tram to meetings at Viborg factories and at barracks. Occasionally they took time to chew the fat with us while waiting for a meeting to begin.

The one thing on which all of them, even Gumberg, appeared united was Lenin—uncritically, it seemed to me when I first knew them. But now the inner-party struggle was blowing up as October drew near, and often one or another of them would appear tense, hurried, distracted, too busy to stop for the long unhurried talks I had come to expect. Fortunately by now I had acquired a bit more of the Russian language, and was no longer so dependent on them. Their lessons were taking effect. Reed was an even more apt pupil, although the time had not yet come when he would begin to reproach me for not being a Marxist.

A week after Reed arrived, he made the following clear-sighted estimate of the political situation in Russia in a letter:

> This revolution has now settled down to the class struggle pure and simple, as predicted by the Marxians. The so-called "bourgeois liberals," Redziasketske [Rodzianko], Lvov, Miliukov, et al., have definitely aligned themselves with the capitalist elements. The intellectuals and romantic revolutionaries, except Gorky, are shocked at what revolution really is, and either gone over to the Cadets or quit. The old-timers—most of them—like Kropotkin, Breshkovskaya, even Aladdin—are entirely out of sympathy with the present movement; their real concern was with a political revolution, and the political revolution has happened, and Russia is a republic, I believe, for ever—but what is going on now is an economic revolution, which they don't understand or care for. Through the tempest of events tumbling over one another which is beating upon Russia, the Bolsheviki star steadily rises.

Reed oversimplified as to the intellectuals and "romantic revolutionaries," many of whom went over to the Bolsheviks, just as many continued to fight them in and out of Russia, and he was not wholly right about

Maxim Gorky at the time. Gorky and his paper, *Novaya Zhizn* (*New Life*), edited by N. N. Sukhanov, were anti-Bolshevik, although they also were opposed to the "compromisers," the Mensheviks and SR's. Gorky was won over at a later period by Lenin, Lunacharsky, and others. Jack's insight, after a week in Russia, nevertheless shows his grasp of the essentials.

To be frank, there was in both Reed and me a good deal of the romantic, of the love of adventure. To picture either of us in September 1917 as having a profound understanding of Marxism, or a devotion to the proletariat as compelling and clear-sighted as that we saw in the Russian-American Bolsheviks, would be wrong. That Reed was if anything more of a romantic than I did not prevent his becoming a Communist, which I did not; it may have accelerated the process.

In Russia in September 1917, at the age of thirty, Reed's flair for the dramatic and picaresque had full play. This was the surface Reed that many saw. Neither the Russian bourgeois types nor the American Embassy majority—though there were exceptions—could quite believe that either Reed or I was altogether serious in sympathizing with the Revolution. The Russian *bons vivants* to whom Gumberg introduced us assumed that we were on the side of the Kerensky regime, but only because the Bolsheviks would be worse and at least Kerensky was trying to keep Russia in the war. Reed loved the farce of these encounters. Unfortunately for the gentle-folk, he would say calmly, the Bolsheviks would be victorious because they had the only program based on the needs of the people. At this, our host or hostess would smile wisely, as if saying, Oh, I know you newspaper correspondents, you have to get your story. It was inconceivable to them that we were not simulating sympathy with the Bolsheviks to obtain news.

This might well have occurred to the Bolsheviks, too. The remarkable thing is that they accepted us as we were, trusted us, patiently explained or vehemently argued, depending on their personalities; Gumberg alone baited us, but he baited the Bolsheviks, too, and his grinning skepticism was not lost on his employers at the embassy, for that matter. Even when he and Raymond Robins were revealing a growing mutual respect, and Gumberg was of invaluable aid to him, Alex could not resist occasionally poking fun.

The American Embassy crowd in general believed either that Reed and I were wide-eyed innocents (in a later period we would have been called "dupes" of the Bolsheviks) and would get over our youthful ardor, or, especially as time went on, that we were dangerous characters to be snooped upon. Our activities were scarcely secret. Our speeches were matters of public record, duly reported in the press—or what our interpreters added—and reported on by Russians employed as agents of the embassy. The news sheets and leaflets we wrote after October 25/November 7 were anything but conspiratorial. We were officially employed by the Soviets' Foreign Service propaganda bureau, working under Reinstein, whose boss was Trotsky, to propagandize the German and Austrian soldiers to throw away their guns and revolt against their Kaiser and their emperor, as the Russians had against their tsar. These broadsides were dropped into German trenches by planes—though planes were few—or, during the "fraternization" period before and after the Brest-Litovsk truce, handed by Russian soldiers over barbed wire to the Germans facing them at the crumbling front. They also went to German, Austrian, and other prisoners.

No one of the Russian-Americans was like another. Each was a distinctive personality. Even among the Bolsheviks there were not only differences but disagreements, on tactics, on interpretations of Marx or Engels. I was not much interested in those theoretical points. "It's interesting," I said to Reed one day, "that they don't seem to have any differences of interpretation of what Lenin says. He never seems to leave any doubt about what he means."

"Don't any of those we know ever differ with him—even if they are agreed on what he means?" Reed wondered.

The time would come when some would oppose Lenin and some would not: the time of the Brest-Litovsk peace. Some historians have indicated that at one point Volodarsky wavered on the timing of the coming insurrection. But I knew him, and I never saw it. And with the third-string Bolshevik leaders, they were united on this question. Not because Lenin's word was law to them. That sort of attitude was definitely *not* a part of the Revolution as I knew it.

Thus I do not say that these Bolsheviks I knew revered Lenin; reverence comes only to dead leaders or is foisted upon subjects of leaders far removed from a people. Lenin was absent only formally; he was very much there, and as intensely alive a man as history is ever apt to reveal. I do say that to them Lenin *was* the Revolution. On the whole they trusted him to use his subtle and wide knowledge of Marxist theory, checked against his close knowledge of the people, and his genius as a tactician to know the moment when the people were ready to seize power, and to lead the way.

They valued Leon Trotsky, who on his arrival from America had recognized in Lenin the only man of action capable of grasping the Revolution at its full tide and channeling it to a valid conclusion. Some of them admired Trotsky, as did John Reed on first hearing him speak and feeling his dynamic quality. Indeed, no one could be in Petrograd in those thrilling September days without being aware that Trotsky was a strong force backing Lenin's position that the time for an armed uprising was near. But personally Trotsky did not inspire any warmth of feeling. His was a rather cold and difficult personality, in which his ego was an unchanging ingredient. It would not be long before I myself was to discover to what ridiculous lengths that ego could go.

Lenin they loved. It was that simple. When it came to Lenin, even the mysterious, fascinating, and dour Gumberg refrained from his otherwise unfailing practice of looking for another's Achilles' heel and celebrating the discovery in words of mordant wit. I may add that Lenin was the only person on either side of the Atlantic among the hundreds who eventually knew Gumberg—and they included many of the great of America after the war—who had this distinction.

There was a reason why these second- and third-string leaders I have been describing—unlike the leading Bolsheviks, who wanted to delay action—were closer to Lenin's point of view. Unlike Kamenev, Zinoviev, Bukharin, and others in the high echelons, they spent their time among the masses. And in September, as Sukhanov put it, "The mass lived and breathed together with the Bolsheviks. It was in the hands of the party of Lenin and Trotsky." My friends knew that Lenin had correctly gauged the revolutionary temper of the workers.

I recall one night when Reed and I and Reinstein traveled to the Viborg side to hear Volodarsky. Reed was enormously impressed with him, as I had been on first hearing him. This must have been in the last half of September, before Reinstein went with us on a trip to the northern front near Riga.

Reed wanted to know if Volodarsky resembled Lenin as a speaker. No, Reinstein said, Lenin never aroused the emotions. He figured the workers and peasants knew quite well what they wanted: an end to the war; an end to the flabby Kerensky regime, which knew nothing but compromise. All power to the Soviets, yes, and the power to be kept and exercised by the workers next time. Bread, peace, land, which they had not got in six months of revolution. The point was to make them think, hard, how to get them. He had on occasion heard Lenin addressing throngs, as for example from the second-floor balcony of the house of the famous ballerina Kshesinskaya, at the time when, all decked out in red bunting, it was occupied by the Bolsheviks as headquarters, before they moved to the Smolny. Reinstein described how more than once workers and soldiers stood silently, lost in thought, forgetting to applaud. Then, as Lenin disappeared within, a sort of low roar would sound.

Volodarsky was not Lenin; none of them was. But he was like a flame. More than a few times I heard him, on the docks and in the mills. To be a great agitator one first has to be agitated; Volodarsky had that qualification. His hatred of the class enemy may have been no greater than that of the others, but his boiling point was low. Alone among the Russian-Americans, it seemed to me, he had vengeance in his blood. Now he was finally able to strike the blow he had been dreaming of for so long, and he drove himself night and day; for him every moment of the Revolution was a joyous one. This is not the first time I have written of it, but still the confession Volodarsky made to me months later, not long before I left Russia, is one of incomparable beauty. Almost shyly, but with that intensity which occasionally lit his face, he said, "In these ten months I have had more joy than any one man should have in all his life."

I presume all the Russian-American Bolsheviks were zealots, if passionate belief in man's capacity to shape his own future and a determination to do all within their power, at whatever risk to themselves, to help direct the forces now unleashed in Russia, where their class was making its choice, made them zealots. Their physical capacity stretched almost to the breaking point, each one did the work of ten men. I had seen, in strikes in America, and in the campaign to elect Debs, this renewing of men's energies, endurance, and above all will, this almost impossible expenditure of energy, despite negligible sleep and food. What men cannot do when they have a purpose! Here there was the same activity projected beyond the possible such as I had seen at home in crises, but more so. In one of its first acts during the Kornilov debacle, the Military Revolutionary Committee had cut the bread ration in the capital to half a pound per food card, and as I recall, this was still in effect. But the Bolsheviks' energy did not flag.

Not that these Russian-American actives were robots, or the humorless type so often depicted in Western literature as professional revolutionaries. The truth is that, with the one lone exception of Trotsky, who as I knew him was devoid of humor, all the Russian-American Bolsheviks loved laughter. They welcomed John Reed's exuberance, his love of life, his hilarious antics, his caricatures of Ambassador Francis pouring out his bonded liquor for the correspondents, of Kerensky addressing troops at the front, or of Rodzianko, a huge, ponderous man like the serf owner Sobakevich in Gogol's *Dead Souls,* whom we had interviewed with Nagel acting as translator.

Rodzianko himself was incredible enough without Reed's caricature of him. For some reason he looked suspiciously at Nagel, who in our opinion looked less like a Bolshevik and was far better dressed than our other Russian-American friends.

"Are you a Bolshevik?" Rodzianko demanded to know, and when Nagel replied no, he was an International Menshevik, Rodzianko expressed himself freely on the Bolsheviks—"These men are licking their chops over the thought of blood"—and declared, "There is nothing to do except wait for the inevitable revolution." His meaning was clear: better see the land drenched in revolution than have the landowners' property rights infringed upon. With revolution, the Bolsheviks could be settled once and for all.

He even said pointedly that the petty bourgeoisie did not intend to obey the mandates of the Constituent Assembly. (He was among the big bourgeoisie, but modestly aligned himself with the small landowners.)

When I asked why the middle class did not offer some program in competition to the Socialists', a program that would give the peasant masses something of their demands, he replied archly in seeming innocence, "The masses on the whole are pretty thoroughly distrustful of the bourgeoisie. Under the old regime we held the offices and positions of the bureaucracy and were looked upon as concurring in what they did, and so we have that heritage to fight against.

"The Socialists say, 'We propose that we take away the coat and vest and trousers of Mr. Rodzianko.' And so Mr. Rodzianko is put in the sorry plight of getting up a party that says, 'I propose to give you workingmen and poor peasants my coat.' But between a party that offers up Mr. Rodzianko's coat, pants, and vest, and a party that offers up Mr. Rodzianko's coat, the people are going to fall for the party of Mr. Rodzianko's coat, pants, and vest."

Except for Yanishev and Gumberg, who was the son of a rabbi, all the Russian-Americans, Bolshevik and non-Bolshevik, were from homes of peasants or artisans. For the Bolsheviks, exile and jails and prisons had been their universities; their experiences as workers in cities from Baku to Singapore, from the Oklahoma oil fields to the Ohio steel mills, their graduate courses. Among them all was the unifying thread of common conscience expressed in action.

Once Peters was named to the Cheka, Jack and I speculated as to whether he would retain the quality of tenderness that Bessie Beatty saw—his essential concern for the human personality. Jack was dead when I saw Peters again after the Revolution; I should have liked to tell him my impressions. Characteristically, Peters had insisted that Lucita Squier, my wife, and I pay a visit to his home. He ushered us into a single large room where he beamed with pride over the Russian family he had acquired, a wife and little boy. The youngster was only a toddler, but clearly he ran the roost. The samovar bubbled, we spoke of old times, of Reed, of the past and the future. He was keen on knowing what Lucita thought of the Russian theater, of the original work of Vsevolod Meyerhold, Tairov of the Kamerny Theater, and the movie directors Eisenstein and Pudovkin. We spoke of Lenin, of course. It was in 1923, and I asked Peters' advice: Should I try to see him, or would it be wrong to tax his strength, presumptuous to take up precious time when he could see so few visitors? Or would I even be permitted to see him? Peters showed his appreciation of my dilemma, and did not commit himself.

The Cheka had been abolished the year before, only to give rise to the

GPU. When I told Peters frankly that I had never been able to picture him as the great sleuth he must be, Peters replied with the same frankness. He deprecated the investigative feats of the Cheka. It was only a matter of catching one White, and he would forthwith give away his companions, or even name "father, mother, sister, brother" to gain immunity. These were not revolutionaries who, tortured, beaten, exiled under the tsars, refused to betray their comrades.

He told how he had got wind of an underground counterrevolutionary group that operated between Moscow and Nizhni Novgorod and sent two Cheka men to Nizhni with forged passes indicating they were approved by the Moscow group. They arrived in time for a decisive meeting, allegedly to give a report on the progress of the plot in Moscow. Having persuaded the chairman to hear the report at the end of the meeting, they sat quietly near the one door in the room and listened. At one point one of the twenty tsarist officers who made up the group became suspicious and whispered to the chairman, who reassured him, and the meeting went on. At another point the nonarrival of certain officers caused restiveness, and an officer went out to determine why they had not appeared. When his failure to return became prolonged, the chairman abruptly asked the Cheka men for their report.

Reaching down into the leather portfolios at their feet, each Cheka man came up with two revolvers. "This is our report!" At this signal, several local Cheka men burst in. They had already arrested the latecomers, along with the officer who went to seek them.

Earlier Peters had ordered certain telephones disconnected and all trains bound for Moscow stopped, in case of Cheka bungling, to prevent the alerting of Moscow conspirators before they were all rounded up.

"Well, is it a state secret how you got on their trail?" I asked.

"Not at all. It all depended on the word of one girl. We decided to trust her. She came to me with her story. She was in love with an officer, but finally chose to betray him rather than the Revolution. When he was drunk he had boasted of new times a-coming. All he would say was 'There will be a change. Then I will not be so poor as I am now.'

" 'But you have money now,' the girl said.

" 'Yes, but not so much as I will have.'

"Then he would be gone for days at a time, never telling her in advance. We put a watch on her man. That's all the story—except that in Nizhni we found stamps, seals, hidden ammunition. Oh, yes. And one of the officers we caught was a Lettish general.

" 'You don't know me,' I said when they brought him before me. He said no, he had not had the honor.

" 'Perhaps you recall the Riga front, and the time when machine guns were ordered up against a Lettish regiment that was unwilling to carry out your orders to retreat?' The General said through set teeth, 'Yes.'

" 'One Lett should help another,' I said. Through him we made five hundred arrests."

Younger than Peters, Voskov had spent ten years in the United States and was twenty-eight when I met him. His was a paradoxical personality. He had a sort of inverted humor that defied analysis. He made a practice of exaggerating the gloomy side of things, so as never to be caught off guard. Why be positive when he might be negative? This gave him, strangely enough, a debonair, positively jaunty air. By all rules of logic he should have been an uncompanionable fellow; in fact, you could find no one who was of a more radiant disposition.

On a trip to the countryside the previous summer, when he had managed to get an old car, I complained mildly of the atrocious roads. He scanned the heavens and said that a thunderstorm would make the road much worse, and that just such a scorching day as this might well end in a thunderstorm. The thunderstorm did not arrive, but the engine stalled. This appeared to cheer him up greatly. He went to work on it with zest and finally we were bumping along again. Then we got stuck in the mud in the bed of a small stream. Grumbling, I got out and tugged and strained to lift the back wheels, and then the front ones stuck. Voskov leaped out, waded ashore, returned with what looked to be about half a tree, did something miraculous, and then, warbling a Russian folk song, drove the car out. "That says in Russian," he said, to my downright annoyance, " 'Here, little bird, take this note and fly away to my lover.' "

He seemed to believe that no matter how bad things were, they could be worse, and probably would be. When they got worse, he became sunshine itself. All of this had to do with surfaces only; beneath it all he believed that the people would inherit the earth through no effort save their own, and that they would do so for a certainty. Like all the other Bolsheviks, Voskov had been trained in a school that left few illusions. His pessimism, I suspected, was cultivated as armor against inevitable disappointments.

In one of my last memories of him in Petrograd, at a time when even an optimist might have believed it would be a miracle if the Soviets survived, Voskov said, with his imperturbable smile, "We must work while we can, because we may be dangling from lampposts before long." It was true enough, every Bolshevik faced this possibility if the counterrevolution, encouraged by intervention, succeeded. This very knowledge seemed to make Voskov begin each day with renewed cheerfulness. One more day without going under, one more day to fight.

And now in September he seemed inexhaustible, worked night and day, but because things were going well, the Bolsheviks gaining with every day, the snatches of song, the smiles were less frequent. It took reverses to bring out the real sweetness in Voskov's nature. Maybe it was because he had known so many that the periods in between seemed somehow unreal. He had been in prison in many places. In Constantinople, for example. Tortured, he bit his lips until the blood came. I asked how he had withstood the beatings and tortures. He was matter-of-fact about it. "The first blow, you see, quite paralyzes the nerves, so they don't respond to subsequent blows." Voskov might be, and was, gloomy with a relish in anticipating tomorrow, but he was serene as to today, and indifferent as to yesterday. As for day after tomorrow, he was sure his two children would have an easier time, but that was all. "We have enough to do now without mulling over the past or getting puffed up about the future," he said.

For all his jocund spirit and inverted humor, Voskov lived by a code of the sternest morality, which embraced not only himself, but Voskova, his comely, strong, hard-working wife (who in later years wanted to help me gather material in the villages), and their children. I can see him now in his Red Army uniform as he bade Voskova good-by in the early spring of 1918. He was one of the young Bolshevik actives whom Lenin rushed to the worst trouble spots as the White counterrevolution gathered force. I am sure it was hard for Lenin to be so unsparing with these fearless, sober, and hardheaded young men, the flower of the Revolution, but he had little choice; were he less reckless with these creative and ingenious young leaders, the seemingly unbeatable march of Denikin, Kolchak, and others could not have been turned back.[4] To Voskova, clinging to him dry-eyed and brave herself, he said merely, "If I die, let our children know that their father expected them to carry on the fight." He knew that the fight would not be easily won, and the coming generation must be revolutionaries too.

That Voskov had the respect and liking of Raymond Robins after the October Revolution I knew. This is borne out by the official text of a wire that Robins, then head of the American Red Cross in Russia, sent Ambassador Francis on April 4, 1918, after Francis had fled to Vologda, which reads in part:

> Reliable report from Petrograd just received assures control there of effective force by Soviet power for all domestic needs. Commander of Red Guard, Waskoff, personal friend of mine, fearless and resourceful. He went to Finland, personally led three assaults on the

---

4. General A. I. Denikin; Admiral Alexsandr V. Kolchak. Kolchak was advancing from the west, Denikin from the south.

White Guards, in which five of his staff command were killed. So long as he commands Petrograd Red Guard, I am entirely satisfied with local situation.

At one point after October, Voskov served as Food Commissar for the Northern Region. My notes from this period, though characteristically I did not put a date on them, read: "As such, he [Voskov] will not bring home one morsel of bread, although he sees his children's mouths gaping with hunger. The children receive ⅛ pound of bread, half of which is made of husks of sunflower seeds. Their bellies yawning, nevertheless the children have the energy to exchange accusations. 'You ate flowers, white flowers,' cries the little girl.

" 'I didn't!' the little boy retorts. Then: 'They were yellow. But you ate flies from the windowpane—dead ones. Mother said you mustn't, they aren't clean.' "[5]

One night Reed and I stood with Voskov looking from the parapet of a bridge at the swift-flowing waters of the Neva beneath us. I said it was like Wordsworth's vision from London Bridge. In the distance were the needle spire of the Admiralty, palaces, and the fantastic bulbous domes of churches. Through the mist could be heard music. "Do you hear that?" asked Reed.

"Yes, I can hear that," Voskov said crisply, demolishing our poetic mood. "And I can also hear the groans of the masses of serfs who built this city."

Voskov had been at some afternoon-long faction meeting when we met him at Smolny and insisted he come along with us for tea and borscht. We wound up in my room at the Astoria Hotel. Voskov clearly was exhausting himself, speaking almost daily at the factory benches or barracks. He seemed unusually preoccupied, and for once, no trace of his fey humor was in evidence.

Reed told Voskov he had talked to a worker the day before who said frankly, "We'll be out on the streets within a week."

Voskov was not letting himself be provoked. He smiled wanly and said, "Who was your interpreter—Albert Davidovich?" (Albert Davidovich was their way of combining my given name and that of my father, who was David Thomas Williams.)

Then, in a matter-of-fact tone, he said, "There really isn't any change in the situation. I mean, there isn't a recognition yet of the change in the

_____

5. The children of the Voskovs were at this time, I believe, in a *Dietsky Dom* (children's home), as was the case with others whose mothers as well as fathers were active revolutionaries, their talents as organizers needed as the counterrevolution gathered momentum.

objective conditions which both of you as journalists have sensed yourselves."

"Recognition by whom? You're not saying Lenin doesn't—" Reed began combatively.

Voskov dismissed the obvious with a tired wave of the hand. "Of course
it is not Lenin who does not sense the mood of the masses. That goes
without saying. He is underground, cut off from us, he complains he is
not told things. But *he* knows both the conditions and the subjective
moods of the people. No, it is others who are no farther from the workers
than a tram ride who don't understand."

As he stood up to go, Voskov said huskily, with something of his customary cheerful pessimism, "We are trying to ride a cyclone. We are such
a small handful. I often feel that ours are pipsqueak voices in a hurricane."
He smiled, shrugged, and added, "You can't stop a hurricane, you know."

"Then roar with it, *tovarish!*" Reed cried, clapping him on the shoulder.
Then, his mood changing with lightning speed, tinged with skepticism,
though perhaps it signified no more than his constant effort as a reporter to
inquire, verify, doubt: "What would happen if the Bolsheviks *didn't*
mount the cyclone? In other words, if the Bolshevik organization decides
against an insurrection at this time?"

Weary as he was, Voskov's eyes flashed as, his hand on the doorknob,
he turned and looked at us. "The people will take to the streets anyway.
Just as they did in July, without us. In July, when we did try to control
the demonstrations, it was too late, they were out of hand. And there was
only a blood bath, and repression. But no insurrection then, even if we had
led it and exercised control, could have maintained itself. Today it is
different.

"We have the organizations today. We have majorities in the Soviets.
We have the factories, solid. We have much of the army, certainly the Petrograd garrison. We have the fleet. And the provinces will come along, most
of the peasants will back the workers once they come out. Albert Davidovich can tell you about the peasants.

"One thing is sure—when the masses move, our place is with them. We
are not all-wise, but the worst thing would be demoralization of the masses
through inactivity. The enormousness of the whole thing at times seems
stunning. To me, too. But Marx tells in *The Eighteenth Brumaire* [of
Louis Bonaparte] that proletarian revolutions differ from bourgeois revolutions in that they are 'ever self-critical,' and even 'Again and again, they
shrink back appalled before the immensity of their own aims.' So, my dear
young American comrades, do not be impatient, and do not misunderstand
us."

Reed and I were affected by his visit, and speculated on how it must feel to cope with a cyclone. Voskov understood well that there were elemental forces on the loose.

But no matter that he and the others had momentary doubts, and were candid enough, felt close enough to us, to let them show. They did not act accordingly. They worked and talked indefatigably. For long stretches they were almost sleepless and seemingly nerveless, quite as if they alone could determine events. But actually they were ready to go where the great wind blowing up—the people—took them, whatever the cost. Their own lives were the least thing they worried about.

A varied group of men, this handful of Communists I knew who had returned from exile after the February Revolution. Uniting them was their common experience, their belief in a society that would regard men as human personalities, not as things, where in time not alone the forms of production would be changed for use, but men themselves would be transformed. All of them, even the anarchists I knew—even Nagel at this time, so far as I know—had a common *ultimate* goal: the end of exploitation of man by man, the finish of a society in which the inhuman processes of capitalist production had alienated man from his work, from his fellow man, and from himself; the eventual attainment of a society in which classes had disappeared and man could work, not to eat, not to sustain himself and enrich a small class at the top, but creatively. They were united, too, by their conviction of the greatness of Lenin.

Among the lot of them, Nagel alone was rigidly dogmatic. When the excesses of the bourgeois press brought about the first suppression of certain newspapers sometime after the October Revolution, it disturbed most of us. Peters said that even as a temporary measure it was a mistake, he thought; Reed and I didn't like it, and Reinstein worried over it. We discussed it, pro and con. But not Nagel. He was open to no discussion; he made it a matter of disloyalty even to question the correctness of the suppression. He was, it seemed, more Bolshevik than the Bolsheviks.

At the time, this meant nothing to us. In 1917–18, tolerance, even of the intolerant, was the rule. Lenin set the tone for it. For example, he said of Nikolai I. Bukharin, a brilliant theoretician, "There is a man with whom I shall never agree. He is too radical." Yes, Bukharin out-Lenins Lenin, Reed and I once agreed; but Lenin continued to work with him.

It never occurred to any of us that Nagel might be assuming any role, and I am not at all sure that he was during the Revolution. Perhaps he was mechanical, but even a mechanical man does not always have to be a hollow man, and later sell out. However that may be, he later disappeared. It was in 1925 that I tried to find out what had become of him. Lucita Squier visited his Russian wife, a lovely girl living in poverty in Moscow with their new baby, and expressed concern over their plight. Learning nothing after inquiring about him, I chose the one sure way to find out about Nagel. And, if the GPU had him, I would straighten them out.

I cheerfully entered the building mentioned in so many histories since then as "the dread Lubyanka prison." Brusquely I stated my mission. I wanted to inquire about a friend who was missing. I was told to enter a room. It was a good-sized room, with a massive table, a few chairs, and not much else. I was gazing out the window when a door opened and three men filed in. They indicated a seat I was to take—one that faced the light from the deep windows. They ranged themselves on either side and across from me. One took notes. Another studied some papers before him. The third, with his back to the light, sat facing me, his piercing black eyes never leaving my face. He was perhaps the most strikingly handsome Russian I ever saw.

I spoke rapidly, telling them about my friend Nagel. I felt somehow I must impress them with his dependability, so I really enlarged on our friendship. I had been through the Revolution with him, he was a Menshevik Internationalist who was thought well of by all of us. The fact that most of the comrades of those days were not here to speak for him made me feel I must come forward.

Then the man with the piercing eyes, the youngest of the three, began in a quiet way to question me. When had I last seen Nagel? Where? How often since 1918? As the questions continued, I was pleased, a bit flattered that so much of my own travels seemed known to them. It was only when he glanced at a page of the records his aide was studying and asked some personal question that had nothing to do with Nagel that I suddenly became aware that it was my own dossier they were studying, and that I and not Nagel was the subject of their interrogation.

"Your friend," my inquisitor said, with a disarming smile that left me cold, "was not all he seemed to you. He was an international spy." I noted the past tense. "We advise you to be more discreet in the future. In your shoes, I should worry no more about *Nagel*."

It was one of life's more uncomfortable moments.

I went to Peters. "All that you could do for him, you have done," he told me.

I was silent. Then: "What did you do with him?"

"Shot him."

But for all Peters' powers, he revealed how powerless he was when it came to his own child. His former English wife, who had followed him to Russia, had placed their daughter in Isadora Duncan's school. Peters, seeing her in a dance in which she flitted about as a gaudy butterfly, took exception. But his wife had control over the child. The dance continued, gauze wings and all. The man who could sign death warrants could find no way of putting a stop to the dance or any other influences his former wife might exert on his child.

Once in those golden autumn days of 1917 Jack Reed and I got in a terrible argument—about what, I do not recall. "Humanitarian! Sky pilot!" he yelled at me.

"Harvard Red! Football cheerleader!" I yelled back.

Bessie Beatty took us both in hand, saying with studied contempt, "You're both acting like small boys. Call yourselves radicals? You're a couple of spoiled American brats. Why don't you learn discipline from the Russian-American Bolsheviks?"

That was, of all the qualities that counted so heavily in this most interesting moment of history—their faith in the historic role of the workers, their hardheaded reasoning, their compassion—probably the most essential ingredient: self-discipline. That, and their relentless optimism, a spirit of courage and daring. Only with both could they have survived the coming trials.

To me personally, humanist that I am, their compassion loomed equally important. Not that they spoke of their feeling for the oppressed, except in flashes: Yanishev's indignation at having a human beast of burden offer to pull him in a ricksha in Tokyo, for example. Like Lenin, they spoke of concrete conditions that enslaved and degraded men, and their words were of hatred of such a system, not love of the workers. It was only at Lenin's funeral that Krupskaya said, "He loved with a deep love all the workers, the oppressed. He never said this, nor did I. I should probably never have spoken about it at any less solemn moment."

It was not only the workers, of course; as Engels said, "Communism is a question of humanity and not of the workers alone."

All these qualities counted in the period when the masses were moving forward to the seizure of power by the Soviets. Would they have stood my friends in good stead during the period of consolidating the Revolution after it was won? How would they have fared when the Revolution entered its later, constructive phases, and they were called on to organize production and administer complex and often prosaic tasks in connection with creating a solvent socialist society? How would Yanishev, Voskov, Volodarsky, Neibut have performed in subsequent periods? Their capacities and records would have assured them places of high responsibility in the new government (Volodarsky became a member of the Central Committee of the party after October). Would their idealism have survived? Would they have been poisoned by power, made arrogant by office? Would they have become insensitive bureaucrats?

Unfortunately there is no answer to this. They never entered into this later period, for the reason that they perished in the counterrevolution. Among these Bolsheviks I knew best, only Peters and Reinstein survived it.

Volodarsky was assassinated in Petrograd in June 1918, when I was in Vladivostok. His was the first of a series of terrorist assassinations by the Social Revolutionaries, preceded by one unsolved attempt on Lenin's life and followed by another traced to the SR's.

Neibut was one of a score of my comrades from Vladivostok who were killed. The Civil War overtook him in Siberia, and he was shot to death by the Whites in Omsk in 1919.

Yanishev was bayoneted to death by a white Guard on the Wrangel front in 1920. He was War Commissar of the Fifteenth Division of the Eighth Red Army. Like Reed, he was buried beside the Kremlin wall.

Voskov, who during the Civil War commanded the Seventh Army and in 1919 the Ninth Division, capturing Orel, died of typhus in Taganrog, March 19, 1920.

All one may say, then, is that these qualities I saw in them held for this early period of the Revolution. Lenin believed that the making of a revolution, the conquest of power by the workers and poor peasants, was much less hard than keeping it. They may have escaped the most difficult period. Even so, ordinary mortals, by their lives and deeds in this year of innocence when individuals as well as another society seemed born anew, they acquired a sort of immortality.

As I look back on this handful of Russian-American Communists, I am aware that the Revolution would have succeeded even were they not present. Nothing would have been different. Even the education of two footloose Americans would have been completed eventually, in all probability; it would only have taken longer. I have devoted this much space to them because they were not only typical of the Bolshevik revolutionary movement, but prototypes of the present corps of young revolutionists in Asia, Africa, and Latin America. And because, in knowing them, I first met Lenin in the spirit, if not in the flesh, so that when I later came to know him I felt at home with him. But perhaps I would have anyway. I rather think so.

· 3 · The Red Cock Crows

When a village hut caught fire in tsarist Russia, the peasants had a phrase for it: "The red cock is crowing again." The smallest villages might consist of one long road, with perhaps a few short crossroads. Invariably, however distant the limits of the village and the strips of land that would fall to some of the inhabitants to plow and seed, the log houses of the peasants huddled together, crowding the roadway. If the red cock crowed on a windy day, sparks quickly caught the straw-thatched roofs and the flames might leap to the ends of the village and reduce the whole of it to ashes. Thus for the peasant in old wooden Russia, the red cock was an ominous bird.

In the long hot summer of 1917, the red cock tirelessly crowed all over the Russian land. The omen now was of a different nature, the heralded disaster visited not on the huts of the peasants, but on the manor houses of the barins and the landlords. After the "July days" of repression, Petrograd and Moscow lay wrapped in an uneasy quiet—and hunger. The countryside, spurred on by another hunger—the age-old hunger of the Russian peasant for land—was, however, in revolt, unmistakable and spreading.

The peasants had been waiting since February for the revolutionary government to give them justice, which to them meant land. They were waiting no longer. As of April, the flow of reports on seizures of land in the provinces had begun.

In mid-July, when I went with Yanishev to the province of Vladimir, all seemed most tranquil on the surface. From the moment we stepped off the train among the rolling hills—not so much hills as undulating billows in that vast land ocean before us—we seemed terribly distant from the roar of the revolution I had heard in June and those first few days of July. Stopping to rest at the highest point in the road that runs over the Vladimir hills, I counted sixteen blue and gold onion-shaped domes glittering in the summer haze. That meant sixteen villages. Every large village had its church, and nearly every small one. In the distance stretched the fields of ripening golden rye, shot through with the blue of cornflowers, where the last part of our journey to the village called Spasskoye (Salvation) would be made on foot. In the nearer distance, below us, where the rolling land permitted a view from the hill, parts of small villages were visible—gray weathered log huts thatched with brown and amber straw, well sweeps with buckets for drawing water suspended at one end, and above all the domes of churches glinting in the sun.

Yanishev had taken off his cap and stood motionless looking over the acres he last had seen ten years ago. A light wind ruffled his hair. I had never been conscious of his hair before; it was getting thin, and with a sharp pang it occurred to me for the first time that he was getting old. How old? I never knew; but forty-five seemed very old to me at the time.

"I feel like a truant," I said. "It's all right for you—you were ordered to take a ten-day rest. But I'm afraid I'll forget all about the Revolution. Isn't this an idyllic picture?"

For a time he did not answer. Then he said absently, still taking in the scene, "You'll find the Revolution is here, too."

The peasant driver we had engaged to transport us part way in a wagon was growing restive. But Yanishev lingered. I waited for some sentimental comment. Hearing none, I grew expansive. This vista, wide and sweeping, this vastness of land and sky, must have helped inspire the scope of the dreams he cherished, which were no less than to make over society, and so man himself, I said. "Can you imagine? It looks absolutely unchanged. The only place conceivable where time has stood still. But it won't be long now!"

It was as if he had not heard me at all.

The immense expanse of rolling land was checkered with little strips and stripes of unfenced fields, narrow plots crazy-quilted in greens and yellows, from the vulnerable green of a second rye crop coming up to the lordly gold of ripening wheat, traditionally reserved for flour for the privileged classes. I thought of the vast stretches of wheatfields at home, in Kansas and the Dakotas, and Iowa cornfields. In comparison these separate plots seemed made for harvesting by a race of Lilliputians.

As we first drove and then walked through successive villages, some very small, I often saw the selfsame long street bordered by the houses of the peasants. This, like the maze of tiny fields, was the product, said Yanishev, of the method of land allocation. What was once a fundamental feature in various European countries—soil held as property in common—had persisted, with many distortions, in tsarist Russia. According to traditional practice, there was a periodic redistribution of the land, both arable and meadows, by each *mir* (whose literal meaning is "world") or village commune, so that each member received the same limited number of narrow plots of land, good and poor, with forests and pastures aplenty for all to use freely.

Only in Russia did the mir survive, and with it remnants of the land-distribution system, archaic and improvident, which kept the peasant's fields small and divided. This explained why the houses were bunched together. The fields he plowed and sowed were not together anyway, and he could not be moving his house every time the land was redivided. Both the abolition of serfdom under Aleksandr II in 1861 and the Stolypin decree of November 9, 1906,[1] had weakened but failed to do away altogether with the village communes.

Before we reached Spasskoye I remarked that it would be interesting to learn what the peasants thought about Lenin. At least it would afford some measure of judging whether all the moderate socialists were justified in blaming Lenin for the seizure of land and the burning and destruction taking place in the countryside. (Naturally, Miliukov was in the vanguard of the chorus attributing all the outrages in the rural regions to Lenin's counsel.) Lenin's was the only voice telling the peasants: Go on and take the land. He added: Do it in an organized way, after the majority decision of the peasantry of a village, *volost, uyezd,* or *gubernia*—and for one sowing, with local committees distributing it for that purpose; remember it is not to be private land, it is to be the entire people's property. More equitable distribution, region for region, can only be by the state power and must await the Constituent Assembly.[2]

In Petrograd, I said, Lenin was blamed for the entire revolt flaming in the countryside. What I wanted to know was: Did the peasant even hear him?

Yanishev warned me then, "Don't ask too many questions. You'll get answers, but not the right ones. The peasants will agree with you because that's their way of being hospitable to a stranger.

1. Peter Arcadievich Stolypin (1863–1911) was a governor of Grodno, then of Saratov, and in 1906 Minister of Internal Affairs. In July of that year he succeeded Goremykin as Minister-President. Cf. G. T. Robinson, *Rural Russia under the Old Regime,* New York, 1932, p. 194: "By the sale of lands, and especially the dissolution of the communes, a prosperous and trustworthy class of petty individual proprietors was to be built up. . . ." A militant pan-Russian nationalist, Stolypin was convinced that only thus could tsarism be bolstered against its liberal and radical opponents.

2. From the outset the Provisional Government had promised a redistribution of the land and a Constituent Assembly, the latter to be elected by a universal, equal, direct, and secret suffrage. It never got around to giving either. It pleaded with the peasants to wait until the Constituent Assembly, when redistribution would be done legally, but it repeatedly postponed the Assembly. Calling of the Constituent Assembly was long an important part of the Bolshevik program, and it continued to be, even after Lenin's return, but with a difference.

"And remember, they'll be polite even to me at first—but wary. Above all, don't ask a young or middle-aged man about himself. Most likely he'll be a soldier home without leave, one of hundreds of thousands voting with their feet against the new coalition government's policy of perpetuating the war.[3] He may proclaim his status of soldier proudly, but again he may be touchy about it, or he may think you're a spy. It hasn't been long since the Miliukov government was sending in agents to 'persuade' the peasants to pacification. And now cavalry troops are entering some of the villages in Kazan province to round up deserters and return them to the front. And peasants have been arrested, even flogged, to get them in the mood to wait, wait until land reforms are *legal*."

As we entered Spasskoye and headed for the home of Ivan Ivanov, I noticed the fire-fighting insignia visible in their fading paint on the corners of the houses. One small board showed a ladder, while a bit farther on was a house with similar boards decorated with water buckets. One house bore the symbol of a long grappling hook. In this way peasants running to put out a fire were reminded where they might find the needed tools to fight it. I told Yanishev I should like one day to see the actual buckets, hooks, and equipment inside.

With all the ceremonious welcome we received in the home of Ivan Ivanov, the excitement of greeting neighbors who dropped in, the old-timers curious at Mikhail Petrovich's return and all of them downright amazed at the appearance of an American, I forgot about my request to see the fire-fighting apparatus. Yanishev did not. In the morning we set out with a peasant, Dvorkin. I took a closer look at the insignia on the houses, and in a couple of them I met the families, saw the equipment, and solemnly discussed fires, all of us avoiding the one topic of consuming interest —the recurring presence of the red cock in 1917, in province after province, from the Black Sea to Lake Ladoga.

"Your houses in the village," I said to Dvorkin, whose penchant for irony

3 The first Provisional Government was one of bourgeois parties, dominated by the Kadets or Constitutional Democrats. After the resignation of P. N. Miliukov, Foreign Minister and long the leader of the Kadets and Russian bourgeois liberalism generally, and A. I. Guchkov, Minister of War, the Soviet of Workers' and Soldiers' Deputies agreed to coalesce with the bourgeois parties and to enter the government. Thus in May five portfolios in the cabinet were given to Soviet representatives. Kerensky had been the only socialist in the first Provisional Government, and without officially representing party or Soviet; now there were six, with Kerensky succeeding Guchkov as Minister of War. Lvov was retained as its head. This first coalition government lasted two months. On July 8, when the uprising of the "July days" had demonstrated it could no longer hold the support of the masses, Lvov resigned. Kerensky hurried off to the front to make speeches which in no way relieved the general crisis of the failure of the Galicia offensive; he left the troops no more zealous than before his campaign, and returned to promote himself as the new head of government. In both the first and second coalition governments the socialist ministers were from the Socialist Revolutionary, Menshevik, and International Menshevik parties, and in both, Kadets remained. The Bolsheviks alone remained outside the government and uncompromised by its policies.

I had already detected, "are they always arranged in this fashion, close enough to assure the complete destruction of the whole village in case of fire?"

"Yes," Dvorkin agreed, with a sly look at me. "When the red cock crows in one house, it often crows for the whole village. But then," he added cheerfully, "we peasants do everything together. We plow and sow and reap together. We pray together, we get drunk together. So we watch our houses burn down together."

"I see," I said. "But isn't it a pity that the gentry didn't build theirs all together, too? It would save a lot of work this summer in some provinces, wouldn't it?"

Yanishev, translating, gave me a warning look. But Dvorkin was not to be cornered. He would not know what went on in other villages, he said; in Spasskoye there were no big estates, of either church or barins. "We have all the land—we just don't have enough."

We were to hear the same plaint in many forms while we were there. It did not tell the whole story. When it was put this way it came from those who *had* the land. Those who had none or almost none were far more numerous. They lived by hiring themselves out in sowing and in harvesting seasons to those who had acquired land, or by getting work for a season in the textile mills of Nizhni Novgorod or the factories in Moscow.

All of Spasskoye knew that Yanishev was a Bolshevik in a matter of hours, but out of politeness no one mentioned it for a couple of days. Meanwhile, he added distinction to Ivan's household, as one who had traveled far and learned much. As the peasants put it, he had "drunk water from nine wells."

The utmost in courtesy was accorded the strange American. This, more than distrust, it seemed, decreed a warming-up period in which only formal questions should be asked me, such as "And how much land do you have?" At first I tried to avoid answering this one, especially at a meeting of the mir to which I was invited on our second morning there. These seventy graybeards represented the peasants who had land. Perhaps they would have no use for an American without any. But when a spry little fellow dressed in worn and faded blouse and pants twice his size dropped by that evening, and for custom's sake asked the same question, I replied, "Not a dessiatine. I don't need land."

"How can a man live without land?" he asked, truly puzzled, and Yanishev's eyes glinted as he translated. "Why, that is more strange than living without vodka, or without ikons, or without children. How can you be sure you are living in this world when you have none of it under your feet? Like a tree without roots, a horse without a manger, or a country without a tsar." Then, seeing my smile and recollecting that the February Revolution had deposed Nikolai II, he added, as he scanned first my face and then Yanishev's as if to read his very fate there: "It's true we have no Romanovs left, but they say a new tsar is coming. Some have already seen him and heard him say, 'Take the land yourselves! What are you waiting for?'"

The same diffidence the villagers showed for a time about Yanishev's party prevailed in regard to his father. A teacher, his father had been taken by the Tsar's police one day. He had expected it, and quietly turned the key in the lock of the school door and surrendered it to them. It remained shut. Under both the tsars who followed Aleksandr II, a deliberate policy had been pursued: to discourage the teaching of the peasantry and allow illiteracy to flourish. There was too much unrest as it was, and revolt and education went hand in hand.

Now, when more and more persons were dropping by to see us, and the samovar was humming and tea and kvass were served, no mention was made of the teacher who had lived among them. Possibly some of the elders who embraced the visiting son so warmly now were the very ones who had put the finger on the teacher. We were told, nevertheless, of a teacher in a neighboring village, who was known far and wide as a bit of a fool because he could not bear to kill a chicken, or even a flea or cockroach. He worried a lot about the killing at the front; and in June, with the news that the Provisional Government, yielding to pressure from the Allies, had ordered a large-scale offensive in Galicia, he who feared to kill a fly went home after classes and killed himself. None of those present failed to share his distaste for the offensive (which after a few days, and serious reverses, had been abandoned as too many peasants in uniform felt the same way). But to take one's own life—that, said one of the villagers, was only done, to his knowledge, among the gentry. He had heard of several cases of suicide among the "masters." But for the peasants, "We die as we live, with fortitude, but we don't invite death. Why should we?"

Alone, in our hayloft bed at night, Yanishev chuckled with amazement that he was received as he was. Twenty years earlier someone would have turned him in to the police if it were even suspected that he was a socialist. Now, after a couple of days, one or two had begun to ask, "Won't Mikhail Petrovich give us a little speech?" Yanishev bided his time. He still was hoarse from his tireless speaking to Viborg audiences in Petrograd. He needed rest. He wanted to wait, too, until there were more requests. Only when some broached the matter directly—couldn't Mikhail Petrovich tell what the Bolsheviks were up to, and just what this Lenin had told the Peasants' Congress?—did he indicate he might. Still he waited, until it was clear that most of the villagers would be there if he spoke, and even perhaps a few from nearby villages. This was exciting to us.

Lenin had spoken to the Peasants' Congress on May 22, before my arrival in Petrograd. Only a couple of days earlier, an Officers' Congress had demanded his arrest. Undaunted, Lenin appeared before the peasant delegates, most of them either intellectual SR's who kept a tight control over the bureaucratic party machinery or the substantial peasants who had acquired considerable land—the type I had seen dominating the mir here. But apparently a few small peasants crept in. Sukhanov describes how "with the absorbed interest of the Peasant Congress, Lenin developed his programme of 'direct action,' his tactics of land seizure regardless of the legally-appointed limits," adding: "It would seem that Lenin had landed not merely in a camp of bitter enemies, but you might say in the very jaws of the crocodile. The little muzhiks listened attentively and probably not without sympathy. But they dared not show it."

Sukhanov was present when a deputation from the Peasants' Congress, seeking a law to stop the widespread sale of land by landlords,[4] called on officials at the Maryinsky Palace. Premier Lvov, Kerensky, and Tereshchenko heard first a soldier delegation from the front, then the peasants. After a flowery beginning in which the officer spoke of his willingness to die for the Revolution, he got to the heart of his "greeting"—"to inform the Provisional Government that we honor it, trust it, and support it to the extent and in so far as it fulfills . . ."

The Premier turned on his heel and left the room at this, and the other ministers turned to the peasants. A gray little peasant earnestly, almost tearfully, urged a law to preserve the land resources, but Kerensky, agitated and pale, interrupted to say there was nothing to worry about, the P.G. was "taking steps." One of the peasants, however, began to point out that the law had long been promised but nothing was done. Kerensky, furious by then, said:

"I said it would be done, that means it will! And—there is no need to look at me so suspiciously!"

Sukhanov explains that these deputations were unlike those of two months earlier.

> Now the intolerable formula about supporting the Government *in so far* as it supported the Soviet had sunk deep into the consciousness of the masses once and for all. The Government itself, however, was very well aware of the impossibility of this kind of existence, which everyone knew to be *by permission of the Soviet*. The naive

---

4. Landlords who feared the march of revolution and the promised land reforms to be passed at the oft-postponed Constituent Assembly, hurried to dispose of their holdings. Rich peasants bid for them, hoping as peasants to forestall expropriation. Many sales were fictitious; landlords who thought small-acreage farms would be permitted sold their estates in small lots to dummy owners. A frequent trick was to transfer ownership to foreigners whose citizenship was in Allied or neutral countries.

officer had struck the chief of the Cabinet on a sore spot. . . . Kerensky was right, the little peasants were looking *suspiciously* at the famous people's Minister. The delegation of peasants had finally arrived at the same point as the delegation from the front.

Yes, it was impossible to live like that any longer.

Yanishev had with him Lenin's speech to the peasants as it was printed May 25, 1917, in one of the newspapers, and reading it to me and having me read it back to him were part of my regular lessons in Russian language here at Spasskoye. We discussed, too, what parts he should stress in his coming speech. This is the speech in which Lenin said in part:

. . . tens of millions of people will not make a revolution to order, but will do so when their position becomes one of hopeless need, when the people are in an impossible position, when the determination of tens of millions of people breaks down the old barriers and can actually create a new way of life.

The Russian people in the mass are only capable of taking a serious step along that new path when the direst need arises. And we say to you the time has now come when that dire need is knocking at the door. . . . ruination is coming closer to us day by day, hour by hour. It is not due to the malice of individuals, but the world war of aggression, to capitalism.

The war has annihilated millions of people, the whole world is bathed in blood. [My plea is for determined advances] along the path to the common cultivation of the soil without the capitalists and without the landowners. [Only this will] lead to the real transfer of the land to the working people.

At last the day was fixed when Yanishev was to speak to the villagers. Meanwhile I busied myself taking part in their holiday feasts, attending christenings and funerals. I even did some work in the fields, fields that had been lustrated (walked round with ikons). Swinging a scythe until my hands blistered, tying up sheaves and rearing an aching back, I began to see that the peasant's life was not one long idyll of peace and beauty as seen from that hillside overlooking the Vladimir fields and villages.

Yanishev spoke from a wagon bed in the village square. It was evening, and I anxiously studied the faces lit by the single flare. Old and young were there, solemn, laconic; the local powers who had welcomed me at the mir formed a solid phalanx close to the speaker.

Poor Yanishev. I did not envy him. It was not that they were openly hostile. At least, only a few were. A man of seventy-odd, whom I had seen standing exultantly, Midas-like, fingering the fat heads of wheat growing on his land, stomped away petulantly early in the evening. The majority appeared to me simply skeptical, perhaps only noncommittal. At the same time in their questions there was often that quality of salty humor possessed by oppressed classes everywhere. That, and the artless honesty of a people still partly rooted in feudalism who had not had the advantages (and the disadvantages) of being educated under a bourgeois democratic society, for whom simple words like "freedom" had a concrete meaning.

"What have the Bolsheviks to say about the land?" Yanishev began. Here he was on sure ground. Anxiously I scanned his face, trying not to see the features that were as familiar as the back of my hand, but to see a stranger's; he did seem rested, and, I felt, sure of his position in the community. He had complied with all the customs as a guest in the village. He had observed protocol. Now he was speaking to a larger audience than the few who in Ivan's home had occasionally got him to conduct brief discussions. His voice rang with confidence. His party was not the only party that stood for land for the peasants. The peasants long had put their faith in the Socialist Revolutionary party, built on the slogan of more land for the peasants, the return of land to the people. Even the Mensheviks were for land reforms. But what in fact had happened since the February Revolution? What had happened since the second coalition government, supported by Mensheviks and Socialist Revolutionaries, headed by Kerensky, an SR, began to rule? Nothing. Absolutely nothing. What were the Soviets themselves, dominated by SR's and Mensheviks, saying about what was occurring in the countryside? All these voices said, "Wait, wait. Meanwhile, deal with the landlords." Everyone agreed, he said, that all land must be the property of the whole people and must be transferred to them without payment, and only a central state power (the Constituent Assembly or All-Russian Council of Soviets) could arrange final disposal.

The differences began, he said, as Lenin had told the Peasants' Congress, when all others said that any *immediate* unpaid transfer of landed estates to the peasantry was an unauthorized act. And Yanishev quoted Lenin's words: "We consider this view to be the most erroneous, the most prejudicial to the peasantry, prejudicial to the tillers of the soil, and the least likely to ensure the country a supply of bread, and unjust."

"Why is only a voluntary agreement between peasant and landowner, between the man who seeds the furrow and the man who owns the land, considered by our provisional government authorized?" Yanishev asked: "Why are the peasants who want to effect the immediate transfer and distribution of the land by local committees accused of unauthorized acts not in accord with the needs of the state? 'That is what we deny, that is what we dispute,' said Lenin. He also said, 'In our opinion, on the contrary, if the landowners retain the land for their own use or obtain rent for it, that is arbitrary, but if the majority of peasants say that the landed estates must not remain in the hands of their owners, and that the peasantry has known nothing but oppression by those landowners for decades, for centuries, that is not arbitrary, that is the reestablishment of justice . . .' "

Since up to then Yanishev was saying what his audience wanted to hear, he had clear sailing—for the time being. So long as he spoke only of the need to kick out the landlords and take the land, they drank in his words. He touched on some of the events that were taking place, both in the countryside and in cities. Nor did he fail to suggest that for both the workers who wanted to kick out the bosses and the peasants who were driving out the landlords, their future lay together; one must support the other. Otherwise it would be as it had been in the other lands when peasants had revolted and won, only to see their gains lost and new repressions enforced.

Lenin, he said, felt the land seized should be divided by the land committees for the coming sowing. But then he went on to suggest what would happen when the bourgeois parliamentary republic was replaced by a socialist republic, how individual farming would give way in large part to the more economic system of large-scale farming.

Here his audience grew restive. It was apparent that they had no use for any such newfangled notions as large model farms. They were bored, indifferent, or downright hostile to all talk of the larger issues of socialism, Lenin's future plans for more tractors, for electricity, for variegated farming and dairy farming.

"Very good, comrade talker," came a voice from the crowd. "The Bolsheviks can do great things. But can they make more land? Only God can do that."

Apprehensively I watched one after another going away quietly to their homes while Yanishev went on talking to his dwindling audience. His patience was indestructible. Moreover, he understood his audience. He smiled. No, they wouldn't compete with God, he replied. But by reclaiming wastelands, by introducing irrigation in drought areas, pouring water into deserts, making the non-black-soil regions richer by introducing fertilizers, they could in effect make more land—vast expanses of plowlands, such as he had seen in America, even larger, as large as Vladimir province. They would see. Harness the horsepower in rivers, light up the dark villages, and have the state pay for moving families from congested areas or marginal lands to richer ones. No peasant ever would have to work again for a landlord or for another peasant.

But to the old guard this was too much. He had his feet on the ground when he spoke of seizing the land. But as for everything that Yanishev said would follow, that was fantastic.

"You are chasing cranes in the sky, Mikhail Petrovich," an old peasant said with dignity, and took his departure.

Out of the circle of light beneath the smoking flare, one by one they drew back and slipped away into the darkness . . . away from the impossible.

" 'As things are, they needs must be. As our fathers plowed, so plow we,' " I said to Yanishev as we plodded homeward to our hayloft bed at Ivan's. It was gallows humor; I felt Yanishev would consider he had failed. Then, more gently, I added, "The young ones and the 'farm hands,' as we call them in the States, and one or two others appeared really interested. After all, they're not the workers at the Treugolnik factory or the Old Parviainen plant."[5]

I went on chattering away, thinking I was cheering Yanishev up. It was not until we were tucked away for the night in the sweet-smelling hay, with the yellow moonlight streaming in through a big square aperture cut in the hayloft wall, that Yanishev found his voice and replied. Biting into a cucumber—a great delicacy—which he had thoughtfully put by for our midnight snack, he smiled at me. "You know, Albert Davidovich, you have it all wrong. I am not in the least discouraged. Not the least bit. I feel rather satisfied that the meeting went so well."

As sometimes happens between two persons who are close, now that Yanishev was taking my side I immediately felt it was quite unreasonable of him. Maybe I was just tired of always being in agreement with Yanishev; or maybe I was more deeply troubled than I had believed at having to concede that my original impressions of the village and the peasants and the mir had been somewhat romantic.

At the end of our first day there I had declared I could live forever (and I did live for some years all told) under those straw-thatched roofs whose eaves hung down like the shaggy hair of some of our hosts and neighbors. On the night before the meeting, however, Yanishev made me grudgingly admit that the huge stoves did add to the congestion of the two rooms that were the rule in most homes. In other ways, too, my first impressions of Spasskoye as a rural paradise faded under the impact of his arguments. The checkered fields were picturesque when seen from a hilltop, but their size

---

5. These were two especially militant groups of workers who on April 12, scarcely more than a week after Lenin's arrival from exile, passed interesting resolutions, carried by *Izvestia*, official organ of the Soviet. They urged the Soviet of Workers' and Soldiers' Deputies to "categorically demand" of the Provisional Government the immediate publication of all secret treaties entered into with the Allies by the Tsar, that it call an international conference for the opening of peace negotiations, and so forth. The Old Parviainen plant workers went further: they demanded the removal of the Provisional Government, "which serves only as a barrier to the revolutionary cause," and the transfer of power into the hands of the SWSD; formation of a Red Guard and arming of the people, and "the immediate seizure of lands by peasant committees and the transfer of the instruments of production to the hands of the workers."

limited the middling peasant to hand plows and harrows for tilling, and to sickle and scythe for reaping. Most of these implements were made by hand from wood taken from the forests. There was metal in the village, good bronze, but it was up in the belfry in the five bells that rang out so clearly in the fresh morning air. I had to admit that Russia's agricultural problem would never be solved by these primitive implements. As for the poor peasants, 80 per cent of the whole Russian peasantry, either landless or with so little land they must hire themselves and their families out to others, I had to admit that the mir itself, with all its ideals of justice and equality, was no longer a "force," as Lenin had said it was not even in 1903.

I had eaten with zest out of a common bowl. All right, I conceded that from a scientific standpoint it was not wise, but I continued to enjoy it. And I had no argument to offer when Yanishev suggested that our hay-mow was doubly attractive because it was a safe retreat from the flea and the cockroach.

Still, there was one thing on which I could agree with Yanishev whole-heartedly: Even in land-hungry Vladimir villages where there was no land to seize, it was obvious that tension was building up. Otherwise Yanishev never would have been welcomed, never would have been invited to tell them "what the Bolsheviks are up to," or "what this Lenin really said." The peasants here might not be hearing Lenin, but there were those among them who were in a mood to hear him.

This was doubly proved the remainder of our time in Spasskoye. Various peasants who had joined the exodus of the elders from Yanishev's meeting now sought him out singly, or seemingly by accident whenever he wandered down the road in the evening. These included a few from surrounding villages. Their talks indicated a cleavage in the village—of youth against elders, of poor against the kulaks—which made for a revolutionary potential. In this simmering village revolt, the old patriarchs, to keep their prerogatives and privileges, were fighting the same losing battle the squires were fighting for their domain elsewhere. For the present, just as the villagers were united in their holiday ceremonies and games, their rituals celebrating a birth or taking note of a death, so they were united in the conviction passed on from generation to generation: The land must belong, it did belong by rights, to those who work it. It was expressed in their saying "The land is no man's, the land is God's."

We took our departure from the village on a bright windless morning and headed for the Volga. We would go by steamer to Nizhni Novgorod, where we would catch a train for Moscow. Our good host and the women of his family seemed genuinely sorry to see us go. Neighbors gathered too, and there were many kisses and embraces exchanged, the women of course looking on, only spectators when it came to such endearing forms of farewell. I promised to return (as I did a few years later), but I could not be sorrowful as I swung my battered suitcase in beside Yanishev's and jumped in the cart that was to lighten the first part of our journey. The trip ahead was too intensely exciting to me. The Volga always had played a part in Russian revolutionary history, and now it was the Volga that drew me.

The boat was crowded. We had obtained second-class passage, but Yanishev wanted to go to the top deck to hear what the gentry were saying— although, to be sure, they might be traveling in second or even third class, pretending to be anything but nobles or landlords. Yanishev was a listener, letting information come to him. I, on the other hand, had to take part in everything. Since I would be certain to advertise our sentiments on the Revolution, I left Yanishev alone with his gentlemen and descended to the fourth-class deck. On these large Volga boats this space was used for transporting anything and everything, including landless peasants. Originally forced to remain in their villages by the debts the mir held collectively, allowed only short-term passports for "going-away work," with the relative easing of passport regulations after the 1905 revolution they had been able to make their way to Moscow or Petrograd.[6] Or they sought work nearer home, in the smaller industries of Nizhni Novgorod, Yarolslavl, Rybinsk, and other Volga cities.

I stood on the lowest step of the wide staircase leading from the comfortable, relatively elegant third-class deck and looked at whole families wedged tightly with their bundles and teakettles between nervous farm animals and crates of produce. The air was fetid. Men dozed sitting bolt upright; children sprawled asleep on boxes. Mothers fed their babies at the breast; others were making tea; a group of young persons at the far end was singing to the accompaniment of a harmonica. The ship's bell sounded monotonously. A foul smell permeated the place. Above, a barely perceptible afternoon breeze stirred the air, but down here there was a sense of suffocation. My recollection is that except for the portholes, whatever light there was came from a type of lantern bracketed along the bulkheads at intervals—a dull but seemingly indestructible glow, like that shed by kerosene storm lanterns in my boyhood in upstate New York.

Thinking I wanted a seat, a big-boned peasant woman near the stairway motioned to her husband and began crowding bundles and sleeping children

---

6. In 1903 the joint liability of the village community for taxes and redemption dues was abolished. Cf. John Maynard, *The Russian Peasant and Other Studies,* London, 1943, pp. 54 ff., on the various steps by which the tsarist government, alarmed by the agricultural riots against the squires in 1905, introduced vigorous reforms which, especially after the Stolypin plan prevailed, brought about the desired weakening of the mir's hold on the peasants. By 1910 not two-thirds but a bare majority vote was required in the mir to allow a villager to leave the mir and claim individual property rights.

closer together to make room. For once I found no word of thanks for this characteristic Russian hospitality. I wanted to say, "Why don't you go upstairs and throw the gentry down here? *You* are the ones who should be basking in those deck chairs now!" Forgetting my scant supply of Russian words in my fury, I pointed to the stairs, to the deck above, and nodded vigorously. The woman only fanned herself with her kerchief in the wretched heat and looked blankly at me and questioningly at her husband, who shrugged, as if to say, "Pay no heed to the daft one." Dejectedly I went up to join Yanishev.

On the lower of the two upper decks I halted at the sound coming from the bow. It was the leadsmen, wielding their graduated poles and calling out the depth of the water. The regularity of their bulletins on the soundings had the effect, to one hearing them for the first time, almost of a chant. I watched them, remembering how Mark Twain described this practice in *Life on the Mississippi*. The Volga, like the Mississippi, is full of treacherous shoals and shifting sand bars, so that a pilot's trade must have called for training as rigorous as that which Twain had mastered with such pride. The landing places were square pontoons built of wood, connected by a sloping wooden bridge to the shore. At times the boat sat down on a sand bar, and there would be a delay till we were pried off again. The leadsmen played their part, but the pilot had to know the river and its tricky bed, especially near the shoreline, like the palm of his hand.

Once we were in the mainstream, I made my way to the upper deck to join Yanishev. Thinking guiltily of the stench-filled air in the pit below, I sank into a commodious deck chair. We were heading downstream. Trailing willow branches dipped into the water from the gently sloping left bank. Along the rim of the steep right clay bank a peasant slowly made his way, a single figure etched against the immensity of endless sky, harrowing his field by hand.

Yanishev repeated what he had heard from a group of landowners. All were in near panic about the peasant revolts, the burnings and the pillaging. A general had voiced their hysteria: "The world used to condemn Russia for exiling and imprisoning revolutionists. Even I in my youthful idealism felt the Tsar was too severe with them. Now look at their handiwork! The Tsar was too lenient. He should have shot them outright."

Lulled by the motion of the boat, by the heat, by the sameness of the sunny skies mirrored in the placid Volga, the two of us grew silent. The steppe stretched unseen a bit to the southeast. Yanishev dozed. Once more I thought of the patient poor below; could they really be akin to those whose anger and vengeance was terrifying the gentlemen Yanishev had described? Heading for historic Nizhni Novgorod, a city even more aged than Moscow, we were passing through the country where the great eastern movement of the Slavs across the vast Eurasian plain began, longer ago than their recorded history, prior to the eighth century A.D.

Life was hard; climate and soil and forestation made agriculture difficult in the central and north areas. Yet because of the type of small village groupings by families and near relatives, and the practice that historians agree prevailed of holding their lands and tools in common and regarding the products of their labor as joint property, there was not the isolation and aching loneliness attributed to frontier life in America. By the end of the sixteenth century the peasants, once free men able to move where they chose, had become serfs in fact; the legalization of the status came later.

The sun was setting. We postponed tea till the crowd had thinned. Even in normal times, Yanishev said, the dining saloon on such boats was small, undermanned, and understocked. The charm of the ever changing sky held me. The earlier cloudlessness had been succeeded by a mackerel sky, the flaming reds and purples in the west faded, and now a rosy stain flung its tint over the fleecy cloud formations. We lingered on to watch the magic coming of the late twilight of a Russian August night—late, that is, compared to the coming short days.

Suddenly we heard cries and a general commotion as men flocked to the other side of the deck. By now the clouds had been swept from the sky except for dark wispy streaks huddling above the high right bank. On the left, the bank rose gently and swelled to a rather high point, where some discriminating *pomeshchik* (landlord) had built a splendid manor house, from which great tongues of fire now reached the dark, cloudless sky.

Its solid timbers were in flames. Smoke billowed forth, thick and heavy, and a fountain of sparks flew up, then high yellow flames swept skyward. A bedlam of choice epithets flew around us in French and Russian, with even a few in German, on this disgraceful Jacquerie. Some passengers paced the deck, their tread funereal, while others clutched the rail, their faces set, doubtless reading their own doom in the glowing embers. I would have remained staring at the scene if Yanishev had not tugged at my sleeve. Bound for a dining saloon, we saw, on the deck below, an arresting figure poised by the stairway. From his appearance he was a stoker. He stood with bared arms, a grimy hand on the polished balustrade, his head cocked in a jaunty manner, eying the last of the holocaust. Yanishev caught his eye and exchanged a word or two. The stoker spat with real eloquence, added, "Another nest of the gentry gone," and with rolling gait swung lightly down the stairs, two at a time.

"Shall we follow him, at least to the deck below?" On the bottom step

I waited for Yanishev, who engaged the nearest group in conversation. I saw no adults sleeping in torpor now. The men appeared animated, talking in groups. Eyes mild and merry seemed to contradict the serious concentration with which they spoke, gestured, argued.

"They knew about it, all right. Got it by the grapevine. A few got unscrambled from the crowd and made their way upstairs. It's no new sight to most of them, I gather." Yanishev spoke with satisfaction on our way up the stairs.

Gone was my own critique of the "docile" peasant, vanished in the smoke of the burning manor house.

· 4 · The Single Voice

After my visit to Spasskoye and the journey down the Volga with Yanishev, I left Petrograd with Alex Gumberg for a trip to the Ukraine. I saw another manor house in flames, had some more talks with peasants. Again I walked through rippling meadows, through clumps of pines and birches whose leaves were now turning yellow, and once more thought how strange that this peaceful scene should cloak the greatest of all agitators in Russia—the Russian land. Again I found a village, this time Gumberg's native Elizavetgrad, which, while not a flaming cauldron of revolutionary fervor, was in the process of awakening. In general I verified my earlier impressions: that should the workers in either or both capitals topple the Provisional Government, the provinces would not be far behind.

Returning to Petrograd, I found reports coming in daily of more burnings and pillaging in the countryside. The peasants were signaling their final distrust of promises. Land and peace they would have. Since three provisional governments had failed to provide them (still another was now being set up), they would manage it themselves. Army desertions increased.

None of this was lost on Lenin, who wrote more and more passionately as September wore on. From his underground hiding place—at first in a hut near Razliv in the environs of Petrograd; then across the Finnish border, where he could obtain newspapers more easily; and, at the end of September, in a Viborg flat—Lenin's public and party letters took on more and more urgency. The gong had struck. Lenin was appealing for insurrection.

His first letters on insurrection, undated for security reasons, were written between September 12 and 14. Addressed to the Central Committee of the Bolsheviks, and to the Petrograd and Moscow committees of the party, they were not published, of course, at the time. But the party circulated them among the various Bolshevik organizations. Word of them got around like wildfire, especially certain apt phrases or sentences, such as "History will not forgive us if we do not assume power now." We heard it from Peters, and Reed loved to let it roll off his tongue as we strode along the Nevsky Prospekt at night.

"You sound like a Greek chorus," I said, "but a chorus with an audience of one."

For answer Jack repeated it, adding, "The man who wrote that line is playing to an audience no amphitheater could hold."

Of course, rumor often distorted those first letters on insurrection. Discussed, argued over, torn apart, and made the subject of wild speculation, they were the topic of conversations behind locked doors and on street corners possibly more than if they had been published.

Probably never in history was a plot to overthrow a government so thoroughly hashed over by all segments of the populace, and so long put off by the plotters. Soon it was no secret that Lenin was meeting with opposition from a majority of the Bolshevik leaders, especially Zinoviev and Kamenev, but also from Riazanov, Bukharin, and others.

A revolution is not like a theatrical performance, with daily rehearsals, a dress rehearsal, and a date advertised for its opening. In Petrograd in September 1917 it was almost as if that were what people expected. It was assumed the Bolsheviks were committed to relieving the distressful situation, recognized in all quarters, by overthrowing the government—a government with or without the Kadets, and whether or not Kerensky was himself a "Kornilovite." It was not unusual to hear portly speculators and landlords saying querulously that the Bolsheviks certainly had their chance now; what was the matter, were they cowards, were they yellow?

From Gumberg, who was attached to the American Red Cross at the time, we heard funny stories of how Ambassador Francis came in one day and took the Bolsheviks to task, in effect, for dilly-dallying on the insurrection. That this was not one of Gumberg's wildest lampoons is indicated by the letter Francis wrote his son Perry in this period:

"The air is always full of rumors here concerning plots of the Bolsheviks, but the outbreaks that are prophesied seem never to occur—it is only the unexpected that happens here."

Earlier Francis had written Dean Walter Williams of the University of Missouri School of Journalism:

The greatest menace to the present situation is the strength of the Bolshevik sentiment, which, intoxicated with its success (attributable in no small degree to the failure of the Korniloff movement), may attempt to overthrow the present Provisional Government and administer affairs through its representatives. If such condition should eventuate, failure will undoubtedly ensue in a short time, but meanwhile there may be bloodshed, of which there has been remarkably little since the beginning of the revolution. . . .

The "Governor," as Harper and other advisers called Francis—and in character he remained the ex-governor of Missouri, the Show-Me state—was confident that the Bolsheviks would not take power, and then, that they would fall. In any event, he could always say that if they did not, it was because his own counsel—to execute Lenin, Trotsky, "and the other Bolshevik leaders"—had been spurned. In his book he reveals how he had suggested this to Minister of Foreign Affairs Tereshchenko of the Provisional Government back in July.

Lenin's first letters on insurrection came at the time of the Democratic Conference, a couple of weeks after the Kornilov revolt was stopped in its tracks. I had managed, after a good deal of fuss and bother about credentials, just to walk in with a group of delegates to the conference. Jack Reed and I, along with Bessie Beatty, were there in the press section, comparing notes with other correspondents, who like us seemed to expect little from this carefully prepared nationwide congress. It had been initiated by the Mensheviks and Socialist Revolutionaries to whip up support for the Provisional Government after the state conference at Moscow a month earlier proved to be more a forum for the Kornilov forces than for those of Kerensky. The moderates, so fearful of growing reaction that they excluded the Bolsheviks from the Moscow hand-picked delegates, in an effort at appeasement, got what they deserved—a swing further toward support of a military dictatorship. Among those setting the tone for the Moscow parley and organizing the Kornilov support was the millionaire Moscow banker Pavel P. Riabushinsky, who told the Congress of Representatives of Trade and Industry a few days before the conference that the "bony hand of hunger" would bring the people "to their senses." The Russian land "will free itself," but apparently not without help, for he appealed: "The merchants are needed to save the Russian land!"

Miliukov recounted the struggle for power that had taken place in August in *Kornilov or Lenin?* Now, listening to the Democratic Conference speeches in a desultory way, Jack Reed and I were discussing the latest reports we had heard via the grapevine of Lenin's two letters on the need for insurrection. No rumor was good enough for Jack, though. He had heard the Bolsheviks were caucusing regarding Lenin's wishes in his latest letter. How to get that letter? "I wouldn't use it now," he said.

I laughed. "Try telling that to Voskov or Volodarsky or Jake Peters or anyone we know."

This was the letter, written to the Central Committee, in which Lenin urged the Bolsheviks at the conference to draw up a statement declaring the necessity for a complete break with the bourgeoisie and removal of the entire present government. Lenin, however, was realistic enough to know that the conference, even if it were to declare itself a permanent revolutionary parliament, would "decide nothing." Thus he recommended that after the party's program was presented briefly to the delegates, "our entire group" disperse to the factories and barracks, "the source of salvation for our revolution." There, in "ardent and impassioned speeches," they should explain the program and put the alternative: either the conference adopt it, all of it, or the people should adopt insurrection.

"There is no middle course. Delay is impossible. The revolution is dying.

"By putting the question in this way [before the factories and barracks] *we shall be able to determine the right moment for launching the insurrection . . ."*

I felt almost sorry for Kerensky when he faced the Democratic Conference and began his lengthy address. There he stood, the man who arose every morning from the bed of Aleksandr III in the Winter Palace and, glancing in the mirror, saw a tall, youthful, round-faced man who by accident had become premier, a man unexceptional but for the persistence with which he continued to see himself as savior of the Revolution. We heard his rounded, eloquent, empty phrases, his voice rising to almost fanatical pitch, then falling in cadences to a whisper. He was making a desperate effort to stem the tide. He appeared pale, his eyes looked fixedly at some point in the big Aleksandrinsky Theater above the heads of his audience, as if frozen with shock, a shock beginning to register itself in his features even as he refused to recognize it.

Along with the "burzhuy," he was in a quandary. The shock of the imminent uprising was as paralyzing to their mental powers as a blow from a whip. Where to turn? Poor Kerensky, after October he remained in a state of permanent shock, preserving the state of mind, the attitude, and even the speeches of 1917, down to this day.

Both Reed and I, as I explained earlier, had missed the Kornilov revolt. There was no missing its results, however. With its debacle had come a sharp shifting of forces. The frenzy of acclaim for Kornilov voiced at the Moscow State Conference was silenced. Then why was his rival Kerensky not strengthened? Why had the Kornilov rout partially engulfed Kerensky himself and strengthened only the Bolshevization of Petrograd? The answer lay in the relation of the two contending men and what they wanted.

Essentially it was the same thing, a dictatorship, although they differed as to choice of dictator. All of this was highlighted more each day as new facts came out about the events of August 22–26. These involved Kerensky-Kornilov parleys through a go-between, used by each man until the time when his bumbling ended his usefulness. It was one of the minor farces that briefly lit up the stage as the sterner drama of the Revolution inexorably unrolled.

The unhappy go-between who made the mistake of appearing to serve two masters was V. N. Lvov (not to be confused with Prince Lvov), a member of the first Provisional Government who served for five months as chief procurator of the Holy Synod. A loquacious and officious gentleman with only the "purest" intentions of saving the bourgeoisie through means of a dictatorship, he apparently was torn between the two, and rushed from one to the other trying to bring them together.

To understand how this abortive *tour de force* could have even got off the ground, we have to take a closer look at the position of the principals in August. Even earlier each man had suffered the other with suspicion. True, Kerensky had made Kornilov his commander in chief, six days after he had yielded to Kornilov's measures, including reinstatement of the death penalty (banned after the February Revolution) for deserters and recalcitrants at the front. This was at the behest of Boris Savinkov, Kerensky's deputy for military affairs. Savinkov was an old-time Socialist Revolutionary conspirator and terrorist, who became the brain of the politically naïve Kornilov, yet remained the pal of Kerensky, his fellow SR. Kerensky was well aware of the hatred he had incurred among soldiers by approving the death penalty and other harsh measures, which were only increasing the desertions at the front. And Kornilov knew that Kerensky would like to replace him.

At the same time, each man, Kerensky and Kornilov, needed the other. The greater the fear of the other, the greater the need, since each feared the rising tide of Bolshevism more.

Lvov was about the last man on earth who should have attempted the role of conspirator. Though groomed and deputized by the archconspirator Savinkov, he just would talk too much. When Lvov appeared at the Winter Palace, Kerensky fell in with his plan—allegedly, the premier explained later, to test his staff and especially Savinkov. And when Lvov returned to Moghiliev, the army headquarters, to assure Kornilov that he, Lvov, represented Kerensky, the test came.

For four days the conspiratorial meetings went on, with Lvov believing himself to be, and representing himself as, the friend and ambassador of Kerensky to Kornilov, and the mediator at the Winter Palace sent by the General and Savinkov. Meanwhile Kerensky, his suspicions growing, installed a high police official behind curtains to listen and act as witness to the final confrontation with Lvov on August 26. It was then that Lvov learned that what he had happily considered an "agreement" had turned into "conspiracy" and "treason." The "agreement" was for the Provisional Government to fade away, in the most peaceful, legal manner, by formal resignation, after transferring power to the commander in chief. But although Kornilov refused to be anything but head of state, Lvov explained, Kornilov had consented to let Kerensky remain in the cabinet as Minister of Justice.

As Kerensky sputtered and fumed and let his listening witnesses behind the paniers know how outraged he was, Lvov, as was later brought out in testimony, pleaded with him that it would be better that way; at least the Premier's life would be spared. Kornilov himself would ensure Kerensky's safety if he came at once to Moghiliev, he had Kornilov's word for it. In Lvov, naïveté went all out and became stupidity. But he *was* honest. So, after assuring Kerensky he was offered a sanctuary at army headquarters, he added a note of nervous warning: It was just possible that Kerensky might be murdered as well as detained. Lvov had heard it from an orderly at headquarters.

And how was Lvov rewarded? Playing the detective, Kerensky got on a private wire to Moghiliev and summoned Kornilov. Could it be that Lvov was representing him accurately? And so on. The result was that Lvov was placed under arrest by order of his "friend" Kerensky. Meanwhile, however, Kerensky, continuing his detective role, went on chatting with Kornilov on the phone, speaking of his arrival at headquarters next day as a matter agreed upon. Trubetskoi, a diplomat associated with Minister of Foreign Affairs Tereshchenko, later told how he saw General Kornilov after this conversation, on the evening of August 26, and that the General was sighing with relief. And when the diplomat asked if this meant that "the government is coming to meet you all along the line," the General said, "Yes."

Lvov, under arrest but not formally charged, spent the rest of the night at the Winter Palace, guarded by two listless sentries and listening through the wall that separated him from the room of Aleksandr III, while Kerensky, happy at the denouement of this strange imbroglio, sang roulades from an opera.

All that can be said is that if Kerensky and Kornilov originally were in one conspiracy together, to purge Petrograd of questionable troops and bring in the Cossacks relied on to support a dictatorship, Kornilov, a stranger to finesse, had shown his hand and revealed that he and Savinkov had their own private conspiracy. And when a wire was received at Moghiliev from Kerensky to halt any movement of troops to Petrograd, Kornilov countermanded it and set three divisions of cavalry in motion by rail.

On the morning of August 27 no word appeared in the press of a Kornilov plot. News of the Kornilov revolt made its way to Smolny, however, and the Bolsheviks went into action at once, contacting the factory committees and Red Guards and dispatching them for defense of the city.[1] The rest is well known: on the twenty-seventh Kerensky declared that a mutiny was in progress and called on the Bolshevik party for assistance. What else could he do? He had to cover up his tracks.

In the spring Lenin had told the Peasant Congress, "Revolutions are not made to order . . ." But everything that had happened since Kerensky succeeded Prince Lvov as premier on July 8 seemed destined to further the growth of the Bolsheviks and the inevitability of insurrection. Their leaders hunted, jailed, the Bolsheviks became all the more trustworthy in the eyes of the workers. The Kornilov coup was a failure, and again it was as if Lenin, from underground, playing it blindfold, were moving his men steadily and triumphantly across the chess board.

And now at the Democratic Conference we were hearing the thirty-four-year-old Kerensky, at the climax of his speech, declaring an end to the hated death sentence. So even he finally knew that when he signed that decree July 12 it was a fatal mistake.[2]

"Doesn't he know it's too late?" Bessie Beatty said.

"He's finally decided that the 'rabble' is more to be feared than the military, so he's repudiating the use of force—for how long?" Reed asked.[3]

"I don't hear him saying anything about the force attempted against

1. After July the Red Guards had to act secretly or conceal their weapons. By October the organizations had spread wide and deep. There was no workshop, no factory without its Red Guard. Headquarters were established in all working-class districts. From the statutes adopted by the conference of Red Guards on October 23, 1917—one hundred delegates representing about 20,000 organized Red Guards at the parley—one reads: "The Red Workers' Guard is composed of workers recommended by the Socialist Parties, factory committees, and trade unions." The fourth statute declares:

"Strict observance of discipline and unconditional obedience to elected bodies of the Guard is to be based not on blind submission, but on the consciousness of the extreme importance and responsibility of the duties of the Workers' Guard and on the fact that the Guard is a completely free and independent democratic organization."

When ordered by Kerensky to disband September 4, the Red Guards serenely ignored the order. Some hid their guns. Some openly refused to hand them over when ordered, and got away with it.

2. It is doubtful that by the time of the Democratic Conference Kerensky, unable to resolve the contradictions of his situation, was in any condition to recognize or define his grave mistakes. Miliukov is quoted by Trotsky (*The History of the Russian Revolution,* trans. by Max Eastman, New York, 1932, II, 348) as describing in these words the Premier as he saw him in this period: "Having lost the ground under his feet, the further he went the more Kerensky revealed all the signs of that pathological condition of spirit which may be called in medical language 'psychic neurasthenia.' " Miliukov, Trotsky adds, attributed the influence over Kerensky held by Kishkin, a Provisional Government minister, a Kadet, and a psychiatrist, to Kishkin's skillful handling of the Premier as patient.

3. The answer came on the afternoon of October 24, when Kerensky, seeking a vote of confidence from the Council of the Republic (also called the Pre-Parliament), promised to crush the revolt of "the rabble" (*chern*) and asked for the members' support.

the peasants here and there. That didn't do him any good, either," I added.

The Democratic Conference seemed a rather silly affair. First the delegates voted for a coalition government. (All the ministers had resigned the night of August 26: first the Kadets, lest they embarrass or be embarrassed in the event Kornilov won or lost; then the others, exactly why we still couldn't figure, but allegedly because Kerensky wanted to have sole power to deal with Kornilov.) Then an amendment excluding the Kadets from the government narrowly won. Since to leave out the Kadets would mean that only socialists were to remain in the government, and Kerensky refused to preside over anything other than a coalition, the delegates then voted by a big majority against the resolution as a whole. They wound up authorizing—as if they had power to authorize anything!—a Council of the Republic, or Pre-Parliament, which they were good enough to say would have no authority, being a consultative, not legislative, body. It was like a broken record sounding squeakily above the roar of the Revolution: a fourth coalition, more futile than the others, was born.

Apparently Lenin's proposal to the comrades never got off first base within their own caucus. The powwow at the Aleksandrinsky Theater closed with no "ardent and impassioned speeches." Trotsky, suddenly and casually released from jail September 4 without explanation, and fairly promptly made chairman of the Petrograd Soviet, was at the conference. In fact, almost everybody was there except Lenin, for whose arrest the "democratic" government still regularly, week upon week, issued new orders. When Trotsky had risen to speak, all the distinguished bourgeois gentlemen—for, as Lenin said, the conference did not represent the revolutionary elements, but the "compromising upper strata of the petty bourgeoisie"—craned their necks to see him. For many it was their first glimpse of the man whom, next to Lenin, they regarded as the most dangerous of the upstarts, the riffraff and jailbirds now running the capital. But we waited in vain to hear any signal, veiled or otherwise, to the "black mobs"— the black-bloused workers—that this was the hour to rise. Sukhanov in his memoirs snipes at Trotsky's speech because in outlining the Bolshevik economic program he did not use the word "socialism." In this Sukhanov pretends to see some deep scheme to fool the masses. Such pedantry we were not bothered with. We were simply straining to catch the word *vostravat* (insurrection).

We trailed after the departing delegates, past the little park across the street from the Aleksandrinsky where the statue of Catherine the Great stood. From the scepter in her hand still fluttered a bit of red bunting, a little the worse for wear.

Reed and I resumed our restless search, going from the Winter Palace to Smolny, from the U.S. Embassy to Viborg, trying to be everywhere at once, seeking out translators to read the papers, sorting over wildly contradictory statements.

We were, like the rest of the capital, wearily, doggedly waiting for something to happen. The suspense was like a fever.

There was on the one hand every threat of disorder. Violence hung in the air almost palpably. Nothing happened. Hundreds of thousands of rifles were in the hands of workers and sailors after the Kornilov revolt failed. At the Putilov plant alone 40,000 workers were just waiting to go out on the streets. At the Grenade works, almost the entire work force was mobilized in the Red Guards. Tension was high at the Reno plant, the Lafern, Sestroretsk, and Obukhovsky factories. In Moscow there were widespread strikes throughout most of the city during the State Conference, in protest against the noninclusion of the Bolsheviks. A month later the workers were in so strong a position they were indifferent as to what the Democratic Conference did or did not do. They had not expected much. At the end of each shift the Red Guards marched and drilled with guns and bayonets, or met and talked of tactics and hunger. Like us, they were waiting for a signal.

Because we figured the Guards would be among the first to receive the signal, we kept watching them.

"How fast are they joining up?" I asked one bearded worker as the Red Guards stood about in a factory yard waiting for their instructor, their guns in hand, older men and teen-age apprentices side by side.

"Recruitment is very slow now. Hardly any at all." He stopped, regarding me with a poker face. Disappointment, surprise, maybe even a certain chagrin may have been written on my face, for I was beginning to react with a sort of proprietary manner to the Revolution. At any rate, the old-timer suddenly smiled and said with a patronizing air, as if pitying my ignorance:

"You see, comrade, almost everyone in the factory was in the Red Guard by the end of August. Who do you think we're going to recruit now? The bosses?"

"What do you do with your guns during the workday?" I asked.

"That depends," he replied. "Most of us fitters keep them leaning against the bench, and have our packs hanging close by us. In the locksmiths' shop they pile them in a corner and wear their packs. It looks like a camp, all right. Oh, we're quiet, we do our work—but we won't be caught napping when the moment comes."

That was the way it was wherever we went on the Viborg side. After the July repression, the Red Guards had concealed their weapons and usually acted with complete secrecy when it came to meetings or membership. Membership fell off sharply for a time. But at the beginning of August recruitment speeded up and the guns came out in the open.[4]

The crisis half paralyzed parts of the city. Little movement took place even on the streets around the Winter Palace, but the workers' districts boiled and seethed, with huge meetings at factory gates or in buildings, and small ones springing up on any street corner. Long queues before foodshops and bakeries would be swept by a rumble as word came that supplies had run out, and yet with all the potential violence, and factories resembling armed camps, there was at the same time a certain order. Not order in the German sense, but the usual casual disorder that passes for order in Russia. As the bearded worker had told me, with some pride, they got their work done. In many plants there were cases of elemental direct action, too—workers putting managers into wheelbarrows and trundling them out of the factory. It suggested the treatment in reverse accorded labor organizers or radicals in backwoods sections in my native land who were tarred and feathered or ridden out of town on a rail. Anything or nothing might serve to set off the dumping of a luckless manager in an atmosphere so charged with tension.

One thing was evident. The transition in power which is the essence of a revolution already had taken place. It only remained for a date to be fixed for an insurrection which would formalize the transition. Only a façade of power remained in the almost empty halls of the Winter Palace. Down near the other end of the Nevsky, where the lights burned brightly until all hours of the night, the Smolny was the real seat of power now. By day the old Smolny echoed to the tramp of ever greater crowds of black-bloused workers, delegations of mud-spattered soldiers from the front, and crowds of sailors in their jaunty beribboned caps.

By this time Reed and I were thoroughly partisan, and alarmed only that the Bolsheviks might not act until it was too late and the government had somehow made arrangements to put down the insurrection when it came. We asked Yanishev, Volodarsky, and Voskov, "What are you

---

4. Edward Hallett Carr, *The Bolshevik Revolution, 1917–1923*, III, New York, 1953, 61, cites official estimates of the numbers of the Red Guard in Petrograd in October as no more than 10,000 to 12,000 (*Bol'shaya Sovetskaya Entsiklopediya*, XXXIV, 1937, 579).

See Trotsky, *History of the Russian Revolution*, III, 184. The Workers' Guard derived its tradition from 1905 and was reborn with the February revolution. The Red Guard or Workers' Guard was not in Petrograd and Moscow alone. In provincial industrial regions, "a reinforcement of the Workers' Guard would involve a complete change of all relations, not only within the given plant but all around it. Armed workers would remove managers and engineers, and even arrest them. Upon resolutions adopted by a factory meeting the Red Guard would not infrequently receive pay out of the factory exchequer. In the Urals, with their rich tradition of guerrilla fighting in 1905, companies of the Red Guard led by the old veterans . . . almost unnoticeably dissolved the old government and replaced it with soviet institutions."

waiting for? For Kerensky to open the doors to the Kaiser?" And now we collared Peters. We knew through Bessie Beatty, who had become increasingly chummy with the disarming Peters, that he had served as courier to Lenin in hiding. Look, we said in effect, we don't know anything about tactics, but we've heard that Lenin is busy these days writing on the need for an armed uprising. Yet Trotsky just speaks of how only a Soviet government can do this or that. No hint of insurrection. You can fool around just so long, and then the workers are going to think the Bolsheviks, too, are windbags, like the SR's and Mensheviks.

Peters was sharp with us, for once. "What do you expect me to do, give you a copy of our secret plan? There isn't any plan. Make up your own timetable. But you can figure out one thing—when 'only a Soviet government' is said, just ask yourself how it's to be achieved. By getting up a petition to Kerensky? By getting promises from Kornilov, and all the generals who sided with him, to keep hands off? Only an insurrection can achieve a Soviet government at this point. That's what Lenin hopes the party members can realize. Our slogan 'All power to the Soviets' didn't mean that at one time. Now we've taken it up again, and in the changed conditions, it means just that."

And he left us. We were sobered, but not satisfied. In any stalemate, morale suffers, and ours did. Perhaps the mood of the masses, fed up with words and talk, was catching. We were discouraged.

Even the contingency we had spoken of to Peters so glibly to needle him—that Kerensky might open the door to the Germans—no longer seemed so wild. Not since our exposure to some of Gumberg's acquaintances. A strange man who loved the picaresque, the fantastic, Gumberg prided himself on getting around in all sorts of circles. He loved to caricature relics of the old aristocracy behind their backs; his sardonic humor reveled in their bland and ludicrous utterances of devotion to mores which in the midst of a revolution could be considered only inhuman or subhuman. Even more he enjoyed the frankly rapacious newly rich, reaping a harvest from speculation, and insisted on our going with him one evening, Jack and I, to the family of a merchant of this type. It was part of our education to see what the Revolution was against, he said; and besides, we could fill up on their caviar and other morsels.

There were eleven at tea, hosts and guests, besides Reed, Alex, and myself. As he had promised, their talk was surprisingly candid. The father, for example, was seeking a mate for the plump widowed daughter, and spoke enticingly of an estate he had acquired in a black-soil province and of course placed in her name. But with things the way they were, and a new law forbidding sales in danger of being enforced now the Bolshies were everywhere, he sought to turn it over to some foreigner. He eyed

Jack questioningly, and Jack bowed to me and unctuously noted that I was a bachelor, but, with a sigh, he himself was tied by holy matrimony. Before we could escape, however, we must have tea—and at tea the talk turned on the possible invasion of Petrograd by the Germans. Again, their candor was almost naïve.

Sadly they seemed to envision rule by the Germans as desirable but, still, not certain. I did not dare glance at Gumberg or Reed. Keeping my eyes on my host, I said, "But you seem to have it pretty comfortable here, all snug; wonderful food. You may not love Kerensky *or* Lenin—but the Germans are starving, I hear. Wouldn't all these things"—with a sweep of my arm indicating the heavily laden tea table, the candlelight, the shimmering cut-glass candelabra, the silver, the thick rugs, the glossy centerpiece of fruit, real oranges and pears such as I had not seen in four months—"be gobbled up?"

"Better the Germans than Lenin and the Bolsheviks," said a steely voice from across the table.

I think it was Alex who, to break the tension, or because it appealed to his macabre sense of humor, suggested that they take a vote. The question as we put it was: "Is it Kaiser Wilhelm or Lenin?" The vote favored Wilhelm ten to one. The nonvoters then took their departure—a bit precipitously, as Alex had heard stories about Reed's pugilistic encounters in the past.

Because many landlords from the provinces were preparing to flee, not so much from a feared German invasion as from the anticipated insurrection, they continued to swarm in the lobbies of the best hotels. Whenever I came into the Astoria, where I had a room for a time, I saw these gentlemen and their ladies, hovering and chattering, like a swarm of blackbirds resting briefly in the branches of a tree before taking wing. Some would spend the rest of their lives in exile, and I would see them in the public library of New York, bitter, dreary, venomous, and futile, in years to come.

The discussions and arguments on seizure continued at Smolny. Even to us on the sidelines, it was a war of nerves. September came and went and October days began. Would talk go on forever? Everyone was on hairtrigger tension, but no one was pulling any triggers. Crowds, crowds, but unlike the July days, no aimless, spontaneous demonstrations—in fact, no demonstrations at all—and no shooting by police and soldiers. The Bolsheviks were in control, in the Petrograd barracks as well as in the factories. They had the guns in both places. The soldiers at least would be neutral. The Red Guards were eager to get going. Kerensky dared not order the Petrograd garrison to the front, for who would obey? Strange as it may seem, Kerensky did not even have the legal right to order the garrison to the front and replace known sympathizers of the insurrection with trusted

soldiers, thanks to the famous Order No. 1. One of the early and most creative revolutionary acts after the February overthrow, it was written by
deputies of the fleet and soldiers, and passed by the Soviet. Under it, all the
Duma Military Commission orders were made inoperative unless sanctioned by the Soviet.

Meanwhile, Lenin continued to appeal for insurrection. For decades
now, and even today, the spate of books coming out about Lenin in the
United States continues to picture him as a ruthless dictator, complete and
sole boss of a monolithic party that seized control in Russia in defiance of
the masses. Even a superficial study of Lenin's letters on insurrection shows
just the contrary. He pleaded and argued and his language became more
and more fiery, but he could not budge the Central Committee. He complained that he was not told anything, that the editors of the party's own
newspaper deleted passages from articles of his before they published them.
(Stalin was the editor in charge then; however, Stalin supported Lenin on
the insurrection issue when it was finally put to a vote.) Lenin's tone became
more sharp; his feeling that the comrades would let slip the one opportunity
of a successful revolution while he was cut off from the masses grew more
apparent.

In his first letter on insurrection Lenin had said, "We are concerned now
not with the 'day,' or 'moment' of insurrection in the narrow sense of the
word. That will be only decided by the common voice of those who are
in contact with the workers and soldiers, with *the people*." But who was
hearing it, this voice of the people? Not the Central Committee that tabled
Lenin's proposals. So it is hardly surprising to find Lenin very much concerned with the day and moment, after learning that at its September 15
meeting the Central Committee took no action on his first two letters, other
than to vote down Kamenev's proposal to destroy all copies and conceal
them from the party.

From then on the hammer-like blows in his letters and articles mounted
to a crashing crescendo that drove the fainthearted in the Central Committee to corner—but only after his declared resignation from the committee
in order that he might appeal directly to the rank and file without being
bound by committee discipline.

To refrain from taking power now, to "wait," . . . to confine ourselves to "fighting for the organ" (of the soviet), "fighting for the
Congress," is *to doom the revolution to failure*.

In view of the fact that the Central Committee has *even left un-
answered* the persistent demands I have been making [for a policy
of insurrection] ever since the beginning of the Democratic Conference, in view of the fact that the Central Organ is *deleting* from my

articles all references to such glaring errors on the part of the Bolsheviks as the shameful decision to participate in the Pre-Parliament
. . . etc., etc.—I am compelled to regard this as a "subtle" hint that
I should keep my mouth shut, and as a proposal for me to retire.

I am compelled to *tender my resignation from the Central
Committee,* which I hereby do, reserving for myself the freedom
to campaign among the *rank and file* of the Party and at the Party
Congress.

This was written September 29. It was a portion of Part VI, the only
secret part of an article, "The Crisis Is Ripe," the first five parts of which
Lenin specified "may be published." (The fourth remains unpublished.)
Part VI, Lenin wrote, "is to be distributed among the members of the
Central Committee, the Petrograd Committee, the Moscow Committee,
and *the Soviets."* Rather a broad distribution!

This further explains why, far in advance, the October Revolution was
discussed widely pro and con by many who were not leaders, who were not
even Bolsheviks. Had Lenin not had the courage and astuteness to air his
impasse with the Central Committee to the cadres below, the October
Revolution might never have come off.

Meanwhile Reed and I were going about in a state of intoxication
mixed with bewilderment. For even among the second and third echelons
of Bolshevik leaders a few were now hanging back, having second thoughts
about quickly seizing power, won over by Kamenev and Zinoviev. When
we heard Lunacharsky was with them, we were thrown by the news, and
figured the whole thing would end in talk. (This proved to be a rumor.
So persistent were the newspaper reports that Lunacharsky took issue with
them and declared in one newspaper that he objected to having his position
libeled and that he was at one with the party. This was in October.)
Valuing Lunacharsky as we did, we ourselves began to doubt. Among
the top leaders with whom I was on speaking terms—Rykov, Bukharin,
Kamenev, Kalinin, Trotsky—only Trotsky was all for insurrection *now.*

Krupskaya, working out of the Bolshevik district administration in
Viborg, at night teaching adult education classes to workers, often read
aloud to members of the district committee from Lenin's underground
letters. Some of them began asking questions, demanding answers. There
was more than one way to break the impasse with the Central Committee,
and Lenin did not scruple to exploit all alternatives. No one knew which
party workers stood for what more than the quiet, unobtrusive, sensitive
Nadezhda Konstantinovna. It was no accident that she had chosen to work
and spend her time in Viborg among the factory people in this period, no
more than it was when in the 1905 revolution she had talked to workers and

soldiers and reported back to Lenin in hiding. She had an infallible ear.

The absent leader had lost out in two skirmishes with the Central Committee. He had been against the Bolsheviks' taking part in the Democratic Conference, and again in the Pre-Parliament. Under the sting of his verbal whip, and as his letters reached wider and wider circles, the Central Committee decided to withdraw the Bolshevik delegates to the Pre-Parliament. On October 9 Trotsky, Volodarsky, and the others left the Pre-Parliament in a body. The move was correctly interpreted as a bid for insurrection.

The previous day Lenin had written to "Petrograd comrades" attending a Congress of Northern Soviets, under the signature of "An Onlooker," making good his threat to go outside official party channels and appeal to the rank and file, as he could do after his "resignation."

As always the teacher, Lenin the "onlooker" reminded them that Marx said "insurrection is an art quite as much as war," and summarized Marx's five rules of the "art." Rule 4 was to "try to take the enemy by surprise . . ." Lenin was far from being naïve. He must have known how little the element of surprise would figure in the insurrection by now—assuming there were an insurrection. Clearly he was more interested now in putting pressure on his own Central Committee than in secrecy; otherwise he would not be appealing to broad groups.

Even the tactics he suggested in this letter seem misplaced, in the light of the actually tranquil overturn of the government I witnessed in Petrograd. My hunch is that they represented less an overestimation of "the enemy" and resistance to the Revolution than an astute realization on Lenin's part that any and all actual plans of armed insurrection, were they discussed and taken up by the militant Bolshevik delegates, including the ready-for-action sailors in the fleet, would help put the hesitant leaders on the spot. Two passages in this letter I will quote, the first to show how careful Lenin was not to criticize the Central Committee to these rank-and-filers attending the Congress scheduled to open October 10, the second to show how, in outlining his "plan," he appealed for boldness.

It is clear that all power must pass to the Soviets. . . . What . . . is probably not quite clear to all comrades [is] that the passing of power to the Soviets now means in practice armed uprising. This would seem obvious, but not everyone has thought or is thinking over the point. . . .

Marx summed up the lessons of all revolutions in respect to armed uprising in the words of "Danton, the greatest master of revolutionary policy yet known: 'de l'audace, de l'audace, encore de l'audace.' "

Applied to Russia and to October 1917, this means: a simultaneous offensive to Petrograd, as sudden and rapid as possible, which must without fail be carried out from within and without, from the working-class quarters and from Finland, from Revel and from Kronstadt, an offensive of the *entire* navy . . .

The success of both the Russian and the world revolution depends on two or three days' fighting.

On October 8 he also urged an attack from Finland, to "smash the Kornilovite regiments" which "Kerensky has again brought . . . into the vicinity of Petrograd." This letter, ending with the passionate words "To delay would be fatal," was addressed to the "Bolshevik comrades" attending the same congress. Since here he was addressing at least party members, he allowed himself some biting criticism of the still unnamed "many leaders of our Party."

Unfortunately Jack Reed and I, speaking October 8 at the Obukhovsky munitions plant on Schlusselburg Prospekt, were not familiar with the contents of this letter, or we would have been better armed when we got into an informal give-and-take discussion with some of the workers afterward. Our talk contained little more than greetings from Socialists in America. It was always surprising to see how important our few words to them seemed. The meeting itself was impressive—ten thousand workers, women as well as men, packed in a building never completed. Petrovsky, the Russian-American shop committeeman, spoke, and Lunacharsky, that gentle-eyed cultured man, a poet. In his speech Lunacharsky did not patronize them, but spoke simply, with as much clarity as I had heard him speak on art. Reed has recorded some of Petrovsky's words, ending, "But let them know they can go too far—that if they dare to lay their hands upon the organizations of the proletariat we will sweep them away like scum from the face of the earth!"·

As usual we lingered to talk to individuals or small groups to try to gauge their thinking. One very intelligent older worker raised an interesting point. The crowd had left, and only a few of us remained, talking. A Bolshevik, he made it clear that most of the men in the plant were sick of half starvation and uncertainty, were disillusioned with the Provisional Government, and "would be with us," would in fact welcome coming out on the streets. Only one thing bothered him: the mood of the people. It was one of despair. Could a socialist revolution be sure of the people under such conditions?

I don't recall how we answered him; only that going home on the rocking, shaking old steam tram, Reed said we had failed to answer him, we did not know enough, we were not good enough. He was plunged into one of his moods, excessively self-critical, ironic, taciturn.

Only later we learned Lenin had dealt with this theme, writing on the same day. Said Lenin: "There are signs of growing apathy and indifference. That is understandable. It implies not the ebb of the revolution, as the Kadets and their henchmen vociferate, but the ebb of confidence in resolutions and elections. . . . The moment is approaching when the people may conceive the idea that the Bolsheviks are no better than the others, since they were unable *to act* when the people placed confidence in them . . ."

However we may have failed to give the right answers after the meeting at the Obukhovsky works, a meeting of several thousand at the same plant the next evening demanded the overthrow of the bourgeois government and echoed the cry "All power to the Soviets!"

When I look back on those fevered days, it seems a miracle that the October Revolution ever took place. Or rather, as some sort of insurrection would have occurred with or without Bolshevik leadership, it seems a miracle that, through the persistence of a single voice, a single stubborn will, the divided party finally acted as one in leading and directing the October Revolution.

On October 7, according to Krupskaya, Lenin, in wig and spectacles and clean-shaven, moved to Petrograd, into a flat on the Viborg side, and three days later attended the historic ten-hour meeting of the Central Committee, called on his insistent demand, to consider the policy of insurrection.

All the rest is well-known history. How Lenin was greeted by the twelve members of the committee of twenty-one who attended, most of whom he had not seen in three months, I never heard, nor is there any indication in the dry official records. If any reply had ever been made to his "resignation," I know nothing of it, nor have I read any mention of one. His remarks include a restrained reproach at his comrades' "indifference to the question of insurrection." After a brief summing up of the "political situation," he said the "technical aspect" was "the crux of the matter." Then, this second reproach:

"Nevertheless we, like the defencists, are inclined to regard the systematic preparation of an uprising as something in the nature of a political sin."

Ten voted for the resolution to prepare for an armed uprising: Lenin, Sverdlov, Stalin, Dzerzhinsky, Trotsky, Uritsky, Kollontai, Bubnov, Sokolnikov, and Lomov. Zinoviev and Kamenev voted no.[5]

---

5. Minutes of the Central Committee meeting of October 10 as published in Valentin Nikolayevich Astrov, A. N. Slepkov, and J. Thomas, eds., *Illustrated History of the Russian Revolution,* trans. by Freda Utley, New York, 1928, II, 298–300, give little indication that, except for Lenin's, any reports save Sverdlov's (on Minsk, the Northern front, and a conference of the "Lithuanian" Regiments in Moscow) reflected optimism as to seizing power at the time.

For example, one paragraph reads: "Comrade Uritzky declared that we are weak not only on the technical side, but in every section of our work. We have passed a number of

Lenin had thrown down the gauntlet. But no date was set. He had insisted in more than one letter that it was imperative the insurrection occur before the opening of the Congress of Soviets, set for October 25/November 7. Lenin again was in hiding, in the Petrograd flat, but his struggle to weld the party together for the insurrection was far from over.

Subsequent events, including an article by Kamenev in a non-Bolshevik paper, Gorky's *Novaya Zhizn*, opposing the party's decision for insurrection and linking Zinoviev's name to his in the opposition, create an air of fantasy when seen in retrospect. Promptly on the day of its publication, October 18, Lenin branded it as strikebreaking in a letter to party members. He followed this with a demand to the Central Committee that Kamenev and Zinoviev be expelled. This battling went on right up to the eve of the Revolution.

Krupskaya has left a record, objective—and yet her restrained words give a dramatic picture of Lenin's aloneness, of the last few days before the October overthrow. They had installed Lenin in the flat of Marguerita Vasilievna Fofanovna, in a large apartment on the corner of Lesnoy Avenue, on the Viborg side, almost entirely occupied by workers.

"Very few came to see Lenin—I, Maria Ilyinishna and sometimes Comrade Rakhya."[6] Krupskaya herself and Fofanovna carried messages from Lenin during this period. On one occasion when Krupskaya arrived she found a military student, a cousin of Fofanovna's, lingering on the stairs. He asked her, embarrassed, who it was who had "stolen into Marguerita's apartment." Yes, he insisted, he had rung and a man's voice answered, but then no one came to the door. After the student had gone, Krupskaya "began to scold" Lenin, who for his imprudence had only the lame excuse that he "thought it was something urgent."

"On October 24th he wrote to the Central Committee urging the necessity of taking power that day. He sent Marguerita with this message. But not waiting for her return, he put on a wig and went to the Smolny himself. Not a minute was to be lost. He met Marguerita on the way and told her he was going to the Smolny and that she need not wait for him."

That evening, Krupskaya and a woman comrade rode in a truck to Smolny "to find out how things were going."

Some accounts describe Lenin's walk into the city, accompanied by Rakhya. For additional camouflage he tied a handkerchief about his jaw

resolutions, but of decisive measures—there have been none! The Petrograd Soviet is disorganised, few meetings, etc. What is our strength? The Petrograd workers have 40,000 rifles, but that won't decide the matter. That is nothing. The garrison, after the July days, cannot instil any great hopes. In any case, however, if we do decide on insurrection, some work must actually be done in this direction. Definite measures must be taken."

6. Maria Ilyinishna Ulyanov, one of Lenin's sisters, and Eino Rakhya (spelled variously in histories Rakhia and Rahja), a militant Petrograd Bolshevik, a Finn by birth.

as if suffering from toothache. They found a streetcar, the last one to run that night, according to one version, and crossed the Liteiny Bridge. Red Guards were on the Viborg side of the bridge, and they breathed with relief. When on the opposite end of the bridge a cadet stopped them, Rakhya pretended to be drunk, and Lenin walked on.[7]

There is no question that Lenin was taking a chance in going into Smolny that night, disregarding a warning that it was too early for him to emerge on the scene. His action can be understood only in the light of one of his last complaints voiced in a note to Y. M. Sverdlov of October 22–23: "How is it you do not send me anything???" In that note he revealed he had been urged not to come in again until the insurrection was a *fait accompli*, in the words "It appears that I shall be unable to attend the Plenary Meeting as I am being 'chased.'"

The letter written to the Central Committee which Krupskaya says he intercepted, going himself to Smolny to make sure the revolution would be under way in the early hours of the next day, began:

> Comrades, I am writing these lines on the evening of the 24th. The situation is critical in the extreme. It is absolutely clear that now, in fact, to delay the uprising would be fatal.
>
> I urge comrades with all my strength to realise that everything now hangs by a thread; that we are confronted by problems which are not solved by conferences or congresses (even congresses of Soviets) but exclusively by peoples, by the masses, by the struggle of the armed people.

Quite obviously, Lenin still did not know the results of the special meeting of the Central Committee held that morning, where it had been resolved to take the offensive at once; he still doubted his comrades. The remainder of the letter, reflecting the same anxiety, in part said:

> We must at all costs, this very evening, this very night, arrest the government, having first disarmed the military cadets (defeating them, if they resist), and so on.

7. Probably more accurate than the current story we heard is that attributed to Rakhya himself. See Astrov and others, eds., *Illustrated History*, II, 347–348. He and Lenin had taken advantage of a quarrel between soldiers and workers at the far end of Liteiny Bridge to slip past and, turning into Shpalernaya Street, "had already covered a good distance of the Shpalernaya when two mounted junkers confronted us and called out: 'Stop! Passports!' I whispered to Vladimir Ilyitch, 'Go on. I will deal with them.' I had two revolvers in my pocket.

"I started quarreling with them roughly and said that no one knew that passports had been introduced and that, therefore, we had not provided ourselves with any in time. Vladimir Ilyitch quietly left us. . . . At last they evidently made up their minds that it was not worthwhile starting a scrap with two vagabonds like us. We really looked like two typical tramps. They rode on. I caught up with Vladimir Ilyitch who had gone on a good long way, and we continued on our journey."

We must not wait!! We may lose everything!

It would be a disaster, or a sheer formality, to await the wavering vote of October 25. The people have the right and are in duty bound to decide such questions not by a vote, but by force; in critical moments of revolution, the people have the right and are in duty bound to direct their representatives, even their best representatives, and not to wait for them.

This is proved by the history of all revolutions; and it would be an infinite crime on the part of the revolutionaries were they to let the chance slip, knowing that upon them depends the *salvation of the revolution*, the offer of peace, the salvation of Petrograd, salvation from famine, the transfer of the land to the peasants.

The government is tottering. It must be *given the death-blow* at all costs.

To delay action is fatal.

Lenin was skeptical to the end (which signified the beginning) of the Bolshevik leadership, but his great faith in the creative forces of humanity never faltered. He was unerring in his timing of the Revolution because of his supreme confidence in his ability to read the temper of the people's mood. He never mistook his own emotions for a public movement, but was like a good barometer which registers the trend of the political weather. In late April, when a wave of optimism swept his party, he fought against illusions, declaring, "So far we are in the minority; the masses do not trust us yet. We can wait." He had no mystic second sight, but as the peasants would say, he could see two feet under the ground. With terrible tenacity, since his student days, he had pursued his goal. But he was the least rigid, the most flexible of men when it came to tactics.

In the darkest days of reaction, in 1912, Lenin had never doubted that the dawn would break. Why should he now, on the very eve of the October triumph? Not that he sat back and waited for it. No, he plunged at once into checking every detail of the mobilization for the armed rising. Most characteristically, he worked closely with the leadership he had but yesterday been chastising—including Kamenev, whom he had sought to expel from the party. Until that day would come when human nature would be changed, Lenin would work with human beings as they were.

· 5 · In the Eye of the Storm

On Wednesday evening, October 25/November 7, Jack Reed, Louise Bryant, and I had a hurried meal at the Hotel France and returned to check on events at the Winter Palace, where we had wandered about like tourists most of the afternoon. It was hardly a guided tour, but no one bothered about us. When a sentinel shook his head dubiously at our Military Revolutionary Committee passes, we simply went to another entrance and showed our American passports; almost anything could be expected of American correspondents. Apparently we were the only ones to whom it occurred to visit the Winter Palace that day. A cordon of soldiers, Red Guards, and a sprinkling of sailors had ringed the palace since ten A.M., we were told, and shooting was expected to begin momentarily.

We saw at once, standing beneath the Red Arch on our return, that nothing sensational was happening. Lights shone from few windows in the great palace built by Peter the Great. Its soft rosy-red-painted exterior was faintly luminous in the gathering dusk. Night comes early in Petrograd in winter; it was probably a little past five o'clock. A few more Guards and soldiers were in the encircling cordon, but all was quiet, tense. Obviously the Winter Palace was still in the hands of the shadow government, whose ministers huddled somewhere within. That was the one thing the American interlopers had been denied—entrance to their sanctuary.

Now under the arch a group of Red Guards and soldiers argued. The soldiers were mystified, muttering angrily at the delay. Why wait any longer? Why not go in and arrest that Kerensky and his crowd? Apparently they did not know that Kerensky had fled early that morning in his own car, followed by a touring car from the American Embassy bearing a small American flag. A bearded Red Guard replied to the growls: "No, the *Junkers* would hide behind the women's skirts. The Women's Battalion's still in there. Then the press would say we fired on women. Besides, tovarish, we are under discipline; no one acts without orders from the Committee."

The soldiers were not satisfied. We left them arguing, and, stepping over puddles, made our way to the Nevsky Prospekt, bound for the Smolny and the opening of the Second All-Russian Congress of Soviets. We had tickets to the ballet in the Maryinsky Theater that night, a new ballet in which Karsavina would dance. But who wanted to see the ballet, or even hear the great Chaliapin singing that night, or see Meyerhold's revival of Alexei Tolstoy's drama *The Death of Ivan the Terrible?*

On the broad Nevsky it looked as if many others, whose dress indicated they might have been ticketholders, had the same idea. Seeing how the crowds strolled along, we involuntarily slowed our pace. The avenue was crowded. I felt lightheaded and lighthearted, and surprised at the lump forming in my throat. I looked around.

There was a curious unreality about the scene. Those who were not parading and peering as if on a sight-seeing jaunt gathered in crowds on street corners, occupied in the favorite Russian pastime, discussion. At each street intersection a few Red Guards or soldiers or both stood carelessly with fixed bayonets. Many of the promenaders were of the vanishing class, it seemed. An elderly woman, shielded against the chill air by a short sable cape, shook her finger at a young Guard and appeared to be scolding him. I caught the words "a day of shame." He grinned at her, his face a mixture of impudence and tolerance. Let the burzhuy rave and protest, he seemed to say; this was his night, his star had risen.

"The whole town is out tonight all but the prostitutes," said Reed. Yes, they were nowhere to be seen, though of late, like flies sensing an approaching storm, they had swarmed in increasing numbers as they plied their trade on the Nevsky.

When we had left the Smolny about four o'clock that morning, after attending a wild meeting of the old outgoing Central Executive Committee of the Soviets, it was clear the real revolution was under way. Volodarsky had led out the Bolsheviks in protest rather than vote on a resolution appealing to the workers and soldiers not to demonstrate, and to the P.G. to transfer land to the peasants and begin peace negotiations. It was a trick, he said. The committee was dying; who would heed such a resolution? Some of the delegates leaving had guns slung over their shoulders. Two ministers had been arrested and were in the basement, we were told. (Unfortunately they were held only briefly, and one of them immediately began organizing forces to try to retake the telephone exchange.) At the moment, Zorin, one of the Bolsheviks, told us, detachments of regiments were on their way to capture the State Bank and the telegraph agency, and soldiers plus Red Guards were to tackle the telephone exchange, which certainly would be stoutly defended.

And there by the entrance of Smolny were a mounted machine gun and a few Red Guards hugging their rifles and eying the machine gun nervously. They had had rudimentary training with rifles, but what did you do with a machine gun?[1] Never mind, they could always use their bayonets. At the same time, we heard in the still, cold dark of the early morning the first distinct sound of the armed insurrection—the distant clatter of a rifle shot, then two more.

By early afternoon, the Nikolayevsky and Baltic railway stations, the State Bank, the telegraph agency, all were in the hands of the insurrectionists. Red Guards and soldiers had fought their way into the telegraph exchange and cut the wires to the Winter Palace, and all principal government buildings had been seized, save alone the Winter Palace. All this had been accomplished without bloodshed. Resistance was slight.

And now what signs of violence did we see along the Nevsky? I remember seeing a soldier tear the insignia from the shoulders of an officer's uniform, but he let the officer go. The only other "violence" I witnessed was perpetrated by a saucy young woman in a shapeless jacket. Ahead of us, mincing along on high heels, was a middle-aged matron in a fur wrap, which she clasped with a careless hand as she looked coyly into the face of her escort. Suddenly the young vixen darted up to her. "Haven't you worn that long enough? I'll try it for awhile," she said, and, snatching the fur, disappeared in the crowd.

As we went on the crowds thinned out. There was no cab to be had, save one driven by a shrunken little man who refused to take us to Smolny. A strange quiet, an easy quiet, almost a serenity seemed to have descended on the old gray city along with the fog. The clop of horses' hoofs on the wooden pavement could be heard as we approached the Sadovaya. We continued along our way, silent for the most part. Even Jack had no appetite for talk. The clanking bell of an occasional streetcar sounded faintly. As we left the paraders behind, our own footsteps clattered in the hushed streets.

While the amiable crowds were strolling along the Nevsky, a few blocks

---

1. Apparently this was the only machine gun in the possession of the Red Guard on October 25. V. Nevsky, a member of the Military Revolutionary Committee, in "October in 1917," in R. MacIlhone, ed., *Petrograd, October 1917: Reminiscences*, Moscow, 1957, trans. by G. Hanna and L. Lempert from Russian text prepared by S. Knyazev and A. Konstantinov, p. 239, lists Red Guard weapons. He writes that "at the Obukhov Factory there were 500 rifles; in the Lesnoi sub-district there were 84, and in the City District there were factories which had 100 rifles and others with only 20. The Red Guards owned a machine-gun and even an armoured car (at the same Obukhov Factory). At the best we had a thousand or two thousand rifles at our disposal while the enemy had all types of weapons."

away an armored car was racing through the night with machine guns at the ready. A revolution as orderly, and even rather gentle and seemingly casual on the surface, as this one appeared to be could not have been so had not a great deal of organizational work and careful planning gone into it. Elsewhere, as in Moscow, the upheaval would be violent, meeting real opposition and costing bloodshed. We happened to be in the calm eye of the storm.

And in the center of it was Lenin, in more ways than one: symbolically, as the most conscious of the conscious forces that would go with the elemental hurricane of the people's movement and give it direction. In a very real sense, too, Lenin was at the center of things; the "workingman K. P. Ivanov,"[2] who had slipped into Smolny the previous night, was gathering all the threads of the insurrection process in his hands.

Certain Western historians depict Lenin as having almost nothing to do with the actual events of the uprising. This is surely a case of deliberate blindness, as self-defeating as the rewriting of history always is, for it has proved impossible to belittle Lenin.

So far as I can make out, the general course followed by the Military Revolutionary Committee, which prepared the groundwork for the events of October 24–25/November 6–7, was pretty much that which Lenin had drawn up in his letter of October 8 (the "Onlooker" letter). It was a plan to "encircle and cut off Petrograd," to "seize it by a combined attack of the navy, the workers, and the troops," a test that "requires *art and triple audacity*."

On October 22 the sailors from the *Aurora* who were on detail guarding the Kerensky government refused to continue and were replaced by cadets. The *Aurora* and the *Zaria Svobody*, with five other ships that had sailed from Kronstadt (the officers saluting and saying, "Aye, aye, sir," when their crews ordered them to fulfill their usual tasks while the ships helped overthrow the government), by now were lying off Petrograd.

"Our *three* main forces—the navy, the workers, and the army units—must be so combined as to occupy without fail and to hold *at any cost:* (a) the telephone exchange; (b) the telegraph office; (c) the railway stations; (d) and above all, the bridges."

2. Lenin escaped to Helsingfors from his hut near Razliv by making himself up to resemble a Sestroretsk workman whose passport he had obtained. D. I. Leschenko, a comrade from the 1905 days, went to Razliv to photograph him, as a photo had to be affixed to the passport. A Finnish comrade, Yalava, an engineer on the Finnish railway, whom Rakhya knew well, took Lenin on disguised as a fireman. Various apocryphal almost-failures have been added to this account, but Krupskaya merely says, "The plan succeeded." (Nadezhda Konstantinovna Krupskaya, *Memories of Lenin*, II, trans. by Eric Verney from the second Russian edition published in Moscow in 1930, New York, n.d., 238.) The wig, with curls coming down on his forehead, was the one Lenin continued to wear until October 26/November 8.

Lenin was not alone in thinking "above all, the bridges." Kerensky had had the same thought. So that was the meaning of the shooting we had heard as we left the Smolny. (Was it only that morning? This day had begun only at noon, but already enough had happened so that divisions of time seemed meaningless.) It had kept on throughout the day. The young officers being trained in the various military schools, known as Junkers, would close a bridge to cut off access to the workers' sections in Viborg. Sailors would get them open again.

In September I had had my first real contact with Bolshevik seamen, and now as the first day of the October Revolution was drawing to a close I was convinced that as class-conscious revolutionists they were hard to beat. At two o'clock that afternoon we had headed for the Maryinsky Palace to attend the regular session of the Council of the Republic. We figured that it might be interesting, since even the council on the previous day gave less than lukewarm support to Kerensky, despite his bragging that he had issued an order for the arrest of all Bolshevik leaders connected with the July demonstrations, and all members of the Military Revolutionary Committee. But a great crowd of sailors at the door of the palace, and others erecting barricades, told us there was no use going in, it was all over. No one had been arrested, we were told. Sailors and some units from the Lithuanian and Kuksholm regiments were lining the stairway inside when "One of our boys from Kronstadt just went in to the assembly hall and said, 'No more council now. Just go along home.' And they went."

We saw them elsewhere, too. I noticed them especially, as I say, because of my visit to the Baltic fleet in Helsingfors. On board the *Polar Star*, yacht of the former tsar, I attended a meeting of the Centrobalt (Central Committee of the Baltic Fleet, a revolutionary-democratic organization) held in a luxurious cabin. After that, I got the erroneous idea that every seaman must be a Bolshevik.

And now to my sensitive eyes it seemed that wherever a group huddled around a fire, or stood as pickets before a government building, sailors were in evidence. It almost seemed that the fleet had come ashore.

This in fact was far from the case. While Lenin's general plan of the objectives to be seized was followed through, the forces he had suggested were neither possible nor necessary. The Centrobalt, contrary to Lenin's expectations, could send only a few destroyers in support of the uprising at Petrograd. In the case of troops from the northern front, which Lenin thought could be sent in part to support the workers if necessary, the units clearly backing the Bolsheviks were little more numerous than the hostile or neutral ones.

Not only were fewer ships and sailors from Helsingfors scheduled to give the workers an assist than Lenin had asked for, but the units directly assigned to rush the Winter Palace were late in arriving. But this we learned only later in the evening.

As we neared the Smolny, out of the dark night we saw pencils of searchlights brush across its pale yellow surface, losing themselves in the lights streaming from its long windows, then picking out the crenellated decoration beneath its roofs. On the street square across from the institute stood armored cars, their engines running, a Red Guard or sailor at the wheel. A cannon with a three-inch mouth stood on the square near stacks of firewood, suitable for quick barricades. They had been placed there the previous night but had not been needed. Kerensky had ordered an attack on the Smolny the previous day, October 24/November 6; but the few hundred who might have carried it out were not forthcoming.[3]

About the entrance with its broad sweep of steps were cannon and machine guns, and armed sentries stood at the doors.

Within, all the corridors were seething, and coming down the stairway in the midst of other delegates, many of them workers in fur caps with guns slung over their shoulders, we spied Kamenev and Lunacharsky. The Petrograd Soviet had met and was just breaking up. But it had been meeting continuously now for days. In fact, the whole of Petrograd seemed to have been meeting since Sunday, October 22/November 4, when sixty meetings took place in one day. I had even been rung in to address one of them that day; Trotsky, having read the reply of the Centrobalt to my greetings, had got me to speak at the People's House (*Narodni Dom*) that day. The big excitement was the Second Congress of Soviets, due to meet here at the Smolny in a few hours. But Jack tackled Kamenev to ask

3. See A. F. Kerensky, *The Catastrophe*, New York, 1927, pp. 328–331. A delegation of several officers and Cossacks from the three regiments of Cossacks summoned to defend the government, called on him at the Winter Palace the night of October 24/November 6, and asked what other forces he had at his disposal. They also reproached him for failing to take "sufficiently energetic measures" in July. After reminding them that as soon as he returned from the front July 6 he "immediately ordered the arrest of all the Bolshevist chieftains," they agreed to "do their duty," but only "on my personal orders." That was at 1 A.M. He ordered them to staff headquarters, immediately sent word to the garrison commander "that the Cossacks could be relied on fully," and at 2 A.M. he received the commander and his chief-of-staff, who "offered" to organize "an expedition of all the forces loyal to the government, including the Cossacks, for the capture of Smolny Institute, the Staff Headquarters of the Bolsheviki."

Parenthetically, before launching this sad tale, Kerensky devotes one sentence to the democratic forces he counted on. "The fighting forces of the Socialists-Revolutionists and Mensheviki were not mobilized in time." Thus it was that (p. 332) "The hours of the night dragged on painfully. From everywhere we expected re-enforcements, but none appeared." The "endless telephone negotiations" with the Cossack regiments always brought the reply that in fifteen or twenty minutes they would "begin to saddle their horses."

Only later did he learn that the Council of Cossack Troops, meeting throughout the night, proclaimed their *neutrality* in the struggle.

what we had missed. Kamenev, his eyes lusterless, rattled through a resolution, speaking in French, and moved on. I had a few words with Lunacharsky. His delicate features were haggard, his collar was soiled, his usually meticulous mustache and goatee were unkempt; obviously he had not slept for days. Realizing he was dead on his feet, I did not press him, only mentioned we had come from the Winter Palace and what about it? Would it be taken soon? "God knows," he sighed. "There is much to be done."

It had not occurred to either Jack or me to ask if Lenin had been there, and when we learned shortly that he had made a surprise appearance at the Petrograd Soviet, his first public appearance in almost four months, Reed was furious. And why hadn't Kamenev even mentioned it? To think we had missed him! Remembering Reed's astonishment at my earlier "confession," I said, "Pretty hard fellow to keep up with—in or out of exile."

We soon ran into Alex Gumberg and Bessie Beatty. A friend of Trotsky's in New York, where he had worked as business manager of the weekly *Novy Mir,* Alex usually knew what was going on in Smolny. But Reed disliked asking him anything and inviting one of his barbed remarks. I had no craft pride to protect, on the other hand, and did not mind admitting I had missed Lenin for the second time.

What had happened was that Trotsky opened the meeting as chairman, presenting the newly won revolutionary power on behalf of the Military Revolutionary Committee, on which he also served, to the Petrograd Soviet. "Or almost newly won." Alex grinned. "Even while he declared that 'the Provisional Government has ceased to exist,' Trotsky acknowledged one little thing was lacking in the new power: the Winter Palace. But he promised that 'its fate will be decided in the course of the next few minutes.' Well, the minutes have passed, quite a few of them, and it still hasn't been taken.

"But Trotsky is a great showman," Gumberg went on. Being a showman himself, he relished the fact that he had even Reed hanging on his words, and he took his time about getting to the part we all wanted to hear. "Things could have become embarrassing for him. After all, he was one of the key men, all of them on the extreme left, SR's and Bolsheviks, on the Military Revolutionary Committee. The men from Viborg appeared a bit restive. Here he was offering the Soviets the keys of the city, and the elders, minus their leader Kerensky, sat in somewhat lonely splendor in the Winter Palace defended by the Women's Battalion and hundreds of frightened Junkers—but still, they were there. Why were the ministers being handled with kid gloves? But before questions could begin to pop, Trotsky saved the situation by introducing Lenin. The place went wild. Prolonged ovation and so on.

"And in the excitement of seeing and hearing Lenin, the men from Viborg forgot about the little matter of the Winter Palace."

For quite a few of the new members of the Bolshevik majority in the Petrograd Soviet, workers from Viborg whose very allegiance to the Bolsheviks may have been rather new, this had been their first glimpse of Lenin. What a scene we had missed!

It was of course part of Lenin's plan, insisted on throughout his notes on insurrection from the underground, and which we know now he battled through successfully in the eventual meetings of the Bolshevik Central Committee, that an armed uprising must take place prior to the opening of the Second Congress. The Congress must be presented with a *fait accompli*. Not that there was any danger that the Congress, with the Bolsheviks in the majority now, would not vote for insurrection in any event. But Kerensky, aware of that, could surround the Smolny and forcibly prevent its convening. Lenin, never counting his chickens before they were hatched, may have been overoptimistic in his estimate of the numbers of sailors and soldiers from Finland posts who were Bolshevized, but he was most realistic in guarding against a surprise move by Kerensky at a time when it was not known how many Cossacks and others from the front would move at his command.

The Congress, originally scheduled for the twentieth, had been postponed until today, the twenty-fifth, the Mensheviks and Right Social Revolutionaries hoping against hope that the government would produce some miracle to stave off a violent overthrow and a take-over by the Bolsheviks. It was this forlorn hope that had inspired the last resolution of the Pre-Parliament, that peace proposals be stiffened and peasants given land—a resolution so worded, however, that it failed to save face for the P.G. (Kerensky, amazed when he had asked for a vote of confidence and got just this, said, quite rightly, that it was a vote of no confidence. He declared he was resigning, which swiftly brought Dan and the compromisers to cajole him into staying, saying the resolution *did* support him.)

"Well, how important is it, after all, that the Winter Palace be taken?" Louise Bryant wanted to know. "Everyone knows the city is in the hands of the Bolsheviks by now."

Gumberg grinned. "Yes, and Bessie here still thinks the Revolution wasn't timed right. She was to have had lunch with the Premier at one P.M. today. Old Francis also is sad that Kerensky has left—but happy he was able to help out a little in making his getaway easy, I hear."

Reed could no longer restrain his impatience. "What I want to know is, what did Lenin say? And what does *he* think about the failure to take the Winter Palace? Did he mention that?"

"I don't know why it is," Alex mused, his voice silky-soft, "but every time I see American reporters, they want to know what took place some-where where they weren't. But wherever there's good food and drink being served, there you'll find them. You were probably having a nice leisurely snack somewhere when Lenin spoke. Anyway, the answer is I don't take notes. And no minutes of the meeting were taken. You'll have to do some digging to find out."

And in fact we did not find out. John Reed's *Ten Days* mentions the "mighty ovation" Lenin received, quotes Trotsky and Zinoviev, from whom one could easily get a recapitulation of a few remarks, but does not quote Lenin. Sukhanov was there, and in his memoirs has Lenin saying in part:

"Now begins a new era in the history of Russia, and this third Russian revolution must finally lead to the victory of Socialism." To end the war, capitalism itself must be overcome. In this, the working classes of Italy, Germany, and England would help. "Within Russia an enormous section of the peasantry has said: Enough playing around with the capitalists; we will go with the workers." And he concluded: "In Russia we must set to work at once on the construction of a proletarian Socialist State. Long live the worldwide Socialist revolution!"

Trying a diversion to forestall a heated retort to Alex from Reed, and a more serious flare-up of the smoldering war between them, I took up Louise Bryant's point and added a controversial quality I knew would catch Reed's attention.

"Is it true that Lenin had trouble persuading even Trotsky that the blow must be struck, and the Kerensky forces must be definitely placed under arrest, before the Congress opens tonight?" I asked Alex.[4]

---

4. All sorts of rumors were afloat since the evening of October 24, when Trotsky told an emergency session of the Petrograd Soviet, reporting in his capacity as president of the Soviet and of the Military Revolutionary Committee: "An armed conflict today or tomorrow is not included in our plan—on the threshold of the All-Russian Congress of Soviets. We think that the Congress will carry out our slogan ["All power to the Soviets!"] . . . But if the government wants to use that span of life which still remains to it—24, 48, or 72 hours— in order to take the offensive against us, we will answer with a counteroffensive, blow for blow, steel against iron." This was a defensive maneuver and Trotsky (*History of the Russian Revolution*, III 360) attributes to it assurances made to Kerensky by Dan later that night that the Bolsheviks would not make an immediate insurrection. (It mattered little, for Kerensky still tried to mount an attack on Smolny.) It also, Trotsky agrees, may have added to Lenin's tension and distrust. Lenin, it will be recalled, was unaware that a decision had been reached that morning to strike without delay; thus his letter written to district leaders, beginning "Comrades! I am writing these lines on the evening of the 24th," and thus his trip, against orders, alone with Rakhya to Smolny on the 25th. (It is also probable that Trotsky was overconcerned with the need of avoiding any appearance of conspiracy.)

See Trotsky on the November Revolution in *Soviet Russia Pictorial*, IV (1921), January 77: "In fixing the Congress for October 25, and in putting on the order of the day, as a capital and essential question, the realization (not the discussion but the realization) of the transfer of power to the hands of the Soviets, we practically fixed October 25 as the day of the Revolution and did it openly before the eyes of 'society' and its 'government.' "

"Doubtless you know more about the Central Committee than I do—I'm not a member," he began. But the full venom of Gumberg's retort was dissipated as Jack exploded:

"If you're implying there's anything deliberate about the delay in attacking the Winter Palace—"

"I'm implying nothing of the sort," I said. "I think it's nothing more than what we heard the Guards saying at the palace square—if they attacked, they'd be blamed for shooting up the Woman's Battalion. I'm not picking something out of the air, though. Peters told me last Sunday that at one of the Central Committee meetings, even those who favored insurrection couldn't agree on the day, so that Lenin was virtually alone. I'm not speaking of Kamenev, Zinoviev, Riazanov, and so on. Trotsky, he said, was so certain the Congress would give the signal for the revolt that he thought it was best to wait—and then it couldn't be said it would be a Bolshevik coup. But Lenin showed them how dangerous that would be. It would only play into Kerensky's hands and give him a chance to get all the Kornilov-type officers to pull their men into the capital. They'd even leave the front unprotected for that, and be thanked by the Allies, so long as the Bolsheviks were prevented from seizing power."

I could see even by Gumberg's poker face that this was not far from the truth.

"All I know is the Military Revolutionary Committee, including Trotsky, has been working night and day to get everything over with by tonight," Jack said stubbornly.

"If you must know, the palace would be taken by now if our friends the sailors had got here on time," Gumberg now said quietly.

Of course Gumberg was proved right. The five ships had been delayed. N. Podvoisky, who with Vladimir Aleksandrovich Antonov-Ovseyenko and Chudnovsky had charge of the operation, had promised the fall of the Winter Palace by noon. But at noon the Kronstadters had not arrived. Even when it became known that Kerensky had left about seven A.M., the plans went unaltered, in case the Cossacks sent from the front arrived. The plan called for the surrounding of the palace in a giant oval of soldiers, Red Guards, and sailors, with the *Aurora* and the Sts. Peter and Paul Fortress ready to fire their cannon if a demand for surrender was not heeded, and the other ships summoned from Kronstadt and the navy completing the circle on the river side. Revolutionary detachments of regiments and Red Guards were to be massed for flank defenses in the remainder of the oval, to prevent a strike from the rear by Junkers and the Cossacks promised to Kerensky by Dukhonin.

Unknown to the Bolsheviks for some time was the fact that the Winter Palace still was in touch with army headquarters at Moghiliev and the staff of the northern front at Pskov, since these phone connections did not flow through the telephone exchange. At the time Trotsky told the Petrograd Soviet the fall of the palace would be a matter of history within a few minutes, he based his estimate on the fact that under urgent pressure from the Military Revolutionary Committee (actually Lenin), the seizure had been set for three P.M. without fail. When four P.M. came and no seizure, but instead news that the palace forces had increased and that the new arrivals had walked in through the besieging lines, Podvoisky said through clenched teeth that it would be at six P.M. "at any cost." But all this we learned later.

It was not until seven that the sailors had come; this much Gumberg told us now. Yet still the opening of the Congress was being postponed, for Lenin's plan had been that the entire city was to be in the hands of the Military Revolutionary Committee before the Congress assembled.

Reed still had not cooled down. "We were talking about what the delay was," he said, that light of battle in his eyes so frequently seen in Gumberg's presence now turned on me with a baleful glare. "And if Lenin really won over the committee, why bring that up at all now?"

"How nervous we're all getting waiting for the Congress to open," Bessie said lightly, and then went on with some news that stopped the squabbling. She had just met Trotsky on the floor above; Alex had introduced her, she said. "The serious thing now is that troops are moving on Petrograd from the front right now." Then, showing that even our little diplomat among the newspaperwomen was not unaffected by our mood, she delivered this thrust to me and Jack: "It seems as if you could have gleaned that much from Kamenev and Lunacharsky. It was announced at the Petrograd Soviet meeting today."

While we fussed and got on each other's nerves, we felt more and more uneasy that the Congress was not convened. Gumberg wandered off, saying he would see us in the great hall later. I noticed he headed in the direction of the Military Revolutionary Committee office in Smolny. Jack, restless as a cat, decided to look into the great auditorium and see if he could pick up any information from Ransome or Price or the Americans Dosch-Fleurot of the *New York World* and Gregory Yarros (really a Russian-American) of the Associated Press. Lenin had slipped through our fingers once; he wanted to find out where he was now and what he was doing. Bryant, Beatty, and I took up a post in one of those unbelievably long corridors of the Smolny, hoping to see one of our Russian-American friends.

Beatty worried aloud for fear that the reported oncoming troops from the front might arrive and storm the Smolny that night and arrest the delegates, while the soldiers and sailors concentrated at the Winter Palace. "Then it would end in a frightful blood bath after all and no one would be better off in the end."

Bryant kept recalling the young Junkers we had seen, some of them resting on dirty mattresses, in the Winter Palace that afternoon, each one trying to outdo the other in the number of French phrases he used. And just as one officer asked her if it would be possible for him to enlist in the American army when it arrived, Bryant related, a shot rang out and wild confusion followed, the Junkers running about aimlessly; no one seemed to be in command.

Beatty now told us that while we were in the palace, she had been pulled inside a doorway on the Morskaya when an armored car and an approaching company of military cadets exchanged shots.

Bryant told Beatty, "We looked through the windows in the front of the palace and saw men running and falling on their faces. Then this little man came out of the palace, walked across the square and planted his tripod, and began taking shots of the women soldiers building a barricade. It all had an operatic air, and a comic one at that. Those poor, miserable cadets!"

Irritated, I said I would rather think of the happy sailors and Red Guards and men from the Petrograd garrison to whom the day belonged. As for Beatty's worry that the Smolny might yet be surrounded, that seemed to me worth thinking about. "Assuming it happened, I wonder if Kerensky would return at the head of the victors."

I decided to go in search of Gumberg. I headed for the Military Revolutionary Committee. I did not go in. The youthful fair-haired acting chairman, Lazimir, a Left SR, the old-time Bolshevik Lashevich, and other members had been in continuous session since Monday that I knew of. So had the factory shop committees downstairs, handing out orders on the government arsenal, 150 guns for each factory. The grim old fort of Sts. Peter and Paul had come over to the Bolsheviks on Monday, as well as the arsenal, and weapons were distributed there. I had seen the factory delegates standing in long disciplined lines Monday night in Smolny, waiting for the slip of paper that would yield them guns at the fortress for their shopmates.

I failed to find Gumberg, but near the Military Revolutionary Committee office I was overjoyed to run into Voskov. He was pale, had what looked to be a three-day growth of beard, and was rushing along, but he stopped to slap me on the back and say in a hoarse happy voice, "It's beginning! The sailors have come now in full force. Now if there aren't any slip-ups! Vladimir Ilyich is insisting: no more delays."

He would have rushed on, but I grabbed his arm. As he still walked on, I walked with him, questioning him. Had he himself seen Lenin? No, Lenin was unavailable. "If you must know, you probably walked right past him in the passageway to the White Hall, if you were there a bit earlier. At least he was there, in his wig and cap and big glasses, sitting

with a few Bolsheviks, while the different parties and factions were caucusing. I hear Dan recognized him, looked embarrassed, and walked on.
Now I think he's gone into an anteroom. Messengers keep going in, and
some come out with messages, too, so I presume he's going on firing away
with questions. Last night and today a number of our men have been inter-
rogated by him. He has to know every detail. Now there's only one thing
left he's worried about— the Winter Palace. But I'm on my way."

He was running down the stairs, and I kept up with him. "One thing,
Voskov. Isn't he going to appear tonight? Won't he be on the podium?"

"How do I know? All I know is that now he's here, there'll be no deals
made, and bloodshed or not, the palace will be taken. And that until it is,
he wouldn't be caught dead facing that congress. It was different this
afternoon. The Petrograd Soviet is largely our men, it's dominated by the
Viborg people. After the palace is ours and the ministers are locked up,
then let the Mensheviks and SR's howl—it will do them no good."

I watched him go, a dozen questions still whirling through my mind.
Why did Lenin remain incognito at this late date? Was there any actual
danger to him even now? It was almost ten P.M. and the delegates were
jamming all the doorways, filling all the windowsills, and all but hanging
from the great chandeliers in the enormous room, I saw as I entered. I felt
apprehensive. Was there really a chance that before the Congress could vote,
those reportedly advancing troops would surround us and Lenin be taken?
I spied Reed sitting far down in the hall, and started elbowing my way
toward him, relieved to see he had dumped his overcoat next to him to hold
a seat for me. On my way to meet him I saw Peters—a delegate, as I recall,
put up by the Letts—seated near Stuchka, their head spokesman. I motioned
to him, indicating I wanted to see him, and he made his way to the aisle,
not looking too pleased about it. I didn't care. I felt I couldn't sit still until
I got an answer. Later he told me how funny I looked—pale, disheveled, as
I stared at him suspiciously. There was such a tumult about us that I was
in no danger of being overheard, but I whispered tensely. He could not
hear me. I stuttered out the words: "Why is Lenin still wearing his disguise? Is he in imminent danger? Are the Cossacks in the city?"

He answered patiently, amusement in his mild blue eyes: "No, no, it's
all right. Comrade Ilyich just wants to take his time, look about a bit, size
things up. That's the way it's been since last night. Getting the lay of the
land, getting control in his hands, but behind the scenes. Why should he be
in a rush to appear in public? Not that he's fooling anybody; everybody
knows he's running the show. And now will you go and let me sit down,
Albert Davidovich?"

At ten-forty the chairman of the Central Executive Committee, Fyodor
Ilyich Dan, a physician by profession and long an editor of all Menshevik

newspapers, rang a bell. His round, clean-shaven face was coldly impassive, as usual. Before he even declared the Congress open, he set the tone of the evening for the minority, once the powerful majority. He would attempt no political speech, he said, inasmuch as his party comrades were at that moment "under bombardment in the Winter Palace, sacrificing themselves to execute their duty." An uproar followed in which he declared the Congress open.

When it was announced the election of the presidium would be by proportionality, the Mensheviks began another commotion. The Bolsheviks won fourteen seats, other parties eleven. Right and Center SR's and Mensheviks promptly refused to take part in the presidium; Internationalist Mensheviks hedged, saying they would await certain conditions. The old body stepped down and the Bolsheviks, minus Lenin, stepped up to the podium: Trotsky, Kamenev, Lunacharsky, Madame Kollontai, Nogin we recognized. The great hall swelled with the rolling applause.

Kamenev acted as chairman. Like everyone else, we accepted this without a flicker of surprise, I recall, although he had opposed the insurrection almost to the end. Kamenev had just announced the order of the day when Lozovsky, an opponent of the insurrection, called for a report from the Petrograd Soviet, and sparring began. My attention wandered during some objections on procedure from the right wing. Peters had dispelled my apprehensions, and now I was simply enjoying myself.

Suddenly a rumble and the hollow boom of artillery were heard. Delegates were on their feet, those at windows peering out. Julius Ossipovich Martov was on his feet, calling for the floor.

"The civil war is beginning, comrades!" he said. His voice was hoarse, hollow, mournful; like many of those imprisoned and exiled, he had contracted tuberculosis. "The first question must be a peaceful settlement of the crisis. . . . The first question before the Congress is the question of power, and this is already being settled by force of arms in the streets! . . . the Congress must not sit with folded hands before the developing civil war, the result of which may be a dangerous outburst of counterrevolution. The possibility of a peaceful outcome lies in the formation of a united democratic authority. We must elect a delegation to negotiate with the other socialist parties and organizations." Again, the hollow booming of cannon sounded through the windows. Distantly, artillery answered.

Every now and then the Bolsheviks would retire to vote, and doubtless to consult Lenin, and return, or other groups would caucus. If the moderates expected Lenin and the Bolsheviks to oppose Martov's resolution—and apparently they did, from the comments that flew around the room—they were disappointed. Why should they? It was the Mensheviks and SR's who had earlier rejected Lenin's offer of a compromise, not the other way around. Lunacharsky announced that the Bolshevik faction "has absolutely nothing against Martov's proposal." A vote was taken; hands were raised among a forest of bayonets. It was carried unanimously.

The Mensheviks, however, did not want to see a united front. A Menshevik officer from the Twelfth Army, Captain Kharash, began a violent denunciation of the Bolsheviks for surrounding the Winter Palace. Another officer said the Congress was "unauthorized" in view of the approaching Constituent Assembly. Soldier delegates interrupted them fiercely, demanding for whom they spoke. Khinchuk, later Soviet ambassador in Berlin, reading a Right Menshevik resolution, demanded that negotiations with the Provisional Government be opened. A Right Socialist screeched out the decision of his faction—collaboration with the Bolsheviks was an "impossibility," the Congress itself "without authority."

Jeers and hoots from the assembly sounded; soldiers from the trenches denounced the officers, urging all to leave as imposters. "Kornilovist!" "Counterrevolutionary!" *"Provocateur!"* greeted Kharash, who claimed to speak for delegates from the front.

In the midst of the tumult Abramovich, representing the Bund (Jewish Social Democrats), said that the firing on the Winter Palace was under way, and the members of the Municipal Duma, the Mensheviks and Socialist Revolutionaries, and the Peasants' Soviet Executive Committee "decided to perish with the Provisional Government, and we are going with them!" He invited all the delegates to go along. "Unarmed we will expose our breasts to the machine guns of the terrorists."

Kamenev shouted for everyone except the compromisers to keep his seat, and out filed some eighty of the determined martyrs.

And now, after Martov saw that it was not the Bolsheviks who blocked any joint action under his unanimous resolution, but the Mensheviks and SR's, the Bundists and varied little groups, he again took the floor. This was his opportunity to do something great. Inveterate optimist that I am, I really thought he would. "He's going to rise to the occasion, I'll bet," I said to Reed.

How wrong I was—and how Jack laughed at me later! I should not have been, as I had had a personal experience with Martov that should have told me that he would not be big enough. Martov had accosted me on the Liteiny Prospekt during one of the huge demonstrations in the first days of July. "What do you think of this?" he asked. I was standing transfixed, gazing at the oncoming waves of thousands and thousands, their red flags and banners rolling down the street in a wide river. As I was still having trouble with the language, I was at first silent, then stumbling. He thought I was sputtering with indignation, as he was. "It is not my revolution," he said. His eyes blazed with anger and his arms pumped up and down so violently I feared his pince-nez might slip from his hand and break on the pavement. A strange spectacle! The great demonstration—a battalion from Kronstadt, twenty sailors deep, powerful men swinging with a steady tramp—was sweeping by while we stood there; and Martov, the old warrior, was suddenly a pathetic figure, storming in impotent rage, a rather ludicrous symbol of the old socialists arrayed against the Bolsheviks. Not that he blamed the Bolsheviks as instigators, to my recollection. Evidently he understood that it was a spontaneous move by the masses. Well, was not this exactly what the socialists had been talking about, longing for, for seventy years? But now that the apathetic masses were in grand revolt, these intellectuals were dismayed. It was they, the intellectuals, who were the custodians, guardians, and directors of the Revolution. How did the masses have the temerity to take matters into their own hands this way? So Martov looked at the defiant ranks passing as if the demonstration were an affront.

Nevertheless, I continued to like old Martov. There was something about him that set him apart from the men like Dan, like Lieber,[5] and certainly like Tsereteli and the others around Kerensky, something that got under your skin. So now I wished the hubbub in the hall would subside a bit so I could hear him; I felt sure he would make a great speech, which would confound the waverers and swing at least his group of Internationalist Mensheviks behind the new Soviet power, willing when the chips were down to work with the Bolsheviks.

I was disappointed. He began, "We must put a stop to the bloodshed." Martov was interrupted; it was only rumors, this bloodshed business, someone called from the floor. No, he persisted, just listen to the cannon. It could not be denied, there was that muffled boom. He introduced a resolution declaring the Revolution was accomplished by the Bolsheviks alone, and by "military plot," and demanding that the Congress suspend its sessions until an agreement was reached with all socialist parties.

So, poor old Martov. In a crisis he always stepped forward fearlessly, conscious of the role of his minority group, always clear in their opposition to the war, to Kerensky's subservience to the bourgeois interests at home and in foreign capitals, to the government's intolerable indecisiveness; and then he fell victim to the same indecision. He had missed the boat again. How blind, how stupid! For now, at this point, when the Right Mensheviks and Right SR's were working against the new revolution, they were in fact counterrevolutionary. Obviously they had agreed in caucuses before

---

5. Mikhail I. Goldman, or Lieber (because of repression in tsarist times most revolutionists had two names), 1880–1937. A leader of the Jewish Bund; after the second congress of the RSDLP in 1903, a Menshevik; a member of the executive committee of the Petrograd Soviet before the October Revolution; resigned from political activity thereafter.

the bell rang that they would walk out. Their numbers had shrunk now, and they could not face being in the minority. But the Internationalist Mensheviks had gloried in being in the minority. In a socialist front that was compromised they bore less of the shame. The Bolsheviks had recognized this in giving them a place in the presidium. And now, what was he doing? Would he send his followers to drag along behind the Mensheviks and SR's they had fought so bitterly? Where could they go now? The people were in the Soviet now, minus their self-appointed mentors who "wear red rosettes in their buttonholes and call themselves 'revolutionary democrats.'" How could the Martov group find themselves?

But Trotsky was giving the answer.

He tells how he was lying on a rug next to Lenin in a bare room close by in Smolny—others say one of Lenin's sisters brought a couple of pillows in to them—while messengers came in giving them notes on how the Congress was going. Lenin decided Trotsky must go in and answer Martov now. There followed Trotsky's short but famous speech, his voice fierce with scorn—possibly more than it needed to be, for these delegates who remained were in no danger of being swayed by Martov's plea for a united front of socialists or anything else. They were the workers who knew that the law ordering an eight-hour day, enacted soon after February, had never been enforced; they were the people whose wives waited in queues several hours for bread; and they were the soldiers such as Reed and I had seen after the fall of Riga in the crumbling front lines, falling greedily on a field of turnips, or crowding into homeward-bound trains, or fraternizing with German soldiers across a barbed-wire fence.

Trotsky's words were like whiplashes. He said in part: "A rising of the people needs no justification. We openly forged the will of the masses for an insurrection, and not a conspiracy. The masses of the people followed our banner and our insurrection was victorious. And now we are told: Renounce your victory, make concessions, compromise. With whom? I ask. With whom should we compromise? With those wretched groups who have left us? No one in Russia is with them any longer. A compromise is to be made, by the millions of workers and peasants represented in this Congress, whom they are ready, not for the first time or the last, to barter away as the bourgeoisie sees fit. No, here no compromise is possible. To those who have left and to those who tell us to do this we must say: You are miserable bankrupts, your role is played out. Go where you ought to be: into the dustbin of history!"

"Then we'll leave!" Martov, emotional, hurt, shouted in his hoarse tubercular voice, beginning to shove his way off the platform.

Sick over this turn of events, wishing to get away from this sorry spectacle of one of the great ones among the intelligentsia unable to reconcile himself to seeing the "dark people" finally doing just what he had bade them do all along, Jack and I hurried out. We would go to the Winter Palace and see what was taking place. It was about one o'clock.

It took us awhile to collect our group. Finally Bryant, Beatty, Reed, and I stood shivering on the Smolny steps. Gumberg was to join us and was negotiating a ride for us—if not to the Winter Palace, which was two miles from Smolny, to somewhere within quick walking distance of it.

"I can understand the others' leaving," I said, "but Martov! Will he really go? Will others? These intelligentsia! They suffer prison, exile, Martov contracts tuberculosis in damp jails and Siberia, all for the people; they make a god of the people. Then when the people rise with the wrath and thunder of a god, imperious, arbitrary, glorying in their new powers, the intelligentsia become atheists. They reject a god who will not listen to them. They cannot control the god, and they creep away to hide."

"That's good, you ought to use it," said Reed.

I was annoyed at his professionalism. But I did.

"Come on, here's Alex."

All of us five Americans save Gumberg have written of our ride in a huge motor lorry. We piled into the back end, where several sailors and a Cossack from the Wild Division (a deserter, I devoutly hoped) stood.[6] The sailors in their caps or tam-o'-shanters, ribbons streaming out behind, and the Cossack in a long cape of shaggy black fur moved over and made room for us among the high stacks of leaflets, guns, and ammunition. In the debonair manner so characteristic of the sailors I had talked with in the Baltic Fleet (part of their supreme self-confidence), we were told, "We are sure to be shot at, you know, but come along; we'll give you a joy ride." One of them made Louise Bryant remove a yellow hatband. A Red Guard cranked up and took the wheel. We were on our way to distribute handbills throughout the city.

As we rumbled and rattled over the cobblestones, the streets looked dark and empty. But with each shower of leaflets tossed in the air, men and women tumbled out of doorways and courtyards and eagerly grabbed them. Gumberg held one up in the half-light of a street lamp at one pause and read aloud:

"To the Citizens of Russia:

"The Provisional Government is deposed. The state power has passed into the hands of the organ of the Petrograd Soviet of Workers' and Soldiers' Deputies, the Military Revolutionary Committee, which stands at the head of the Petrograd proletariat and garrison.

6. The "Wild Division" or "Savage Division" was made up of volunteers from among the mountain peoples of the North Caucasus during World War I.

"The aims for which the people were fighting—immediate proposal of a democratic peace, abolition of landlord property rights in the land, labor control over production, creation of a Soviet government—these aims have been achieved.

"Long live the revolution of workmen, soldiers, and peasants!

"Military Revolutionary Committee of the Petrograd Soviet of Workers' and Soldiers' Deputies."

Gumberg said dryly, "They've been printed and ready for delivery since ten this morning. Pretty optimistic. But the optimism failed to trickle down to the military geniuses conducting the cat-and-mouse game at the Winter Palace. They want to make so sure their operation succeeds that they wait for almost the whole navy to arrive, and then they keep sending in ultimatums to the palace, setting new deadlines beyond which they will fire if the ministers don't give in, and then giving them another chance."

At the juncture of the Ekaterina Canal and the Nevsky, barricades had been erected and we were turned back. The truck went on its way, and we walked back to the Kazan Cathedral, where we were again halted. There across the wide street we saw a crowd of men lined up, confronting some twenty sailors who barred their way. It was the self-proclaimed martyrs of a few hours earlier. (The Congress had opened at ten-forty P.M. and it was now about two A.M.) With them were wives and friends and the mayor of Petrograd and rightist socialist members of the City Duma.

"Let us pass! Let us sacrifice ourselves!" they pleaded.

A sailor replied: "Go home and take poison. But don't expect to die here. We have orders from the Military Revolutionary Committee not to allow it, and not to let you pass."

They huddled together, and another spokesman tackled the sailors, in less heroic words. What would be the tactics employed against them were they "suddenly to push forward?"

"Why," said a sailor, "we might spank you, but we just will not kill you, nary a one of you."

At this, the group was addressed by one of its members, Minister of Supplies Prokopovich, who should have been with his fellows in the Winter Palace but was one of two arrested on his way to answer Kerensky's summons about six o'clock that morning, and later released. "Comrades: Let us return," he quavered. "Let us refuse to be killed by *switchmen!*" Stiffly they began to march in the direction of the Taurida Palace, where the Duma met.

After being let through the cordon of sailors by virtue of our Military Revolutionary Committee passes, we advanced only to be stopped by Red Guards. We looked too bourgeois for them. Back near the cathedral, we found a sympathetic Red Guard, there as a sort of commissar (the word was being used more frequently now) with an army detachment. After examining our passes, he sent one of his soldiers with us to get us through the lines.

As we reached the Red Arch three shots rang out. There was no return volley, and on all sides of us Red Guards, soldiers, and sailors were running toward the palace. Gingerly we picked our way over cobblestones now carpeted with broken glass. A sailor called out, "It's all over! They have surrendered!"

There was a rush for the one small entrance that was open. We clambered over the barricades behind the Guards and sailors and ran toward the great palace, now streaming with light. Our blue-sealed passes gave us entrée; a Red Guard at the door waved us forward. Within, the Junkers were being disarmed and set free. A squad of sailors mounted the stairs to arrest the Provisional Government ministers. We were motioned to a long bench by the wall, and from there watched the procession down the broad stairway of the members of the cabinet, each with his escort.

All the ministers descending the stairs before our eyes were there in the Winter Palace by no virtue of election. As Miliukov had explained to a partly enthusiastic, partly jeering audience after the February Revolution (they accepted Kerensky as Minister of Justice with enthusiasm then), there was no time for elections. No force at the time, even the Bolsheviks —who were complacent, I gathered, until Lenin's return—had seriously challenged this procedure. So the people who made the February Revolution had not put them in office. They put themselves in office, and even those like Tereshchenko who would have supported a return of the Romanov dynasty, but were not so flagrantly marked by the old regime as Miliukov and Guchkov, had grimly clung to their position. It was accurately named a provisional government. It could rule *provided* it had the support of the masses. Never were the masses enthusiastically for the government. It was a government by consent, but it was a reluctant consent at best, and now the consent had been withdrawn.

"It's a mistake to let the Junkers go," Gumberg was complaining. "How softhearted do they have to be? Do they think the Allies are going to bless them just because they save bloodshed? But it's their revolution."

"First you have them underconfident, then overconfident," Reed said.

"And that can be just the way it is!" Alex snapped.

Before we got into another first-class wrangle, I cut the conversation short, little thinking I would be agreeing wholeheartedly with Gumberg in a few days about the Junkers. I suggested we try to get upstairs now, as they seemed to be on their way. The ministers were to be taken to the Peter and Paul Fortress, where a secondary headquarters of the Military Revolutionary Committee had been set up.

Someone, Antonov or Chudnovsky, as I recall, gave us permission to enter the Malachite Hall, just as guards were being posted there and all the inner rooms were being searched for any hidden cadets or possibly any of the advance groups of sailors who had broken into the palace earlier, only to be disarmed and held prisoner. It was here in the great hall with its huge windows facing the Neva that the P.G. had held its meetings and the ministers had spent most of their time while waiting for the Cossacks who never came. But toward evening they had left the Malachite Hall, whose windows were too close to the guns on the turret of the *Aurora* beyond Nikolayevsky Bridge and the guns of the Peter and Paul Fortress.[7] A vivid description of the ministers' feelings before they retired to an inner room, where they seated themselves at a big round table in semidarkness, the light from the only lamp shielded from the windows by newspapers (even though the study faced only a courtyard), is given by P. Maliantovich, Minister of Justice in the P.G.

[In the] cold light of a grey sunless day . . . a panorama of the city could be clearly seen through the crisp air. From the corner window we could view the crowded expanses of the mighty river. Indifferent, cold waters. . . . Hidden alarm seemed to hang in the air.

Doomed people, lonely, abandoned by all, walked around in the huge mousetrap, occasionally getting all together or in little groups for brief conversations. . . .

Around us was a void, inside of us a void, and in it we felt the growing reckless determination of total indifference. . . .

The moment when we should issue a brief and decisive order would come inevitably. What order?

To hold out to the last man, to the last drop of blood? What for?

When a power was not defended by those who organized it,—was it needed? If it was not needed, if it had outlived itself, to whom should it be turned over, how, and on whose orders? . . .

We did not have behind us the authority of an order issued in the name of the people; we enjoyed verbal sympathy but actually we were being abandoned.

I remember Antonov's pale face, his ascetic features, his wild red hair beneath his picturesque wide-brimmed felt hat, and his general air of intense calm which belied his most unmilitary exterior as he departed with the sixteen ministers, three aides, and their guard of about fifty sailors and soldiers and Red Guards.

I learned from one of the sailors that upstairs, as Chudnovsky had

---

7. The fortress guns would not work either.

made out a list of the ministers present, Antonov had asked, "Comrades, are there any cars?"

Someone replied, "No cars," and others said, "Let them walk! They've done enough riding."

Antonov shouted for silence, then after a moment's thought said, "All right, we'll take them to the fortress on foot."

In ensuing years Western historians have been wont to speak disparagingly of Antonov, and the fact that no cars were handy did mean that the ministers were harassed and followed by an ever growing crowd that grew uglier, their demands to have the ministers turned over to them grew more insistent. Curiously, an incident on the Troitsky Bridge, when an approaching car began firing on the men on foot, saved the day. This served to divert the crowd, and Antonov's screams, "Don't fire! We're friends!" at last halted the firing, and they made their way safely into the Peter and Paul. But if Antonov had a gift for getting into predicaments, that is not unusual in a revolution, and my own later contacts with him including in the next few days a predicament from which I was instrumental in rescuing him—convinced me that he had other considerable talents, including a cool head and a complete lack of fear.

Of course, Gumberg did not spare Antonov that night, but why Antonov more than Chudnovsky or Podvoisky, I do not know. Why had not Antonov, who had been a Bolshevik since 1903, was a military man of sorts, and as secretary of the Military Revolutionary Committee was relied on by Lenin, acted sooner? Gumberg asked. Everyone knew—Lenin had been telling them long enough, said Gumberg—that a successful insurrection was impossible without the Bolshevik forces from the Baltic fleet. Antonov knew Dybenko, knew the situation in Helsingfors. Yet, when Smolny had received a telegram from Helsingfors on the night of October 23 that ships were being held in readiness to move as soon as Smolny sent word, why was not the reply: Start now? Fortunately the sailors sent two torpedo boats at the time, without instructions. And as soon as Kerensky had ordered all the swing bridges save the palace bridge opened, and the same night had the left-wing papers shut down, why, instead of sending detachments to unseal the presses, had not the Military Revolutionary Committee ordered an attack on the Winter Palace then? And why in hell had the Military Revolutionary Committee released the two ministers arrested without orders by Red Guards?

Even as I hurried up the broad staircase, the walls of which were hung with tapestries, I heard Reed mutter to Gumberg, "Well, as you say, it's their revolution. Too bad you didn't make it yours, and then you could have had some say-so in it, huh?"

From the Malachite Hall we managed to make our way into the

inner study—reputedly once the study of Nikolai II—where the ministers had sat about a round table, or walked up and down, or tried to sleep on sofa or chairs during the last seven hours or so before their arrest. It was to be sealed and searched, so we had only a few moments there, under watchful eyes. We snatched up a few scraps of paper, with an occasional sentence of that final order they were debating, the words usually ending in idle jottings and doodling.

Leaving the palace, we saw a young Bolshevik lieutenant standing at the only exit open. A table was nearby. Two soldiers searched all who left, to make sure no valuables were taken. The lieutenant repeated over and over, "Comrades, this is the people's palace. This is our palace. Do not steal from the people. Do not disgrace the people."

Shamefaced, a few big bearded soldiers yielded their loot—a blanket, a worn sofa cushion of leather, a wax candle, a coat hanger, the broken handle of a Chinese sword.

Strange, wasn't it, Reed said, that long before the end, after the departure of the Cossacks (some two hundred), the Women's Shock Battalion, and hundreds of the cadets, the only visible defenders were a crowd of frightened children—for the cadets were mere boys. None of the defenders had been wounded. "All the wounded were on our side," the lieutenant at the door told us, and this was confirmed. Five sailors and one soldier were killed, and many wounded.

We were in a somber mood as we made our way back to Smolny. We dreaded what we might find. We were afraid the new minority parties might have perpetrated further mischief in their exploitation of the Winter Palace business. We knew by now that the ominous boom from the *Aurora* that Martov had dramatized had come from the firing of blank shells. But the exchange of rifle and machine-gun fire followed; what had they made of that?

As Reed analyzed it, the delay had played into the hands of the moderates, and the cannon's boom probably had affected Martov, always emotional, so that he had jumped the gun on his own group.

"At any rate," Gumberg said with finality, "the storming of the Winter Palace will go down in history as the great anticlimax of a revolution that in other respects was dramatic just because it was so unassuming." You had to know Gumberg to realize this was not altogether sardonic, that saying it was "so unassuming" was another way of saying it was so unanimous. But I always argued with him on principle, if possible before Jack could begin.

"Oh, I don't know about its being so anticlimactic," I said. "They made a greater haul than the Parisians did. When the Bastille fell they freed exactly seven prisoners, most of them petty thieves, I believe. At the Winter

Palace they captured fourteen, and at least they weren't *small* thieves."

It was late when we again entered Smolny. We learned that a recess had been called to allow caucusing. Trotsky had introduced a harsh resolution against the departing members and their "criminal attempt to smash the All-Russian Congress." Sukhanov had insisted on an emergency conference of Martov's faction meanwhile, to take issue with Martov. As he wrote later, "No place was left for neutrality or passivity. This was frightening, and far from natural to us." Martov, "a victim of Menshevik indecisiveness," won, fourteen against twelve, apparently with a few abstentions. "I felt that I had suffered a disaster worse than any before in the revolution. I returned to the great hall completely numb."

We arrived in time to hear the applause from Kamenev's announcement that the Winter Palace had fallen and the ministers were under arrest. Then he read the names. Tereshchenko's brought high laughter and applause, and Palchinsky's angry hoots and cheers. With the departure of the Martov group, only the Left SR's and the small Gorky faction remained to do business with the Bolsheviks. But the audience seemed not a bit concerned. After the deafening applause died down, a Left SR began a speech about the injustice of arresting the ministers. Trotsky replied, his language bristling with epithets, to which his audience responded eagerly. It did not seem to matter to the workers and peasants there that he failed to make the main point: that if the ministers were turned loose (as the too good-natured sailors who adjourned the Pre-Parliament had turned loose Miliukov and several other former Kadet officials), they would have been immediate focal points for a counterrevolution—as indeed they were when they did get their freedom a few days later.

Then Lunacharsky was reading, in a voice that seemed to me husky with emotion, far more than when I had heard him read a poem at one meeting of workers, a statement that went in part:

"Basing itself on the will of the enormous majority of workers, soldiers, and peasants, and relying on the achievement in Petrograd of a victorious rising of the workers and garrison, the Congress takes the power into its own hands. The Provisional Government has been overthrown. The Congress decrees that all power throughout the country be transferred to the local Soviets of Workers', Soldiers', and Peasants' Deputies, who must preserve genuine revolutionary order."

The resolution was passed with two no votes and twelve abstentions.

It was well after five o'clock in the morning—and after the adoption of a resolution urging soldiers and railway workers to stop all troop trains being sent by Kerensky, Kaledin, and others against Petrograd—that Krylenko, bleary-eyed from lack of sleep, waved a telegram from the podium. "Comrades! From the northern front! The Twelfth Army sends greetings to the Congress and announces formation of a Military Revolutionary Committee that has taken over the command of the northern front! General Chermissov has recognized the committee, and Commissar of the Provisional Government Voitinsky has resigned!"

Soldiers embraced each other and wept; the hall rocked with emotions let loose. Petrograd was safely theirs. Workers staggered happily under their guns, drunk with fatigue, and, delirious with the power and poetry of the night, jostled each other good-naturedly on their way out.

It was six in the morning as we stood on the steps of the Smolny, stretched our aching muscles, and looked at the sky in vain for any rising sun. In the cold iron-grey dawn the soldiers and the Red Guard standing with their backs to us, warming their hands at a little bonfire in the square, seemed the only stable, reassuring human force in a world that otherwise remained a great question mark. How great it would be to feel really a part of all this! Instead, we had to face the insistent doubt. What would our own country do now? What side would it be on? How would it receive the news of this newborn republic still weak from the trauma of its birth? For that matter, what would happen in Moscow? The provinces I for one did not worry about—but I could be wrong. Wearily we started the search for a droshky.

· 6 · Red-Letter Sentence

"Comrades, we shall now take up the formation of the socialist state."

Mechanically I repeated the words after Lenin—in English—and noted John Reed, seated next to me, writing down the sentence. Satisfied that he had it and I could get a fill-in later, I continued to stare at the man who had pronounced these words I have since written so often and termed the red-letter sentence of the Revolution.

You will not find that sentence in any of the newspaper accounts of the second session of the Second All-Russian Congress of Soviets of Workers' and Soldiers' Deputies on the night of October 26/November 8. The minutes of the Congress were not preserved, if they were taken down at all. The parliamentary stenographers had walked out of Smolny, where the Congress was held, when the Mensheviks, the Right Social Revolutionaries, and the Bundists made their sorry exit the previous night.

John Reed recorded it in his unmatched *Ten Days That Shook the World,* and in the same year (1919) I wrote of it in my *Lenin: The Man and His Work*. It is only now, comparing what we wrote, that I find our versions differ slightly. Reed says:

"Now Lenin, gripping the edge of the reading stand, letting his little winking eyes travel over the crowd as he stood there waiting, apparently oblivious to the long-rolling ovation, which lasted several minutes. When it finished, he said simply, 'We shall now proceed to construct the Socialist order!' Again that overwhelming human roar."

Acknowledging Reed's greater accuracy as a reporter, I stick to my version. Either way, it is a great sentence. Though still unincorporated in Lenin's official works, it has found its way into histories. Trotsky deigns to consider it "wholly in the spirit of the orator," adding gratuitously, "Reed could not have made it up." Whoever it was, Reed or I, who strayed a bit from the words as we originally got them, the discovery that we were not in agreement on them is just further proof that things do not happen with the utmost nicety and precision in a revolution.

Not alone John Reed and I, but hundreds in the Smolny's great Hall of Columns were seeing Lenin for the first time that night. Or if we did see him the previous night, we had not recognized him as the Lenin of newspaper photos. Most of these were old Blackleg (tsarist police) photos, showing him with beard and the prematurely bald head he acquired quite young. Many stories were afoot about Lenin in disguise, and some have been added since, including one that he had had a hard time getting past a guard at the Smolny entrance on the night of the twenty-fourth. Having seen how freely anyone and everyone walked into Smolny that night and every night, I put little credence in that. But true or not, some of them are good stories, among them that of Bonch-Brueyvich. According to Bonch, Lenin was still in disguise save for the soiled handkerchief binding his jaw up until the time Smolny received news of the fall of the Winter Palace and the arrest of the ministers. It was then that Lenin decided to spend the rest of the night at Bonch's apartment, and as they prepared to depart, Bonch suggested Lenin take off his wig. Lenin handed it to him and Bonch promised to put it away, saying, "It may come in handy someday, who knows?" Another version of Lenin's quitting his disguise has him absently taking off his cap when he entered the room where the Military Revolutionary Committee was meeting. The wig came off with the cap, and when he realized it, he laughed with his audience, slapped it on his head, and then removed it for good.

From the moment that Kamenev, presiding, said, "Comrade Lenin will now address the Congress," my eyes were riveted on the short stocky figure in the thick worn suit, a sheaf of papers in one hand, who walked quickly to the podium and swept the spacious hall with his rather small, penetrating, but merry eyes. In that I was no whit different from the rest— whether it was Raymond Robins, whom I could see staring at Lenin with those large burning black eyes (he was there early and stuck it out until five in the morning), or any one of the mass of soldiers, sailors, workers, and peasants from provinces near and far. What was the secret of this sturdy balding figure who was so hated and so loved? When I turned my eyes from Lenin, it was to watch the peasants. Most of them were SR's, and the Left SR's predominated among the delegates.[1]

I heard only occasional phrases in the proposed proclamation on peace, which was addressed to "the peoples and governments of all the belligerent nations." The issue of peace was painful and clear, and so the

1. Of the total 670 delegates only 300 were Bolsheviks. The Socialist-Revolutionaries came second with 193 delegates. Of the SR's, 169 were Left SR's.

The storming of the Winter Palace on the evening of November 7, 1917. "As we reached the Red Arch," Williams writes, "three shots rang out. There was no return volley, and on all sides of us Red Guards, soldiers, and sailors were running toward the palace. . . . A sailor called out, 'It's all over! They have surrendered!'"

Albert Rhys Williams. In 1904, as a young man of twenty-one, he entered Hartford Theological Seminary.

In 1922 Williams posed in Greenwich Village for a publicity picture for his third book, *Through the Russian Revolution*.

In 1945 he was still vigorous and active in attempting to shape American attitudes toward the Soviet Union.

John Reed and Louise Bryant, in a photograph probably taken at Croton-on-Hudson, New York, before the Revolution.

Raymond Robins, whom Williams met shortly after Robins arrived in Petrograd with the Red Cross Mission to Russia. In the period after the October Revolution he was virtually a back-door ambassador to Smolny and one of few American officials who urged cooperation with the Soviets.

Charles Kuntz's passport photo. In 1917, when Williams met him, he was a pacifist and had "come to see the Revolution straight from a New Jersey chicken farm." The spectacle of "The Professor" marching down the Nevsky with a rifle was resounding evidence of the power of the Revolution to recruit and inspire.

Lenin in Sverdlov Square, speaking to the soldiers before they leave for the front.
(JOHN REED COLLECTION, HOUGHTON LIBRARY, HARVARD)

May Day in Vladivostok, 1917, before the Revolution. Williams spent two months there in 1918 before he left for home.

document he was to read needed no introductory remarks, he said calmly, briskly. He spoke in the manner of one who had spoken to the same audience only yesterday, or punctually once a week. There was no hint of the fact that, as Krupskaya says, "The whole of that last month [before October 25] Lenin lived exclusively for the insurrection, he gave himself up to it entirely, he thought of nothing else and infected the comrades with his enthusiasm and his confidence."

Reading, he called for "a just and democratic peace," which meant an "immediate peace without annexations . . . without reparations." There was nothing in the proclamation contrary to the platforms of the various socialist parties, I noticed, and this puzzled me at the time. It differed little from a resolution proposed by Martov and passed, 122 to 102, at the final session of the Pre-Parliament, in which immediate guarantees of peace and land were called for—when it was too late. The language was mild. "In accordance with the sense of justice of democrats in general, and of the working people in particular, the government conceives . . ." Why, this could not be our fire-eating Lenin!

Although "no indemnities, no annexations" had become a slogan of moderate socialists, there was a difference now. Kerensky, Lieber, Dan, and other moderate leaders had repeated the words "no annexations" but done nothing to realize them. Lenin gave them life, not through oratory, but by the direction which his party was taking. It was annexation if any nation was "forcibly retained within the borders of a given state." It was "seizure and violence" if any incorporating nation did not accord another "the right to decide the forms of its state existence by a free vote, taken after the complete evacuation of the troops" of the former. And: "The government considers it the greatest of crimes against humanity to continue this war over the issue of how to divide among the strong and rich nations the weak nationalities they have conquered. . . ."

The entire first part of the second session, which opened at nine o'clock, unlike the agonizing delay of the first session, had for me an almost dream-like quality. I stared at the speaker, trying hard to imagine how he felt now that the Revolution and his party had become one—and the expression of that unified power clearly dominated by one man, Lenin.

Of this last, however, Lenin appeared to be completely oblivious, to a point that left me vaguely irritated and dissatisfied. It was as if he were not dignifying his role sufficiently. Without him, there would have been a second revolution, I was convinced—but not this type of revolution, virtually bloodless so far, a revolution before which resistance melted away. Kerensky in his memoirs describes, with incredible naïveté, just how the expected resistance evaporated, his petulant concern seeming to lie alone in proving that he did all in his power to bring in the Cossacks to quell the uprising and liquidate Smolny.[2] Lenin, on the other hand, was silent on his own role as catalyst—that night and in all he wrote afterward.

My impression now is that the sentence went almost unnoticed in the great hall. For a moment I craned my neck and looked around. Of the men who sat quietly in jackets or greatcoats, unconscious of the smells and the body heat permeating the otherwise unheated hall, with eyes glued on their leader, how many had taken part in the events of yesterday? I recalled the jeering remark some wiseacre from the embassy had made to me and Reed at the Hotel France, where we ate the previous day. "Your friends the Bolsheviks seem to be less than geniuses at military strategy. Of course, what can you expect? Trotsky running that so-called Military Revolutionary Committee—an orator, a conjurer of words, but hardly a military man. And Antonov—what is he, a poet? Yet you'd think they would put some defense around Smolny. If Kerensky had been less fearful, he could have taken Smolny with a few hundred men. What do they have in front even now? A bunch of logs, not enough for a respectable barricade, and a couple of machine guns manned by workers who never shot one." Reed had retorted that Kerensky had waited for his few hundred, and they never came. Moreover, Kerensky would not touch Smolny with all the SR's and Mensheviks around there.

It was the sort of carping we had heard prior to the uprising when the Bolsheviks were taken to task for delaying it. Now the critics complained that the Guards were amateurs and the leaders not military strategists— the very critics who insisted the insurrection was a Bolshevik *coup d'état* accomplished by a military conspiracy.

Now, in the early part of the session, it was as if the masses, tired, exalted at their own triumph, but bewildered too since it had come so easily, were in a sort of suspended animation. Perhaps, too, they were surprised they were still here. For just as Petrograd, with its geat squares and broad avenues, was admirably suited as a stage for revolution, with ample space for enormous masses to deploy themselves, so were the straight avenues ideal for the processions to be mowed down by raking fire from cannon and machine gun. Well, it had not happened, and its not happening still stunned the imagination.

In my little volume on Lenin I told something of our reactions on seeing him that night of October 26/November 8. It was our first glimpse of the man whom we knew up to now only through his younger disciples.

---

2. Ironically, the only force Kerensky found ready to do even partial battle for him was the same Third Cavalry Corps which two months earlier Kornilov had appointed for the overthrow of Kerensky. At its head was the same Cossack General Krasnov. See Kerensky, *Catastrophe*, pp. 324–370.

I described, as many others have done since, his way of rocking back and forth on his heels, his thumbs in his vest at the armholes; his voice, in which we heard "a harsh, dry note rather than eloquence." I could have let it go at that—this rather homey picture of a man who seemed so utterly at home in this great hall filled with the reek of massed human bodies and cheap tobacco and faced with a thousand pairs of searching, questioning, intent eyes. But I continued:

> For an hour we listened, hoping to discern the hidden magnetic qualities which would account for his hold on these free, young, sturdy spirits. But in vain.
> We were disappointed. The Bolsheviks by their sweep and daring had captured our imaginations; we expected their leader to do likewise. We wanted the head of this party to come before us, the embodiment of these qualities, an epitome of the whole movement, a sort of super-Bolshevik.

I have been asked since if I played down our reactions deliberately, using an inverted play of the dramatic, a sort of Chekhovian heightening of drama by means of the anticlimactic. This doubtless was partly true. But Lenin did represent something of a riddle to our American eyes, so used to political figures remote from the throng, surrounded by servile lesser lights, watched over by Secret Service agents, their every appearance planned with care by publicity men, speech writers, and campaign managers, and wrapped in ceremony. What perplexed us was the combination Lenin offered: a man so completely at ease, and yet so lacking in what is called a commanding presence, so pedestrian—at first sight—in his approach. For example, that initial sentence, not a part of his notes, but tossed out casually. On the lips of any U.S. leader, Socialist, Democratic, or Republican (unlikely thought!), it would have rolled forth with rhetorical embellishments. At the very least there would have been allusions to the dawn of a new day, or imperishable phrases on freedom, or a grave reference to the Almighty. Even Debs often spoke of God, though for him Christ was always the rebel and crusader, driving the moneychangers from the Temple —and with violence.

So we had to adjust to this peculiar mixture—Lenin's detachment, as if he were an understudy for the great actor who would be back in his role in a night or two, and at the same time his complete ease and total lack of self-consciousness. They were of course opposite sides of the same coin, his deeply ingrained faith in the revolutionary initiative of the people. This gave him a remarkable freedom and, as I have noted again and again, a joyousness. All through that winter and until I left Moscow for Vladivostok in the spring of 1918, through all my associations with Lenin I marveled at this freedom, which of course accounted for his fearlessness (for himself) and his lack of pretension. Not that it kept him from attacking every problem that came his way, and routing out those that did not, but even so, his humor and happiness bubbled up at every opportunity, expressed in a hundred little ways, even his walk, his way of devouring a newspaper with his eyes, or the voraciousness and exactness with which he tackled each new task. Ransome, when he returned to Petrograd in 1919, wrote after interviewing Lenin, "Walking home from the Kremlin, I tried to think of any other man of his caliber who had a similar joyous temperament. I could think of none." To Ransome it was because "he is the first great leader who utterly discounts the value of his own personality."

When Lenin first walked across the platform to the podium that night, with no more aplomb than a seasoned professor who has appeared daily before his class for months, a reporter seated nearby at the press table, whispered that if Lenin "were spruced up a bit you would take him for a bourgeois mayor or banker of a small French city." It was a superficial witticism, but it was stolen by many of us and many who have written since then; never funny, the remark became threadbare. The scene itself belied it: the intensity of the listening faces throughout his reading of the peace proclamation, the immobility of the audience—hulking shoulders in greatcoats barely shifting, peasants (some of them the real agricultural proletariat) wary, intent. Then he was finished—and the surge forward, the wave on wave of applause that broke and beat upon the hall. A voice in the back of the hall boomed *"Da zdravstvuyet Lenin!"* ("Long live Lenin!") and was echoed and re-echoed by "Lenin! Lenin!" from every part of the enormous hall.

Then he spoke again, in explanation of the proclamation. "The workers' and peasants' government," he said, for as yet it had no other name, "created by the revolution of October twenty-fourth and twenty-fifth, and basing itself on the support of the Soviets of Workers', Soldiers', and Peasants' Deputies, must start immediate negotiations for peace." I for one began to see why the proposed peace proclamation itself was so simple; he first of all wanted to ensure peace. To ignore governments would be to delay peace, so the appeal would be addressed to both people and governments, and "we must . . . help the peoples to intervene in questions of war and peace." They would insist on all their program, a peace without annexations and reparations, but, not to make it easy for their enemies to say it was useless to begin negotiations, "the point is included that we are willing to consider any peace terms and all proposals. . . . that does not necessarily mean that we shall accept them. We shall submit them for consideration to the Constituent Assembly, which will have the power to decide what concessions can and what cannot be made." He went on to say that henceforth secret diplomacy was out. He declared unhesitatingly that the government "will act openly in full view of the whole people."

The fixing of the proposed armistice for the duration of three months— although they would not preclude a shorter one—was explained as a "desire to give the peoples as long a rest as possible after this bloody extermination, and ample time for them to elect their representatives. This proposal of peace will meet with resistance on the part of the imperialist governments —we don't fool ourselves on that score. But we hope that revolution will soon break out in all the belligerent countries; that is why we address ourselves especially to the workers of France, England, and Germany. . . .

"The revolution of October twenty-fourth and twenty-fifth has opened the era of the social revolution. . . . The labor movement, in the name of peace and socialism, shall win, and fulfill its destiny." There was something quietly confident, more serene than threatening, more a low-keyed paean of joy than braggadocio, about the end of his remarks. I here use the version Reed and I agreed on, as I like it better than the official translation, which I relied on earlier. Besides, we were as able reporters as the Russian, and the official version is simply culled from the daily papers there in lieu of stenographers' verbatim records.

By vote of the audience itself, it was decided that only spokesmen for political groups should speak, each limited to fifteen minutes. Left Socialist Revolutionaries and Internationalist Mensheviks (including the *Novaya Zhizn* or Gorky faction, but not Martov's more significant group) had separated themselves from the Right SR's and Mensheviks the previous night and remained with the Revolution. Now both voiced complaints. They had had no time to study the document or propose amendments, said the first. Only a government made up of all the socialist parties would be able to act on the program, said the other. Still, they were in agreement with the proclamation. Various other groups voiced support, some speaking with eloquence and fire—Ukrainian Social Democrats, Populist Socialists, the Lettish Social Democrats, and so on. Then a deep-voiced delegate arose as an individual to protest, and was heard. How was it, he asked, that the program called for peace without annexations or indemnities, yet it was promised all peace proposals would be considered?

"We want a just peace, but we are not afraid of a revolutionary war," Lenin replied. He amplified this, in part, as follows:

"Probably the imperialist governments will not answer our appeal— but we shall not issue an ultimatum to which it will be easy to say no. If the German proletariat realizes that we are ready to consider all offers of peace, that will perhaps be the last drop which overflows the bowl—revolution will break out in Germany." (That Lenin later decided the German workers would not revolt in time to save Russia from a Brest-Litovsk peace had nothing to do with his estimate at this moment, nor his general confidence in the imminent collapse of capitalism in Europe—but what is imminent can be regarded by a Marxist with a long view, strategically, or with a short view, the tactical view.)

"For some of our terms we shall fight to the end—but possibly for others will find it impossible to continue the war. Above all, we want to finish the war." Forgoing ultimatums was not a sign of weakness. And from the official version I take this remarkable passage: "Our idea is that a state is strong when the people are politically conscious. It is strong when the people know everything, can form an opinion of everything and do everything consciously."

At 10:35 Kamenev called for a vote. The appeal to the peoples and the governments of all belligerent nations was adopted unanimously; one delegate had raised his card to vote no, but at the commotion round him he lowered it. It was done—the first transaction of the new government. Men smiled, eyes brightened, heads nodded. This was something like it! This hardly formed new government was willing to signal its offer to the world without waiting for the Constituent Assembly. (We would see before too long how Woodrow Wilson, unable to ignore the challenge, virtually adopted it in his Fourteen Points.)

Near me a burly soldier stood, tears in his eyes as he embraced a worker who also had risen and was clapping furiously. A small wiry sailor from the Baltic fleet—from the ribbons on his cap, one of those Beatty and I had visited with only weeks ago—flung his cap in the air. A Viborg man, his eyes hollow from lack of sleep, his face gaunt beneath his beard, looked around the hall, dazed, and, crossing himself, muttered: *"Pust budet konets voine!"* ("May it be the end of the war!")

From the back of the hall someone struck up the "Internationale," and at once we were all singing it. Ever since, I have never been able to hear the strains of that most familiar of all workers' songs without seeing that throbbing, solemn, rapturous throng of men and women, and, crowded about Lenin, the entire Bolshevik leadership, standing and singing.

Then we sang the slow, solemn funeral march, beginning "You fell in the fatal fight," in memory of those killed in the February Revolution and buried in the Brotherhood Grave on Mars Field. The men and women in the hall—not an audience, for it was after all their day, their evening, belonging to them—again applauded, stamped their feet, turned to their neighbors with shining faces.

Sukhanov, who had fought against the Martov line in his group's caucus the previous night, and narrowly lost (about 12 to 14), describes his feelings as he witnessed this scene from the back benches of the hall reserved for the public, where he "felt torn away and separated from everything I had been living by for eight months that were the equivalent of a decade."

The whole Praesidium, headed by Lenin, was standing up and singing, with excited, exalted faces and blazing eyes. But the delegates were more interesting: they were completely revivified. The overturn had gone more smoothly than most of them had expected; it already seemed consummated. Awareness of its success was spreading; the masses were permeated by the faith that all would go well in future too. They were beginning to be persuaded of the imminence of peace, land, and bread, and even beginning to feel some readiness to stand up positively for their newly acquired goods and rights.

Applause, hurrahs, caps flung in the air . . .

But I didn't believe in the victory, the success, the "rightness," or the historic mission of a Bolshevik regime. Sitting in the back seats, I watched this celebration with a heavy heart. How I longed to join in, and merge with this mass and its leaders in a single feeling! But I couldn't . . .

Then Lenin was at the podium again. The seething hall became silent, the provincial delegates leaned forward, faces stern. He was reporting on the next item, land. Earlier Kamenev had announced the latest measures of the Military Revolutionary Committee: abolition of the death penalty at the front, and thus throughout Russia, restoring one of the original bans enacted soon after the February Revolution; release of all political prisoners; and the freeing of all the peasant members of local land committees arrested in seizing land without benefit of the P.G. All these announcements met with loud applause, from the peasants no less than the soldiers. But now that Lenin stood before them, another sheaf of notes in hand, on the subject of land, they were withdrawn, withholding judgment.

At first Lenin spoke, without glancing at his papers, his great bald head thrust slightly forward, his mobile mouth and bold chin more prominent than they would be in the future with his customary beard. This armed uprising, Russia's second, clearly proves the land must be turned over to the peasant. The government just overthrown and the compromising SR's and Mensheviks "committed a crime when they kept postponing the settlement of the land . . . and thereby brought the country to economic dislocation and a peasant revolt." Their talk of riots and anarchy was deceit. "Where and when have riots and anarchy been provoked by wise measures?"

"The first duty of the government of the workers' and peasants' revolution must be to settle the land question, which can pacify and satisfy the vast masses of poor peasants." He would read the clauses of a decree "your Soviet government must issue." Then in a matter-of-fact voice he said that one of the clauses embodied the Mandate to the Land Committees, compiled from 242 mandates from local Soviets of Peasants' Deputies. This peasant mandate was compiled by the newspaper *News of the All-Russian Soviet of Peasants' Deputies* (a daily paper expressing the Right SR line as undeviatingly as the *Wall Street Journal* speaks for finance capital in the United States). And, said Lenin, it "shall serve everywhere to guide the implementation of the great land reforms until a final decision on the latter is taken by the Constituent Assembly."

Except for that, the clauses were not remarkable. Besides the Mandate they numbered five. "Landlord ownership of land is abolished forthwith without any compensation." All estates, including those of church and crown, with all livestock and buildings, would be under the disposal of *volost* land committees and *uyezd* Soviets of Peasants' Deputies pending the Constituent Assembly. Land of ordinary peasants and Cossacks would not be confiscated. Since property would belong to the whole people, any damage to confiscated property hereafter would constitute a "grave crime" punishable by revolutionary courts. The local committees should take all necessary steps to ensure the strictest order during confiscation, to draw up inventories, and to determine which estates were to be confiscated, and their size.

He then began reading the Mandate, which had been printed in Petrograd the previous August 19 and might well have been written by the *narodnik* theoretician Tkachev in the nineteenth century. I was fascinated with lines such as "All the small streams, lakes, woods, etc., shall pass into the use of the communes, to be administered by the local self-government bodies"; and the bit about how land would be "subject to periodical redistribution."

This was more what the peasants wanted, or thought they wanted, I thought, than what the Bolsheviks historically had wanted for them. "Land tenure shall be on an equality basis, i.e., the land shall be distributed among the toilers in conformity with a labor standard or a consumption standard, depending on local conditions." Holy smoke! After all of Marx's blistering of Proudhon and Bakunin and the slogan of "equality" and its alleged meaninglessness! Lenin was deliberately doing what he had done in the peace proclamation, stressing what any democrat, and any peasant or soldier, wanted and understood. He was beginning cautiously.

I forget now at what point Lenin stumbled over the words, held up the paper, peered at it more closely—and was relieved by one of the numerous persons on the platform, who finished the arduous and not very thrilling (save to the peasants) reading of the 1,100-word Mandate.

Around the issue of tenure alone many fights would be waged—as many had been in the past, when the matter was one of theory alone, uncomplicated by practice.[3] Now the question of what was "utopian language" would be settled, not by semanticists and in the long run not by men with guns—which may come in handy in seizing the means of production, but cannot be the main force in the relations of men to each other and a man's relation to his own labor, so qualitatively different in a socialist economy.

Most surprising of all was the fact that nowhere in the extremely sparse summary Lenin had added to the "Peasant Mandate" was there a word to the effect that all land belonged to the people as a whole; only that "confiscated property" would. Sukhanov and others complained that there was a contradiction in Lenin's saying all private property in land was abolished forever and in the "Model Decree" provision, which excluded from confiscation not only the land of ordinary peasants, but all the land of Cossacks. This just was not so. Lenin's provision, and his alone, set forth that "the land of ordinary peasants and ordinary Cossacks" was not to be confiscated. It gave no special privileges to rich or well-to-do Cossacks, of whom there were many. As for farm implements, only those owned by peasants with little land were exempt from confiscation in the Mandate. And while Lenin stated that "landlord ownership" was to be ended once and for all, it was the Mandate worded by the peasant SR's that declared, "Private ownership of land shall be abolished forever," just as it was the Peasant Mandate that specified, "The employment of hired labor is not permitted."

Reed, not having had my summer experience in the provinces, could not understand my intense excitement. All the dreamlike quality of the hours up to midnight now had vanished for me.

"So now let's see the SR's object to *that* one," I was muttering bitterly. "What are they going to dig up to complain about now? They can't plead unfamiliarity with *this*!"

"Then why are you so worked up?" Reed wanted to know. "Those Welsh forebears of yours weren't farmers, they were miners. Or do you expect to settle here behind a plow? You can't, you know—you're not a citizen, and hired hands aren't to be permitted."

As I expected, the objections were being formulated. We could see the heads bobbing, hands gesticulating among groups of Left SR's and Inter-

3. Historically, Marxists held that the SR theory of allotting land on a basis of a labor standard or consumption standard was unrealistic, for a family might have twelve mouths to feed and be able to supply only five workers. See Carr, *Bolshevik Revolution*, II, 45: Lenin felt that the slogan of distribution of land on the basis of equality had a revolutionary significance "in the bourgeois-democratic revolution," but could provide no lasting solution. It was something the peasants wanted at the time, but the Bolsheviks would *help* the peasantry shift to Socialist slogans.

nationalist Mensheviks. But Lenin was heading them off. Taking the wind out of the sails of his opponents, he said with disarming candor:

"Voices are being raised here that the decree itself and the Mandate were drawn up by the Socialist Revolutionaries. What of it? Does it matter who drew them up? As a democratic government," he went on coolly, even blandly, "we cannot ignore the decision of the masses of the people, even though we may disagree with it. In the fire of experience . . . the peasants will themselves realize where the truth lies."

"Pretty cool," Reed remarked, nudging me.

"Life is the best teacher," Lenin said in part, "and it will show who is right. We must be guided by experience; we must allow complete freedom to the creative facilities of the masses. The old government, which was overthrown by armed uprising, wanted to settle the land question with the help of the old, unchanged tsarist bureaucracy. But, instead, the bureaucracy only fought the peasants. The peasants have learned something during the eight months of our revolution; they want to settle all land questions themselves. We are therefore opposed to all amendments. We are writing a decree, not a program of action. Russia is vast, and local conditions vary. We trust that the peasants themselves will be able to solve the problem, better than we could do it. They themselves must arrange their own lives."

Both the Left SR's and the Internationalist Mensheviks demanded time to caucus. Reed and I went outside during the caucusing.

"No mention tonight of the dictatorship of the proletariat," Reed said. "A stressing of 'our democratic government' and democratic ideals."

"I don't know any good reason why a socialist government can't be a democratic government," I said.

Bessie Beatty and Louise Bryant caught up with us and we began walking back and forth and around the square before the Smolny. Only October, yet we shivered, after the heat of the hall. Night was crowding out day by now, and in any event our nights had been long and packed with events. If we had slept all night we would have slept eighteen hours on end. As it was, we slept hardly at all, snatched meals as we could, and had lost count of the days and hours. Had it been only twenty-four hours ago that we trekked back to Smolny from the Winter Palace, after watching the ministers departing for the Peter and Paul Fortress? And now, just as we left the hall, Trotsky had announced that the ministers would be released. This was in answer to some fiery denunciation of their imprisonment. It had been decided that day to hold them under house arrest only; it was a detail, he said wearily, that would be taken care of next day. There had not been time. He could have been much sharper with the critic, I thought, but mildness seemed to be the order of the day.

We were tired. We stopped to warm our hands at a bonfire at the outer gate, where a soldier in a high astrakhan hat worn over one ear stood with his back to the fire—one of several bonfires dotting the dark night, most of them tended by two or more soldiers and a Red Guard. They had helped themselves to the cordwood now that the barricade seemed useless. Our man looked lonely. I wondered how he felt, watching the thousand delegates go by that night, and if he wished he were inside.

"*Chto delaetsia?*" I asked him. ("What's it all about?")

He muttered a reply in which I caught the words "the cursed war" and "hunger." Bryant was trying to get Reed to ask him something else and Reed was ignoring her. He offered the soldier a cigarette and then asked him for a light. Taking a sliver from an unburned stick of firewood, the soldier lit his own, then gave Reed a light. Suddenly he straightened up, his bearded emaciated face animated, his eyes glowing fiercely in the firelight, and with his left arm (his right held his bayoneted gun) raised a clenched fist, saying in a loud voice, "The world needs bread! The world needs happiness!" His somber eyes followed us accusingly as we turned away.

Out of earshot of the Guard, Reed asked Louise, "Why did you have to act as if he were Exhibit A? He thought we were making fun of him— or slandering his revolution, or God knows what!" Then, his mood changing like lightning, he said softly, "Happiness . . . bread . . . yes, and there may be both of them yet."

"Just the same," said Bessie Beatty as we trudged after Jack and Louise, "I'd hate to be in Lenin's shoes. They expect so much. I just saw Robins. He says there was only three days' supply of bread when the Winter Palace fell—whenever that was. Yesterday? Anyway . . . Lenin has promised them so much—"

"He has promised them nothing," I snapped, "except the chance to run this poor bankrupt, bewildered, bruised, and suffering Russia themselves."

We went back into the Smolny.

At two o'clock the vote was put on the land decree. One vote was against it. The peasants went wild with delight.

But the counterrevolution was gathering its forces. The Military Revolutionary Committee was sending messages to all army committees to be on the lookout for Kornilov, to bring him to Petrograd for imprisonment in the Peter and Paul, and for trial. He had escaped from his guards at the Bykhov jail. Feeling at home so long as the Provisional Government was in power, he had taken to his heels at news of the new revolution. A call for agitators went out to go to the front. More soldiers piled into the hall, awaiting assignments.

It was almost seven when we climbed on a trolley for home.

• 7 • Antonov the Bolshevik

The next day (October 27/November 9) Reed and I went to Smolny with our hearts set on getting new passes that would enable us to go to the new front. Kerensky, determined to retake power, had a valuable ally in General Pyotr Nikolayevich Krasnov, a tsarist general who, thanks to Kornilov, had been made the head of the formidable Third Corps. These Cossack troops were considered so loyal that, to be on the safe side in case the masses got out of hand, Kerensky early in September had ordered them (in a coded telegram purporting to come from Krasnov) to return from the German-Russian front and spread themselves in Tsarskoye Selo, Gachina, and other suburbs of Petrograd. Now they were on the march, with Kerensky said to be at their head.

And now there were reports that the advance guard representing the new government, factory workers, and occasional army units, going to meet them, had been driven back from Gachina. But Red Guards were streaming out of the city on roads leading south. Factory whistles were sounding. If work had to stop, it stopped. That was by order of the Military Revolutionary Committee.

We saw some of the posters on our way out to Smolny. "To the District Soviets of Workers' Deputies and Shop Factory Committees: *Order*. The Kornilov bands of Kerensky are threatening the outskirts of our capital. . . . The Army and the Red Guard of the Revolution are in need of immediate support of the workers." The committees were to recruit "the largest possible number of workers," who were "to collect all available plain and barbed wire, as well as all tools for digging trenches and erecting barricades." In larger type: "All available arms to be carried on persons." And in even larger: "Strictest discipline must be preserved and all must be ready to support the Army of the Revolution to the utmost." It was signed by People's Commissar Lev Trotsky, president of the Petrograd Soviet of Workers' and Soldiers' Deputies, and Chief Commander Podvoisky, president of the Military Revolutionary Committee.

Coming out of Smolny were workers with blankets and teakettles strapped on their backs, with revolvers or guns, spades and hand grenades. Among them were women and boys with picks, blanket rolls, and fabric bags containing tea, bread, and other foods.

Reed and I anticipated no difficulty in getting passes. We had got temporary passes from the War Revolutionary Committee on our second trip to the Winter Palace, so why should there be any problem now? But at the entrance to Smolny we were stopped. One needed a pass even to get in. Things had changed in a day. Discipline had come to Smolny. In the hubbub, Reed and I were separated.

My passport finally got me in the building. A pass to accompany the Red Guards going to battle the Cossacks was another matter. All of Smolny suddenly was bristling with order, functionaries, and commissars. I was shunted along from one to another, higher and higher, until I finally was pushed before Lenin himself. There I stood, credentials in hand, thinking how fortunate I was. But Lenin took one glance at my credentials, signed by Morris Hillquit and Camille Huysmans, and shot me a quizzical look. To me the names of Hillquit and Huysmans were perfectly respectable.[1] Not to Lenin. He handed the letters back to me, quite as if they were from officials of the Union League Club, with one word—a laconic "Nyet."

I do not remember just where I ran into Reed again, or what his experiences had been. I recall racing here and there looking for someone to intervene with Lenin, without success. We were determined, just the same, to go with this ragtag army.

The following day found us outside Smolny just when a car was starting for the front. Getting into it were Antonov-Ovseyenko and the sailor Dybenko. We were with Gumberg, who coolly climbed in, motioning to us, and in answer to Antonov's protests explained it was most important to have two American correspondents cover the story and give to the world the true picture of the workers' heroic defense of the Revolution. Antonov sighed but submitted. Weighed down with all the problems that had settled on his slender shoulders—he was now no less than commander-in-chief of all the armies of the Russian Republic—he refused to allow one more problem, which simply meant less leg space in a battered old car, to disturb him. And Dybenko, commissar of marine forces—now twenty-eight years old, a dashing figure with curls showing under his astrakhan hat tipped

1. Camille Huysmans was a prominent Belgian Socialist who adopted a Centrist position at the Second International.

rakishly on the back of his head, a closely clipped fan-shaped goatee, and curved mustachios—had no objections.

We were not anxious to reveal the fact that after Lenin had said no, we had, through Gumberg, talked our way into getting to the front—and not just with the Red Guards, but with the heads of the army and navy. So Reed put the account of the journey in the mouth of "a Russian acquaintance of mine, whom I will call Trusishka," and had himself and me going to the front by railway.

(In picking this pseudonym for Gumberg, Trusishka—from the Russian word *trus*, for "coward"—Reed was indulging in the peculiar feuding that they carried on against each other with equal ingenuity and animus. That Reed extended it into his book was no more petty or unjustified than an act that Reed privately attributed to Gumberg which resulted in the cancellation of Reed's appointment as Soviet consul to America in January 1918.)

Since then, however, one of the persons we were protecting, Dybenko himself, has left a memoir of the October days which reveals the two eager-beaver American correspondents as bumming a ride with the two most important military commanders of the day. In Dybenko's lively and detailed account, "The Great Upheaval," he relates how on October 28, while bound for Tsarskoye Selo, he ran into Antonov-Ovseyenko on the staircase at Smolny and they decided to go together. After great difficulty they obtained a car.

"When we were getting into the car, two civilians insisted that we take them along. Both looked like journalists. I found out subsequently that one of them was John Reed who wrote the famous book *Ten Days That Shook the World*. Antonov-Ovseyenko allowed Reed and his companion to travel together with us."

Dybenko complained he had had nothing to eat or drink since leaving Helsingfors the previous morning, and Antonov agreed to halt the car at the first possible eating place. The chauffeur stopped at a little food shop on Suvorovsky Prospekt and, returning with some sausage and bread, asked the commissars for money to pay the proprietor. Neither had a kopek. One of us paid the bill—very likely Gumberg, newly employed as an aide to Raymond Robins.

We were on our way, just about to leave the environs of the city, when the car broke down. Dybenko stopped an approaching car flying a small Italian flag. Whether the occupant was the Italian consul, as he insisted, claiming diplomatic immunity, or had adopted the flag as a ruse, not uncommon in those days, our commissars did not bother to find out. When he refused to be placated by promises of the car's return, and the use of our car when it was repaired—with a straight face Dybenko said it would be soon—he was told we were on urgent business of the Revolution, and we climbed in.

We made our way through a constant stream of groups of armed workers and soldiers (the sailors were on their way, as Dybenko constantly told everyone we spoke to) going to and from Gachina. There were no full army units as such, no marching, but heavy plodding through mud, and a variety of footgear, some pitifully inadequate. But it was impossible to pity them, the members of this unprofessional army. Dybenko and especially Antonov seemed a little horrified at the fact that even as we got closer to the front and the soldier-worker concentrations grew thicker, there seemed to be no one in charge. "Who is commanding you?" they stopped to ask every now and then. If the men knew, it was always someone they had elected on the spot, simply for their own little group.

The fact remained that even the workers in worn, outlandish costumes, with old-fashioned guns and teakettles bobbing on their backs against all the ammunition they could collect, had an air about them. They were there because they wanted to be there. So were the soldiers, some of them stepping along smartly in spite of the mud, in trim warm uniforms and greatcoats, such as volunteers from the famed Grenadier Regiment.[2] But at this time, early in the siege, the Red Guards seemed more numerous; in equipment, they seemed halfway between the workers who up to now had had no training and the sprinkling of troops from the Petrograd garrison.

In any revolution contingency plays a role, and one more incident, which Dybenko omits from his account, impressed Reed and me as characteristic of these days when human will had to persevere against lack of experience, supplies, and order.

Before we reached Pulkovo we stopped at Narvaskaya Zastava. At the edge of the town several hundred of the Petrograd workers were waiting. Some were completing the digging of trenches, some brewing tea over a fire. All seemed to be busy. If they were nervous they did not show it. Antonov asked who was in charge, and for once we were quickly sent to a Red Guard commandant. Morale was high, said a young worker; the men were deployed in what he felt would be the best positions. All was in readiness for the Cossacks. Let them come! "Only one thing," he added apologetically. "You see the men with their guns. But—we have no ammunition."

Antonov replied with a confident air that at Smolny and in the Peter and Paul Fortress there was no lack of ammunition, and besides, more was coming from factories still in production. "Here, I will give you an order."

---

2. The Grenadiers became well known when some of its officers and men were arraigned on a charge of refusing to go into attack at Tarnopol. Two leaders were acquitted, but more than one hundred Bolshevik soldiers were imprisoned at Kamenets-Podolsk, where they remained until the October uprising.

He fingered his pockets, first his overcoat, then his jacket and vest pockets. "Has anyone a scrap of paper?" he asked mildly. Dybenko had none, either. Reed and I both took out our packets of paper, folded, dog-eared, and began going through them rather carefully to get a blank page. Meanwhile Gumberg whipped out his notebook and offered a sheet.

"A pencil, too, comrade," Antonov said blandly. "I seem to have none."

I shall not recapitulate all of our wanderings at and around Tsarskoye Selo, including the Whites' headquarters in the huge Ekaterina Palace, where the officers were slightly startled to see our old Bolshevik passes, with which we had crashed the gate at the fall of the Winter Palace. It is enough to say that they were most polite, but felt that our lives would be worth something less than a plugged nickel with those passes on the arrival of Kerensky. We might stay the night in the officers' mess and return the next morning early and obtain new passes. A colonel could not say just when renewed fighting would begin. The Cossacks were nearby. He even admitted sadly he was not sure of the outcome. The garrison was divided, and today, after the battle, many had gone away, taking as much artillery with them as possible. The soldiers who remained were not exactly *for* Kerensky—and neither was he, the man claimed—but most of the officers were. "We are," he smiled sorrowfully, "in a most difficult position."

It was some comfort to learn that the defenders of the Revolution were not alone in being confused and uncertain of their fate. They were without officers to lead them, but here were Kerensky forces with plenty of officers and no soldiers—or none the officers were sure of.

Late that night a wire was sent to various army and navy groups signed by Lieutenant Colonel Muraviov, "Head of the Defense of the City of Petrograd and Petrograd District," which related that Kerensky had sent a "lying telegram everywhere and to all" that Petrograd's defenders had laid down their arms. "The army of the free people does not retreat and does not surrender," Muraviov continued indignantly. "Our army left Gachina to avoid the bloodletting between itself and the misled brother Cossacks." It had taken up a position, he said, "which is now so sound" that if Kerensky and his forces were tenfold stronger "there would be no occasion for alarm." His telegram, a yellowed copy of which I retain in my notes, concluded: "In our armies the morale is excellent. In Petrograd all is quiet."

We decided we would return to Petrograd that night. The colonel sent his orderly with us to the station, and we returned to the city by rail. We found conditions in Petrograd to be exactly as the wire stated. All was quiet. It did not remain that way long.

Without waiting a single day, the counterrevolution had begun testing the new government. It was not found wanting.

Just how this was so, how within a few days the victorious worker-soldier-sailor troops came streaming back into Petrograd and the counter-revolution in both capitals was driven underground, still is a matter of magic to me. Antonov without a pencil, Dybenko hungry without a kopek, their car breaking down on the way to the front where they were to plan the battle of workers without leaders or ammunition against the fierce Cossacks—these incidents were typical of the Revolution. To one who loved all of it, they are no less a part than the first boom of the *Aurora* (a blank shell, at that), which so aroused Martov's righteous indignation at the Congress.

Later, when I was better acquainted with Antonov, he told me he also returned from the front to Petrograd that Saturday night of October 28, and was questioned in minute detail by Lenin as they pored over a map. I can picture Antonov, almost dead on his feet from fatigue, as Lenin asked his pointed questions. What forces were holding the railway line Gachina-Lissiho-Tosno? How reliable were they? Were they strong enough to hold out if the enemy tried to seize the Petrograd-Moscow railway (so vital to connection with Moscow, where, contrary to Lenin's expectation, resistance to the Bolsheviks had been far and away more substantial than in Petrograd)? Where were the Putilov workers and those of the Tube works? Were they to be sent just anywhere, or assigned to key trouble spots? It was clear he felt they should be sent to trouble spots. And the sailors from Helsingfors and Kronstadt, who should be arriving now—he, Lenin, had instructed them to bring their own supplies, but were the soldiers and Red Guards getting enough bread and ammunition? And how about demolishing railway bridges and lines over which the enemy might be entraining for Petrograd? And now, about that armored platform car the Putilov workers were planning to turn out (Lenin himself had gone out, talked to the workers, and ordered it)—where did Antonov think it could be used most effectively?

Poor Antonov. At the end of the conference the other members of the War Revolutionary Committee saw he was in no condition to return to the front as the general in charge. Instead, he was put to bed.

Dybenko also returned that night to report to Podvoisky on the confused situation in the Pulkovo sector, and writes: "After leaving Podvoisky I met Vladimir Ilyich in the next room. He was calm. He was smiling as usual."

But Antonov was out early the next day, and instead of commanding armies, turned up as my fellow prisoner on the first day (and the last, for the present) of the counterrevolution in Petrograd. When, on that Sunday, October 29, I found myself, along with Bessie Beatty, a captive of the Whites in the telephone exchange, and, wandering around as correspondents do even in such circumstances, opened a door and there beheld Antonov, it was just part and parcel of the way things happened in Petrograd.

For two American correspondents to get in such a fix was the easiest thing in the world in Petrograd at this point. Having managed successfully up to now in poking our noses into various spots considered dangerous as well as none of our business, Bessie Beatty and I thought nothing of making our way into the telephone building. It had been one of the first government buildings seized by the Bolshevik forces on October 24, and we figured it would be one of the first to be seized by the counterrevolution. It was of course a vital center for Petrograd, connecting Smolny with the regiments and the Peter and Paul Fortress; a million wires ran from the massive stone citadel, which faced flush on the Morskaya, only a couple of blocks from the War Hotel, where many of the correspondents stayed. During the night the few Soviet sentries guarding the building had been taken by surprise. Twenty Junkers disguised as Red Guards, guns slung slantwise over work clothes, gave the Red Guard password and told the sentries that they were relieving them. The sentries stacked guns and turned to go, only to be faced with twenty pointed pistols and, empty-handed, forced to enter the building as prisoners.

Later in the morning this scene was reenacted in the War Hotel, other student officers forcing the Soviet guards into the basement, after the trick of showing a false Military Revolutionary Committee paper stamped with its blue seal and giving the password. It was only a few steps to the telephone building, and there I verified that it was the first place struck. A French officer was giving orders and Junkers were hastily finishing a barricade of sorts. He demanded to know what I was doing there. Showing my passport, I said casually I was an American correspondent and had dropped in to see what was up. I was just wondering if I could get away with asking him innocently what *he* was doing there, and deciding against it, when Beatty dropped in. This was too much. The French officer informed us this was no tea party, and, placing guards over us with instructions not to let us get to a telephone, sent us upstairs. Shortly we could hear the whine and crash of guns, shot by attacking Red Guards and sailors hidden behind some pillars, or shooting from neighboring roofs, from behind chimneys, or through windows across the way.

So I have accounted for our being there. But how account for the commissar of the armed forces getting himself in such a predicament on this particular gloomy Sunday in Petrograd? And did he appear chagrined, did he seem nervous or panicky, or even embarrassed by loss of face, when I opened that door upstairs and saw him? I cannot recall that he did.

The details of the counterrevolution that was meant to strike terror into the heart of Petrograd during a lull in the Gachina offensive, and how it was stopped, no longer seem too important.

I write of it now for only one reason—to amplify the profile of Antonov, who in one respect typifies the best of the young Bolshevik leaders. Each of these men, like Lenin, saw himself first of all as a representative of the party. Their singularity—for, without the genius of their leader, or even a suggestion of it, each was distinctly an individual—was none the less because of this. With each one, the overriding principle of their ethic, to act collectively, to submit to the collective thinking of their party, detracted not a whit from his own individuality.

One can write about the Revolution as being masterminded by highly competent directors, or one can write as if it were a casual affair, a series of events in which accident was the decisive ingredient. Either, of course, is a distortion. Without organization and plan it would have petered out, or ended in a gigantic blood bath and the victory of reaction. Yet contingency cannot be ignored.

Vladimir Aleksandrovich Antonov-Ovseyenko was thirty-three at this time. He had been a Bolshevik since the age of nineteen. He came from a military family and himself was a former petty officer. During the war he ran a newspaper in Paris, *Nashe Slovo* (*Our Word*), a sort of military review, where he worked for a time with Trotsky. Antonov was no youngster. As a young officer he had taken part in the Sebastopol insurrection of 1905. Possibly the most faithful of the Bolshevik leadership working directly with the sailors, on his release from prison on the day of the Kornilov campaign he went at once to Helsinki to mobilize the sailors. A caption under a photograph of Antonov-Ovseyenko in Trotsky's *History of the Russian Revolution* credits him with being "perhaps, next to Trotsky, the principal figure in the actual insurrection." Trotsky blamed the slowness with which the Winter Palace seizure was carried out in part on "the personal qualities of the principal leaders. Podvoisky, Antonov-Ovseënko and Chudnovsky, are men of heroic mould. But after all they are far from being men of system and disciplined thought." Trotsky saw Antonov as "naturally an impulsive optimist, far more apt at improvisation than calculation." Apparently he found a more serious handicap in Podvoisky's tendency to act in timid fashion, overestimating the enemy, due, he says, to the fact that in July Podvoisky had been too impetuous.

Thinking back on it now, I would say that during the entire telephone-building incident Antonov revealed neither noticeable optimism nor pessimism, but rather, whatever his native emotional equipment, a quality quite valuable in a revolution. From his appearance one would expect him to be flighty, sensitive, and interested in the abstract. I found him on the contrary to be almost phlegmatic. He reacted quickly enough, but betrayed no surprise. He reminded me, not in appearance but in conduct, of a seasoned trade-union organizer who keeps a poker face during contract negotiations with the boss. Possibly he had been through too much in the last few days to be taken by surprise. I suspect, however, that beneath that shock of reddish hair he had a quick but well-ordered mind, and, more importantly, one thoroughly disciplined. Whatever his background, he had acquired this seeming stolidity which stood him in good stead.

Antonov was something like Yanishev in size and stature and in disposition, too. And now he looked over the top of his spectacles at the young Junkers with a combination of sternness and knowingness I found rather impressive.

Certainly he was not where he was because of impetuousness. But it might be said that he had not thought seriously enough of his own safety. Things happened very fast in Petrograd in those days. When we had left it, Reed and I, bound for Gachina, all was quiet. On the surface, old Petrograd had become almost placid, so far as I could see. Streetcars ran again, the droshky drivers plied their trade, the number of robberies greatly diminished. The Foreign Office building was empty—the clerks and petty officials and straw bosses had stormed out when Trotsky demanded the secret treaties, which were to be published by the Bolsheviks in full, as Lenin had promised—and the bank clerks had quit, but all the buildings were safe enough, and guarded only by a nominal patrol. Not a hand was raised against the Bolshevik power. But that was a couple of days ago. Now the plot of bitter-end reaction, led by the Committee of Salvation and the Council of the Republic,[3] and aided covertly by many individuals in foreign embassies who could not abide the thought of a Bolshevik victory, was out in the open. Sabotage was not enough; it must be armed uprising. In this they had enrolled the cadets, convincing them that Krasnov and Kerensky were about to enter the city and would be met by sections of the garrison still "loyal."

According to the plot, key buildings of Petrograd all were to have been retaken at dawn. It was sheer luck, and awareness on the part of a Soviet official, that the plan, with a map marking the chief target and chief re-

3. It is interesting that the appeal issued by the Committee for the Salvation of the Country and the Revolution recognized the revolutionary situation and that it was dealing with revolutionary masses. "Contrary to the will of the revolutionary masses," it said in part, "on Nov. 7 the Bolsheviki of Petrograd criminally arrested part of the Provisional Government, dispersed the Council of the Republic, and proclaimed an illegal power." As all parties but the extreme tsarists and Kadets were made up of revolutionaries, albeit moderates becoming more moderate by the minute, the Committee, which included the presidium of the Council of the Republic, the old Central Executive Committee elected by the First Congress of Soviets in June, and others, actually appealed for counterrevolution in the name of the revolution: "Civil war, begun by the Bolsheviki, threatens to deliver the country to the horrors of anarchy and counterrevolution, which must affirm the republican regime and transmit to the People forever their right to the land." The Committee organized strikes in the ministries, spread stories of outrages which proved to be fabrications, and made futile calls to the people to refuse to recognize the Soviets.

serves, was uncovered the previous night. As a result, a part of the Chemical Division of the famous Grenadier Regiment was sent to disarm and take prisoner the cadets of the Pavlovsky and Vladimirsky schools for officers. (There was bitter resistance at the latter, and considerable bloodshed.) But the telephone building had fallen to the cadets by the time Antonov made his way in his car along the Morskaya. The barricade, when he saw it, had thrust out across the street with an opening through which certain vehicles were allowed to pass. And what a prize these beardless youths got when, by stopping one car, they decapitated by one-third the War Revolutionary Committee's troika leadership. But if they had seized the entire committee it would have made little difference. The self-organizing instinct of the Russian masses plus the discipline of Bolshevik-trained cadres would have come into operation, as it did despite all the slip-ups at the Winter Palace, including letting Kerensky escape. In this sense the defense of the October Revolution was a built-in mechanism. And now an important difference pulled military operations more tightly together. Lenin's eyes and ears were on everything. No longer did he have to write notes from the underground, or meet secretly with a few trusted comrades.

Still, Lenin notwithstanding, such things did happen. If the story of Antonov's being captured on his way to direct the recapture of the building is bizarre and both comic and near tragic, it was not more so than many other details I learned about later in this greatest of all revolutions. Krupskaya and a woman worker catching a ride in a truck from Viborg to see the Second Congress open the night of October 25; Lenin hustling out himself to a factory to order an armored car; Peters depending on an American correspondent (Beatty, at ten P.M. Friday, October 28) to translate the peace decree into "newspaper" English to be cabled to English-speaking countries—none of these things seemed unusual at the time.

And it was only later that I learned, in connection with the petty problems that loomed so large to those responsible for the Winter Palace assault, the explanation for Antonov's unkempt, mud-spattered appearance when he arrested the ministers. The Peter and Paul Fortress was to be the main stronghold of the attackers, in contact both with nearby army units and with the *Aurora*, where Antonov was giving directions. At a signal, the army units deploying along Millionnaya Street, the Nevsky Prospekt, and other streets near the palace would open the bombardment. The signal was to come from the fortress. When all units were ready for action, the *Aurora* and her big gun, the fortress and its guns, and the army units in position in the streets, a red signal lamp would be hoisted on the fortress flagstaff. The *Aurora* then would open fire, at first with blanks, in hopes that the ministers would respond to an ultimatum delivered by messenger, and submit. If the ultimatum brought no results, the fortress would follow with live shells aimed at the Winter Palace, and if the P.G. ministers still held out, the *Aurora* would use live shells.

But the guns that looked so threatening atop the fortress parapets were only for effect; they were not usable. A few three-inch guns were found in the arsenal yard of the fortress, dragged outside the walls, hidden behind heaps of rubbish, and after nightfall hoisted onto a rise of ground between the walls and the Neva By-Pass Canal. (They could not be fired from behind the walls as the palace was too close.) Once they were mounted, however, and a few shells located, there was a dearth of trusted artillerymen. There was no help for it, a few must be used from the artillery company in the fortress—definitely not one of the units in sympathy with the Bolsheviks. Under threat of dire punishment if orders were refused, the unit was ordered to send a small group to man the guns. They reported the guns could not be fired: there was no oil in the recoil tubes, they might burst at the first round. A trusted Bolshevik who knew the guns was sent for. The ultimatum was dispatched to the palace from the fortress before the fortress guns could fire a shot.

But then it developed that no red lantern could be found throughout the fortress. After a frantic search, the agreed-on assault hour of nine long past, a lamp was found. But for it to be seen, it had to be attached to the flagstaff. Tregulovich, whose task was to attach it, failed in his first efforts.

This was the state of affairs when Antonov, furious over the delay in showing the signal, arrived at the fortress, having left his post on the *Aurora* with blood in his eye. Told of the troubles by G. Blagonravov, fortress commissar, he set out to inspect the guns himself, for who could be certain the "neutral" artillerymen were not sabotaging them? A recent rainfall had left huge puddles in the fortress yard. Antonov's weak eyesight, the darkness of a moonless night, and his haste meant that he kept running through puddles, splashing mud around generously. Then Antonov and the fortress commissar lost their way, stumbling through the pitch-black darkness of the labyrinthine passages of the ancient prison before emerging on the Neva bank. To make matters worse, heavy rifle fire was coming now from the Winter Palace, and an occasional burst of machine-gun fire. Well, that was to be expected. What they did not expect was that their own soldiers were aimlessly sending rifle fire from the fortress walls in the general direction of the palace winter garden, which meant in the direction of the Neva embankment.

Arriving at the guns, they found two Bolsheviks inspecting them. The artillerymen's report was verified: patches of rust could be made out on the guns, and there was no oil in the recoil tubes. At least Antonov's trip was not all in vain: he returned to the *Aurora* to find three sailors, expert gunners, who volunteered to risk their lives in shooting the old guns. (The ministers surrendered without their services, however; the guns were never fired.)

So it was in these ways that the miracle of the Revolution had taken place. Could we expect all to run smoothly from then on? But the counter-revolution at this point had no more support than Kerensky had had before he fled from Petrograd.

Antonov himself describes the indecision and confusion that reigned in the telephone exchange when a gale of bullets from outside gave the signal that the Bolshevik forces were storming the building. The Junkers could not make up their minds what to do. "The booming kept on increasing, shots crackled. Then unexpectedly the door opened and, with a couple of trembling Junkers, before me stood the rather well-known figure of Williams, correspondent of an American socialist newspaper. . . ." (The *New York Post* was decidedly capitalist, but never mind.) Antonov continues:

" 'I am coming forward as a mediator with an offer for you. The Junkers want to free you, on condition of safety for their lives and prevention of violence,' said Williams.

" 'All right, I will answer for the safety of their lives, let them bring their weapons here,' I answered."

Antonov describes how he saw below, through the broken door, "the armed crowd with T. Stark, machine gun in hand, at their head." (Stark, a commissar of the Military Revolutionary Committee, with a small detachment of sailors had occupied the government news agency on October 24, and thereafter was made the first Soviet director of the agency, before going to Afghanistan as ambassador.)

Then Antonov adds laconically: "With a few words I quiet the excitement, I order the guard to set out with the arrested men. . . . The crowd discontentedly grumbles, threatens with punishment the trembling Junkers, but is quieted down and I without hindrance lead the arrested men to their destinations. . . ."

It really was not so simple. Antonov's first few words were simply drowned in the cries of the sailors and Red Guards shouting for vengeance on the Junkers.

Among the Junkers were some of the very young men Reed and I had seen at the Winter Palace when we wandered unhindered in the rooms after Kerensky's flight. Then they had sworn to die in defense of the Provisional Government. It looked as if they presently would be given their opportunity. Now, however, their one concern was to live—an indication of their good sense.

Bessie Beatty had argued with me that the Junkers were little more than boys, and that they had entered into this venture not wholly on their own volition, but instigated by former tsarist officers and others such as the French officer. Yes, I said, but during the siege of the Winter Palace, so carefully maneuvered to avoid bloodshed, lives were lost—and none of them defenders.' And the Red Guards and sailors who swarmed over the glass-strewn courtyard and into the Winter Palace at last had not been consulted when the Junkers who remained were allowed to go free. If they had had their way, the cadets would have been not only disarmed, but locked up. Actually it had been Chudnovsky's original plan to let the Junkers free *with* their arms. This was too much for Antonov, who demanded to know "how far this forgiveness will go—if we catch Kerensky are we to pin a medal on him?" And Chudnovsky retreated. So the Junkers were given a lecture and their freedom on parole. And now they had used it in this fashion. Some of the gunfire we were hearing, I reminded Bessie, was directed on the men storming the building, and some were bound to die (as they did).

Antonov was sparring for time, and was carrying out to the best of his ability the Bolshevik policy of avoiding bloodshed if possible. In his shoes, I would have considered my life worth about a nickel. But he was calm, confident, almost mechanical. He betrayed no fear—and no imagination.

"You must not touch them," he said in even, sensible tones. "They are our prisoners. I promised them life."

"But *we* didn't," a member of the sailors cried.

"We will hand them over to the tribunals, the people's courts," said Antonov.

"And the tribunals will free them. They tried to kill us. We will kill them," a Red Guard replied.

Even then Antonov behaved as if he were sure reason would prevail, as if he had confidence in their revolutionary discipline, which he mentioned more than once. I guess it was I who was not so sure. Not being the type to stand by reflectively in such a moment, I went into action.

Squeezing Antonov aside, I faced the sailors from the top of the stairs.

Now I know I have written otherwise about the episode that followed. This is because a frightened delegation from the City Duma, which for some reason had wandered into the telephone building at some point, went back and reported to the Duma that with Antonov I had saved the day and prevented bloodshed. This in turn inspired a glowing account in the Socialist Revolutionary newspaper *Volya Naroda* (*People's Will*) on October 30, and even hit the Associated Press.[4] So in my book I felt (1)

---

4. *New York Times*, November 14, 1917, p. 2, under the head, "American Girl and Man with Cadets," said in part:

"The seizure of the Central Telephone Exchange by the military cadets was made possible by deceiving the Bolsheviki guard, to whom the cadets presented forged credentials from the that I had to live up to this heroic stuff to some extent; (2) that no one would believe me if I told the truth; and (3) that if I did, it would downgrade these brawny tough sailors and militant Red Guards who had faced death to get past the barricades and into the building. What! depict them as crying down Antonov's plea for discipline, and then show them melting at a poem I recited in English? And when not one in a hundred understood a word I said, and when if they had understood they would have been even more bewildered because what they were hearing bore no immediate relevance to the situation?

So I wrote that I made a speech reminding them that the eyes of the world were on them, or some such. And Beatty wrote an eloquent passage, too, about this speech I never made.

The truth is that all I had learned so carefully of the Russian language, Yanishev's patient coaching, all Voskov's lessons in song and story, all failed me at that point. I could not remember a single Russian word. That was not the worst. I could not even think in English.

Poetry I can always recite. On every occasion I can call up any one of a hundred poems. On this occasion the poetry recall was less voluntary than a sort of reflex action. I began saying the first poem I thought of, and why that one, I do not know. I had a strong voice and I let out all the stops.

> Shall you complain who feed the world?
>   Who clothe the world?
>   Who house the world?
> Shall you complain who are the world
>   Of what the world may do?
>   As from this hour
>   You use your power,
> The world must follow you!

Charlotte Perkins Gilman's poem was gibberish to them, but as I declaimed it with a great deal of passion and vigor, and used my arms to flail the air, they saw I was highly exercised over something. Momentarily my performance topped theirs. The mob spirit that in another moment might have prevailed was dissipated.

There were limitations, at that, to their willingness to listen to me.

Lenine government. Two Americans spent Sunday with the cadets who defended the building. They were Bessie Beatty of *The San Francisco Bulletin* and Albert Rhys Williams of Boston.

"Panic soon seized the defenders. The officers in desperation cut the buttons and insignia from their uniforms, while others discarded their uniforms and telephone calls were sent in every direction asking for help. Finally M. Antonoff and Mr. Williams were sent to parley with the Bolsheviki, who gave their word that the men would be spared if they surrendered. The military cadets were led out one by one and formally delivered to the victors."

Before I could get to the second stanza, let alone the third, with its "Stand all as one!/See justice done!/Believe and Dare, and Do!" there were unmistakable signs they had reached that limit. The cry that shut up so many embarrassed speakers in Petrograd from June to this October 29 rang in my ears: *"Doloi!"* (*"Down!"*).

In her account of the telephone-building episode, Bessie Beatty recalls that one of the sailors recognized me and called out, *"Americanski tovarish!"* It is possible. It was just four weeks since she and I had been royally entertained by the Centrobalt. All I remember hearing was the *"Doloi!"* before Antonov confidently led the way down the staircase, and a scuffling behind me. Some of the Junkers had to be dragged down by their fellows before they filed out of the building, each with two guards.

We were to see the Junkers again sooner than we anticipated.

Meanwhile, that night Bessie and Peters and I got together. The fighting around Gachina had subsided temporarily, but "Lenin is taking no chances," Peters said. Order was being brought into the chaos of yesterday at the front, and the Soviet forces were consolidating their positions. It was in response to a phone call from Lenin himself to Helsingfors that earlier that day (October 29) the cruiser *Oleg*, the battleship *Respublika*, and the destroyer *Pobeditel* arrived in Petrograd and anchored near the Nikolayevsky Bridge. Just in case.

"When he made this call," Peters said, "it was just two days after he'd faced Congress and spoken of the weariness of the armies of the world. Now he was asking for detachments to be sent posthaste for defense of the Revolution. A hell of a note that he had to."

"What did he tell the sailor comrades on the other end of the phone? Was he conciliatory, tactful, or what?" asked Bessie.

"No, just frank," Peters replied.

"You mean about the lack of order, trained men, and so on at the front?" I asked. "Did he say they had retreated at first?"

"That's what I'm talking about." Peters was weary, and a bit sharp. "He was completely frank—said the army units sent to make a stand against the Cossacks had retreated with the first shelling by the Krasnov-Kerensky forces.

"He knew the sailors would respond. He said they should bring their own food, each detachment, and asked if they had any reserves of rifles and bullets. If so, they should please send as many as possible."

"Is it really so bad?" Beatty asked quietly.

"No, not bad, not good," Peters said. "It's just that—well, no one else has smashed state power and set out from the first day relying on the workingman. We're just human. Podvoisky and Chudnovsky were quite content with the turnout toward the front—the morale of the Red Guards was high. But Lenin convinced them that no amount of revolutionary enthusiasm will win anything without sufficient arms and organization."

When Lenin heard that a majority of the Petrograd garrison—by now used to ignoring commands they did not agree with—had turned a deaf ear to both Krylenko and Podvoisky when they appealed for support at the front against Kerensky's forces, he was furious. The regiments, he told Podvoisky, must leave the city *instantly*. Did he understand? He would answer to the Central Committee if there were a moment's delay! Peters added: "You're going to try to return to the front? You'll find the soldiers there, all right."

Lenin, said Peters, was all over the place, sticking his nose in, asking questions, demanding, threatening.

"He sounds terribly nervous," Bessie said.

Peters, who was very fond of Bessie, looked teasingly into her eyes and shook his head. "That shows how little you know," he laughed. "It's one thing Lenin is *not*. He's going here, there, everywhere, walks in unannounced, snaps at you, maybe. But he's relaxed about it. It's a thing I can't explain. Look, this will tell you. Podvoisky was hurt because he figured Lenin didn't trust him enough, didn't let him alone to do his job." Podvoisky was doing most of the inside work of running the Military Revolutionary Committee then. "So Podvoisky told Lenin, 'I'm resigning.' Lenin said, 'Then I'll have you shot. You can't resign.' Five minutes later he was smiling, it was all forgotten. Podvoisky did not resign.

"Take it any way you want to. I just heard about it. I wasn't there. My guess is he knew Podvoisky was bluffing and he could bluff, too."

Then, while we were coming up for air, he said: "You know, no one but Ilyitch is so aware that the Revolution may have a very short life. And no one but Ilyitch is so sure the people will win out. I can't explain it."

The Sts. Peter and Paul Fortress is on a small island in the Neva River, distantly facing the Winter Palace. On Friday, November 3, Bessie Beatty and I, Boris ("Daddy") Reinstein, and a Russian-English émigré and correspondent of the London *Telegraph* named Mikhailov made our way across the long Troitsky Bridge, a winter wind at our backs. The first snow had fallen on Wednesday, and now Reinstein, peering out across the misty Neva, sniffed the air and decided more snow was due. When I first arrived in Petrograd I never tired of watching the swift current of the Neva underneath the great bridges, or of hearing the gentle lapping of the water against small boats in the canal as a barge glided through. Already the early winter of Petrograd was creeping up on us, and soon the tinkle of the first ice would be heard.

By the time we reached the other end of the Troitsky we were chilled and thoroughly depressed. We were on our way to visit the prisoners, old and new, in the ancient Trubetskoi Bastion. This was the notorious prison section of the Peter and Paul Fortress, the most lugubrious reminder of tsarism in a city where on the whole so few of the emblems of tsarism had been removed for the reason that they were so thoroughly and massively built into the city. Built by Peter the Great in 1703 before he began building the city itself, the fortress had held such eighteenth-century pioneers against serfdom as Pososhkov and Radishchev, as well as plotters against the court, and all the current revolutionary victims of the tsars had landed here for a time.

We were not bound for the fortress as prisoners, but as a committee to investigate conditions. The idea of this committee had come from the City Duma. After the telephone-exchange affair of Sunday, a Duma delegation approached Bessie Beatty and me and urged us to serve on it. The Duma wanted to track down reported cruel conditions and mistreatment of the former Provisional Government ministers being held in the Trubetskoi Bastion, to verify whether they were suffering hardships, lack of food, and damp, cold, overcrowded cells. We were assured that the American Red Cross approved the idea of a committee of correspondents to investigate.

The previous day, Thursday, we had talked it over with Raymond Robins and found that this was true. So that afternoon we met with Prison Commissar Aleksandra Kollontai, a very elegant and erudite lady, mistress of many languages. Deceptively mild-looking, with her serene gray eyes and brown hair touched with gray, she was a tigress as an agitator, burning up the class enemy with her words, as her tense, lithe body paced a platform before her audience of Viborg workers and soldiers. "A traitor to her class," as some of the old aristocrats we met in the Astoria Hotel lobby indignantly termed her, she had the honor of being among the top Bolsheviks sought by police in July, and had been arrested and imprisoned with Trotsky, Lunacharsky, and the others. As we talked, she sipped her tea, ate a piece of black bread and butter, and, at our questions about plans for her ministry, seemed amused. "Heavens, I have no plans. If I became a minister I would be just as stupid as all other ministers," she said. (Later she was ambassador to Sweden and Norway and still later to Mexico. Kollontai was the only leading Bolshevik to rise to the defense of Lenin back in April when he announced his April Theses at a meeting of Bolsheviks and Mensheviks.)

In all about 250 prisoners had landed in the prison since the fall of the Winter Palace. The Junkers arrested in the assaults on the officers' schools, the telephone exchange, and the many hand-to-hand fights that raged over the city October 29 had been sent to Peter and Paul or the Kronstadt

Fortress. This influx greatly taxed the supplies of food on hand, in a prison where since the February Revolution the only prisoners were a few representatives of the tsarist regime. (The many Bolsheviks jailed in the July days were released by October.)

Except for one cell that we found too crowded, we reported that the cells were "dry, clean, warm, spacious, relatively well ventilated, equipped with modern sanitary conveniences, and in general in a much better state than the majority of American jails with which we are familiar."

Virtually all the prisoners we spoke to found it not unreasonable that in the first twenty-seven hours after the fall of the Winter Palace, food and supplies were slim. Almost all said they had no complaints on food or conditions at the present time. In one cell, some Junkers wanted to talk to us outside the presence of the guard, and he withdrew. We then listened to their story of their terrifying experiences when they were taken to the fortress through mobs who wanted vengeance. Arrived at the fortress, they were surrounded in the courtyard by an enraged crowd, joined by some of their escort guards, who wanted to stand them against a wall to be shot, "but the resolute action of a commissar and of a majority of the guards prevented this." Two officers, including an aide to the commandant, confirmed this, adding that some of the Junkers, terrified, started to flee despite guards' warnings. Shots followed, killing three and gravely wounding a fourth. When this was reported to Smolny, Lenin himself intervened, ordering "the most energetic measures" to safeguard prisoners, including the ministers, from violence.

The sight of Junkers munching sweets from boxes sent in by friends and families assured us they were not suffering the dreadful hardships envisioned by the City Duma gentlemen. And it seemed almost too much of a good thing when we entered Tereshchenko's cell and saw him, handsome and bland as ever, sitting cross-legged on his cot smoking a cigarette. He spoke to us in flawless English, addressing most of his remarks to Beatty, a favorite of his, and I was pleased to note that her usually big heart did not run over with sympathy for him.

Besides Tereshchenko, Palchinsky, Kishkin, Rutenberg, Vladimir Burtsev, and other members of the cabinet or leaders of the Kerensky regime, whose one complaint was that they were not allowed to receive visitors, we interviewed some of the pre-October prisoners. In Cell 55, for example, was General V. A. Sukhomlinov, now seventy, Minister of War under the Tsar, who told us the Tsar was "a good fellow, the father of Russia." Of all the various administrations during his eight months' incarceration, he liked the present Bolshevik regime best for one reason—he was allowed to see newspapers.

Our most interesting prisoner was no less than the notorious S. P. Beletsky, chief of police under the tsarist regime and, until the February revolution, Minister of the Interior. A large-framed man with gray hair and shrewd brown eyes, he was extremely suave. This man so close to the court during all the hysterical period of Rasputin's power had been a favorite of Rasputin, and privy to all the intrigue that went on at the time when all the Rasputin clique, including the Tsarina, were considered Germanicized.[5] When he was a prisoner of the Provisional Government he had bombarded its Special Commission of Inquiry with notes informing on his former pals, the most extreme reactionaries. Now he made it plain he had no use for Kerensky. He described the former premier as "sickly" and "a hysterical man, not able to run the country."

He volunteered that he had followed Lenin's movements ever since the split in the Social Democratic party occurred. Then he let us know that during the past July days Kerensky's agents had come running to his cell to see if he could help indict the Bolsheviks and especially Lenin. "Many came here to ask about Lenin," he said, peering at us through his hooded eyes. "Was he a German agent?" Then, virtuously, "They were government men, so I was less than frank."

To us he said, "Lenin is a man of principles and ideals." And he spoke of "an Austrian *provocateur*" who was among those who ran to the Kerensky regime with tales of German gold and Lenin.

When we left his cell Beletsky shook hands, bowing over Beatty's ceremoniously. But Reinstein and Mikhailov, the two Russians in our party, put their hands behind their backs.

It was at the Peter and Paul Fortress that I made the acquaintance of an unusual man, G. Blagonravov, commissar of the fortress after the October Revolution. I suppose I must have mentioned my having been held prisoner with Antonov by the Junkers a few days earlier. At any rate, something I said prompted him to describe the night when the Winter Palace fell, and his impressions only added to my respect for Antonov.

At the fortress Blagonravov received a note from Antonov, brought by a Red Guard, asking him to prepare cells in the Trubetskoi Bastion for the arrested ministers. Eventually the terrified ministers, who had come very near death on the bridge, and a heavy escort of workers and soldiers, headed

---

5. Cf. Michael T. Florinsky, Russia: *A History and an Interpretation*, II, New York, 1953, 1145–1146, 1362–1363. Rasputin's growing power over the court through the Tsarina was shown in the appointment of several ministers and reached a climax in August 1915, when Nicholas decided without consulting his cabinet that he would take over the supreme command of the army—which was then in full retreat. When ten ministers objected, the Empress declared, "The ministers are rotten." It was the German-born Empress, under the guidance of Rasputin, who dominated Nicholas II.

Historians now disagree on the amount or degree of Germanicization of the court, but at the time the German-born Empress was suspect—and it was certain she exerted her power, unlike the ineffective Nicholas.

by Antonov, gathered at the gate, where they found five ministers and their guards who had been separated from the others outside the Winter Palace. Antonov counted them, and they filed in.

There was something wrong with the electricity. So, in the stuffy little guardroom, by the flickering light of a smoking oil lamp, Antonov called the roll. Blagonravov described the scene, the ministers looking small, defeated, and pathetic, yet inescapably comic, too, in their injured dignity, as they sat on the edge of the rough benches, while all around were the triumphant faces of the workers and soldiers, their faces grimy with mud and smoke, guns in hand, shoulders back, their shadows gigantic against the wall as they stood surveying their pitiful prizes.

Others have told of how Antonov, after drawing up the protocol, read aloud the names of the prisoners and asked them to sign it. Before reading it, however, he took off his wide-brimmed felt hat, placed it on a table before which the ministers were seated on low benches, then took out a long comb from a vest pocket and went to work on his hair. He combed it over his face, parted it, then combed it back, tucked it behind his ears, put his comb away, and took up the paper. When it was duly read and signed, Antonov said with a faraway look in his eyes (he was probably almost unconscious with exhaustion, but exalted—and why not?) to the soldiers and sailors standing to the rear of their august prisoners, "Yes . . . yes. This will be an interesting social experiment." A pause, then: "And Lenin! If you only knew how splendid he was tonight! For the first time he discarded his yellow wig, and how he spoke! How wonderful he was!"

All this may have made Antonov seem absurd to the ministers. But I have no doubt that the men who were the real victors that night, the Red Guards and soldiers and sailors crowding around, were not in the least offended by Antonov's hair dressing. I am only sorry I was not there then to see their eyes kindle at his words about Lenin.

At three A.M. on October 31 a telegram from the front reached Smolny. The Kerensky forces had been smashed. But again Kerensky had escaped. And Krasnov, in the palm of Lenin's hand, nevertheless was held in the Peter and Paul Fortress only for a time, and after being paroled became one of the most ambitious and successful of the generals leading the Whites against the Red Army, before his final defeat.

It seemed a long time since the twenty-fifth, when Volodarsky introduced a resolution in the Petrograd Soviet, generally attributed to Lenin himself, which quietly spoke of the insurrection as "in rare degree bloodless and in rare degree successful."

In the November 2 *Pravda* the defeat of Kerensky was announced.

After describing the victory of October 25 as bloodless, the declaration read in part:

> The revolutionary army came out by the will of the All-Russian Congress of Soviets in order to fence off and defend the cause of peace and the transfer of land to the people which it began. If the blood of brothers was shed—KERENSKY MUST ANSWER FOR IT.
>
> And at the same time in the rear, within the city, the agents of the Bonaparte Kerensky aroused the Junkers to insurrection against the whole of the Petrograd garrison and began military action. The soldiers, sailors and Red Guard rebuffed the attack. Again blood was shed—IT IS ON THE CONSCIENCE OF THOSE WHO PUSHED THE JUNKERS INTO BLACK DEEDS.

· 8 · In the Balance

The weather was turning cold. The last of the leaves had disappeared from birches, maples, and oaks. Ice was edging puddles in the courtyards and sidewalks. The fever of the masses, mounting to a high point in the contagion of a common danger, had subsided. Fighting in Moscow and in Petrograd and its environs was over. The Soviets were supreme. But bitter days lay ahead.

Only six months had passed since, in answer to Tsereteli's fatalistic claim that there was no single party that would alone assume the power, a voice had replied, "There is." Now Lenin's party was in power, and Lenin found a troubled country on his hands: cold and hunger, the old order collapsing, and in Lenin's words, "the new order . . . being born amid indescribable sufferings."

For six months Lenin and his party had pointed to the weaknesses of the coalition government: the failure to stop the speculators, the breakdown of the railways, hunger in the cities, broken promises to the peasants, slowdowns and stoppages in production, the criminal failure to supply the needs of an army bled white to fulfill the Tsar's commitments to the Allies. Now, with power, the Bolsheviks must face the music, come up with a viable economy, without the capitalists and landlords. For this there was no blueprint.

"Marx gave the workingclass an objective," said W. C. White in his book on Lenin. "Lenin gave it a party, a road map, and tools for its journey." But Lenin had no road map ready, nor did he pretend to. There was nothing written about such matters in the Bolshevik textbooks. Nor even in those of the Mensheviks.

And tools? He had only the confidence that the workers would provide them. In speeches everywhere, at factories and before peasant groups, he urged initiative from below.

The enemies of the Bolsheviks sat back and waited confidently for them to fail. Miliukov, the most conscious leader of the bourgeoisie, recalls this: "The victory of the Bolsheviks was complete and final." When Moscow fell to them, that meant the provinces, all of Russia. "At that moment everybody still believed that the victory would be brief and that the Bolsheviks could not retain the usurped power." The other parties predicted the Bolsheviks "could give the people whom it had deceived neither peace, nor land nor bread, nor 'socialization' of industry . . ."

A deceiver Lenin never had been, nor was he now. At every point he let the people know what they faced. In January he was to report: "You cannot expect . . . that socialism will be delivered on a silver platter."

He did not even promise that their experiment would last. On January 11 he was to say, "Two months and fifteen days—that is only five days more than the preceding workers' power lasted . . . the power of the Paris workers at the time of the Paris Commune of 1871." Reviewing their initial steps at the Third Congress, he said, "The workers and peasants have not yet sufficient confidence in their own strength; owing to the age-old tradition they are too much accustomed to waiting for orders from above."

The Mensheviks and Right Social Revolutionaries and other moderate parties, and Miliukov's Kadets, who had been declared enemies of the people, were in open opposition to the Bolsheviks. For the time being Lenin and his party depended on the Left Social Revolutionaries to organize the peasants in the orderly division of the land. In many areas the Left SR's had to contend with the Right SR's and the kulaks in trying to convert the surviving mir or land committees into Soviets. For the time being the Bolsheviks would go along with the Left SR policy of "partition," which Lenin conceived as mistaken, as it did nothing to point the way to socialism or the goal of socialist production, but not "harmful." Overwhelmed as the Bolsheviks were with the need of halting the catastrophic decline in production and getting grain to the hungry cities, they had no time to organize the poor peasants' committees then. It was not until 1918 that Lenin was to write, "It is only in the summer and autumn of 1918 that our countryside is experiencing its October (i.e., proletarian) revolution." This was after the committees of poor peasants began to function, and by this "we passed the boundary which separates the bourgeois from the socialist revolution."

Certainly if any segment of the populace could be said to be the immediate beneficiaries of the Revolution, it was the peasants. This had its formal expression in Petrograd in a happening of great historic interest. The old Executive Committee of the Soviet of Peasants' Deputies, controlled by the Right SR's, refused to have anything to do with the new government at Smolny. But the First Congress of Soviets of Peasants' Deputies, despite their leaders, decided to join the Soviet of Workers' and Soldiers' Deputies. The decision came at the end of a long stormy debate. The peasant deputies then marched out to Smolny to merge with the big Central Soviet, which thus became the Soviet of Workers' and Peasants' Deputies, signalized by the emblem of the hammer and sickle.

As this happened at night, what would have been historic in any event became high drama as the parade of peasants turned into the dimly lit Nevsky, where I stood. Searchlights played upon the marching men out of the velvet darkness. The deputies marched with brisk step to the "Marseillaise," smartly played by a military band. Big flakes of snow were falling in long slanting lines to meet the glistening bayonets of the long slanting rifles in the hands of a military escort. Here and there torches were carried by the marchers. They lit up the white-lettered banners of red borne on poles. It was a short procession, I should judge at the most not more than ten minutes in passing. Out of the dark it came upon me, a blaze of light and color and briskness, and in a few minutes it vanished into the dark and I was left standing alone, until, recovering my senses, I walked swiftly to overtake it.

At Smolny I witnessed the formal wedding of the peasants and the soldiers and workers. I heard, as I wrote later, an old muzhik cry out, "I came here not walking on the ground but flying through the air." It was at this time that the Bolsheviks took the Left SR's into the government in what Lenin explained to the Peasants' Congress was "an honest coalition, an honest alliance," as it reflected that of the peasants and workers. It could be an honest alliance "at the summit," he explained, only if the Left SR's were more definite in stating their belief that it was a socialist revolution. Abolition of private property in land, introduction of workers' control, nationalization of the banks—they were not socialism, but merely measures that would lead to socialism, he said. The Bolsheviks did not promise the workers and peasants "milk and honey immediately," but an unwavering struggle which, if the close alliance of workers and the exploited peasantry continued, would lead to socialism.

What followed, however, was only a temporary honeymoon, presently to be disrupted by requisitions. (And a temporary uniting of Bolsheviks and Left SR's. The latter quit after the Brest-Litovsk peace was confirmed in March.) It was the beginning of the long struggle, still in progress—the struggle not only for the real socialization of the land, but for the transformation of the people on the land. (The peasant saw the land as alienated, and now reclaimed from the landlord; he did not see himself as alienated. Only when he became a *social* producer, a part of the community of city *and* country, would he fulfill his old dream or regain his identity.)

As I later heard Lenin say (in January at the Third All-Russian Congress), "Every politically conscious socialist says that socialism cannot be imposed upon the peasants by force. . . . We know that only when experience has shown the peasants, for example, the kind of exchange there must be between town and country, they will themselves, from below, on the basis of their own experience, establish their own connections. On the other hand, the experience of the Civil War has demonstrated to the peasants that there is no other road to socialism except the dictatorship of the proletariat and the ruthless suppression of the rule of the exploiters."

Meanwhile, in the honeymoon period, things were not so simple. In many provinces, especially those remote from Moscow or Petrograd, the rich peasants got richer and the poor peasants became only less poor. Still, the wastage of wealth, the burning of manor houses, the looting, in which sailors and soldiers had often joined the embittered peasantry, had stopped.

Other than the peasants, few groups obtained immediate tangible rewards from the October overturn. Some workers, limited in number, moved up out of cellars or down from attics to occupy more decent quarters. The *Lumpenproletariat,* the vandals and looters, for a time enjoyed sating their appetites for vodka and choice wines. Prior to October the raiding of vodka distilleries had not been unusual, the raiders making up for their arrears in thirst. Now the winecellars of the aristocracy were invaded, until the Red Guards, following stern warnings to those taking part in "wine pogroms," put a stop to it.

The peasants had their land, but for that class on whom lay the chief responsibility for the Revolution conditions grew progressively worse. Before 1917, the excessive mobilization of manpower in the army and factories drained the countryside. Serious decline in production nevertheless had occurred. Now, after October, production shrank even further. Because of hunger in the cities, many of the factory proletariat, most of them recruited from the provinces, returned to the land. Railroads were in worse shape than ever. Lenin's urgent appeals for peasants to be paid in needed items from factories, so that the grain would come to the cities, had little effect in view of the dearth of such items and the breakdown in transportation. And there was a fuel crisis.

All this after three years and seven months of war, in which two and one-half million Russians were killed and four million wounded; there were 350,000 war orphans and 200,000 deaf, dumb, or blind. In World War I the Russians lost more than Belgium, France, Italy, and America combined. Of 70,000 *versts* of railway in European Russia, only 15,000 *versts* remained undamaged in the war or civil war, according to Carr.[1] And twelve million soldiers were demobilized either by their own leave prior to October or by the Revolution.

---

1. Carr, *Bolshevik Revolution*, II, 192, is speaking of railway damage by 1919, but it was bad enough in 1918. The fuel crisis aggravated the industrial breakdown; in the winters of 1918–19 and 1919–20 "cold was probably a greater cause of human misery and human inefficiency than hunger."

Then what was it that held the masses in their allegiance to the Soviets, which meant, as well, their allegiance to the Bolsheviks? How did the Bolsheviks retain their trust? Reed and I had many discussions on this.

Already in December we could see that if the Revolution gave the workers increased cold, hunger, and hardships, it was giving them compensations. A sense of triumph still hung in the frosty air. Decree after decree inaugurated socialist reforms. Most of them written by Lenin himself in 1917–18, they abolished all the old restrictions based on race, nationality, religion, and sex. They were like a bulldozer clearing away the old obstacles and taboos that kept the lowest strata chained to misery and impotence; on the barricades the workers had removed the barricades to life.

Nowhere was the meaning of October—passionate protest against the past, earnest for the future—more evident than in the fashion in which the rather prosaic decree on the people's courts was carried out. And here it was that the ability of the people to transcend their old habits of thought and action was most apparent.

In the early days of the October Revolution the Workers' Tribunals functioned with fascinating irregularity, unpredictable restraint, and almost mercifulness toward the bourgeoisie. Fierce proclamations and warnings were issued that "looters, marauders, and speculators are declared enemies of the people," one of them closing with the words: "To the pillory with saboteurs! Ostracize the criminal hirelings of capital!"

But in this time of trial and error, sublime innocence and undimmed hope, it was the Revolutionary Workers' Tribunals that dispensed justice, and the one sentence we heard uttered with most frequency and with awesome severity was that the guilty should be "held up to the shame of the international working class." (Most of the old courts had refused to recognize the authority of the Soviet power, but they were permitted to operate if old laws were invoked only to the extent that they did not contradict the "revolutionary conscience and the revolutionary conception of right.")

On the bright, frosty morning of November 28, Agursky, the Russian-American anarchist who became a Bolshevik, Bessie Beatty, and I crossed the Dvortsovaya Bridge over the Neva and trudged through the snow to the palace of the Grand Duke Nikolai Nikolayevich. The ducal music room, spacious and with walls paneled in rare woods, had been chosen for the debut of the Workers' Tribunal. Defendants included Countess Sofia Panina, a leader of the Kadets and Minister of Public Welfare in the Kerensky cabinet. A decree of the same day ordered the arrest of all Kadet leaders as public enemies charged with conspiracy in the Kornilov revolt, but the Countess was in court on the specific charge of having removed 93,000 rubles belonging to the Ministry of Education. A few workers were in the throng awaiting the arrival of the judges, but they were out-numbered by well-dressed men and women, friends of Panina and other defendants. Among the latter was the former tsarist deputy V. M. Purishkevich, notorious organizer of pogroms, and ringleader and originator of the Black Hundreds. A grand duke failed to appear, but General Bandirev and a minor defendant or two were there ready for trial.

Everything had been done to make this debut of the Revolutionary Tribunal seemly. At the last minute it had been discovered that something had gone wrong with the electricity. The only light came from two kerosene lamps with red shades, placed on the semicircular table at one end of the room, draped in red. At one point the women clustered near the prisoner Panina, who sat on a bench with soldiers at either side, were all aflutter when another soldier carried in a machine gun and placed it with a flourish on the table. The machine gun, it developed, was simply evidence in the case against Purishkevich, who had been caught with it and incriminating counterrevolutionary papers in a raid by Cheka men.

The hubbub quieted when the court filed in: the president, Zhukov, clean-shaven, with a lean intelligent face and distinctly at ease, and the six judges—two peasants, two soldiers, two workers. The president's white shirt and collar stood out among the black blouses and peasant shirts with cross-stitched work. All but the president sat stiffly, their faces solemn with responsibility, on the brocade-upholstered chairs. The commandant, who stood at one end of the table, interested me most. His padded brown canvas coat was in itself a symbol of proletarian dictatorship; his high sheepskin hat was like that worn by the soldiers, but worn jauntily. He was about twenty-five.

The Countess' case alone consumed a good deal of time, chiefly because her main witness was a worker, and the prosecutor, who also appeared from the crowd and was a worker, wanted to educate her defender. Neither one paid much attention to the charge, the witness pointing to her good works, in particular the *Narodni Dom* (People's House), in which he had learned to read, so that "She gave me the possibility of thinking." Obviously he scored a point when he added: "We want the world to see how generous the Revolution is," and urged that she be given her freedom. Then came the earnest voice of the prosecutor, Naumov, also a factory worker, who said in part:

"Comrades, all this is true. The woman has a good heart. She tried to do good with her schools, her nurses, and her soup kitchens. But if the people had the money she received out of their blood and sweat, we could have our own schools, our own nurses, our own soup kitchens. The comrade worker is wrong. The people must learn to read because they have the right, not out of any one person's kindness."

Panina took the stand and admitted she took the money and placed it in a bank so the Bolsheviks could not get at it (the nationalization of all the banks had not yet been effected).

The tribunal panel (one of six such panels, who rotated, serving a week at a time) retired to deliberate. Half an hour later they filed in, their faces even more solemn. Bessie Beatty was agitated. "Everyone's talking about the guillotine," she whispered. "Peters told me there will be no guillotine, but they'll send her away. I just know it will be a stiff sentence."

Zhukov read the verdict to the silent courtroom. It was a long one, replete with clauses about the sacrosanct nature of the people's property. We had to sit through an exhaustive preamble, which would have been ample as a prelude to a death sentence, before we had any inkling of the sentence. Then these words were uttered by Zhukov with all the awesomeness he could muster: "And this Revolutionary Tribunal moreover *holds the citizeness Panina up to shame before the revolutionary working people of the world.*" The worker judges, who had hung on every word, now glanced at each other in a self-congratulatory way, as if to say, "We showed her!"

A few of Panina's thoughtless admirers broke into applause, but were quickly shushed by her more knowing friends. (A few days later the missing funds were turned over to Lunacharsky and she was released.)

To defend the General, there were not only soldiers who had served under him and testified in his behalf, to the fury of those who wanted him to get a stiff sentence for disobeying Krylenko's order summoning him to a council, but trained lawyers who employed chicanery and split-hair legal subtleties to confuse the court. When he was sentenced to three years, there were cries of "Shame! Shame!" from the audience. No one was satisfied, neither his accusers nor the bourgeois crowd. Zhukov threatened to clear the court if the commotion was repeated.

The commandant called the case of Vladimir Purishkevich, and there was a stir as the monarchist deputy, arrogant disdain in his smile, stepped forward together with his counsel: the Pushkins, father and son. The Tsar's most dependable anti-Semite, who had been involved in the famous Mendel Beilis case in 1913, among other frame-ups, was clever, all right. Agursky, himself a Jew, whispered to me furiously that the Pushkins were Jews! A list of witnesses for the prosecution, some ten or twelve, among whom three names were Jewish, was read aloud. When the defense objected to one name on the theory that the witness would not tell the truth, it was decided by the tribunal to withdraw the witness, even before he was heard. "This leniency is simply liberalism, it is absurd!" Agursky whispered. But this was not all. The Pushkins, with many legalistic arguments, wanted the evidence separated into two parts, with the court proceeding first to consider the defendant's past activities insofar as they bore on the charge of plotting a counterrevolution. Then his own witnesses would be heard, to reveal how he always favored support of the Provisional Government. (Actually Purishkevich had had a leading role in the pro-Kornilov clique that dominated the Democratic Conference in Moscow the previous summer.) After that, said his lawyers, the court should consider the evidence that was purportedly found on his arrest November 3/16.

The court ruled that it would take this proposal under advisement, continuing the case to another day. Agursky was disgusted. "If they're going to go into all Purishkevich's past crimes, they'll still be hearing evidence a year from now," he said. He had a point there. Among other things, Purishkevich had organized the grand dukes' plot to forestall the revolution by fomenting a "revolution at the top," the main plank in his program being the murder of Grigory Rasputin, the illiterate Siberian mystic who held sway over much of the court, including the Tsarina. When the assassination was accomplished—in Prince Yusupov's palace in December 1916—it brought a sense of relief to the liberals and a brief wave of optimism to Purishkevich and the other monarchists, but failed to save the dynasty.

(Purishkevich later was found guilty and sentenced to a short prison term, but escaped. He is credited with organizing a regiment of officers and Junkers he sent to serve with Kaledin. After his disappearance he turned up in the Caucasus, where he joined up with General Denikin, and later published one of the Black Hundreds magazines. He died a natural death in 1920 in Novorossisk.)

Then the court turned with equal seriousness to the case of a boy charged with stealing a bundle of newspapers from an elderly woman news vendor. He readily admitted he stole the papers. The worker-judges took a hand in questioning him. What did he do with them? He sold them for one ruble and sixty kopeks. What had he done with the money? He had felt out of sorts, depressed, and as he had always wanted to see an opera, he had gone to see one at the Narodni Dom, he said cheerfully. "And did you feel better after you went to the theater?" one of the judges asked. The boy nodded briskly. He was ordered to sell something, as he was penniless, to repay the old news vendor—who, they reminded him, was not a capitalist just because she had a kiosk. He said he had nothing to sell except what he wore. After looking him over and deliberating on his garments, they chose his overshoes—they were not too much to give her. Sadly, reluctantly, he removed them and handed them over. Then he smiled. "Anyway, I heard the opera."

Thus the Workers' Tribunals. The mildness of the retribution they exacted was a conscious Bolshevik policy. In the moment of their victory, the masses found it possible to show compassion to their class enemy.

At what cost was this early compassion indulged in? If they had been less merciful—just slightly less merciful—at the beginning, we perhaps would not have to write that bloody story of counterrevolution and intervention. On the other hand, if they had not indulged in this mildness, we would not have this chance of telling how at the start they tried to conduct a civil war in a civil manner.

It is especially remarkable that there were not more instances of violence and revenge in the weeks and months following October when it is considered how intemperate, to put it mildly, were the expressions from soldiers sent to relatives, the Soviets, and the Bolsheviks, as revealed in the Central Archives of Military History. One soldier's letter to his relatives reads in part:

"I ask you, without any by-your-leave, to send the cattle to graze on the land of the landlords. And plow up the land without asking them, the fat-bellied dogs. They have drunk our blood long enough. See to it that you take everything into your hands at once, and we will return home with our rifles."

Only too soon would come the time when all the clemency of the early months after October would necessarily change. Within two or three years, we find a deep harshness. Steel has entered into their constitutions, and a blood-and-iron regime. This was after the harsh terms of the Brest-Litovsk peace treaty with the Central Powers, and the constant violations of the treaty by the Germans, and the intervention of the Allies, making common cause with the most brutal of the would-be dictators among the White generals, Kolchak, as well as Denikin and others.

Even now in December, so soon after the October victory, Lenin was not averse to lecturing the comrades on the need for vigilance. Voskov quoted him as saying, "The workers do not yet understand their own power; that is but natural. But there are, God help us, 'revolutionaries' who want us to turn the other cheek when we catch a saboteur, or a Purishkevitch with documents showing the details of a counterrevolutionary plot. No, they should be shot! These 'revolutionaries' are intimidated because the bourgeois press jackals rail at us as dictators. *Where* do we have a dictatorship? And what will happen to our revolution without it? But no, we have confusion, talk—and our enemies will do us in unless we stiffen our spine!"

And Trotsky writes of Lenin's saying, "If we are not ready to shoot a saboteur or White Guardist, what sort of big revolution is that?" According to Trotsky, the repeal of the death penalty was hurried through on Kamenev's initiative, "probably in the Revolutionary Military Committee and apparently on the very morning of the 25th of October . . . Lenin was not yet there. . . . When he learned of this first legislative act his anger knew no bounds." But though Lenin called it "madness," Trotsky writes, to repeal it would, " we told him," create "an extraordinarily unfavorable impression."

Actually the Bolsheviks, whose earliest battle had been against the anarchists and the Social Revolutionaries for instituting in their despair the tactic of terror and depending on a minority to overthrow the Tsar, did not object to force or terror on moral grounds, but because force alone could not win. And at the Third All-Russian Congress Lenin drew stormy applause when he said: "Not a single problem of the class struggle has ever been solved in history except by violence. When violence is exercised by the working people, by the mass of exploited against the exploiters—then we are for it!" That it never should be a weapon in the hands of the few went without saying.

But for now, for the hungry but joyous days and weeks that followed the repulse of the Kerensky-Krasnov forces to recapture Petrograd, there was this flowering of kindness and generosity, and it prevailed no matter how much Lenin warned against it.

Despite his heavy duties as assistant to the head of the newly formed All-Russian Extraordinary Commmission (Cheka for short),[2] Peters was glad enough to take time out to talk to Reed or me or Bessie Beatty. When Bessie, concerned over the rumors she heard, asked him if the guillotine of the French Revolution was going to be revived now,[3] he replied (differing with Trotsky as to the date): "On October 25 the Provisional Government was overthrown. On October 26 the death sentence was abolished. We will never restore it—unless," he hesitated, "unless we have to use it for our own—if any of our men should turn traitor. What else can you do with a man who betrays his own cause? And there are so few of us to do the work, we must take everyone who offers."

Reed and I were working for Boris Reinstein in a new bureau of propa-

2. When the Military Revolutionary Committee was discontinued, a section on security, under Felix Dzerzhinsky, military commandant of Smolny, remained; a decree of December 7 ordered it reorganized as "the All-Russian Extraordinary Commission" (Cheka for short), for the purpose of "combating counterrevolution and sabotage." The decree itself apparently was kept secret and was published for the first time in *Pravda*, December 18, 1927. But the fact of Cheka's existence was no secret.

3. More than any other Bolshevik, Trotsky was given to fierce public utterances in the first few weeks after the October Revolution. When the Kadet party was outlawed he declared: "At the time of the French revolution more honest men than the Kadets were guillotined by the Jacobins for opposing the people. We have not executed anyone and do not intend to, but there are moments when the fury of the people is hard to control" (*Izvestia*, October 30/November 12, 1917). And after the suppression of the Kadet party he pooh-poohed the "mild terror" under way against "our class enemies," warned that within a month the terror would take on more violent forms, and added: "The guillotine will be ready for our enemies and not merely the jail."

ganda set up under the Foreign Ministry. We were writing flyers, pamphlets, and leaflets to be distributed among German troops at the front, urging them to get rid of their Kaiser just as the Russians had forced the abdication of the Tsar. We dropped in on Peters one day after work in our corner of the Foreign Office. Peters was on the top floor of the old police station on the Korokhavaya, formerly used by the Cheka's predecessor. The Cheka was set up by decree of Sovnarkom (*Sovet Narodnikh Komissarov,* or Council of People's Commissars), December 7, replacing a section of the now disbanded Military Revolutionary Committee entrusted with combating counterrevolution and sabotage. Most of its duties were investigatory and in general maintained certain socialist standards, though Reed and I often challenged Peters on these, sometimes unjustly. (Even the anarchist Makhno, writing about the summer of 1918, when he was a political prisoner of the Cheka, described its organizing former political inmates of the Moscow prison into an investigatory commission to interview others on tyrannical supervisors, who were then arrested and brought before the Cheka for questioning.)

On this particular day Peters appeared tired and depressed and defensive. He told us of a certain officer who, pretending to be a Soviet commissar, had gone through the better hotels requisitioning pocketbooks. He had amassed quite a sum before he was caught in the act.

"So what happened? Did the worker-judges hold him up to the shame and reprehension of the international working class? Or was his name published as an enemy of the people?" Reed asked. These were the two awful fates so regularly imposed.

"Life imprisonment," Peters said laconically.

I protested. Hadn't others caught in worse acts merely got a few weeks in jail?

"But you see," said Peters, "this officer had taken a girl of sixteen and seduced her, and he was altogether a bad man. He can rot in prison for all I care."

"Well, did he get life for seducing a girl, or for theft and impersonating a commissar?" Jack wanted to know. Then, before Peters could answer, he changed his tack, in one of those swift reversals that characterized Reed, who in the constant process of questioning, analyzing, often saw the yes of a thing as soon as he had stated the no.

"I don't care what you do about some lousy officer," he said, "but what I don't get is why so many of the big shots got away. Kornilov, for example. The Bolsheviks come to power, and Kornilov, held a prisoner, gets wind of it and just decamps. Kerensky rides out of Petrograd openly, and then slips out in a sailor's disguise while Dybenko is parleying with Cossacks a few feet away, arranging their surrender. And Krasnov—he comes to Peter and

Paul and then is released! We're writing these tracts telling the Germans how to get rid of their oppressors—and how do we explain that the Revolution lets theirs escape? But what the hell?" he said, laughing and hitting Peters on the back. "Better wait till we make ours before we tell you what you're doing wrong."

"Wonder what the Germans who read our tracts would say if they knew it was a couple of Americans telling them how easy it was to make a revolution," I said.

It was true. It was borne out by one of our sheets, with photographs, that were sent to the front lines, where Russian soldiers would pin them on the barbed wire separating the lines, or simply hand batches to the Germans. Explaining the nature of a revolution, the flyer read: "It is easy to make. Autocracy rests only upon the servitude and acquiescence, the passivity, of the people. When they vanish, the Tsar disappears."

Telling Peters about it now, and making him laugh, we cheered him up. He reminded us that Lenin hadn't made it sound quite so easy when he addressed the Navy Congress and, speaking of the mutiny in the German fleet, added: "Whereas it was quite easy to drive out a band of nitwits, like Romanov and Rasputin, it is immensely more difficult to fight against the organized and strong clique of German imperialists, both crowned and uncrowned."

"And it isn't so easy," Peters said now, in a softened mood, "to immobilize the generals and counterrevolutionary leaders without losing the goals of the Revolution in a wave of anarchistic debauchery. But you're right, we let many slip out of our hands. It's all very difficult. Don't forget the wireless message sent by Lenin and Krylenko to the soldiers and sailors. But Dukhonin was butchered just the same."

We were silent. General N. N. Dukhonin, the last chief of staff under Kerensky, became after Kerensky's flight the first commander in chief of the new regime. On November 8/21 Dukhonin was ordered by the People's Commissars to open immediate armistice negotiations with the enemy command he faced at the front. At this time, few of the generals were taking the October Revolution or the Soviet commissars seriously, and Dukhonin refused to obey the order. Dismissed, he declined to accept dismissal. The Council of People's Commissars at once branded Dukhonin an enemy of the people, appointed Ensign N. V. Krylenko as commander to succeed him, and sent Krylenko and a military expedition to Moghiliev, army headquarters. A wireless message signed by Lenin and Krylenko was sent on November 9/22 "to all regimental, divisional, corps, army, and other committees, to all soldiers of the revolutionary army and sailors of the revolutionary navy," stating the facts and urging them not to "allow the counterrevolutionary generals to frustrate the great cause of peace," but to "place them under guard in order to avert acts of summary justice unworthy of a revolutionary army and to prevent these generals from escaping the trial that awaits them." The wire urged the men further to "Maintain the strictest revolutionary and military order," yet uged with equal emphasis that the regiments at the front elect representatives to begin negotiations with the enemy.

When the punitive expedition under Krylenko arrived, Dukhonin offered no resistance. Some of his officers and a few troops who were not in sympathy with the Bolsheviks left Moghiliev. Control of the town on November 19 was handed over by order of the local Soviet to the Bolshevik Military Revolutionary Committee. Krylenko was established in headquarters, most of the officers arrested with Dukhonin were released, and all seemed quiet enough. Nevertheless, a group of drunken soldiers dragged Dukhonin out of Krylenko's railway car and murdered him. But not before Kornilov, Denikin, and other officers imprisoned at Bykhov were released by order of Dukhonin (it was knowledge of this that had inflamed the soldiers). Making their getaway to the Don, the other generals by now (December) were organizing their Volunteer Army of Whites, together with Alekseyev. The counterrevolution was on the way.

"I know," said Reed, running his hand through his mop of unruly hair. "But you can't expect the average soldier to understand the meaning of 'revolutionary discipline' yet. And you know, they understood a lot, at that. They knew that Dukhonin's ordering the release of those generals was jeopardizing their revolution."

"Anyway," I said, "it strikes me that, despite the few acts that of course get headlines all over the world, the Russians in general have a deep streak of forgiveness in them. I hear that in the provinces the peasant juries are notoriously on the side of the prisoners. That reminds me of what Yanishev told me—the word 'criminal' has no counterpart in the Russian language."

Reed, wrinkling up his nose, began to tell me not to romanticize the peasant. Reed was always a great one to tell the other fellow not to romanticize. "But you Bolsheviks do go too far in being nice," he grumbled.

Though few have pictured Peters as having a sense of humor, he had a nice sense of irony. He now said to Reed, "Well, some of the excesses in the countryside may be regretted, but not criticized for lack of imagination. Just heard of a few landless peasants in one village where the mir staunchly refused to become a soviet or divide the land. Seems they chased after the kulak who was leading the resistance, and he climbed up into the church belfry and rang the bell—a signal for help. So what they did before aid could arrive was to hang the kulak bellringer with his rope.

"No, comrades, Yanishev's is the better way. He was called to a factory in Viborg where there was trouble. The foreman complained that *he* wasn't the owner, and that his feelings were hurt when the men told him they were running things now and he was only a 'vermiform appendix,' quite without function. Yanishev talked to the committee and suggested that until they learned all the foreman knew about production, they'd better keep him around and not make his life miserable."

Later on, when Uritsky headed the Petrograd Cheka in 1918, Voskov told us he was with Uritsky when some relative of the Romanovs, whose name and title I did not record, was brought before him. A decree had been issued to the effect that no male Romanov could reside within the Petrograd district.

"Here was this great Romanov before two Jews, one of them me, the boy who used to dig apples out of the gutter and fish out delectable bits of garbage with a nail on the end of a stick. So Uritsky tells the Romanov with great delicacy that the decree is for his own protection as much as anything else. 'But I can't leave the district, I can't go anywhere, because I have no servants left,' he replied.

" 'Well,' says Uritsky, pointing to me, 'here's a man who gets along without servants. I get along without servants. Try it. Go and earn money somewhere, and then maybe you'll be allowed to return.'

" 'But I can't get a position in the Soviet government,' the man said with some force of logic. 'A Romanov in the Soviet government—it wouldn't look right.'

" 'There are other means than political service,' Uritsky said, not unkindly and with utter seriousness. 'Go and work in a garden. The spring is coming on, you know.' "

It was Volodarsky's resolution, actually written by Lenin, Trotsky told us, that was passed by the Petrograd Soviet on October 25, in which the insurrection was described as "in rare degree bloodless and in rare degree successful."

What irony that Volodarsky (at a time when I was in Vladivostok) was the first Bolshevik of several to be assassinated in cold blood on the streets of Petrograd by Social Revolutionary terrorists! That was on June 21, 1918. And on August 30 Uritsky likewise was murdered and Lenin wounded. It was only after Volodarsky's murder that retaliation began; it was only after the White terror that the Red terror commenced. Stirred by Volodarsky's murder, Lenin wrote on June 28 to Zinoviev, who had been made president of the Petrograd Soviet in February. His words seem moderate enough, in my opinion, having seen on many occasions how workers in factories looked up to Volodarsky. The tragic thing is that

Lenin, when the first attempt had been made on his own life, issued no such warnings.

> Only today we learned in the Central Committee that Petrograd *workers* wanted to answer the murder of Volodarsky with mass terror but that you (not you personally, the Petrograd Chekists and Petrograd Party Committee) restrained them.
> I resolutely protest.
> We compromise ourselves . . . *we put a brake* on the *perfectly* proper revolutionary initiative of the masses.
> That is im-poss-ible.
> The terrorists may think we are weak sisters. This is tensest war-time. We must foster energetic action and demonstrations of mass terror against counterrevolutionaries, and especially in Petrograd, whose example is decisive.

And I feel I must say it, because I was there when it happened, and there in the weeks following, seeing everywhere the reactions to it: It was Lenin's fault more than anyone else's that when he himself first was shot at, he minimized it, he muffled the people's anger over it. Why? Because—and this was borne out a hundredfold as I came to know him—he himself was deeply marked by this typical Russian forgiveness. It had its wonderful aspects. It was what allowed him to excoriate Kamenev and Zinoviev repeatedly, and then work with them the following day. Even in this happy victorious period, both quit their posts, and so did Lunacharsky, but Lenin made short shrift of forgiving them.

Charles Trevelyan, the British historian, wrote, "A revolution breeds neither saints nor devils." But there was this period, before the Revolution had to answer terror with terror, this period before intervention and the bitterness of civil war, when a relative handful of men and women—I knew some, I ate and slept and worked and later drilled alongside them—in trying to wrest order from chaos, in selflessly following the most selfless of them all, Lenin, were very nearly saints.

Today historians agree that Lenin's policy of peace now, peace while we build an army that can fight the imperialists, saved the Revolution. The narrow margin by which he won, by which his coldly realistic tactics finally prevailed against a policy that was overwhelmingly popular, forms one of the great dramas of history. As for me, my real acquaintance with Lenin was to begin in December, and become deepened during those trying months ahead.

• 9 • Internationalism in January

One of the peculiar conditions that made for complexity in the developing crisis over Brest-Litovsk in January was that the debate was taking place when the Bolsheviks were flushed with success. It was a heady wine, the glory of that October, and no less intoxicating in the ensuing weeks that saw the popularity of the Revolution registered in countryside and cities.

In Lenin's words, "In the course of a few weeks, having overthrown the bourgeoisie, we crushed its open resistance in civil war. We passed in a victorious triumphal march of Bolshevism from one end of a vast country to the other."

Revolutionary ardor burned strong. Faith in the proletariat of other lands was an indissoluble part of the Revolution. For what other reason than a burning faith in the workers of other countries would Reed and I have been called upon to speak at factory meetings in September?

More than one monarch, more than one "liberal" democratic party in power in the West trembled in fear that the dread virus of bolshevism would spread to workers whose unions and parties so far had been obligingly patriotic. In America, the editors of *The Masses*, including Reed, were under indictment, and the hysteria was building up against the IWW and the foreign-born which would become the Red crusade of 1919–20.

So far as its public image went, the United States government was not at all worried about bolshevism. Had not its President, Woodrow Wilson, gone out of his way, in sending greetings to the Provisional Government in May, to speak of war aims in what sounded for all the world like Lenin's words on self-determination in his April Theses?[1] More than this, had he

1. Wilson, in a message sent May 26, said in part: ". . . No people must be forced under sovereignty under which it does not wish to live. No territories must change hands except

not eloquently set forth in his "Fourteen Points" of December 26, 1917/ January 8, 1918, the very principles incorporated by the Russians in their peace decree? And although the Fourteen Points were not addressed to the Soviet government, but to his own Congress of the United States, he made specific reference to the peace negotiations in progress at Brest-Litovsk, and it was perfectly plain he considered the Bolsheviks there the legitimate "Russian representatives."

That Wilson felt moved to make this sympathetic speech, whatever his reasons, showed that many of Lenin's points—beginning with his April Theses description of the conflict as a "robber's war"—had put all the parties to the war on the spot. It was dramatic proof, too, of the disturbing thrust of this unheard-of confrontation in a burned-out village (Brest-Litovsk) behind the German lines, where untrained diplomats—a worker, a peasant, and intellectuals—faced representatives of the German high command across a conference table on which a newfangled instrument, a radio receiver, carried their speeches to the world.

Surely it was the Bolsheviks speaking into this thing to whom Wilson paid tribute as "sincere and earnest." The President, whose second-term campaign slogan in 1916 was "He kept us out of war," told the Congress:

It is the voice of the Russian people. They are prostrate and all but helpless, it would seem, before the grim power of Germany, which has hitherto known no relenting and no pity. Their power, apparently, is shattered. And yet their soul is not subservient. They will not yield either in principle or in action. Their conception of what is right, of what it is humane and honorable for them to accept, has been stated with a frankness, a largeness of view, a generosity of spirit, and a universal human sympathy which must challenge the admiration of every friend of mankind. . . . Whether their present leaders believe it or not, it is our heartfelt desire and hope that some way may be opened whereby we may be privileged to assist the people of Russia to attain their utmost hope of liberty and ordered peace.

It is not hard to see why illusions were so easily come by in this period. Not only were they current among most of the Soviet leaders; they penetrated to the masses, and certainly two perspicacious but still human Americans were not immune. As for me, I entertained all sorts of hopes

for the purpose of securing those who inhabit it a fair chance of life and liberty. No indemnities must be insisted on except those that constitute payment for manifest wrongs done. No readjustments of power must be made except such as will tend to secure the future welfare and happiness of its peoples." *Russian-American Relations, 1917–1920, Documents and Papers*, compiled and edited by C. K. Cumming and Walter W. Pettit, at the request of the League of Free Nations Association, New York, 1920, p. 25.

of United States rapprochement of one kind or another with the Soviets, or even a French–United States–Red Guard stand against the Germans, after an encounter with Jacques Sadoul, a military aide with the French Embassy, whose role as a maverick was similar to that of Robins.

At the same time, the work that Reed and I were doing in itself had a marked effect on us. Day in and day out, we appealed to the Germans to revolt, until we could hardly conceive that they would not. When permission was granted for the massive distribution of Wilson's Fourteen Points, they were printed at the same large plant we used for the printing of a daily paper in German. Trucks were loaded with stacks of both, and together Wilson's output and ours went to their destination, the front. There the words of the silver-tongued President had the same distribution as our plain, simple words. They were thrown over into the German trenches, or handed to the German and Austro-Hungarian soldiers at appointed fraternization points. Our paper, *Die Fackel* (The Torch) had become *Der Völkerfriede* on December 19/January 1, and because, with the temporary armistice, distribution was easier than before, its importance was escalated.

This Bolshevik-American cooperation in getting Wilson's propaganda (and ours) to the Germans set off gusts of the always ready wit of Karl Radek. (A gifted journalist and publicist, a Pole educated in Germany, Radek was our editor by now; for a time we had worked directly under Reinstein.) When we came to think of it, this bit of cooperation went from subechelons (Reed and me and our copy) to Colonel Robins, head of the American Red Cross, and from Red Guard truck drivers to Lenin.

The paper also went to prisoner-of-war camps throughout Russia. Carr declares that "Thirteen numbers of *Der Völkerfriede* appeared down to January 10/23, 1918 (the last in the British Museum file); its career was ended by the Brest-Litovsk treaty." I must correct this, as I have a stack of crumbling issues of *Der Völkerfriede*, and the latest copy I have is dated February 11/24, 1918. I am not at all certain that later issues did not appear. I certainly shall not attempt to refute Carr on another point, that "What is perhaps most surprising about these journals is the intellectual character of their appeal; some familiarity with the basic tenets of Marxism is assumed in the reader." This was true, but Reed and I also worked on broadsides and flyers that at our insistence were less intellectual, more dramatic, and filled with photos that told the story in a simpler way. That they hit home was attested to by the reactions of the Austro-Hungarian prisoners of war who, according to what Trotsky said December 9, had offered to fight against the Kaiser's troops if the front again became active. As for General Hoffmann's often quoted statement that "Immediately after conquering those Bolsheviks, we were conquered by them. Our victorious army on the eastern front became rotten with Bolshevism," perhaps it is not immodest to think we played a minor role there. At any rate, from the People's Commissariat of Foreign Affairs we used to send out daily more than half a million newspapers in five languages—German, Hungarian, Polish, Serb, Czech—and occasional one- or two-page flyers in Rumanian, Turkish, Croatian, and other languages.

The wide distribution of Wilson's speech both within Russia and among the German troops represented a minor triumph for the Americans. It also involved interesting developments, as it had required an interview with Lenin (December 29/January 11), arranged by Gumberg for Robins and Edgar Sisson. Sisson, a former *Chicago Tribune* man and *Cosmopolitan* magazine executive, was the Petrograd representative of President Wilson's wartime Committee of Public Information.[2] It was Robins' first such interview (and I believe Sisson's only one), although Robins had seen Trotsky, also through Gumberg's maneuverings, within a few days after the October Revolution. It revealed, too, that despite Lenin's skepticism, he was willing to oblige Robins. He commented that Wilson's speech was "a great step ahead toward the peace of the world," said he had no objection to its distribution, and made inquiry about the implementation of the speech. Apparently Robins and Sisson let that one go by.

On January 7 Trotsky returned from Brest-Litovsk to report on how things were going. Two days earlier General Hoffmann had placed a map on the table and, drawing a line, reminded the Russian delegation that "the victorious German armies [were] on Russian soil." Moreover, they would not retreat from that line (marking off almost all of Poland, Lithuania, and White Russia on the German side, and half of Latvia and the islands off the Moon Sound) until Russian demobilization was complete. As for the Ukraine, he was cagy; that would be for the (anti-Bolshevik) Ukrainian Rada to decide.

The same day Trotsky returned, Lenin began his "Theses on the Question of the Immediate Conclusion of a Separate and Annexationist Peace." But while the theses were read the next day at a meeting of about sixty leading party functionaries, none appeared in print until February 24. (February 1, old style, had become February 14 as the Gregorian calendar went into effect.) It was only on February 23 that Lenin finally won a bare majority in the Central Committee. Meanwhile, during all this time, there was what he later termed a "conspiracy of silence"[3] as to his arguments and theses.

---

2. The committee was headed by George Creel in the U.S.

3. On February 28 Lenin attacked a resolution by the Moscow Regional Bureau of the party and at the same time thanked the Muscovites, who he said "were the first to reply" to his arguments for the peace, and who by stating their position broke the "conspiracy of silence" which had existed "over the *essence* of my arguments." "The very essence of my

Quite naturally, then, Reed and I were torn and wavering in this January period in regard to Brest-Litovsk, as were many of our comrades. I knew only that wartime censorship of the foreign press was unable to hide all the evidence that a prolongation of the war was becoming hateful to both sides. When Lenin, on October 16, 1917, stated the reasons why that was the propitious time to seize power, he pointed to the mutiny of the German fleet, which augured that "we shall have all proletarian Europe on our side." Since then, signs of unrest had multiplied.

We gathered from hints dropped by our Bolshevik friends that Lenin agreed for a time to let the Brest-Litovsk parleys drag out, playing for time, but that he was skeptical, and that he had definite disagreements with most of the leadership, even those who supported him. It was a vulgarization, Reinstein said quietly, ever to think for a moment that Lenin was playing a nationalist or patriotic role. He simply wanted the comrades to shed their illusions.

These illusions were of various kinds. One was that the German high command would be forced by unrest at home to take a conciliatory attitude on many questions to be raised at Brest. Another was that Wilson would break with Lloyd George and England and recognize the Soviet government independently if he could not get joint action. It was assumed by almost everyone that Wilson would prevent Japan from landing in Siberia. Overshadowing all other illusions, however, was the fervent belief that all Europe, and first of all Germany, was on the verge of revolt.

In the face of all this, who could believe the German workers and peasants would obey the orders of their officers and kill their Russian brothers, in the event the Soviets scorned all German terms and declared a "revolutionary war"? So argued the youthful and fiery Nikolai Bukharin, a party theoretician whom Lenin would later term a "favorite" of the party.[4]

---

theses . . . is that we must accept this extremely harsh peace *right now*, at once, while at the same time seriously *preparing* for a revolutionary war (and accept it, moreover, precisely *in the interest* of such serious preparations)."

Characteristically, Lenin thought it "quite natural that comrades who violently disagree with the Central Committee over the question of a separate peace violently condemn the Central Committee and express their conviction that a split is inevitable." He added: "All that is the most legitimate right of Party members, which is quite understandable." But he found "strange and monstrous" the Muscovites' statement, "In the interests of the world revolution, we consider it expedient to accept the possibility of losing Soviet power, which is now becoming purely formal." And, he said, "more humiliating than any humiliating peace is humiliating despair." See "Strange and Monstrous," in Lenin, *Selected Works*, II, Moscow, 1960, 613–620.

4. From Lenin's last letter, begun on December 23, 1922, continued on December 24, with an addition of January 4, 1923, called "Lenin's Last Will and Testament" and revealed here by Max Eastman in 1926, and finally published four years after Stalin's death in the Soviet Union. Lenin's *Selected Works*, III, Moscow, 1961, 792–793, calls it "Letter to the Congress."

For a time things went well—when it was only a question of negotiating a truce. The first negotiators, Joffe, Kamenev, Sokolnikov, Madame Bizenko, and Captain Metislavsky, flanked by a worker, a soldier, a sailor, and a peasant as plenipotentiaries of the new order, stated their position— the same as the peace decree—emphasizing national liberation. These were accepted by German Foreign Minister Richard Von Kühlmann as a basis for discussion. They even were able to get two novel clauses in the truce: that the Germans would not pull out troops on the Russian front for the west unless they were already under orders to be moved (Hoffmann later minimized this, but it was solemnly agreed on), and the right of publicity and fraternization of soldiers at the front.

On the day that I met Lenin for the first time (I preferred to forget the earlier brush-off in regard to my credentials) I had only a fuzzy idea of what the inner-party struggle over Brest was about. It was on January 1. I knew that when the formal peace-treaty negotiations opened on December 9, following the truce with the Central Powers (Austria-Hungary, Turkey, and Bulgaria now ranged alongside German high diplomats and field marshals), some hedging had begun on self-determination. The Central Powers showed their hand by saying that Lithuania, Kurland, and parts of Estonia, Livonia, and Poland should be liberated from Russia. At the suggestion of the Bolsheviks, the party was adjourned again for ten days, while for the third time Allied Powers were formally invited to be present. But when the parleys resumed, the very day after Wilson's speech had rung in every world capital, Britain, France, and the United States again were missing. Now General Hoffmann and Von Kühlmann got down to plain language. Trotsky was heading the Soviet delegation for the first time. Radek was along, not as a delegate, but to ensure Petrograd press coverage.

It was a part cut out for Trotsky. He loved this forum for sparring with Von Kühlmann and Count Czernin, the Austrian foreign minister, on the principle of national liberation. His speeches seemed aimed only to further the effect of a document penned by Trotsky, to which both Lenin and Trotsky affixed their signatures, addressed "to the toiling peoples of Europe, oppressed and bled white." They did nothing to get on with a peace treaty.

It was in this atmosphere, with the Petrograd masses being propagandized at home and the German soldiers and workers hopefully hearing the same message wherever they might be, as well as the workers of Belgium, France, Austria-Hungary, and Bulgaria, that I went to the Mikhailovsky Manège on January 1. I had been invited to speak at the first Socialist Army meeting.

An armored-car battalion was entraining for the south, the first beginnings of an organized revolutionary army. The new recruits, most of them from the Red Guards—in other words, factory workers, young, some appearing little more than boys—began arriving at two-thirty. Among them were a few experienced soldiers, doubtless picked for high revolutionary consciousness. The factory lads stood about shivering and stamping their feet. There was no electricity. The only heat came from a wood fire burning in a single stove at the far end of the vast interior. The men were awaiting Lenin and a general pep talk before they departed. Except for the few soldiers, the men wore any kind of coat. Guns, a tin pail, and a roll such as peasants carry formed their equipment.

Banners of red were tacked around the walls here and there, but there was an awful coldness and dreariness about the place. Two armored cars with red banners, and further decorated with fresh evergreens, stood outside the building; inside, another decorated car served as a platform. On either side within the great long building were rows of formidable dun-colored motors.

While waiting for Lenin, some of the men asked questions. The grand *nachalnik* (the boss) answered all questions by saying they were going to fight against the counterrevolutionaries or the imperialists. By four o'clock the building was pitch-dark. Revolutionary songs were struck up; a man with a balalaika mounted the decorated car, followed by another with a tambourine and a third with an accordion, and, to pass the time and keep warm, men formed into an elongated ring, held up candles, and danced the favorite dance of the particular village from which they came, packs and guns still on their backs. Still Lenin did not come. Three times their song was interrupted by an auto horn, they waited, and it was a false alarm.

It was about seven o'clock when Lenin finally arrived. There were cheers for him, but it was not much of a reception. He did not seem disappointed, but climbed briskly up onto the top of the decorated car. He said that things had been going well, very well, up to now, but that they must be prepared to suffer setbacks now and then. It was a dispassionate statement of the situation as he saw it.

It was the first—and the last—of the numerous times I heard Lenin that he seemed to miss fire. I did not understand why at the time. Even in 1919 when I wrote my volume on Lenin I think I missed the real point when I attributed it to Lenin's overwork. In looking back now at that whole glowing period, I see that I was looking for the same type of speech to which the new army fledglings (referred to for the first time at that meeting as the Socialist Army, not the Red Guard) were accustomed. I expected assurances that the international proletariat was on the march; boasts that we were showing the German generals and statesmen at Brest-Litovsk a thing or two, and they would have to give in on self-determination for the occupied countries; and that they, the new army contingent (not yet christened the Red Army) were bound for the front, but it was a front now bound to inactivity by our truce, and we expected them back to live for the glorious results of October.

Whatever Lenin said, it was not that. My notes, made later, were sparse, and I have not found an official version of this talk, if there was one.

Mirsky says of Lenin that "whatever seemingly unpopular policy he adopted, this never affected his popularity, for, as he came to be understood, his policy was always consonant with the real, if unexpressed, will of the people. . . ." I think that was generally true, but there were periods before the unpopular policy was understood, and this was one, and I was in the midst of it, and not even aware of it at the time. I saw only that his speech was unpopular, and that he made no effort to make it otherwise.

I felt that something special was demanded of me. When Lenin stepped down and Podvoisky said in the same dry manner Lenin used, "An American comrade to address you," and I was climbing up on the big armored car, I was trying to make up my mind. Should I, dare I, speak in Russian? By now I had been there seven months. My natural Welshman's love of words made it easy for me to pick up languages, and besides, it was talk or perish there. Still, I had to confess that my four years of Greek, six of Latin, and one of Hebrew were little help to me.

Seeing me standing there undecided—I was a little grim about it all, as if it were a matter of life or death—Lenin said kindly, "Oh good. You speak in English. Allow me to be your interpreter."

That decided me. "No," I said recklessly, even a little pompously, I suspect, "I shall speak in Russian."

Lenin was delighted. His eyes twinkled, his whole face lit up with the laugh wrinkles in play, becoming the face of a gnome, no less elfin because of that high forehead and balding head. He positively looked forward to the diversion my Russian would afford.

I began with a few stock phrases, which I now knew by heart. These I wrote down when I got home that night, with my execrably spelled Russian beneath, so I can say precisely what they were. "Long live the victorious, unconquerable Russian army! Long live united, powerful Russia!" Then, with the words of President Wilson's Fourteen Points still ringing in my ears: "Long live the lasting union between America and Russia!"

Of course these phrases got a big hand, but I felt they were perfunctory. I was groping around for something serious to say, but meanwhile, why not lighten the tone? So, more haltingly but still going at a pretty good clip, I said it was true I spoke Russian very badly, but that was for only one reason. "The Russian language is a very difficult language. When I tried to speak in Russian to an *izvoshchik* [driver of a droshky] yesterday he thought I was speaking Chinese. Even the horse got a little scared." That brought a booming roar of laughter from the audience, and Lenin was laughing hugely. Only Podvoisky, I noticed, remained solemn-faced.

But then my struggles began. I tried to tell them how the sight of them, raw recruits in their new uniforms, fresh from factory benches, moved me. Knowing there was division in the party and among the masses about the whole matter of a separate peace with the Germans, I wanted them to know that I was not unaware that the Revolution was in danger, that Petrograd itself might be in danger. So far, the audience had been polite; no matter how a foreigner butchers their language, Russians are charitable. So with each pause while I searched for words, they covered me with applause, and that gave me a breathing spell. But now I had reached the climax. If it came to a showdown, if a great crisis came, I wanted them to know that I would . . .

They were hanging on my words now. No applause. I could feel the sweat break out. Then I felt Lenin's eyes boring into me and turned to face him. "What word do you want?" he asked softly, in English. The laughter was gone from his face. His eyes still were merry, but he was encouraging me to go on.

"Enlist," I replied.

"*Vstupit,*" he said.

So I went on. I would, I said, enlist in the Socialist Army. There was not much more to the speech, but from that moment on, whenever I was stuck for a word, I turned to him, he quickly supplied it, and I went on without the awkward pauses.

I had more or less by chance hit upon the magic factor that the masses at this point wanted. My very presence was visible proof of the current internationalism, so that their own revolutionary ardor rose, and the applause swelled and mixed with the friendly laughter prompted by my Anglicized pronunciation of the words Lenin flung up to me.

This socialist comrade so unmistakably American, offering to enlist if necessary, had given a new twist to the internationalism that was on the lips of so many speakers in those days. For here was someone saying, not that the Revolution was immune to German attack, not that the German brothers never would assault a socialist land, helpless and urging peace on the world, but that if it were attacked, he would join them.

At the end, in my atrocious Russian, I assured them that in America there would be revolution, but I did not say when. "I am very sorry, the American working class is very conservative." And I wound up, "Long live the Revolution! Long live the Socialist troops! Long live the International!" ("Da sdrastvooyet Revolutsia, da sdrastvooyet Sotsialistecheskia voeska, da sdrastvooyet International!") (Reproduced as I wrote it that night, it illustrates why Lenin's teaching impulses were aroused; from that time on I was his pupil, and quite a challenge to his skill, at that.)

As I climbed down, Lenin was most cordial. "Well, that's a beginning in Russian, at any rate," he said kindly. Then he added with a special seriousness, "But you must keep at it, hard." Turning to Bessie Beatty, who had come along with me, he said, not in a bantering way, or to be gallant, but with complete seriousness: "And you, you must learn Russian, too. Put an advertisement in the paper asking for exchange lessons. Then just read, write, and talk nothing but Russian." And to both of us: "Don't talk with Americans. It won't do you any good, anyhow," he added humorously. And to me: "Next time I see you I shall give you an examination."

Lenin left, the car in which he was riding pulled away, and we were making our way on foot from the Manège slowly, in the press of the crowd, when three shots rang out. Three bullets had been fired at him, crashing through his car. Fritz Platten, Swiss Left Socialist, who was seated next to Lenin in the rear seat, was wounded in one hand. This was the first attempt on Lenin's life, made by a would-be assassin hiding in a side street, who escaped.

Shaken, Bessie Beatty and I hurried through the crowd. We had to find out for certain that Lenin had not been hit. "To think that he stood there, talking to us." Bessie was in tears. "Maybe it wouldn't have happened at all except for that. Maybe the assassin wouldn't have arrived if he'd left right away." I had had the same unreasoning, useless thought myself, but now it was some relief to take her to task. "Isn't that just like a woman?" I fumed. "Maybe waiting for him so long, the man got nervous and missed, too." We were both very tense even after we learned that Lenin was safe, for that night.

Weeks before this assault on Lenin, Reed and I had reported to our Bolshevik intimates how one wealthy speculator had told us, in dead earnest, that he had a million rubles for the man who would kill Lenin, and knew nineteen others who were prepared to match that sum, or better. He was one of the *bons vivants,* newly rich from war profits, running goods by the underground to Germany, who loved to entertain newspapermen. Gumberg had introduced us, and we went to his home on the prospect of a lavish feed; we were not disappointed.

On January 27 we ran into Bill Shatov at the Maryinsky, where we had good seats at four rubles to see *The Barber of Seville.* Shatov was worried that the Smolnyites were minimizing the danger of General M. V. Alekseyev, who was organizing his volunteer army of White Guards in the Caucasus. "Sure his forces are small, but they've burned their bridges. What's death to them? So they'll fight. For to live under the Bolsheviks is to give up all the privileges that made life worthwhile to them."

Later we went to the Empire Café, which had been "nationalized" into the International Café now, and Shatov kept on. France was pouring money into the hands of these White wretches, and the English were feeling about, ready to follow suit, he said. Good old Bill. For an anarchist—and he remained one, even years later when a friend of mine discovered him running a bank in Rostov, he was still an anarchist—he was a very practical guy, and always loyal to the Bolsheviks. When I asked Peters about it the next day, my journal reminds me, it began to look as if Shatov was right:

"Peters today looks to no great danger from that quarter, says that the danger is the lack of bread. He blamed the Ministry of Supply for the reduction in the ration to a quarter pound a day, saying that two days earlier there had seemed to be ample to continue without such a cut."

The fact is that there were so many things to worry about that the growing belief in internationalism found fertile soil. And as the negotiations at Brest-Litovsk worsened, the need to believe in internationalism grew. It was a humiliating situation to be in, for all the brave face put on by the negotiators. If they were not to acquiesce to a "brigand's peace," as Lenin termed it, the Soviets must get aid. Internationalism was no longer just an amiable, desirable idea or ideal; it was imperative.

But what was imperative could not be ordered. Lenin, skeptical, was willing to give it a chance. He waited, not too hopefully, while Trotsky, arrogant, confident before the German generals, used brilliant invective and masterful logic to challenge the imperialists of all nations, hoping to get the German masses to move. As Lenin wrote later, "We sent broadcast the clarion call of the international working class revolution." But the proletariat of other countries did not take up the call.

The greatest of the meetings on internationalism was held on International Day, in the Cirque Moderne. The meeting was unique—not in its enthusiasm, but in what it was enthusiastic about: fraternity, a new social order, the outlawing of wars of aggression, the affirmation of the goodness of the rest of mankind, along with the workers' and soldiers' own new feeling of importance. Others have argued that this internationalism abroad in the Russian cities and penetrating the provinces was temporary, and that I cannot deny. But it is no mean thing that for a brief period these rough soldiers and the men and women from the factories were swept up by these emotions, which presumably are to animate all mankind in some more or less distant time. They were, if you please, premature citizens of the world. From the little community of the mir they had leaped to a concept of a community that would embrace the entire world. Granted that in the hatred engendered by the intervention, this spirit would lapse, falter, and never regain the freshness of that moment. Still, for a time, backward, war-scarred, hungry Russians not only had become the "vanguard of the Revolution" that Marx saw as a possibility late in life, but were the precursors of what one day all mankind, hopefully, shall be.

Heightening interest in the Cirque meeting was a street demonstration held December 17 and hailed in *Pravda* the previous day under the headline TOMORROW IS THE DEMONSTRATION! The story follows:

> Let the orderly ranks of the workers, soldiers, and peasants flow in a mighty stream through the streets and squares and their appeals to the toilers of all countries to rise under the red banner of proletarian revolution in the common struggle for peace and socialism loudly resound.
>
> Through the solidarity and organization of proletarian ranks we shall show all the enemies of the Soviet Power the uncrushable force, the united will of all toilers ready to rise as one man to defend with their bare breasts the great cause of proletarian revolution.
>
> The radiant dawn of peace and socialism is already rising high!
>
> Long live a democratic peace and socialism!

All these events, the demonstration, the Cirque meeting, and a later official meeting in Smolny noted by the historian Carr, actually were meant as preludes to the organizing of the Third International, which never got off the ground in 1918, thanks to Brest-Litovsk and intervention. Speakers included Karl Hogland, "The Liebknecht of the Scandinavian countries"; Mayor Lindhagen of Stockholm, Egede Nissen, mayor of Stavanger, Norway; Comrade Rakovsky of Rumania; and Reed and me. The multilingual Aleksandra Kollontai translated for all of us. Hogland and Nissen had spent time in jail and were paid high tribute by *Pravda*, and now that it was known that Reed had been indicted, the *Pravda* reporter's enthusiasm so ran away with him that he had Reed already sentenced to twelve years in prison.

The lengthy *Pravda* account gave few direct quotes from any of the speakers, and I am not at all sure Reed exaggerated as much as it would indicate. After the item about his twelve-year sentence "for his struggle against the American Imperialists and for his support of the Russian Bolsheviks" came this paragraph:

> Comrade Reed in his speech reported that the American Socialist Party had grown and strengthened during the years of the Imperialist war and that the events in Russia would spur the further development of the class struggle in America which was attaining especially sharp forms.

Actually, there were signs aplenty that the class struggle was sharpening at home. Never in the history of the United States had there been so many and so violent strikes as in the years 1913–17. But the Socialist party at home, as in Europe, had split on the very question of supporting the war, one group becoming "patriots," the other sticking by the interests of the international working class. I doubt very much if Reed, who was bitter about the defections at home, gave general praise to the American Socialist party.

A tattered copy of what is now a collector's item, a little magazine called *The Year of Revolution* edited by Eugene Debs, may be found in the shelves of the New York Public Library. It contains an article I wrote for the issue (the magazine's first and last) celebrating the first anniversary of the founding of the Russian Soviet Republic. Since that part of it concerning the Cirque Moderne meeting has been borrowed by others, and because more than anything I have since written it gives the flavor of "The Spirit of Internationalism," its title, I have no hesitation in quoting it now.

> It was in the dead of winter, a bitter cold day, when we came with a procession streaming across the Troitsky Bridge. Between the minarets of the blue-domed Mohammedan Mosque and the shining golden spire of the Church of Peter and Paul, lay the new Cathedral of the proletariat. It was a great, low, rambling, gray bordered structure called the *Cirque Moderne*. There was a black mass of people jammed up against the entrances.
>
> "Why don't they open up and let the people in?" I asked as we passed the crowd and entered a back passage into a great, black cavern. It was a huge pit, dug out of the earth with hundreds of girders to support the monstrous, arching roof. But we could see neither the floor nor the roof nor the seats in a wide sweep rising tier on tier around the arena. In fact we couldn't see anything at all, as, guided by Kollontai, we stumbled through the dark, damp passages and up some stairs and came out upon a few rough boards which served as a platform. There was no light in the place because that day there was no coal in Petrograd.
>
> "Why don't they open the doors and let the people in?" I repeated.
>
> "There are fifteen thousand here already," Kollontai replied, "and the place is packed to the roof!"
>
> The deep silence made that statement incredible. A candle was lighted so that the face of the speaker might be visible—a tiny flicker in the dark.

Kollontai said: "Go ahead, speak!"

It seemed foolish to talk to the vast void. But in a venture of faith, I raised my voice and blindly flung my words out into the night.

"Comrades! I speak for the American Socialists, Internationalists!"

Like a blast from the pit came an explosion of fifteen thousand voices:

"Da sdrastvooyet International!" (Long live the International!)

That word was like a match tossed into a powder magazine.

"Long live the International!" That phrase could always be depended upon to set fire to an audience. When it fell in broken Russian from the lips of a foreigner it started a conflagration.

And with what spirit they sang the *Internationale!* Not the way we sing it here, with part of the singers guessing at the words and another part guessing at the tune and the majority of us spectators —in Russia every revolutionist is sure of every word and every note and sings it as though his life depended on it. . . . In its singing they found strength, an affirmation of the militancy of their faith, a sharpening of the edge of their fighting spirit.

But in all truth now, as when I stood upon the bridge of the battleship *Respublika* and 11,000 sailors made the turrets ring with their greetings to the American internationalists, it was both a thrilling and a humiliating experience. The faith that they put in our internationalism had little existence in reality. I felt that they pictured me as a representative of millions of American sailors, soldiers, miners, railroad men, steelworkers, and longshoremen, all on fire with the same flame. And I was acutely conscious of those little bands of intellectuals in the New Jersey Socialist locals I had addressed during my campaigning for Debs.

Many in the audience had never met, or had not been sure they had met, an internationalist. We were real, authentic, blown-in-the-bottle foreigners, symbols in flesh and blood. We did not even look the part. (But neither did the mayor of Stockholm.) In retrospect, we were not so misrepresentative. In America we did live up to our promises to tell the world about the great October Revolution. In Russia, as we stood before audiences and spoke, we knew that the movement in the United States was important, but not so powerful as our audience wanted to think it was. At home, on the contrary, the movement in Russia that we represented to our audiences was much greater than that audience conceived—or could conceive.

·10· Prelude to Battle

The Bolshevik party leadership, divided before October, was just as divided after the successful insurrection. Carr's estimate is that dissension reached proportions unheard of in that party "and perhaps rare in any other." I would only add that to Ivan Ilyich it seemed the normal course of events, and he was as unruffled as ever. Now all the skirmishes of November and December were mere preludes to the decisive battle shaping up over Brest-Litovsk.

Obviously, any struggle for party unity would have to wait. Now that I think of it, there was little talk about party unity. That came later. It was taken for granted that there would be an Opposition, and on Brest-Litovsk the divisions were deep and widespread. The storm clouds of peace or war loomed overhead, but everyone expressed himself, for or against. At times Reed and I were on opposite sides, at times both on the same side, and the next day both on the opposite one.

A large measure of tolerance was a part of the very air we breathed in Petrograd, so that everywhere one heard men argue passionately, all but come to blows, then wander off arm in arm. Everywhere open debate went on, in and out of the party. In later years I was to recall this openness. No one huddled in fear, or was silent lest he make a mistake. It was this that remained in my mind as essentially Russian, and the hallmark of the early Bolshevik days.

Meanwhile, all the dissension which had been growing apace in the United States Embassy and assorted agencies was heightened because of tensions over Brest. Lines were shaping up sharply there. Boyce Thompson and Robins moved cautiously in support of the new government, at least to the extent of believing in its viability. Colonel William V. Judson, military attaché, initially intransigent, even threatening an American blockade, was won over to the side of the Robins-Thompson group, along with Major Thomas D. Thacher, Major Allen Wardwell, and others.

Unlike Ambassador Francis, who regretted Lenin and Trotsky had had not been shot[1] and according to Gumberg still yearned for the return of Kornilov, Robins had been the first to recognize that Kerensky was finished. Even Francis was glad to get Robins' reports on what went on at Smolny. (Francis, writing in his memoirs on the only occasion he himself visited Lenin, reports, "Lenin was pleasant in manner throughout the meeting." He returned to the embassy nonplused, Gumberg related, saying, "That anarchist is likable, you know.") Robins had argued Thompson into agreeing that the only way to find out about the Bolsheviks was to talk to them, and Thompson had sanctioned a visit to Smolny. Judson had had a forty-five-minute interview with Trotsky, and Trotsky had then approached Robins and Robins had received the Bolsheviks' cooperation in moving Red Cross supplies stalled at distant points, and in apprehending contraband shipments destined for Germany. Judson's interview actually had been made with Francis' authorization, although he later nervously denied it. Robins and Judson were strongly convinced, in view of the Bolsheviks' weaknesses on the international front, that they might be persuaded with some United States support not to conclude a peace with Germany; they were even hopeful of winning Francis' support.

In the midst of all this, things at the embassy had become further complicated, and the Ambassador's huffiness grew more pronounced just as he had seemed on the verge of admitting that the Bolsheviks were the *de facto* government and the United States might exploit their need of a friend. This complication arose from the Ambassador's association with Madame Matilda de Kram, wife of a Russian officer. Francis had met her on the boat coming over. When it was pointed out to him that she was one of a group under suspicion as German agents, he brushed the charge aside. In October and November the De Kram–Francis relationship flourished, and she was a constant visitor at the embassy. When Robins, Judson, and others noticed secret material disappearing and one day saw Francis showing her a letter, they investigated. It developed she was on the secret list of the Inter-Allied Passport Bureau, and some member of the staff warned the State Department, which sent explicit orders to Francis to suspend all relations with Madame de Kram. Francis, furious, said it was all a lie, and

1. "Had the Provisional Government at this time arraigned Lenin and Trotsky and the other Bolshevik leaders, tried them for treason and executed them, Russia probably would not have been compelled to go through another revolution. . . ." David R. Francis, *Russia from the American Embassy*, New York, 1921, pp. 141–142, 143.

continued to see her. Then Judson called upon the Ambassador and showed him her dossier. Francis cavalierly dismissed the entire business. The association continued.

Robins was a man of great magnetism and intense personal convictions. Soon after his arrival I had been his guest in a big restaurant. To the strains of "The Marseillaise," dancing girls in scant attire had sallied out on the floor. It seemed a bizarre combination to me, but Robins liked the music better than the usual melancholy airs and thought the dancing lively. When I noted his looking at my third cigarette, I reminded him he was almost a chain coffee drinker. He replied with a glint of humor in his eyes, "Anything against coffee in the Bible?"

Now, shortly after Robins' initial sortie to Smolny, he asked me to lunch one day. It seemed not at all odd to me at the time that I should be sitting with this man of affluence, a conservative, and speaking of how to help foment revolution. Of course, it was revolution in Germany he wanted fomented. And, he said, at the embassy the previous night they had been discussing a certain appeal issued by the Bolsheviks to the German masses, in effect asking them to revolt. Was I familiar with it? Yes, I said, if it was the "Appeal to the German Soldiers" signed by Trotsky.

"It must be that. I hear Trotsky wrote it for the men at the front—like those things you're working on now. But, if it's as it has been represented to me, I want it to have much wider distribution. I'd like to get it into Germany itself—in large amounts." He eyed me narrowly.

Robins had not taken me into his confidence, naturally, on his trials with Francis or his long-range campaign along with Thompson to influence American policy. Doubtless he knew I knew about these matters, however, and that I might even have heard that Thompson, who had planned to leave for home via Vladivostok, had changed his mind when Thomas S. Lamont agreed to meet him in London, where they would try to influence the British. Such things got around by the grapevine fast in Petrograd, especially when one was a friend of Robins' ordinarily taciturn and discreet aide Gumberg and his favorite reporter, Bessie Beatty.

Without elucidating further, he merely said now, in a casual tone, "What's more, that document, signed by Trotsky, should be proof to the world that they are no German agents."

I laughed. "That's so. The appeal doesn't actually say, 'Rise up and throw out your Kaiser,' but the implication is there—pay no attention to your officers, refuse to fight your Socialist brothers, come to our help, and so forth."

"With massive distribution of this appeal," Robins said, "the disaffection now brewing in Germany—not only in the fleet, but among the workers, according to reports—might flare up into something big. I'll tell you—get me permission to have the thing printed in huge quantities, and the Bolsheviks' cooperation in distributing it widely, and I'll give a hundred thousand rubles toward it."

I set out for Smolny, confident enough. I knew Trotsky slightly, had spoken from the same platform with him at Narodni Dom three days before the October Revolution. He had even asked me for a copy of the speech I had made in the Baltic, and though I did not have any, I felt quite set up about it—until Peters, who had asked me to speak and come with me, told me Trotsky had questioned my political views and opposed my speaking until he gave him a newspaper clipping on my reception by the sailors.

Getting past the two Red Guards stationed on either side of Trotsky's door in the Smolny, each with a gun with fixed bayonet resting on the floor in the usual unmilitary stance of Red Guards, was no problem. Trotsky had spent only a few months in New York, and I had heard he was more comfortable speaking German than English, so I tried my German. He did not invite an informal approach, as Lenin did, so I avoided trying my Russian on him. I came to the point at once: Robins was impressed with what he had heard about the appeal "To the German Soldiers," signed by him, I began.

"Robins wants it distributed widely inside Germany as well as at the front, and he will give a hundred thousand rubles to see that this is accomplished."

I had not specified that the 100,000 was to pay for the printing, but that seemed obvious to me. Not to Trotsky. As if stung, he jumped up and shouted that "your friend Robins" had given Breshkovskaya two million rubles "to put patriotic dope into the people." I stood open-mouthed, realizing he had not understood anything but the 100,000 rubles. "I will have you know that your friend Robins cannot bribe the Bolsheviks!"

It was a noisy performance, and before I recovered my breath the door opened, the two Red Guards came flying in, and all I saw were those shiny bayonets pointed at me. With an accusing finger Trotsky pointed at me and in Russian ordered the Guards to take the "agent of the imperialist power" away.

By this time he was no longer shouting, but I was. "Listen! You can't arrest me! I'm no agent of imperialism, I'm working for the Bolsheviks— right in your Foreign Office, which you never enter!" I yelled at Trotsky, and sat him down hard. He looked at me, astounded. The Guards stood gazing at me quizzically, and then one put a hand up to his whiskers to hide a grin. The whole thing had been pretty absurd, and even Trotsky, a humorless man if I ever knew one, must have felt a bit sheepish. I know I did, once I was safely outside that office and on my way, not to prison, but to the Foreign Office.

Later Trotsky and I made it up, with Volodarsky, now People's Commissar of the Press, playing intermediary.

It was true that Trotsky almost never entered the Foreign Office building. Once the secret treaties had been published serially in the press, Trotsky seemed to feel his duties were about over. I am sure he had no idea, until my loud voice announced the fact, that Reed and I were doing anything in that big, now almost silent building.

Our propaganda bureau was the busiest place there. Most of the clerks had quit or sat about doing nothing. Next door to us was the Department of War Prisoners, where in an elegant room German and Austrian war prisoners came to report on the effect of our propaganda and to plot further bolshevization of prisoners. When we went in to talk to them, we had to sign our names in a book and remain silent as to whom we saw and what we heard. Louise Bryant was convinced the Black Hundred had access to the book through some undercover man among the prisoners, as she began to be tailed wherever she went.

Reed, Beatty, and I were invited by Maria Spiridonova to celebrate New Year's Eve with the peasants of the Left Social Revolutionaries. This was in the heyday of their partnership in the ruling Soviet power with the Bolsheviks, so there would be much to celebrate. Just the same, Spiridonova told us, it was to be an evening purely of fun—no political speeches.

We set out for 6 Fontanka Place, where we were to be guests of the Left SR Executive Committee, in high fettle, hiring a sleigh and paying the izvoshchik the exorbitant extra fare he deemed appropriate for the holiday. We all admired Spiridonova, who had worked with Lenin and the other Bolsheviks at the All-Russian Congress of Peasants and was largely instrumental in swinging a majority to the Soviets for the coalition government. Reed thought her the most striking and powerful woman in Petrograd. On the way, we speculated as to whether, in the coming Constituent Assembly, the Left SR delegates from the provinces would follow their leaders, or be confused. By now it was a foregone conclusion that the Constituent Assembly would be allowed to meet, but unless it supported the Soviet and all the chief Soviet legislation to date, it would be broken up.

"It's going to give Lenin a very bad name in the West," Beatty observed as we flew along the snow, the wind in our faces.

"But not here, and that's what counts," Reed said. "Would you have Lenin bow out and let the C.A. take over? That's what the Kadets and the

old military gang would like to see. No one cares about the C.A., really—
I mean the workers don't."

"But the old peasants do," Bessie argued.

"You mean," I put in, "the old-time intellectual revolutionaries who
were put on the ballot long before the October Revolution, and were voted
in as delegates because the peasants had no way of distinguishing Right and
Left SR's, as the tickets didn't say. It was a trick. Besides, I thought this
evening was to be minus politics."

As we entered 6 Fontanka, a hall that used to be a law university and
now served as headquarters for the peasants, we saw a sign that read, "All
peasant comrades who are anarchists will please sign their names here."
Four names were written in the allotted space.

It was a festive party, with roast pig and pastries of meat and stuffed
cabbage, and there were singing and dancing, and even a diversionary fire
when a lamp overturned. Men put it out with their coats while Spiridonova
motioned for the singing to continue.

But even here the debate intruded. Not the surface debate raging in
embassies and among correspondents over the Constituent Assembly. That
had all been settled, and was accepted here. The radical Left SR's had
seen the realism of Lenin's arguments—that with the Provisional Government in power, the C.A. might have been a progressive force, but with
the proletarian revolution already a fact, it would be only a rallying ground
for those who wanted to use it against the people. The debate that impinged
on the festivities here, however briefly, was concerned with more important
issues—the shadow of Brest-Litovsk and the resolution of the trouble in
the Ukraine, where the power first had swung to the Soviets and the
Revolution, but now was challenged by the reactionary Rada.

The toastmaster, the Left SR Markim, now People's Commissar of
Posts and Telegraph, could not bear to see an evening wasted altogether in light talk and merriment. An intellectual, with a pale, poetic-
looking face and mournful eyes, accentuated by the light of the candles
that lit the long tables seating more than a hundred guests, he at last rose,
rapped for attention, and began, "Unless we break the last chain that binds
men—nationalism—the Revolution will be broken. We cannot let nationalism divide the people."

An old peasant from Moldavia shook his head vigorously. "Lenin will
not allow that. Lenin is very wise."

"Ask Lenin," Markim went on. "He will tell you, he is always telling
us, everything must come from the bottom. It is we, you, you peasants,
who must initiate—"

But his voice was drowned in gay protests. The guests did not want
to be serious this night. So Kamkov, People's Commissar of Justice,

started a mad whirling dance in the adjoining narrow hall, and it was decided to try Markim "in the name of the Right SR party and the Constituent Assembly." The trial proceeded with many jests at the expense of their right-wing erstwhile brothers; playing their parts, they condemned Markim before any evidence was presented. The only thing to be deliberated was the punishment. It was decided he must forfeit his dessert.

Reed planned to go home to face trial with the other *Masses* editors, but he wanted to cover both the C.A. and the Third Congress (set to open January 10), so he postponed his departure beyond that of Louise Bryant, who was leaving Petrograd on January 7. Knowing that much would be made of the C.A. at home, he wanted to stay long enough to assess any aftermath in Petrograd.

In April, and again and again since April, Lenin had stressed that a republic of Soviets was a higher form of democracy than the usual bourgeois parliamentary republic. During the Kerensky regime the C.A. was considered the apex of parliamentary democracy, and a legitimate demand for the Bolsheviks to voice. Now it was outdated.

Headed for the Constituent Assembly on Friday morning, January 5, I was walking up the Liteiny chatting with old Mark Andreyevich Natanson, a former Populist and long-time member of the SR Central Committee who was now with the Spiridonova group, more numerous by far by now than the Right SR's who had captured most of the seats at the C.A. He was telling me how he had gone up to Lenin to talk over the C.A. at one point. Vladimir Ilyich, he said, had bluntly said, "We can't let the Constituent Assembly cost us the Revolution, you know. We will have to break it up, and then where will the Left Social Revolutionaries be? With us?" And the old Populist, after a bit more talk, was won over, and said, "Very well, if it comes to the revolution or the C.A., break up the C.A., and by force." He could not then speak for his party; some might waver, but he thought not.

Then, as Natanson and I approached the Nevsky, we saw groups forming for a procession, their great red banners proclaiming, "All power to the Constituent Assembly." Two days earlier the city had been proclaimed in a state of siege; people were warned not to demonstrate or enter the district around the Taurida Palace. Lenin had ordered a Lettish regiment to stand guard.

We saw a red banner being carried over the Aleksandr II Bridge. Suddenly there was the drumfire of a machine gun, and a precipitate riot. As we swung down one street, we saw Red Guards manning a barricade of wood across the street. In the effort of the Soviet to prevent bloodletting by restraining any provocation from its side against the burzhuy, blood was spilt.

I had no ticket, but at the entrance a sailor recognized me and I made my way into the spacious lobby. This was the palace Catherine the Great turned over to Grigory Potemkin, her long-time favorite, with a stroke of the pen. It lay gleaming in the sun, spread over what appeared to be several blocks, its new pale-yellow paint and the snow on its roof giving it a festive air out of keeping with the heavily armed guard surrounding it.

In the lobby I spoke to Vladimir Bonch-Brueyvich and to the Commissar of Justice I had met at 6 Fontanka. I saw Kollontai, looking feminine and pretty, her usual poised self. I pointed to the cleaners and decorators still touching up parts of the big hall, and asked her if they were packing gats. She gave me a reproving smile, as if I were a naughty boy, and chattered away about the coming international meeting.[2] I told her I had no pass but had hopefully left my credentials with the press officer for the next day. She heard the question in my voice but ignored it.

There was Lunacharsky, waiting in line for his lunch with all the rest. This was going to be a well-fed bunch. Most of the delegates had come armed with sandwiches in case they could get no food, and candles in case the Bolsheviks turned out the lights.

Volodarsky came over to tell me about the meetings held throughout the city on January 4. Neibut was there too, hoarse after speaking far into the night, preparing the troops for defense of the city. All the C.A. delegates who could be trusted, he said, had been taken around to speak in a whirlwind campaign.

I walked into the spacious semicircular chamber and went into the press gallery, situated just behind the podium. No one asked me for a pass. I found Reed and Louise Bryant. Bessie Beatty, Edgar Sisson, and Gumberg were sitting in a box reserved for Robins, and with them was Trotsky's secretary. Next to Robins' box was that of Olga Kameneva, wife of Kamenev and sister of Trotsky. She was surrounded by soldiers with a veritable armory of revolvers strapped to their hips.

Neither Reed nor I could abide Sisson. Reed's favorite epithet for him was "the weasel." It was not so much Edgar's sharp, narrow features and narrowly set eyes that suggested the analogy, or even his movements,

2. On January 24/February 6, 1918, what was hailed as an "international socialist conference" was held on the premises of Narkomindel (Carr, *Russian Revolution*, III, 116–117). Present were Bolsheviks, with Stalin in a leading role, Left SR's, and representatives of several border countries and Scandinavia, together with Petrov and Reinstein, representing respectively the British Socialist party and the American Socialist Labor party. They passed resolutions urging "a revolutionary struggle . . . for immediate peace" and for support of the Soviet government. A few days later a delegation including Kollontai, Berzin, and two SR's was appointed to go to Stockholm. It set out at the height of the Brest-Litovsk crisis and was turned back in Finland. Not until after the armistice of November 1918 was any further effort to organize a new international movement possible. On December 19, 1918, Gorky, then anti-Bolshevik, presided over an international meeting convened by the Petrograd Soviet, in Petrograd.

although he slithered here, there, everywhere. It was what Jack called his "air of earnest furtiveness."

Sisson had been en route to Petrograd when the October Revolution took place. Appointed by George Creel, director of the United States Committee on Public Information, Sisson was there on an appropriation of $250,000 and under President Wilson's orders to stress America's "friendliness ... unselfishness ... and desire of helpfulness." The war aspects "would take care of themselves if a bond were forged" between the two peoples. But that was when Wilson and his cabinet blandly declined to see the handwriting on the wall. So when Sisson disembarked at the Finland Station on November 12/25 with a good deal to catch up on, he was to all effects and purposes pursuing the policies laid out for him. Finding that Robins was the man who had the contacts at Smolny, the one official who got around, he made friends with him and was won over to his theory of action—that if they could count on some United States aid and support, the Bolsheviks might be kept from making a separate peace with Germany. The Ambassador seemed to have no policy at all except to insist that the Bolsheviks could not last.

When, not long after Sisson's arrival, Judson had interviewed Trotsky (on November 18), Sisson had been all for it, even cabling Creel importantly to advise the President and say it was based on a policy that had his approval. He was new then, and philistine that he was, boasted of putting in a good word for the Brigadier General.

The first visit had been reported in *Izvestia*. Judson, making it clear he spoke only for himself, not officially for his country, spoke of the coming formal peace parleys (a temporary truce was in effect), and made up for his earlier embargo statement. Trotsky had agreed to waive the previous affront, assured him every step would be made public at Brest-Litovsk, and hoped that at some stage the Allies might intervene in the peace talks. And when, at a later interview, Judson had broached the plan that the Russians try to secure the holding of the German troops already on the eastern front, Trotsky was "amiable and responsive" and declared the armistice commission "would be given instructions accordingly." This Judson had reported to Francis, and Robins, pleased as punch, told our little friend Beatty about it.

Later, on December 15, Joffe, heading the Russian delegation, obtained an adjournment for ten days after Minister for Foreign Affairs Von Kühlmann indicated what the Germans meant by self-determination: that Lithuania, Kurland, and parts of Livonia and Estonia already had shown their preference for Germany. Robins wasted no time, rushing to Smolny, where he found Trotsky furious, worried, and most concerned about what the U.S. would do if the Russians walked out for good. It was then that

Judson and Robins went to Francis and, as we now know, obtained his full authority to "go to Trotsky and inform him the [United States] would render all assistance possible."[3]

At the time we didn't know that Robins sent cables via the embassy wire with Francis' reluctant approval to Henry P. Davison, the House of Morgan figure and head of the American Red Cross War Council, urging that pressure be brought on the Wilson administration for full recognition; or that Francis, unknown to Robins and Judson, had his own ideas of what a German peace should be, and informed Washington that if a separate peace proved unavoidable, "it should favor Germany to [the] extent possible in order to make it the more unacceptable not only to the allies but to pacifist and proletariat throughout the world."

But then, on the night of December 19/January 1, had come the cable for Judson's recall. And this still rankled with Reed, who said darkly now, "Remember, Sisson was all sweetness and light and bragging about sending the cable approving Judson's mission to Trotsky. But not long after, the boom falls, and old Judson, stunned, is recalled. I'm not saying Sisson was trying to get him fired. I am saying he's a busybody. And—something has happened to him since then.

"Robins may not notice it. But the great newshawk is busier than ever—and busier having me tailed. I don't have the lowdown, but I suspect Washington told him to tend to his knitting. Not that he will. But if he'd just leave me alone! He's always trying to ferret something out of me."

"I get the feeling something's happened with Sisson, too, but maybe it's just that he feels like an expert on Smolny now, since he went there once with Robins and saw Lenin. Anyway, I'm happy not to have him barging in on us at the Foreign Office any more. I always felt he was too interested in the War Prisoners office next door and that list of visitors they keep. Others than the Five Hundreds can institute a shadow," I said. Reed was silent.

"We ought to get hold of Gumberg today," I said without thinking—but at that same moment I could see it just was not the day to get Gumberg and Reed within reach of each other. "Oh, well, Beatty can tell us later how the Colonel made out with Lenin. I'd like to have seen that."

"The Colonel probably quoted the Bible to him."

Reed was less sympathetic than I with Robins' rather obtrusive enchantment with religion; having been converted to the ministry in the Klondike,

---

3. William Appleman Williams, *American-Russian Relations, 1781–1947*, New York, 1952, p. 121, cites this quote (National Archives, Record Group 59, Francis to Lansing, January 1, 1918, and Judson Diary, December 31, 1917, in the Judson *Mss* at Newberry Library, Chicago) and adds: "Even the British and French admitted it was a great opportunity and agreed to support the decision."

where he had also acquired a comfortable fortune by gold mining, he felt it his mission to bring the Word to all and sundry, and particularly the workers.

"Wonder if Lenin has heard about Thompson's idea: 'Let's make them *our* Bolsheviks.'" Reed laughed. He loved that. Robins had told it to us. He was not so disingenuous as Thompson, although without doubt he saw the same opportunities beckoning for United States capital if Washington could be made sensible to them—opportunities of getting in on the ground floor as the one power befriending this new government whose far-flung plains and mountains contained such riches, whose people would need so many things United States industry could produce.

"Gumberg may have been putting on an act, but it's a wonderful act. You might make it even better, Jack—and undoubtedly will. He does a takeoff on old Francis when he hears of Thompson's proposition, 'Let's make them *our* Bolsheviks.' The Ambassador takes it very seriously. What if in making them ours, before we succeed in changing them, and bringing back law and parliamentarianism and all that, they bolshevize *us*? Francis himself doesn't dare go near Smolny. They're not going to bolshevize *him!*"

"And right he is." Reed was solemn as a judge. "There is too much at stake. For what would he do with Madame de Kram then?"

"There's the Winter Palace," I offered. "Why should a lot of rough workmen have it all to themselves?"

Mayor Lindhagen of Stockholm, a Socialist, came through the press gallery and whispered to Reed, "It's going to be a real Wild West show—everyone seems to be carrying a gun."

It was four P.M. when the assembly opened. In the press gallery we all stopped debating as to exactly where we would hide if the shooting began —flat on the floor or behind the pillars. Sverdlov, chairman of the Central Executive Committee of the Soviets, opened the proceedings. Election of a chairman was to follow. Meanwhile he read all these documents everyone knew the Right SR's would never agree to: the Declaration of the Rights of the Toiling and Exploited People; the resolution the Bolsheviks had been thoughtful enough to prepare for the C.A., offering full support to the Soviet as supreme power, and everything that it had done. Not much was left out: independence to Finland, withdrawal of troops from Persia, the right of Armenia to self-determination, workers' control of factories, seizure of landed estates without remuneration, and determination to march with the Soviet "firmly on this road until the final victory from the yoke of capitalism is won through international workers' revolt."

There was commotion in the press gallery, scornful interjections by reporters as they wrote. I glanced around and found three soldiers breathing down my neck. They evidently took it on themselves to look into this bourgeois-looking crowd up here.

Viktor Chernov, who had been beaten into retreat by little Spiridonova, was running against her for the chairmanship. It was a foregone conclusion he would win. In the intermission, while they were counting votes, I went up to Lenin. He recognized me immediately. (It had been only a few days since we shared the armored-car top at the Mikhailovsky Manège.) I introduced Reed, who was meeting him for the first time. Lenin was the calmest man in all the Taurida that day, I am sure. He asked with interest how my Russian was coming along.

"Can you understand all the speeches now?"

"There are so many words in Russian," I said. And although this is the sober truth—a paragraph of five lines in English becomes ten or fifteen in Russian—this amused Lenin, and he laughed.

Then he said, most earnestly, "You must go at it systematically. You must break the backbone of the language at the outset."

I could see that Reed was virtually bursting with the desire to get an exclusive story, but Lenin launched into a recital of his own method of tackling a foreign language: first, learn all the nouns, learn all the verbs, then all the adverbs and adjectives, then the prepositions and conjunctions; then learn the grammar and rules of syntax—most important; then keep practicing, every day and upon everyone.

Leaning over the box, his eyes alight, Lenin drove his words home, his fingers jabbing the air.

Then, eying us with that faintly skeptical, shrewd, but merry look which was a good deal like a Russian peasant's, and which merited Radek's favorite name for him, "the sly muzhik," Lenin asked how our work at the Propaganda Bureau was coming along. Reed and I were both surprised that he had any idea we were working in the Foreign Office building. "You ought to print your propaganda in English as well as German," he advised. "Then the soldiers reading it in German would see that it was passed along to the English front in time."

Back in the press gallery, Reed and I were the object of envious, even hostile, glances, and were besieged in various tongues. Come on, let us have it, what's the strategy going to be? What did he let you in on? Even Ransome looked skeptical when we insisted that Lenin had not said a thing about the Constituent Assembly. "Then what the devil was he so explicit about?" Just telling me how to get on with my study of the Russian language, I replied meekly. Oh, yeah? The Premier of the Russian Republic takes all that trouble to help you with your Russian? A likely story!

When the ballots were counted, Chernov had 244 to Spiridonova's 151. One speech after another denounced the Bolsheviks. By now more factory workers, sailors, and soldiers had begun to drift into the boxes, filling up empty seats behind distinguished guests, balancing on railings, shouting, *"Doloi! Doloi!"*

Then Tsereteli, Minister of Posts and Telegraph in the old coalition government, arose. He had not been seen in public since the Council of the Republic. Like Tereshchenko, he exercised some charm over our women reporters, and I could hear Louise Bryant utter rapt little adjectives as his sentences rolled forth. "He has that majestic air," she said.

"And you'll be given the air if you keep that up," Reed said.

Already the soldiers in back of us were muttering. "You're giving us the same old thing, siding with the burzhuy," one said. And at the back of the chamber a voice sang out, "Yah, you're working with the Kadets now." The Kadets, who were subject to arrest now, had stayed away, but the objector was right, they were supporting the C.A. It was the one hope left, to which all the embassies, the moderate Socialists, the Kadets, and even the monarchists clung. A slim hope.

When the Bolsheviks demanded that the assembly vote on their proposals, first of all on support of the Soviet, then on the decrees on peace, land distribution, and workers' control of industry, the majority voted to take up first war and peace, then land, and finally the question of "a federated republic." The Bolsheviks asked time to caucus. A half hour was granted. It was midnight, and it was obvious what was going to happen.

During the intermission, which stretched to two hours, I went into the lobby and saw Kollontai again, the intrepid Dybenko at her heels. Now the Marine Commissar and in charge of the defense of the Taurida, he looked a little bored, as if this assignment, defending the palace with all this military hardware against the delegates and their sandwiches and candles, were beneath his skill.

The beautiful and cultured Kollontai, widow of a tsarist officer, was one of our favorite commissars. And though her fellow Bolshevik Central Committee members felt it most inappropriate when she suddenly vanished with Dybenko shortly after October, reputedly to an idyll in the Crimea, and even wanted to expel them both, Lenin intervened. Telling the committee he would deal with the offenders, he summoned Kollontai and Dybenko, told them they had been remiss in leaving their posts without permission, and said that if it were in his power to do so, he would sentence them to spend five years together. This was Jake Peters' story.

So, I thought, seeing Dybenko striding after Kollontai now, at least they seem to be serving out their sentence so far. I am sure Lenin liked to confound the busybodies on the Central Committee. He hated gossip, hated hurting people even when it was to fight on issues, but refused to hurt them over foolish things. In exile he made it a matter of principle never to interfere in the private lives of his fellows.

The story of the rest of the assembly has been told and retold—the negative votes on the Bolshevik proposal, the walkout of the Bolsheviks, Spiridonova's vain attempt to get at least a consent vote on the Soviet government's peace platform, and Spiridonova's walkout, followed by all the Left SR's. Chernov, who earlier had presented the Right SR program, which would substitute the C.A. for the Soviet power, now launched the Right SR proposal on the land, but before discussion had more than started, a Kronstadt sailor named Zhelezniakov sauntered down one of the aisles to the presidium and announced that the assembly must go on home now, "the guards are tired."

Some of the guards fixed their bayonets. Chernov demanded to know on whose instructions the sailor dared to order them to retire.

"Commissar Dybenko."

The guards yawned. The members remained in their places, the bayonets in theirs. Chernov began reading still another decree.

This was too much. A soldier yelled out, "Why wait? We should arrest them all!"

Another voice shouted, "Kill the counterrevolutionary Chernov!"

The delegates, summoning all the dignity they could, straggled out. Some of the Bolsheviks remaining in the palace surrounded Chernov and led him out. As he left, he called up to the press gallery, "You can tell America that we do not recognize this dissolution of the Constituent Assembly. The C.A. will be called again!"

It never was. On the morning the C.A. was dispersed, Jack took it into his head to go on patrol duty with the Red Guards in front of the Foreign Office building. It was all pretty silly, for the C.A. deputies who trailed away in the small hours from the Taurida had no forces, and represented nothing but the dying gasp of the socialists who had lost out. It was right for Jack, however, as it gave him a chance to work off his fury over the way the embassy had begun to set sleuths after his wife. The flatfeet who occasionally followed Reed after his arrival in September only faintly annoyed him, and he brushed them off like insects. But when Louise Bryant had been tailed, it upset her, and this upset Jack.

Reed had calculated that the news of his marching up and down with a gun over his shoulder, along with the Red Guards, would bring a swift complaint from Sisson, and thoroughly enjoyed it when it came. The newshawk approached Reed in all solemnity. He dwelled on Reed's "good family," noted that he was in fact a Harvard man; all of this hurt the Ambassador all the more, when such things as this patrol came to his attention.

Couldn't Reed see that the Bolsheviks were just using him for advertising purposes? Great, said Reed. If the Bolsheviks needed him for advertising, he hoped he could oblige them. At this, the weasel, white-lipped, prim, lugubriously earnest, asked him to cease all his activities on behalf of the Bolsheviks, and to promise him not to speak at the coming Third Congress. Reed told him he was deeply touched by his concern and what he could do with it. He promised Sisson nothing.

·11· Straws in the Wind

The boycott of the peace parleys by the democracies continued, despite the efforts of Raymond Robins and his group. The Western capitalists feared bolshevism almost more than German militarism. They were on the horns of a dilemma no less than the Soviets. The Soviets needed help, and were divided. Some had scruples as to accepting any help from any imperialist government, and preferred revolutionary war to a separate peace; others had doubts as to what they could get; still others, inflamed by the successes they had had, felt that by Trotsky's bold stance at Brest their position was strengthened and German revolution nearer.

In the newness and unique quality of this revolution, one did not look for consistency. Boyce Thompson was attacked in the Bolshevik press "as being the representative of Wall Street and trying to get the Trans-Siberian for the Morgans and copper interests for himself." But by the time he left Petrograd, Thompson was an ardent advocate of recognition of the Bolsheviks, leaving Robins to keep close to Smolny, while, as Robins put it, "it was wise for him to leave and to cooperate at the other end." Thompson had stopped off in London on his way home and, with Thomas W. Lamont, a Morgan partner, had conferred with Lloyd George, who offered enthusiastic support for some joint action friendly to the Bolsheviks. At home, Thompson organized businessmen and saw Senators, and in 1918, when I returned, was still working with Robins to gain consideration for the new republic.[1]

---

1. In 1918 Thompson was speaking publicly but Robins, who had been asked to keep silent by the State Department on his return in June, with Thompson opened a long campaign to argue against intervention as opposed to U.S. interests. He saw government officials and Senators on behalf of American-Russian relations, keeping his silence until he testified on March 6, 7, and 10 before the Overman subcommittee of the Senate Judiciary Committee.

204 · JOURNEY INTO REVOLUTION

There were other Wall Street men recognizing the reality of the Revolution, since they could not wave a wand and make it disappear. Thomas D. Thacher, son of a prominent New York lawyer and himself later a judge, shared a platform with me and denounced intervention before the Economic Club in the Boston City Club on December 20, 1918.

But the man on whom the situation had its most lasting effect was Raymond Robins. A dramatic, complex personality, he was a man who retained his deep loyalties even when to others they appeared conflicting. He owed his presence on the Red Cross mission to Theodore Roosevelt and until Roosevelt's death was unswerving in his devotion to him. Roosevelt had obtained Robins' appointment to the mission after declining to head it himself; he was indebted to Robins, who had broken Democratic party ranks to support Roosevelt's third-party campaign. And Robins stuck with Roosevelt in 1916 when the Democrats, because of Robins' influence with the labor vote, urged his return to the fold. He had begun his political life in Chicago as a crusader for fair voting practices. With Harold Ickes he ran reform candidates in an attempt to oust the control of John Coughlin and Mike Kenna. Like Ickes, he was anathema to the *Chicago Tribune*. He and Ickes were largely responsible for electing and keeping in office a reform mayor, William Dever.

Although staunchly procapitalist, Robins displayed decided realism when it came to the Bolsheviks. "At stake is not what we think they should do, but what they are going to do, and this is what I keep trying to tell Washington," as he put it.

So it was not in the least surprising to me that Robins, as his role of back-door ambassador grew in importance, became more and more impressed with the Bolsheviks. This seemed almost inevitable, surrounded as he was with so much pessimism and suspicion, from the Ambassador on down to Arthur Bullard, on his daily jaunts to the embassy from Red Cross headquarters at the Hotel Europa.

Bullard was the latest addition to the sycophants around Ambassador Francis. Having been brought by Sisson late in November from Moscow, where he wrote for Creel and associated closely with U.S. Consul General Maddin Summers, Bullard became head of the Information Bureau's press section in Petrograd. A former writer for *The Outlook*, and known to me as a fellow contributor and ardent socialist, he was Creel's single experiment with sending over a "sympathizer" with the Revolution. Working for a new master, he had adjusted with alacrity. Even before leaving home, his initiation to the Committee on Public Information was to write, with Ernest Poole, the committee's most catchy brochure, *The Red, White and Blue Book, or How the War Came to America*. And in Moscow, like a chameleon emerging from Summers' vest pocket, he had taken on the

Consul's antipathy for anything Bolshevik (in Summers, it was anything to the left of the monarchy). In Petrograd, part of his job was to keep in close touch with Summers. No longer did he speak, as I had heard him speak, of the inevitability of "honest-to-God class war." Having swung away from the radical stance, he skipped the liberal and went reactionary— the full swing of the pendulum, as he later entitled his book on Russia.

In a burst of confidence, I told Robins that Reed and I had dubbed the Information Bureau the Intelligence Bureau after two illuminating little incidents. One, Bullard himself confessed that he was investigating one of our Russian-American friends. I wondered if I had gone too far, but Robins' glowing eyes took on an extra glow and he demanded, "And the second?"

I explained that Bullard, who was a great talker anyway, and always liked to tell the story of his life, persisted in seeking me out and unloading unwanted confidences. He liked to tell me how much he admired the Bolshevik leaders, Lenin, Trotsky, Lunacharsky, Kamenev, Kollontai. Kollontai especially interested him, as she had lived in Brooklyn and believed, so he was told, in a single standard for the sexes—or, as he called it, free love. (What Brooklyn had to do with it I could not say.) And then one day, in his bland way, he told me he had great respect for Lenin. Yes, he said, he had tried, and was unable to find the least black mark against his character. He himself, personally, would vouch for Lenin as "a man of complete integrity." He looked thoughtful, and then, when I said nothing, volunteered this inside information: With the intelligence services of the British, French, Italians, and Americans, he had "gone over the record of Lenin's life with a fine-tooth comb," and after prying into every nook and corner, gave it up. Not a trace of scandal could be found. No, sir, he said with an amazement that I found singularly distasteful, there was nothing in the record—"not even making a pass at another man's wife."

Robins appeared quietly furious. He was a man of great dignity despite the bluntness and informality he liked to assume, and he did not always reveal his inner feelings. He would have made a good poker player. When he wrote his wife (December 7/20), "Our diplomacy is past speaking about. . . . Each hour I am expecting my recall for my services," I am certain that his intimates had no inkling of these sentiments. He and Judson were "expecting to be reprimanded," the same letter continued. But when Judson's recall came, even the stoical and all-knowing Gumberg seemed jolted. "Well I am almost an anarchist as a result of this experience with the diplomacy of organized government," he continued to his wife. Yet to me he spoke only confidently, even about Ambassador Francis; it was true the old gentleman still did not distinguish between an anarchist, a socialist, a Bolshevik, and a Social Revolutionary, Robins said indulgently, but he no longer thought Lenin and Trotsky were German agents. As for his own staff, Robins could not praise them warmly enough; and this is reflected in the same letter to his wife, when he wrote: "All the men of the Mission are with me heart and soul. . . . Many others here are like-minded and they gather to me as each storm breaks."

The thought of those two Wall Street gentlemen in London trying to sell the Bolshevik government to various members of London's high officialdom must have acted as a tonic to Robins. Apparently Lamont and Thompson, visiting such men as John Buchan, later Lord Tweedsmuir; Sir Edward Carson, in the confidence of the War Cabinet; Admiral Reginald Hall, chief of British Naval Intelligence; Lord Reading; and Montagu Norman, governor of the Bank of England, found them all of like mind. (And writing of it later, Lamont says, a bit unnecessarily, these officials were "all of them hard-headed men.")

At a long breakfast at 10 Downing street, Lloyd George declared himself "strongly in favor of attempting more active cooperation with the new Soviet Government." He was "for something realistic that—even though the chances were against it—might conceivably serve to hold Russia in the war." He proposed a joint Anglo-American Mission of possibly only two or three men, with this in mind—even though Russia might be kept in only "in a purely defensive relation." Then the Prime Minister said the soldiers of the Russian Army, "with no weapons, food or warm clothing, badly led almost to the point of treachery," had reason to return to their homes from the front. In the midst of these moving memories, as Lamont recaptures that turning point in history in which he momentarily played a role friendly to the *enfant terrible* among nations, he stops to apologize for the British Prime Minister. "When he was speaking the Red Terror had not shown its head . . ."

With Lloyd George's farewell ringing in their ears, "You will return, both of you, at once, and see your President. He is full of liberal ideas. He will be ready to act with me," Thompson and Lamont landed in New York on Christmas morning, "never doubting" the President would see them. But Wilson refused. It was reported to them that he did not want to talk to anyone who would "throw away a million dollars" to keep Kerensky in power. So they wrote a memo to him.

William Appleman Williams reports that when, encouraged by certain Senators and other figures, Thompson again sought an interview with the President, it was solemnly explained to him that the President had "a cold."

Certain terms of the Lamont-Thompson memorandum appear equivocal. "Recognition of the Bolsheviks is not essential. Contact is. . . . At the same time it does not bind the Government in any degree. This committee [as proposed by Lloyd George] would deal with conditions. It would work through any and every group in the attempt to arouse Russia to the German menace."

In any event, the stillborn proposal of Lloyd George did not go so far as the standby messages drafted by Robins and initialed by the Ambassador on December 20/January 2. In an early January talk I had with Robins he hinted at these by speaking of "tangible support" the old gentleman had consented to give him which had proved of aid in dealing with Trotsky. One of these documents (neither was sent) we now know promised, in the event the Central Powers refused to conclude "a democratic peace" and Russia was "compelled to continue the war," that Francis would urge upon his government "the fullest assistance to Russia possible." This included munitions for the Russian armies as well as supplies, extension of credits, and technical assistance. And, significantly, the Ambassador said that if hostilities against Germany were seriously pursued by the Russian armies "now under the command of the people's commissaires," he would recommend formal recognition of the government.

In the second, Francis said he was reliably informed that assurances of United States support might decidedly influence the Bolshevik leaders in the event of failure of peace negotiations. Thus he considered it his duty, "notwithstanding previous cables," that he have representatives communicate to the Bolshevik leaders the assurance that, in the event the Russians continued to fight Germany, "I will recommend to the American government that it render all aid and assistance possible." Penciled in the margin was: "To Colonel Robins: This is substance of cable I shall send to Dept. on being advised by you that peace negotiations terminated and Soviet government decided to prosecute war against Germany and Austria-Hungary. D. R. F. 1/2/18."

On January 10 Reed and I were back at the Taurida, where the C.A. had met five days earlier, this time for the opening of the Third Congress. We were waiting for Reinstein, who had decided that Jack and I should draw straws to see which of us would represent the American comrades. Of course, whichever one of us spoke, it would be the usual thing, extending greetings from the Socialists of America—who were by now split over the war, so that we would be representing only part of them.

"I have a hunch," I told Jack now, "that the weasel has got wind of this consul business."

The State Department had been querying Francis as to Reed's activities, for Washington had been alerted by the American Consulate that the Reeds probably would be "carrying papers" when they left Petrograd. Both Louise Bryant and Reed had gone to Trotsky prior to her departure in order to get permission to travel as diplomatic couriers. In that event, their luggage would not be rifled or lost, as some of hers was en route to Russia, it seemed. Each was taking the notes collected over months, all kinds of posters, documents, and newspapers, and Reed was taking samples of all the stuff we had got out for the Bolsheviks. Trotsky had unquestioningly given Louise Bryant courier status. As for Reed, he said he would do better than that: he would make him Soviet consul in New York. It was just the sort of thing that would appeal to both Trotsky and Reed, and if Trotsky hadn't been so humorless, I would have considered it nothing but a spoof from start to finish. I never was sure, nor am I now, how seriously Reed took it, although he enjoyed the idea thoroughly.

"How would Sisson know about it?" Reed asked.

"He knows everything about it, you may be sure, and not through his paid flatfeet. Haven't you told almost half the American colony about it yourself?"

Arno Dosch-Fleurot, correspondent for the *New York World*, was one of those he had told. Reed had said to him, "When I'm consul, I suppose I shall have to marry people. I hate the marriage ceremony. I shall simply say to them, 'Proletarians of the world, unite!'"

"Whether or not he knows about the consul appointment," Reed said, "Sisson probably will do everything he can to keep me from going home. If he weren't such a *little* weasel I'd punch him in the face today."

"Oh, he isn't all-powerful. Besides, he doesn't want you *here*. Just your presence sends the Ambassador's blood pressure up."

Reinstein came along and we drew straws. As luck would have it, I won. I felt rather miserable. I did not need to. When I had said my piece, during the part of the program featuring guests from other lands, the irrepressible Reed decided he would speak, too, and speak he did. Reinstein gave him a flowery introduction that really overshadowed the speech, dwelling on the trial that awaited Reed with other indicted editors of *The Masses*, comparing him with Liebknecht in Germany and working up the crowd greatly.

When Reed finished he resumed his seat beside me and said, "We never got such a reception at home."

Trotsky was back from Brest-Litovsk, and both of us, along with the more than one thousand delegates in the big square glass-domed auditorium, newly draped in red flags, were wild to know what he would report and what Lenin would say on the peace negotiations. Our speeches were short and hardly profound, no more than any visiting fireman's was expected to be. All the stranger, then, is the importance placed on them by a highly respected U.S. historian who, some forty years later, in one of a series of books on U.S.-Russian relations, devotes some 650 words to them, coming up with the conclusion that Reed and I believed fervently in the imminence of revolution in the U.S.[2]

Since the quotes used by the historian do not suggest any such conclusion, the implication is that it was obtained from the parts of our speeches he failed to quote. His version, he says, is from a translation of Russian into English found in the archives of the American Embassy in Petrograd and revised slightly by the author to make it more grammatical. But the quotes used by the eminent historian correspond closely enough to the version used by Sisson thirteen years after the event and attributed to *Izvestia* of January 11 to make it pretty obvious that what lay in the embassy archives was in fact the same translation of *Izvestia*. Sisson uses the entire account of both of our speeches and Reinstein's introduction of Reed, and neither that nor the *Pravda* story of January 12 (two translations of which appear in my files) suggest any belief on the part of Reed or myself in the imminence of revolution in America.[3]

On the contrary, especially considering my previous experience with an interpreter at the First Congress, both newspaper accounts, though full of jargon neither of us would use, indicate surprising restraint on the part of the interpreters who followed us. Even Sisson, to whom both Reed and I seemed to make "a stammering, sorry show" of ourselves, failed to detect our belief in imminent revolution at home.

But then Sisson, whose book came out two years before the recognition of the Soviet Union by the U.S. proved that Robins had been right all along, had not discovered that the best way to discredit his enemy Robins was to paint him as a romantic and visionary, isolated from such pros as Maddin Summers and Francis. And since men who shared Robins' beliefs

---

2. George F. Kennan, *Russia Leaves the War*, Princeton, 1956, pp. 358–360. "Reed, like Williams, used language which clearly endorsed the Soviet brand of parliamentarianism as opposed to that of the Constituent Assembly. He reiterated Williams' confidence in the imminence of social revolution in the United States."

3. Kennan omits the quote attributed to me (not a direct quote) in both the *Pravda* account and the *Izvestia* story as quoted by Edgar Sisson, *One Hundred Red Days*, New Haven, 1931, pp. 257–258 n.

"Comrade Williams says that he is the representative of the proletariat highly developed in the capitalistic sense, but an exceedingly conservative proletariat" (*Izvestia*).

". . . although even in a capitalist country developed to the highest degree, the proletariat is very conservative" (*Pravda*).

To omit it was essential in order not to make ridiculous his "imminence of social revolution in the United States," which he pulled from the air. Kennan puts direct quotes in Reed's mouth when neither newspaper did. And he omits the ensuing sentence, which makes it obvious that Reed, in speaking of his knowledge that the "victory of the proletariat" is "not a dream but a reality," was speaking of Russia, not the United States. He also omits the characterization of America attributed to Reed (*Izvestia*) as "the conservative country of the ruling imperialists." Or (*Pravda*) "the country of deep-rooted reaction and the reign of capitalism." Had Reed felt this proletarian revolution was a "reality" in the U.S., he would not be returning to face trial but to be hailed as a hero, as he was at the Third Congress.

in 1917 included the "romantics" Thompson and Judson, and the British newsmen Ransome and Price, it served Kennan's purpose not to stress them, but to utilize Reed, and even Reed's companion, as copy.

Learning that Lenin's speech would not be given until the second day of the congress, and that Trotsky would report only on the third day, I left the press gallery to prowl around the corridors.

I ran into Arnold Neibut, whom I had seen again in Petrograd a few days earlier. He was going to send a dispatch to his Vladivostok paper, *Krasnoye Znamya,* and said he would quote Reed and me.

"Why, what did we say?"

Oh, he said, nothing special, but there wasn't much to write about that first day.

"It will get lively tomorrow, with Lenin's report—but I hear he will talk about everything *but* peace and war tomorrow," he said.

"But what else can there be to say?"

"Plenty." Neibut eyed me. "Lenin is still pretty much alone, I gather, and the real battle lines won't come out at this Congress even with Trotsky's talk. Trotsky should trim his sails a little, in view of the lousy terms they're offering at Brest, but he'll try to put a good face on things."

I wandered off, mulling over Neibut's words. I felt he saw things more clearly, having been away from Petrograd. There was something compelling to me about his quick lithe movement, his intensity, his openness. Suddenly I heard a familiar voice, low, mocking, inescapable as the clack-clack of typewriter keys. It was Alex Gumberg.

I asked him, partly to irritate him, as I knew he would tell me very little, what was the most that all these interviews between Lenin and Robins and Sadoul, which I assumed he was masterminding, could accomplish. "Ransome, for example, says the democracies don't dare to recognize a socialist government and wouldn't even to keep Russia in the war in some minimal defensive way. Even if the Soviet refuses to make a separate peace, that is."

"I like to hear what your newsmen friends come up with."

"Oh, it's not only they. Shatov claims that the Allies are flirting with Kaledin in the south."

"Don't make the mistake of thinking everything's a *fait accompli* one way or another," Gumberg said, putting on his inscrutable look, which meant either that he knew nothing about the Kaledin business or, if he did, it was none of my business. "But if Lenin thinks it worth while talking to Robins or anyone else, maybe you newspaper fellows should let him." Having vented his sarcasm, he said in another tone:

"Lenin is in the great Marxist tradition—he's treading cautiously, trying to see if one group of the great powers can be played off against the other, before both of them get together and eat up Russia."

I told him I had seen Robins and that he seemed sold on Lenin as well as Trotsky now.

He grinned. "Oh, the Colonel? You know the Colonel doesn't stop halfway. By now he's attributing some of his own best ideas to Lenin. Even puts into Lenin's mouth some remarkable convictions about America. He'll be having Lenin think Theodore Roosevelt is a man of the people next. He believes every word he says, too.

"He has lots of facts about America—which he selects, of course—and Lenin loves facts. He likes Robins, too. Told me so."

I was glad to hear it, but there was something else on my mind. "Alex, what do you know about Sisson's badgering of Reed? And from how far up does it come? And why is it being intensified just at this time?"

For the first and last time I saw the urbane Gumberg flush, but he remained Gumberg, in perfect control, bitterly unpleasant—and objective. "You can tell your pal that all the embassy knows about that consulship gambit, which has not been announced, and never should be. And it's not only Francis that's against it. When Robins heard of it he said, 'Jack already hears the salute of guns hailing his arrival as the first Soviet consul in America. It's just the thing to appeal to his sense of the romantic. But it won't help relations between the two countries.'

"Also, you can tell him that he might as well forget about it."

"Well, is that all there is to it, just this consul thing? Or are there any stumbling blocks going to be put in his way?"

Gumberg never lied to me, and I think he was truthful when he replied, "None that I know of. Like what?"

"Look, don't be a bureaucrat, Alex. You're the last person I thought would ever turn stuffed shirt. You know darned well the main thing Jack is interested in—getting home and writing his book. You wouldn't believe the amount of notes and sources he's accumulated. He fools around, sure, he goes on patrol duty, he makes a big deal of this consulship thing, but he's deadly serious about his work. And you know very well that for weeks he was sending stories not knowing his magazine had folded. Well, what do you think? No one writes without wanting publication. He wants to get home." I walked away angrily.

I went back to the press gallery. Reed was excited, as he had managed to talk to Georgi Vasilievich Chicherin, who had preceded us in speaking. Chicherin, who had been in the tsar's diplomatic service, and active since the 1905 revolution, recently had arrived from England, and was now Acting Commissar of Foreign Affairs while Trotsky was in Brest. He had brought shouts of applause when he said, "Comrades! The proletarian-peasant government of Russia has freed me and my comrades from the prison into which we were thrown by the English imperialists, leaders of world reaction. . . . These English imperialists, who are accustomed to decide the fate of peoples, were the first to yield to the demand of the proletarian government to free us." Reed was convinced, now that he had spoken to Chicherin, that there was real revolutionary ferment in Britain.

I began to argue that he couldn't count on that. "If you hang onto revolution in Germany, in Britain, or wherever, you're seeing things through rose-colored glasses. You fall into the same trap as the Bukharin group, or you get carried away like Trotsky with what might happen."

"Not at all," Reed said. "We don't know yet what Lenin's *Theses* say. But I hear that he is rather rough on the comrades who make the mistake of thinking he's for nationalism. He does not discount revolution in Germany, for example, as I get it—he just won't say *when* it will occur."

"Exactly," I said heatedly. "And that Russia must sign the peace or the Germans will wipe out the October Revolution, while the Allies will turn their heads!"

Trotsky left Petrograd for Brest-Litovsk January 15/28, but not before reporting to the congress, at a session that included also the members of the Peasants' Assembly. He said in part: "The bourgeois governments can sign any kind of peace. The government of the Soviets cannot. Either we shall be destroyed or the power of the bourgeoisie throughout Europe will be destroyed. We have left the imperialistic war and we shall never return to it. I cannot say that the Russian revolution is assured of victory over German imperialism. More than that, I declare that anyone who says that the Russian revolution will not under certain conditions be obliged to accept an unfortunate but not disgraceful peace is a demagogue and a charlatan. We cannot give you a pledge that we will not conclude a separate peace. If we gave such a pledge we should make the Russian army dependent upon French and American gold. We are strong because we are rousing the people's conscience to protest in all countries. The conversation between the Russian revolution and German imperialism is not finished yet. We shall still say our say there and we will not bend our banners." And he asked to be allowed freedom of action, promising he would not sign a nondemocratic peace. He was given a free hand.

Meeting Robins after the speech, I heard him say it was "the greatest forensic effort" he had ever heard. "He got away from the stigma of the revolutionary war-party crowd," Robins said. "And with that remarkable denunciation of imperialism, he goes back to Brest-Litovsk to play his greatest card—the revolution in Germany. The Germans wouldn't be frightened by any revolutionary army that is all but nonexistent. So he is playing all he has—revolution in Germany."

Before the week of the congress ended, news came of strikes in Germany, and reports were received of Soviet victories in the Ukraine and the Don which greatly weakened for the time the Rada groups. Before going on to Brest-Litovsk on January 15, Trotsky termed the strikes "the first recognition of our methods of conducting peace negotiations that we met with from the proletariat of the Central Empires," and claimed the road the delegates were pursuing at Brest was the only one by which the revolution could ensure its development. Even the British Labour party had come to life and issued a statement.[4]

If the mood of the congress had been one of hope and confidence before —and it had—as it wound up, with the added presence of the peasant deputies in full force, it was buoyant beyond belief. Every distant province was represented in this multinational, multicolored throng, many of them picturesquely dressed in their national costumes, expressing by their presence, their songs, and their applause their belief in the future of this government of workers and peasants. And now with the latest news it seemed that this socialist republic might not be so all alone.

Lenin reflected the surging hope in his speech the last day. His first speech, on the second day, had been thoughtful. Marx and Engels had said, "The Frenchman will begin it, and the German will finish it." But today, he said, we can see that it is easier to start a revolution in countries that are not so rich and not so able to bribe the upper section of their workers. The pseudo-socialist parties of western Europe accomplish nothing. "Things have turned out differently from what Marx and Engels expected. . . . The Russian began it—the German, the Frenchman, and the Englishman will finish it, and socialism will be victorious." But Lenin was careful not to say it would be victorious in Russia.

Now on the last day he referred to reports of Soviet victories over the Radas in the south, and of the strikes in Germany in the last few days, and said:

"We are not alone. You have read the news of the revolution in Ger-

4. On January 15 (Western calendar) the British Labour party came to life, issuing an address to the Peoples of Russia and Central Europe and declaring: "The British people accepts the principle of no annexations for the British Empire. This applies in our case to the Middle East, Africa, and India. . . ." It called for the "defeat of militarism on both sides, and . . . the victory on both sides of moral and intellectual fair dealing." To the Peoples of Central Europe it urged they give the same self-determination to members of their states as the Russians gave to Finland, Kurland, Lithuania, and Russian Poland. It even said, "Do not let your Governments drive the British people, as they are driving the Russian people, into the terrible choice between continuing the war and abandoning the only principles that can save the world."

many. The flames of the revolution are drawing nearer and nearer to the old order. It was not a theory, an idea of cloistered people, that we, who formed the Soviet, inspired other countries to make similar attempts. The toilers had no other way of putting an end to this butchery.

"We close this historical Congress of Soviets when everything seems to indicate that the world revolution is growing and that the time is not far distant when the toilers of all lands will unite in one state and together build a new socialist edifice." This was the end of the talk, and it brought down the house.

It was a part of the paradox of the period that, moved and exalted as we felt as we left the Taurida that evening, for we had never heard Lenin when he let himself go as he did in this closing session, we soon fell silent as we walked on past the departing crowds.

"Maybe I like Vladimir Ilyich better when he's sort of sour, at least down to earth, the way he was the other day, better than when he too gets hopeful," Reed said quietly. It was almost a question.

"I know," I said. "You're afraid, when you see everyone else being so emotional all over the place, you're afraid he's catching the fever, and what would happen then?"

In all the excitement of those last days of the congress, about the last thing Reed seemed concerned about was the matter of his appointment as consul general to New York, although by then it had been announced without much fanfare. Jack was too engrossed in the world horizon, which alternately seemed forbidding and storm-racked and glowing with hope, to be aware of the small ominous cloud hanging over his own head.

• 12 • War of Nerves

Lenin's closing speech at the Third Congress may have satisfied the delegates but not Reed and me, and this we were more than ever sure of in the sober light of the next day. The debate over Brest-Litovsk still raged, dwarfing the importance of all else, especially the minor furor created by the announcement of that post of consul general for Reed in New York. Bolshevik and Left SR newspapers began seriously discussing whether the gauntlet thrown down by the Germans should be taken up or whether their terms should be acceded to in order to gain a "breathing space." In the eyes of the extreme left, Bukharin, Radek, Dzerzhinsky, and others, Germany would never dare advance. And yet no word came publicly from Lenin. This omission was what now seemed odd in his closing speech; we had no knowledge yet of that "conspiracy of silence" over the essence of his arguments which he would expose in late February.

We asked ourselves why our first reaction to that moving last speech of his was to feel it answered the questions when it did not even speak of peace. We came to the conclusion that unconsciously we had fallen under the spell of the dogmatists. These included Bukharin, Radek, Dzerzhinsky, and Joffe, as well as some of our Left SR friends who publicly had not yet opposed a separate peace, and most of the anarchists we knew. Without quite admitting it, we had felt that a separate peace would be a betrayal of international socialism, and that the Soviets must maintain a rigid and equally hostile approach to imperialism, whether Entente or Central Powers. Hearing Lenin, we were jubilant—prematurely, we began to suspect. Figuring this out freed us of that feeling of sadness, doom, and disaster which followed the Congress the previous night—when, for all the world like two elder statesmen guarding the Revolution, we adopted a sort of patronizing pity for Lenin and hoped he was not becoming gullible.

"You're just a softhearted poet, Reed, that's what," I said blithely. "No backbone, no real grasp of dialectics."

"And you should end your days as a Welsh ballad singer. And probably will—a traveling troubadour."

We had it figured out now. Lenin, with his ear perpetually to the ground, and not wanting to get too far ahead of the people ("like a good union organizer," Reed said), simply paid recognition, on the final day of the Congress, to the will toward international solidarity which so gripped the psychology of the Russian masses then.

"Especially the proletariat of the cities. But Lenin is still 'the sly muzhik.' It takes time to organize a new army, and it couldn't be done without the peasants. And no amount of international pie-in-the-sky will make up to them for some peace *now*. Besides, as I get it, he can't start to prepare the people while the Bolsheviks' leading body is divided. He may be thinking the time isn't far off when he'll go to them again over the leaders' heads; but meanwhile he's hedged in by rules. And whatever the Central Committee's final decision is, they all have to go along with it, even Lenin. Reed, you and I would make terrible Communists."

"Speak for yourself. It's whoever can argue best that wins. More than you can say for the Democratic and Republican parties."

"Yes, but you're such a rotten arguer, Jack."

We decided to see what Peters made of it. The soggy snow lay in dirty, uneven heaps in streets that had not been cleared in weeks. A hint of thaw and coming spring was in the air. We climbed up the stairs to the top floor of the old police station on the Korokhavaya where Peters had his office. How had he interpreted Lenin's latest speech? Each of us told him our "analysis." Each of us he smacked down—without sarcasm, gently, as was his way. I was wrong; it was not that the high mood of the congress called for such a speech. "Lenin is always honest with the workers." It was not that Lenin would simply go along with the majority in the committee, either. "Lenin is no flutterer in the wind. He was responding to changed objective circumstances. A million workers on strike in Germany —it's something to consider.

"He's willing to let Trotsky try his hand at stalling a while longer. So long as they can keep the parleys going, there's that much more chance of the German revolution."

We were subdued, even if we were not entirely "clarified."

Lenin's Theses still went unprinted, but before Reed left Petrograd (about January 24/February 6) Reinstein gave us a skeleton version of key points in the "Theses on the Question of Immediate Conclusion of a Separate and Annexationist Peace." Even the title was typical of Lenin. No whitewashing for him, no pretense it could be any democratic peace. Reinstein was present when some sixty Petrograd Bolshevik leaders heard them on January 8. What he considered key points included:

• The socialist revolution in Europe will, of course, take place. Confidence in final victory is based on scientific analysis. Propaganda must be increased, and fraternization at the front.

• The tactics of a socialist government could not be based on a prediction that the European, especially the German, revolution would be within six months, or any such time, or at all.

• It was not a question of choosing which imperialism was preferable. The only consideration was how best to develop and strengthen the one socialist revolution that "has already begun," in one country. And this should be done precisely because it would benefit world revolution.

Reinstein said the issue was not whether world revolution was at stake; no one group was more in favor of it than another, it was basic to all. The issue was simply whether to refuse to accept any peace save one that was without annexations and indemnities. The group was split into three main camps, Lenin's strongest opposition by far the revolutionary-war group headed by Bukharin. Trotsky already had shifted some in his position, his "third force" role flexible and reminiscent of his role in the early exile period after 1903, when he veered from Mensheviks to Bolsheviks. Lenin earlier had called this unprincipled in Trotsky, Reinstein said. "But now Lenin needs him. He has few supporters. And, " he said with a smile, "he is rather rough on those he does have."

At the January 11 meeting, when instructions were voted for Trotsky's directions at Brest, two small happenings were described to us that illustrated Lenin's essential character. Lenin would change his viewpoint to fit changing circumstances, but he refused to water down or sweeten the circumstances. And twice when one of the few supporters he had at the time spoke out in his favor, it was only to be corrected by Ilyich. He wanted support, but not on opportunistic grounds. Each point must be fully understood—concretely, and on its principle. He would flay others with fiery invective for invoking principle by "the revolutionary phrase," for placing principle on parade. But his own was built-in.

"Stalin and Zinoviev each made an effort to come to Ilyich's rescue," Reinstein said in a very dry manner, quite unlike his usual sweetness. "Stalin said there is no revolutionary movement in the West, no facts, only a potential movement. Zinoviev said that by making peace we would strengthen chauvinism in Germany and for a while weaken the revolutionary movement everywhere in the West, but this was better than 'the ruin of the socialist republic.'

"Lenin would not have either argument. Stalin was wrong. Of course there is a mass movement in the West, Lenin said, but the revolution over there is not yet under way. And if the Bolshevik party changed its tactics because of that, we would be betraying international socialism. Zinoviev was wrong, too; the conclusion of peace would not slow down the movement in the West. But if we do believe that the German movement could develop immediately if the peace talks were broken off—if it were a question of sacrificing the Russian to the German proletariat—then we must sacrifice ourselves, because the German revolution would be much more powerful than ours, and infinitely more important.

"But such was not the case. Germany, he said, was 'only big with revolution,' whereas 'over here we have a lusty infant,' a socialist republic 'screaming with all its might.' "

"So what was the end result of all this?" Reed asked Reinstein.

"It was beautiful!" Reinstein said, looking out the windows of the Foreign Office building at the gathering dusk, a smile lingering on his lined face. "Oh, the result? Trotsky had his way."

But Lenin had won two Americans over to his side, anyway.

Even Robins had attended the meeting of January 8 where Lenin read his Theses. Gumberg was able to arrange for it, as it was not a formal Central Committee meeting, but an enlarged meeting. Robins found Lenin's twenty-one theses "crushing," but saw that Lenin let Trotsky sway the meeting, and later asked Lenin why. Lenin said he was willing to let Trotsky put off the peace, or save them from it if he could. "But I wanted the comrades to know what I am thinking. . . ."

On February 26 in Christiania, Reed received two cables from America. One, signed by Lincoln Steffens and Reed's wife, Louise Bryant, read: "Don't return, await instructions." By this time Reed was already in Christiania, on his way home.

The second was signed by Steffens, the writer and editor who had made Reed his protégé when, on leaving Harvard, the youthful poet went to New York looking for a writing job:

"Trotsky making epochal blunder doubting Wilson literal sincerity. I am certain President will do whatever he asks other nations to do. If you can and will change Trotsky's and Lenin's attitudes you can render historical international service. Steffens."

Reed's biographer, telling of the cables and lamely trying to excuse Steff's idiocy, which Steff himself would not have done later, fails to tell what Louise Bryant told on the witness stand in 1919: that Steffens came to her from George Creel, chairman of the wartime Committee on Public Information. But Reed did not need to know that Steffens' cable was inspired by Creel to know it was a lemon. He cabled back that if a group of revolutionary leaders, including Eugene Debs and Bill Haywood, asked him to, he would go back to Petrograd and see what he could do; otherwise he would not.

However, Reed was in no danger of returning home for some time. Sisson had seen to that.

In addition to the cable Jack sent Steffens, another document is added proof that it is not the hindsight that often overtakes men in their later years that makes me certain that, despite our veerings and setbacks, Jack and I reached a certain understanding of the complexities of Brest-Litovsk before his departure. Although Jack's letter to Robins, dated January 11, 1917— showing that even as good a newspaperman as Reed can be absentminded about dates, for it was of course 1918—which I shall reproduce here, does not directly mention Brest-Litovsk, it makes it amply clear that Reed was under no illusions about Allied motives. I give it in full, too, because the document also reveals the pressures Reed was under as he sought a ship to the United States, and breathes his sense of his own dignity and purpose and his uncompromising integrity.

My dear Colonel Robins—

I have been thinking over all you said.

Now I know you will pardon me if I speak my mind, for I do it with the greatest regard for and belief in you, as well as the greatest admiration for what you have done in Russia.

Am I wrong when I think that your main objects are: first, to crush German autocracy—second, to further the legitimate greatness of America?

As for me, I am working for international democracy *from below*—the only way I believe it can come. There are conflicts, as you know, between our two ways of thinking. But I don't think you judge me right when you call my method a "strait-jacket" formula. However . . .

Now I think that this affection for the Bolsheviks on the part of the Allies is inspired by the glad belief that Russia will join them once again in their war aims, which, according to Woodrow and Lloyd George, are still a little Alsace-Lorrainish, if I may put it so. The Allies don't yet want a really democratic peace—and of course Germany doesn't. I myself wouldn't fight for anything less, nor work for it. Therefore I wouldn't work for any one of the allied governments, *unless at the same time it furthered the cause of international democracy*. On this point we can come together somewhat.

I am in favor of putting over such parts of the President's speech as agree with the general democratic interest. I am in favor of this not for money, or statements from the Ambassador, etc.

I appreciate very much all you have done for me, and am most grateful for anything you can of your own free will say to signify that I am not corrupted by anybody's money—neither the Germans' nor the Americans'—that I am working for things I believe in, and am willing to sacrifice for, and that I have not knowingly violated my agreement with the State Department.

It would also be of great help to me to have a statement from the Stuffed Shirt to the effect that I am *not* the dangerous dynamiter and German spy that he has described me in official dispatches to his Government—and mine.

I should of course be also grateful if both or either of you could honestly say that I have done my best to aid the cause of democracy against autocracy—the Germans' as well as our own—while I was here. But I wouldn't like to be put down by anybody as having served the interests of the United States or any other capitalist Government, for I haven't—if I could help it.

Let me add that your personal friendship and kindliness in personally lending me this money when I needed it, without any thought of obligation on my part, I shall always remember. I may have to call upon you even again, and I want you to believe that I do so because you are a friend of mine, for whom I would, and will, do as much if ever I can—and not because I wanted to bleed you.

Yours very truly,
[signed] JOHN REED[1]

Ambassador Francis initiated the move to have Reed's consul appointment canceled and asked Robins to try to persuade the Soviet government that it was unwise. Robins asked Gumberg, and of course Gumberg was delighted to oblige. Therefore I dismiss as suspect Sisson's claim that it was really *his* accomplishment and that Gumberg was doing *his* bidding. Kennan writes that Gumberg says he himself told Jack he had had it canceled, but does not say when he told him. Francis and Sisson are his

1. Robins MSS (Wisconsin State Historical Society, Madison), which also contains an IOU from ARW to Robins on an American Red Cross letterhead, in his handwriting, reading:

Petrograd
Feb 20 1918.
One year from date I promise to pay Raymond Robins
Six Thousand Roubles   6000
Value Received   Albert Williams

It is not surprising that both Reed and ARW were forced to float a loan from someone. Their pay from the propaganda bureau of the Foreign Affairs department was 50 rubles a month, the same as the pay provided for Red Army men in February.—ED.

sources for saying Reed knew before he left Petrograd that he was not to be a consul. I do not recall that Jack was told about it officially in Petrograd; but as I was never too sure how serious he was about the post that he and Trotsky had cooked up between them, I may simply have forgotten. My notes only say that "Reinstein told us" what had occurred, and these are undated, without any indication that "us" meant Reed and me, though it usually did. I knew later that at home the story of the cancellation was not printed until February 18 in *The New York Times*. Under a London dateline, the story, headed, "Drop Reed as Consul?" related that "a belated dispatch from Petrograd" said Reed had left Petrograd as a private citizen, his appointment withdrawn. The story alluded to "a previous dispatch from Stockholm" which "said Reed had arrived there on his way to New York to take the post of Consul."

I give Sisson full credit, however, for the dirtiest, most vindictive, and foulest trick one ex-newspaperman ever played on another.

Francis had given Reed a letter directing passport-control officers and censors to pass him without examining his papers until he reached home, where, the letter made plain, they would be examined thoroughly—a fact Sisson fails to mention when bragging of his exploit. Obviously Sisson and most of the other American personnel must have known about Francis' letter, and thus known Reed's papers would be searched on his arrival. But this was not good enough for Sisson.

It is impossible to assign a rational motive to an act so vindictive as Sisson's. In any event, it gave Sisson a strange pleasure, judging from his words printed long afterward,[2] to recall that it was he who engineered Reed's being detained in Christiania. Reed arrived there February 19 (the Russian calendar by now was the same as the Western calendar). The boat on which he had passage to New York sailed on February 22. The consul at Christiania told Reed the State Department had ordered him to withhold Reed's visa. He was not under arrest, he just could not get home—not until April, when the next boat sailed. He rented a room and made a start on his book, *Ten Days That Shook the World*.

Sisson gives two versions, some thirty pages apart or less, of why he took the trouble to see to it that Reed was exiled in Christiania for two months. Both are guardedly worded, but in the first version it seems he was afraid Reed would serve as consul when he got home; and in the second, that there never had been any intent to have Reed as consul, and that it was all a

2. "He [Reed] left Russia . . . with so much rumor circulating as to what he was to do upon his return to the United States that it seemed advisable that he should be received at home with some care. He was delayed so long in Sweden [sic] that I reached the United States not long after he did. In the State Department at Washington I found waiting for me his papers." Sisson, *One Hundred Red Days*, p. 259.

trick, directed at Sisson personally, of course, to get Reed home safely with his "papers."

It is with satisfaction that Sisson notes that he himself was home not long after Reed got there, and that all Reed's papers were waiting on his desk for his perusal. He fails to explain just how he worked this feat. He says he kept the consulship-appointment paper, adding, as if it were a truly magnanimous act, that he returned Reed's notes. "Handsome and spoiled, I am afraid that Jack Reed never quite grew up." Shedding crocodile tears over Reed's fate, he adds, "Poor, brilliant, unhappy Reed!"

Well, it takes a lot of nerve to patronize John Reed, but less when he is dead. Sisson waited until 1931 to do it.

I believe Lewis Gannett wrote the most effective reply to Reed's detractors, friend or foe, when he recalled the Reed who returned from Russia in 1918: "He began calling himself a communist; old friends said of him that a good poet had been spoiled by politics, which wasn't quite true: all politics, and especially revolution, was poetry to Jack Reed."[3]

Interestingly enough, Sisson at no point in his book goes into the business of what the evidence was that Gumberg uncovered to get the consulship revoked, or even mentions how he performed his mission. Max Eastman has written a more interesting and flamboyant account of the consulship cancellation than mine will be, in which he puts Gumberg in the act of stealing the evidence from a drawer in Jack's desk. This will be my first touching on the matter in print, and I do so now only because Jack's biographer dealt with it so elliptically, and other accounts have been so overstressed, if not downright malicious.

And since the eminent historian Kennan spends some six pages in his account of the revocation of Reed's consul appointment, and finds that two documents were involved, of such an incriminating nature that

---

3. The first revolution covered by Reed was the 1913 Mexican Revolution, for *Metropolitan* magazine and the *New York World*, his reporting bringing from Walter Lippmann the following:

Dear Jack,
    Your first two articles are undoubtedly the finest reporting that's ever been done. It's kind of embarrassing to tell a fellow you know that he's a genius, but you're in a wild country just now. I can't begin to tell you how good the articles are. If you keep it up we'll all be able to sit comfortably at home and know all we wanted to know. That's the only immoral thing about your work. You make it unnecessary for the rest of us to stir. You have perfect eyes, and your power of telling leaves nothing to be desired. I want to hug you, Jack.
    If all history had been reported as you are doing this, Lord—I say that with Jack Reed reporting begins. Incidentally, of course, the stories are literature, but I didn't realize that till afterwards. They were so much alive with Mexico and with you.
                                                                                    Affectionately,
                                                                                    Walter

(John Reed Collection)

With its forty thousand workers, the Putilov factory (a steel plant) played a vital role before and after the October Revolution. Among other factories, Williams and John Reed visited it in their search for information after the Kornilov revolt failed. This photograph was taken in January 1918.

Thousands of soldiers and workers before the Winter Palace, listening to the harangues of Bolshevik leaders.

Boris Reinstein, for whom
Williams and Reed went
to work in the Propa-
ganda Bureau immedi-
ately after the October
Revolution. He helped
them both with the Rus-
sian language. (JOHN REED
COLLECTION, HOUGHTON LI-
BRARY, HARVARD)

Lying off Petrograd, the cruiser *Aurora* fired blank cannon shots at the Winter Palace to signal the fall of Kerensky's Provisional Government. When Williams, Reed, and the others arrived at the palace, Kerensky had fled, though the ministers were still sitting around a table, in session.

Imperial soldiers join the Revolution in Petrograd, riding on the footboard of a motor car with red flags flying from bayonets. (CULVER)

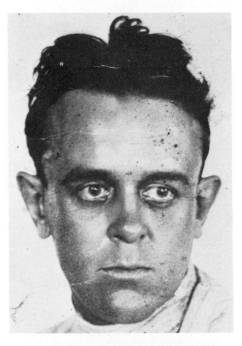

John Reed, after his arrest by Finnish authorities and his imprisonment at Abo early in 1920. Reed had been trying to return to the United States and had stowed aboard a Finnish ship bound for Sweden. He was held incommunicado for several weeks. (JOHN REED COLLECTION, HOUGHTON LIBRARY, HARVARD)

Louise Bryant, Reed's wife, was with him when he arrived in Petrograd. She returned to the United States in January 1918, then went to Russia a second time in 1920, disguised as a sailor. She was with Reed when he died of typhus in Moscow in October 1920.

Cossacks on whom General Kornilov depended to capture Petrograd in order to force a change of government. But the well-organized propaganda of the Bolshevik workers persuaded them to desert Kornilov and join the uprising of the people. The banner reads, "Down with Kornilov." Williams, who was away from Petrograd early in August, returned in time to see the failure of the "Kornilov affair." (CHARLES PHELPS CUSHING)

Tsar Nicholas II was sent to join his family at Tsarskoe Selo the day after his abdication on March 2, 1917. Here he exercised by gardening and chopping wood. Later the royal family was exiled to Ekaterinburg at the foothills of the Urals, and there shot probably on the night of July 16, 1918. (BROWN BROTHERS)

"they were shocking to Lenin," I find myself in the position of defending a man who needs no defense.

Frankly, relating who said what and why about that consul business would seem pretty unimportant to me were it not thus elevated to a new status by a critic who would seem to be more radical than Lenin and at the same time to be justifying United States policy by slandering Jack. I am Jack's friend. I was there. I knew pretty much what went on, and if I did not, I did not read Lenin's mind. And I did know Jack. Not to settle the score now would be a shame.

First of all, since the only "document" that Reinstein spoke of in his account to me was written by Jack for Colonel Robins, at the latter's urging, I see no reason to think Gumberg had to steal anything; certainly he knew just where to look for it—probably a drawer in Robins' desk. Copies of both documents are now in the Robins collection at Madison, Wisconsin.

At any rate I will recall what I remember about the circumstances surrounding this document Reinstein spoke of. I do not remember the date or approximate date of Robins' request to Jack. I do remember that the Reeds were broke at the time, so I judge it was before we got any pay for writing captions and stories for the Foreign Office's Propaganda Section. Jack had been cabling *The Masses* for money in vain. Since in normal times the magazine had no money, Jack assumed it was more of the usual. He had no idea at the time of *The Masses'* troubles with the Post Office Department, or that a grand jury was investigating the editors, including himself. So he mailed his copy rather than cabling it—and grumbled, hilariously at times. His revolutionary magazine, he would complain to all and sundry, could not scrape up money for cables on the only revolution of its kind in history. The editors couldn't even manage postage to tell him they were shipping him a bag of potatoes and onions and canned corn beef at the earliest opportunity.

It seems that Robins and Thompson, having learned that the concept of Revolution held by the people in the chancelleries and embassies bore little resemblance to the reality, and deciding that it was a great elemental popular movement of the people and would last, had revived and completely renovated one of their schemes. This was the idea of a newspaper. Originally, before October, it was to keep Kerensky in power and Russia in the war. Now they conceived of starting an official daily American newspaper in Petrograd that in the long run would help American businessmen sell a lot of needed products to a democratic Russia, and in the meantime might create a friendly attitude toward the United States, which they hoped would keep the Russians from making peace with Germany. Since they were confident at the time that they could obtain first *de facto* recognition and then *de jure* recognition for the new socialist republic, the plan was not so outlandish as it might seem today. There were other foreign newspapers published there, including the *Journal de Russie,* the *Entente,* and a paper in English, the *Russian Daily News.* When Robins asked Jack for some of his technical knowledge in the form of what he called a "prospectus," he was turning to someone well known as a professional reporter, and with some knowledge of layout acquired on *The Masses.* But Jack was embarrassed. He had joked around about *The Masses'* finances and his own impoverished condition, and he wondered if Robins were just giving him a task as a handout. Besides, he had some scruples about it. (There was never even a suggestion on anyone's part that Jack be attached to the paper, let alone edit it. A hornet's nest like Jack would be the last thing they wanted, and besides, they knew they couldn't get him. So Granville Hicks was confused on this point.) Finally Reed agreed to do a technical job for Robins.

I assumed it was only a dummy he had to get out, showing the number of pages he envisioned, and a sample makeup for page one, with sample headlines and type size and possibly type faces indicated. I heard him grumbling and fretting over whether a routine thing like this was a violation of revolutionary ethics. No matter what its pronounced goals or its limited and selected readership, such a paper would mislead the masses. And so on. Getting a little tired of all that, I told him I thought better of the masses, and so should he.

One day he mentioned that Robins had come by their hotel and he had turned the thing over to him. "Anyway," he said triumphantly, "I dummied in a line under the masthead: 'This paper is devoted to promoting the interests of American capital'!"

I remember too the embarrassment of Louise Bryant when she later found that Robins had tucked a thousand-ruble note under some object on a table in their hotel room; but they took it because they were broke.

Reinstein said that Gumberg put the "newspaper thing" in Lenin's hands. Edmund Wilson, in his study "Lenin: The Great Headmaster," finds that Lenin "tended to trust people perhaps excessively," and I agree. In this case, however, his trust embraced Gumberg and left Jack out in the cold. Naturally, he would think Gumberg disinterested. I feel certain that Lenin weighed whatever words Gumberg spoke on this occasion without its ever occurring to him that Gumberg might have some personal axe to grind. So I can see him confronting Trotsky, possibly half jokingly, when he was back from Brest—for certainly weightier things were on their minds —saying, as Reinstein told me he said, "Why do you trust a man like this, who works one day for the capitalists and the next day for the Revolution?" But as I told Reinstein at the time, "Too bad someone couldn't have let him

know that there's bad blood between Reed and Gumberg. After all, couldn't
the same thing be said of Alex? He really does have a foot in each camp.
I'm not saying he won't serve them both. But where does he get off crying
out that Reed works for two masters?"

By that time, however, Lenin had acted, and the consul appointment
was formally canceled by Chicherin.

Despite Sisson's omission of any mention of it, Kennan accepts Gumberg's version that one of the two documents Gumberg presented to Lenin
to obtain the consul cancellation was Reed's proposal for a newspaper, a
proposal he submitted to Sisson! Kennan declares he has looked over a
copy of each document and that both "were indeed curious ones to flow
from the pen of John Reed."

A copy of a typed nine-page document headed *Russisches Tageblatt*,
dated November 27, 1917 (which was only two days after Sisson arrived in
Petrograd from the United States, assuming Reed used the Western calendar), is among the Robins manuscripts, which together with the Gumberg manuscripts are in the Wisconsin Historical Society's archives at
Madison. It does not bear the name of John Reed, nor is it attributed to him
by any notation affixed to it. It is not in Reed's familiar typing (no words
are crossed out with dollar marks; in fact, it is letter perfect, and its neatness
does make it a queer thing to have issued from any newspaperman's typewriter). It could very well have been retyped, however, and some of the
phrasing sounds like Jack's; some does not. The document clearly states
it is for a newspaper to be published in English, not Russian, as Kennan
states.

It might even be a combination of something Jack wrote, rewritten
later and added to at a time when Sisson and Robins were close, for in a
December 21/January 3 cable to Creel, Sisson declares, "Presently may be
desirable to start our own newspaper." The only thing that definitely sounds
unlike Jack in the November 27 document is the sentence: "If Gumberg
could be persuaded to stay, he would make a wonderful thing out of the
business management. I know something of his record in New York." The
fact is that the document is entirely innocuous, as innocuous as the other
one; though this is the one that Kennan says "must have made Lenin jump."
Interestingly enough, Kennan uses not a single quote direct or indirect
except Reed's assurance (he assumes it is Reed's) that the paper will be
welcomed by the Soviet government. He does not use the paragraph that
immediately follows:

> Trotsky says Russia needs capital for development, and in a non-
> Socialist world Russia can not be wholly Socialist. But under a really
> democratic regime in Russia, foreign capital will not be permitted to

grab the country and enslave the nation as it has done in Egypt, Turkey, Mexico and other "backward" places. Any movement by American capital, based frankly on the fact that Russia needs capital but will not be throttled by it, and that American capital needs dividends but will not attempt to throttle Russia, will be welcomed.

In the "Declaration" the purpose was stated to be "to promote American business in Russia, and friendship and understanding between the two peoples." And the declaration ended with the following:

This newspaper recognizes unqualifiedly the right of the Russian people to shape their own destiny. We will obey whatever laws the Russian people see fit to make. We will not interfere in Russian politics.

As can be seen, even though the document in the Robins collection has no dummy attached bearing the words that Reed told me he dummied in below the masthead, no one on either side of the Atlantic could find anything "shocking" here.

The other document cited by Kennan in his account of the consulship business (one copy of which is in Harvard's John Reed collection and another in the Robins collection) was entitled by Reed "Skeleton Report." It is a typed summary, with his name typed on the first page (I have no doubt this is Reed's, as there are various words crossed out by use of the dollar mark), of interviews with Left SR's and Bolsheviks in government. It is a report of their thinking on future trade and commercial relations with capitalist states, especially the United States, and nowhere goes as far as the actual relations that Lenin encouraged and put into effect to the limit of his abilities. For example, those interviewed by Reed opposed outright any concessions. Kennan, however, has quoted some 20 words from the report of more than 1,000 words—the only passage that might possibly be misinterpreted—and on this manages to give the impression that Reed is betraying the working class, a matter Kennan feels rather sad about. The line is: ". . . the Russian Government is prepared to recognize the necessity for the establishment of a restricted capitalistic state within the bounds of a Socialist state. . . ."

Obviously it could not be much of a "capitalistic state" Reed had in mind when he warned that any capitalists dealing with Russia would find rigid enforcement of such items as government of industry by the workers; confiscation and nationalization of natural resources; public ownership of land for the benefit of the peasants; socialization of banks, "and in general the utmost restrictions upon capital." Foreign or domestic capital would have to be sought for building some railroads, but here, as with public utilities, "this will be with the strict understanding that they are to pass into the control of the Government within a fixed time." All those interviewed agreed that compensation "should not take the form of either concessions (commercial or otherwise) or of a preferential commercial arrangement."

Does this sound like the betrayal of socialism that seems of such concern to Kennan? Significantly, after outlining the great need for locomotives, with spare parts, and steel and pig iron in immense quantities, Reed added in italics: "*Technicians, mechanics and railroad organizers are not wanted.*" Russia had plenty of expert mechanics and technical men, the commissar-to-be of railroads told him, "and if more men are needed, or more knowledge, men will be sent to America and Europe to study." Foreigners coming there to run railroads or industries would try to manage things as they had in their own countries, and "would run up against the new source of power in all Russian affairs—*the control from below.*" (His italics.)

There would be time later for complicated planting and harvesting machinery, after the government's plan for agricultural education bore results. Now what was most needed, he said, were simple tools, spades, shovels, plows, hoes, rakes, axes, tractors if simple ones.

He placed first importance on items for the Public Welfare Department, under our friend Kollontai. "Before anything else the Russian people have got to have food, especially canned stuff, shoes, clothes and cloth, and enormous amounts of milk for the babies—*immediately.*" (Reed's italics.)

Kennan suggests also that possibly "Reed's curious proposals were designed, with tongue in check, as a device with which to whet the appetites of American financiers and persuade them that American business had a future in Russia even under Bolshevik power."

If they were "designed, with tongue in check" and so on, was this without Lenin's knowledge, and was it thus that he was so shocked? Just in the event Mr. Kennan's curious interpretations are made in honest ignorance of Lenin's position, I will quote what Lenin told Louise Bryant in later years in what is marked in the John Reed collection as the first interview Lenin gave after the blockade:

> I told Americans, Colonel Robins for one, early in 1918 that it was to the interest of the United States to be friendly to Soviet Russia. As long ago as that I pointed out the desirability of commercial relations both from our point of view and America's. We offered concessions to foreign capital. American business men now arriving in Moscow agree with us. Outside of all political questions the simple fact remains that America needs our raw material and we need American goods.

Only a few days after Reed left Petrograd, I ran into young Allen Wardwell. Wardwell and Thacher were aides of Robins', and were dubbed the "Bolsheviks of Wall Street" by Gumberg. I was glad to see him. What was new with Sisson? I asked. What was he ferreting out now?

What, I hadn't heard? He and Robins had broken, for good, it seemed. "Sisson has made a discovery—Lenin is in the pay of the Germans. He's had some trouble justifying the immediate situation. As Robins said when he talked to Trotsky initially, 'Mighty peculiar kind of German agent.' Sisson and the Ambassador have become very cozy."

"And where is Gumberg?"

"Oh, he no longer works for Sisson, only for the Colonel. I guess Gumberg was in on one scene between Robins and Sisson. The Chief said later that just as the situation was at its most tense and acrimonious, he looked away from Sisson and saw Gumberg in the corner of the room, 'laughing like a hyena.'

"So Sisson, I suspect, is sending messages in code to Washington, trying to undermine everything Robins is trying to accomplish. But the Chief is still trying. He rushed to see Trotsky the moment he returned for the Third Congress, and made a special report to Francis. I think the Ambassador is getting frightened. He repeats, 'Nothing will make me flee. Even if the Germans come, I must hold the fort.' "

Of course, we didn't take seriously this new "discovery" of Sisson's. No sane government believed the German-gold myth any longer. Even had we known that Sisson was working with Semenov, the discredited one-time editor familiar to every embassy as a peddler of forged documents, it wouldn't have seemed important to us.

Sisson puts the date of his final break with Robins as February 11 (January 30). His parleys with Francis on Semenov and his attempts to procure newer and better German-gold documents he places as beginning February 5 (January 24). He says Robins showed him his first set of the German-gold documents on February 2. William Appleman Williams, the historian who exhaustively studied the Gumberg and Robins manuscript collections, states that Gumberg "obtained the first set of documents for Sisson"—not because he believed them valid but in answer to what appeared to be a casual request for a curiosity.

Robins testified before the Overman subcommittee later: "There were more forged papers of one kind and another in Russia than ever before in human history. There were forgery mills of the old Okhrana, the secret police, forged against the revolutionists, and of the revolutionists forged against the Okhrana. Passports and letters were forged in great numbers. You could not beat it in a million years. I could prove anything by all the documents you want."

Written years after he finally released the documents in a sensational series (the second installment of which was spread across page one in San

Francisco the day I landed there, September 16, 1918), Sisson's book tries
to make up for anything they lacked in the way of authenticity by a most
remarkable purple passage. He says he was convinced Lenin was a German
agent the day that he and Robins interviewed him on January 11 (or
December 30, by the old calendar).

When did this occur to him? Obviously not on January 11, or at least
no mention was made of it in a "serial letter" he began to his wife January
13. He does not say when the letter was completed. He quotes the letter,
more than 1,500 words. It was chatty. He said it was the first time he or
Robins met Lenin, for while he himself "had channels running to every
seat of power, I have camouflaged as a newspaper man. . . . Even on this
occasion I went only as the head of the American Press Bureau."

He described Lenin: "short, sparsely bearded, a bronze man in hair
and whiskers, small, shrewd eyes, round of face, smiling and genial when
he desires to be. And this time he did." And on Lenin's reaction to the
President's Fourteen Points speech, in addition to quoting Lenin's favorable remark, Sisson fairly bubbles over:

> He was as joyous as a boy over the President's humanly understand-
> ing words to Russia, and his recognition of the honesty of Bolshevik
> purpose.
> "Yet I have been called a German spy," he said, and smiled and
> threw up the palms of his hands.
> His only criticism was on the colonial clause, which is the only
> weak clause in the message. When he went unerringly for it, I knew
> that he had the gift for finding the cracks in any armor. But he
> wasn't fanatic and took the practical view that the word "equitable"
> could be turned in a Bolshevik direction no less than in an Imperial
> direction.

The letter continues to relate all the busy activities occupying Sisson
since the interview to get the President's speech out in roughly about two
million copies (including use of *Die Fackel*). Then, several pages after
the letter ends, Sisson returns to his meeting with Lenin, which "I described
in my letter as it was." Then: "In early retrospect of the meeting, I per-
ceived, however, that none of my distrust of Lenin was lessened, although
my respect for his ability had increased. On Robins the effect was different.
Some fire in him was lighted. Lenin, too, must have observed something
malleable in him. Mischief came of the contact between the two." He
never places when this afterthought, or "early retrospect," takes place, but
says that he and Robins "in a day's time"—whether a day after the unnamed time of retrospection or a day after the interview is not clear—were

"acridly debating Lenin; while the break was delayed, it had its beginning then." Then his own inner vision is described in mystical language.

As I turned over the incidents of the session with Lenin a lower stratum of my mind began to send its message upward. When it broke through I found myself repeating Lenin's sentence, "Yet I have been called a German spy!" Without incentive from us he had spoken from inner compulsion. We had heard the voice of his brooding. The subject was one he hugged to himself, however unwillingly.

None of this feeling did I put in my letter, as I had suggested to my wife that the letter be shown to George Creel—and he might show it to others. A letter was no place for analyzing a mental problem.

He does not say whose mental problem, but the assumption is that it was Lenin's.

He confided in Robins, and Robins resented his conclusions. Sisson says Robins contended Lenin "spoke from hurt innocence." (Robins always spoke in picturesque, vivid language. Such cloistered, motive-seeking language I do not recognize as his.)

If ever a man had a hard shell it was Lenin. I could not conceive a tenderness of covering. I could imagine, instead, that as a dictator he felt his prestige subject to injury from imputations of servile dealings and that, confronted by two innocents like Robins and me, he had used the chance to get us to proclaim a denial for him. Where Robins saw a sensitive person I saw a calculating one.

If Lenin had not used the outright words, "German spy," I never would have used them in reference to him. They are only popular catch-words. But they enshrined themselves in the brain of this maker of catch phrases. That is their significance.

Whether this is meant as an apology to the American taxpayers for all the money it cost them to buy the documents turned out by Semenov, to bring up to date the "evidence" when he might just as well have stopped at reading Lenin's mind, I have no idea.

If it seems strange that I should clutter up a chapter on the long three-month Brest-Litovsk period by such trivia, it is because they were used to whip up the spirit for intervention in America. True, they were regarded with enough suspicion so that the most high-powered chicanery was used to get an academic committee to approve the documents, and the abysmal confession of his own part in this left by Sam Harper makes painful reading.

Poor Russia! As if the new socialist state did not have enough troubles on its hands, the weasel had to be stirring up this nonsense again. But Lockhart, we may assume, fortunately was not the "innocent" that Sisson pictures himself. Without mentioning Sisson by name, Lockhart describes "one American intelligence officer" whose "chief contribution to the war was the purchase of a stack of documents, so palpably forged that even our own secret service would have nothing to do with them."

Just the day before Jack left Russia, Trotsky, on January 28/February 10, led the delegation out from Brest-Litovsk. The Germans, at last preparing their ultimatum to their fractious, intransigent opponents, were interrupted by Trotsky, who, after a bitter attack on the Germans' intrigue, concluded with the declaration that "Russia, while refusing to sign an annexationist peace, for her part declares the state of war with Germany, Austria-Hungary, Turkey and Bulgaria at an end." Trotsky and the delegates returned to Petrograd, apparently feeling not only self-righteous, but satisfied they had confounded their adversaries. The day before the walkout they had learned that the Central Powers and the Rada had signed a separate peace that day in which the Rada gave the Germans carte blanche over the desperately needed grain of the Ukraine. It was the birthday of Prince Leopold of Bavaria, so the peace was signed with a salute in his honor, fired with permission of the Kiev Rada delegation, since under the treaty of peace the city of Brest-Litovsk went to the Ukraine. All this on the very day after the Russians had insisted, citing the widely known Soviet victories at Kiev and elsewhere in the Ukraine, that the Rada no longer existed. Then there was the Germans' seizure of the Moon Islands, part of Estonia. They were of only defensive importance to the Soviet, but in the hands of the Germans they were a menace to vital centers, including Petrograd.

I looked up Gumberg, who was not inclined to optimistic predictions. I wanted to find out just how realistic it was in the present crucial state of affairs for Robins, Sadoul, and now, as I heard it, Lockhart to expect their countries to offer help to the Soviets—not as a delaying tactic, the better to sink their knives in Russia, but on the up-and-up. And if they did make a legitimate offer, what then?

"Robins is being realistic," Alex said. "It's just now, now that Trotsky is back from Brest having played his trump card and lost—though he doesn't think so, he still doubts the Germans will advance—that the capitalists have a chance to do themselves a good turn. If they don't, they're playing with fire. Because no matter what is said by any faction in the Bolshevik leadership, it just could be that the Bolsheviks will survive with or without the United States, Britain, and France.

"If we turn aside from them now, it will mean a long period of reaction for us—because once my government starts out on a new path, all its spokesmen defend it, and it rolls along, and it's awfully hard to reverse it. This now is the crossroads for America—as well as Russia."

It was the first and last time I heard Gumberg speak more than two serious sentences consecutively. I realized only later he had not committed himself at all on whether he thought Robins would win out—either in getting the Bolsheviks not to sign the peace, which seemed less likely now, or in getting Washington to treat his ideas seriously—or whether in his opinion his boss would be left holding the bag.

I stayed away from the subject of Reed, but Gumberg could not. Reed was wrong about a lot of things, he said, but right about one thing: Sisson.

I couldn't let his remark about Jack go unnoticed. What was Jack wrong about?

"Oh, he has to make such a point of wearing the Revolution on his sleeve," Alex said. "You guys who suddenly discover revolution are all the same. No idea of tactics. Reed, now. You mark my words. He won't go to jail. Harvard boys don't go to jail. But he's dying to be a martyr. He must proclaim his principles—for how long? He'll make a lot of noise and then sputter out, like a wet firecracker. Wind up on Wall Street."

"What about your old *Novy Mir* pals who've become bureaucrats and run around now with briefcases under their arms?"

Catching Gumberg with his guard down was another first and last for me. Always he had kept up his pose of being the cynical observer of the human comedy, uncommitted, uninvolved. He had never pretended to be a Marxist or not to be a Marxist, nor did he now. Nor did he admit that his mask hid a real concern for both his adopted country and his native land. This involved no contradiction; in my opinion, and in Reed's, too, if the United States recognized the Bolsheviks and the Soviet power, both Russia and America would be better off. And though Alex and not Reed would wind up on Wall Street, many knowing people would say on his death that, keeping always out of the limelight, this strangely fascinating, provocative, mysterious Gumberg played as important a role in the long effort to obtain recognition of the Soviets as any other one person.

· 13 · The Germans March

On January 28/February 10 Trotsky's formula of "sticking the bayonet in the ground" was played to its final conclusion at Brest-Litovsk. Seven days later the Russians were notified military operations would resume the next day. Trotsky still felt it was a bluff. Actually marching orders had been given by the Germans while he was on his way back to Petrograd.

In the forthcoming week the Central Committee met in almost continuous around-the-clock session. With the Germans approaching, the committee still was split. Lenin's fight, already stretching out for weeks, was just beginning. On receipt of Hoffmann's message, Lenin put a motion to propose to Germany that the peace parleys be resumed. Voting for it, besides Lenin, were Stalin, Sverdlov, Sokolnikov, and Smilga. A bare majority defeated it: Trotsky, Bukharin, Lomov, Joffe, Uritsky, and Krestinsky. The same six then voted to delay renewing negotiations "until the German offensive is sufficiently apparent and until its influence on the workers' movement is revealed." Lenin persisted. If the German offensive began, and no revolution took place in Germany and Austria, should peace be sought? On this, Trotsky shifted position and backed Lenin, making a majority of six, against which Joffe alone, the mild head negotiator at Brest preceding Trotsky, stubbornly voted no. There were four abstentions.

On the following day Dzerzhinsky was present, voting with Lenin's opposition, and Zinoviev, who voted with Lenin. In the morning Trotsky, repeating that they must see what effect the new situation had on the German masses, again voted against immediately offering to continue negotiations, and the motion failed to carry, seven to six. Then came the news of the actual advance. This was the evening of February 18. Not only did the Germans march, but, as Lenin was to write on the twenty-third, the old Russian army was "refusing to fight at all." And at Dvinsk, which was taken by the Germans that first day of the advance, Russian officers were "already going about wearing their shoulder-straps." Later on the evening of the eighteenth there was a rumor that the Germans were moving into the Ukraine. Trotsky then again switched to Lenin's camp, reluctantly, and a motion to contact the Germans with an offer to sign the original German terms, while requesting further negotiations, carried seven to five.

That night Sovnarkom, or the Soviet Central Executive, voted on the proposal. The Bolsheviks, bound by the decision of the Central Committee of the party, supported it without exception. Of seven Left SR's present, four voted for it, although their party later disclaimed the vote. A wire was sent at once to the Germans at Brest-Litovsk. But General Hoffmann, having prevailed over Germany's more temperate Von Kühlmann in refusing to consider Trotsky's strange proposal as anything but an end to the temporary armistice, and backed by Ludendorff, Hindenburg, and the Kaiser, now was feeling his oats. He let the Russians wait for their answer —and in the meantime, the Germans kept marching.

Those four days we waited were lived by all of us in a sort of sleepwalking intensity. Wild rumors swept Petrograd daily. The verified facts were bad enough. After Dvinsk fell, Trotsky's suggestion that the Central Powers be queried about their demands without mentioning peace brought Lenin's response that this was "joking with war," that "We are writing papers and in the meantime they [the Germans] are seizing rolling stock. . . . History will say that you have delivered the revolution [to the enemy]. We could have signed a peace that was not dangerous to the revolution." It was then that Trotsky, instead of voting for his own resolution, voted for Lenin's. But now the Germans *were* finding this kind of war a joke, as Hoffmann later wrote. What little of the old Russian army had not demobilized was doing so in a hurry, melting before insignificant German forces. But the Germans did not stop.

Curiously, in this situation there were some who now leaned more toward the revolutionary-war group than ever, saying that the Germans would attack in any event.

For me personally the entire debate now seemed almost academic, so long as I did not hear it; whenever I did, it was different, for though they were lacking in dynamic leadership, the left group, which included my dear friend Kollontai, had many powerful spokesmen. I had seen the Germans in action in the early days of the war,[1] however, and now I had all too

1. In England when the First World War broke out, I became war correspondent for *The Outlook* and on my experiences in Belgium wrote *In the Claws of the German Eagle* (New York, 1917).

realistic a vision of their appearing any day goose-stepping down the Nevsky.

After weeks of trying to use reason and persuasion with the Bolshevik leadership and the Left SR's with whom they shared the government, Lenin once more took his case beyond them, appealing to the people. Under the pen name of Karpov he attacked. And when after two articles on successive days Lenin still found the Central Committee almost evenly divided, and against him on crucial votes, he wrote a third, signed "Lenin," revealing himself as the author of the first two.

On February 21 I devoured the first of these, Lenin's *Pravda* article "The Revolutionary Phrase," and on each of the next two days the shorter articles written the day of publication. I wished that Reed were around to savor the language of the first.

> If the desire for a revolutionary war on the part of, say, the Petrograd and Moscow party organizations were not a mere phase, we should have witnessed between October and January a different [set] of facts: we should have seen demobilization firmly opposed . . . tens of thousands of agitators and volunteers sent to the front . . . regiments formed and coalescing into a Red Army and resorting to means of terror to stop the demobilization.

The demobilization of the army by the Soviet Socialist Republic before the war with a neighboring imperialist state was ended was the insurmountable result of the social composition of a backward country with a peasant economy, reduced to economic ruin after three years of war. Mirsky, summarizing the article, continues:

> From October onward the Revolution had had too triumphant a progress. This had spoiled the revolutionaries and made them lose the habit of reverses. They must reacquire it: "If you are not able to fit in with the circumstances, if you are not prepared to creep on your belly in the mud, you are no Revolutionary, but a windbag, because no other way is open to us, because history has not been so amiable as to bring the Revolution to maturity at the same time in all countries."

Of the half-dozen favorite arguments advanced by the revolutionary-war group that Lenin answers in the article of February 21, the last interested me most because it had bothered me most. Lenin called it "the most specious and most widespread" of all. His opponents argued, he says, "this obscene peace is a disgrace, it is betrayal of Latvia, Poland, Kurland, and Lithuania." Looking at it theoretically, Lenin asks, "Which should be put first, the right of nations to self-determination, or socialism?" and answers, "Socialism should." He goes on:

> Is it permissible, because of a contravention of the right of nations to self-determination, to allow the Soviet Socialist Republic to be devoured, to expose it to the blows of imperialism at a time when imperialism is obviously stronger and the Soviet Republic obviously weaker?
>
> No, it is not permissible—that is *bourgeois* and not socialist politics.
>
> Further, would peace on the condition that Poland, Lithuania and Kurland are returned "to us" be *less* disgraceful, be any less an annexationist peace?
>
> From the point of view of the Russian bourgeois, *it would*.
>
> From the point of view of the socialist-internationalist, *it would not*.
>
> Because if German imperialism set Poland free (which at one time some bourgeois in Germany desired), it would squeeze Serbia, Belgium, etc., *all the more.* . . .
>
> Examine the behavior of the Anglo-French bourgeoisie. They are doing everything they can to drag us into the war against Germany now, they are offering us millions of blessings, boots, potatoes, shells, locomotives (on credit . . . that is not "enslavement," don't fear that! It is "only" credit!).
>
> The Anglo-French bourgeoisie are setting a trap for us: please be kind enough to go and fight *now*, our gain will be magnificent. The Germans will plunder you, will "do well" in the East, will agree to cheaper terms in the West, and furthermore, Soviet power will be swept away. . . . Please do fight, Bolshevik "allies," we shall help you!
>
> And the "Left" (God save us from them) Bolsheviks are walking into the trap by reciting the most revolutionary phrases. . . .
>
> We must fight against the revolutionary phrase . . . so that at some future time people will not say of us the bitter truth that "a revolutionary phrase about revolutionary war ruined the revolution."

But I too had a revolutionary phrase to remember. Now the memory of it was a spur in my side, goading me to action. Not just any action, but a specific, meaningful action, which seemed all the more imperative when I saw the *Pravda* headline the next day, over a proclamation from Sovnarkom:

THE SOCIALIST FATHERLAND IS IN DANGER

In order to save the exhausted, tormented country from new war trials, we have made the greatest sacrifice, and have announced to the Germans our readiness to sign their peace terms. Our emissaries departed in the evening of February 20 from Rezhitsa to Dvinsk, and thus far no answer has been received. The German Government . . . manifestly does not want peace. Carrying out the commission of the capitalists of all countries, German militarism wants to choke the Russian and Ukrainian workmen and peasants, and to return the land to the landowers, the factories to the bankers, and the power to the monarchy. The German generals want to establish their "order" in Petrograd and in Kiev. The Socialist Republic of Soviets is placed in the greatest jeopardy. Until the moment when the proletariat of Germany will rise and conquer, unstinted defense of the Republic of Soviets against the hordes of bourgeois-imperialist Germany will be the sacred duty of the workmen and peasants of Russia.

There followed a number of items resolved by the Council of People's Commissars. The entire power and resources of the country were to be at the disposal of revolutionary defense. All Soviets and revolutionary organizations were to be responsible for defending every post "until the last drop of blood." Railroad organizations and cooperating soviets would make every effort to prevent utilization of the railroad system by the enemy; in case of retreat, tracks were to be destroyed, railroad buildings blown up and burned, and the entire rolling stock sent into the interior.

All foodstuffs in danger of falling into the hands of the enemy must be destroyed "unconditionally." In such cases the local soviets were to be charged with supervision, and their presidents held personally responsible.

The workmen and peasants of Petrograd, of Kiev, of all the towns, villages, and hamlets along the line of the new front "shall mobilize battalions for the digging of trenches" under the eyes of the Red Guard.

All doubts about what I intended to do vanished. It was too late to go back to America. I rushed back to Smolny, the newspaper under my arm. I wandered about the corridors.

Where did one go to enlist in the Red Army? For I meant to make good my promise to the raw recruits, the first contingent of the Red Army, although then it was not called that, on the day when Lenin had to supply the Russian word for "enlist." I had promised to do so in case of emergency.

Now, little more than a month later,[2] there was no doubt that this indeed was an emergency. *Vstupit* I would.

I felt self-conscious about it all, however. I wanted to do it in the most unobtrusive way. There would be plenty of Russians enlisting today, after *Pravda's* editorial—actually the opening gun for the first meaningful drive for recruitment of the Red Army, which had been created in a decree of January 15. But I did not want to ask any of the Bolsheviks I knew where a foreigner could enlist. I decided to ask a stranger. I did—at least two. One was a worker, who got the idea I was asking *him* to enlist. He assured me he was not afraid to die, but what did Lenin want—should they make peace, or should they fight? I began making my getaway while his arguments pursued me. And why should an American stick his nose into it, anyway? I kept retreating.

Then in another corridor, as far away as I could get, I summoned my courage and approached a sailor. I made myself understood. He nodded quietly, as if it were the most usual request in the world, and said he would take me to the right place, and we set off.

That was the way I happened to fall into Bukharin's hands. I knew Bukharin, of course, but he was one of the Russian-Americans (he had at least spent a short time in New York) I knew least, and it never would have occurred to me to go to him, of all people, on this quest.

But it was too late. The sailor, saying merely that here was a comrade who wanted to join up to defend the Revolution, left Bukharin and me together, and Bukharin piloted me along while he jabbered away enthusiastically. At first I paid little attention, preoccupied with the step I was about to take. Then what he was saying took on a pattern. It was all about the revolutionary initiative of the masses, and how Marx had cautioned against the French Revolution, too, but then was moved and thrilled when the sans-culottes demonstrated their revolutionary initiative.

I reminded him that the glorious French Revolution had become Bonapartism.

"Exactly," he said as he opened a door and, taking my arm, led me in. I was disturbed by his "Exactly." Did he simply misinterpret me, or was he just paying no attention?

"Listen, Bukharin," I said. I spoke rapidly. I sensed some sort of intrigue in which I would be used as a pawn. "Let me make myself perfectly clear. I'm no theoretician, and you are. But it's an easy thing to do as you do, kindle the revolutionary ardor of the workers—an easy thing when stomachs are empty and hope is cheap."

2. At long last the revision of the old calendar was made effective, the old February 1 becoming February 14.

I had not noticed where we were, but now, just as I saw the ingratiating smile on Bukharin's face, I was aware that we were in fact in Lenin's ante-room. I protested. I had simply come to Smolny to join the Red Army, not to see Lenin. I did not want to be served up to Lenin as a representative of the iron battalions of workers of all lands who would rush to preserve the Soviets if only they refused to sign the peace. But while I argued with him, Bukharin was waiting for that inner door to open, and at the same time effectively holding onto his live Exhibit A.

I could have pushed him aside and fled. But I did not. Instead, along with Bukharin, I found myself watching fascinated while the doorknob clicked, and some hand within, possibly Lenin's, held it, turning it back and forth, presumably while farewells were said. Bukharin crept up close to the door, and when the visitor emerged he seized the door while it was still ajar, opened it wider, and virtually pushed me through it.

I was catapulted into the presence of Lenin. He was in the act of walk-ing to his desk, his back toward me. He turned, understandably surprised at being thus confronted with an unannounced caller.

I was greatly embarrassed, and after blurting out something to the effect that I had come to join the Red Army, I felt still more embar-rassed. How would it be if every recruit came to tell Lenin about it before signing up?

I tried to explain about Bukharin. From the gleam in Lenin's eye at the name I got the idea he had caught a glimpse of Bukharin in the offing, or at least surmised that he had something to do with this sudden intrusion of mine into his office.

To Lenin, Bukharin's position on the need of an implacable stand on Brest-Litovsk which would inspire the German workers to revolt and save the Soviet workers' and peasants' government was intoxication with the revolutionary phase. Lenin himself did count on international support of the workers, but it was not imminent, immediate—and the advancing German forces were.

He took some time to expand this thought, probably as a means of drawing out my ideas—something he always did, whoever his visitor, whatever the topic discussed, I had been told.

He talked, then, about the folly of dying for the Revolution as an end in itself. Better to live for it. Keep alive. That was the real job. If all rev-olutionaries died for the Revolution, the Revolution would die with them.

"Of course," he said, "you journalists, well-wishers, and so on are more of a moral than a military factor. But I am glad, very glad, you made your decision." He looked at me directly, seriously. I was relieved that there was no hint of sarcasm or amusement in his voice or manner.

I started to explain about my pledge atop the armored car, and was pleased to see he remembered it perfectly well. We both spoke in English, however; time was too short and I was too tense to attempt Russian.

"It looks very bad for us just now," Lenin said. "The old army will not fight. The new army is largely on paper. Pskov has just been surrendered without resistance. That is a crime. The chairman of that Soviet ought to be shot!"

He was silent for a moment, then continued: "Our workers have a great capacity for self-sacrifice and heroism, only they are without military training or military discipline. The soldiers in the old army are tired, war-weary, but give them a little rest and they will fight well."

In these brief sentences he summed up the situation. Now he added, "All I can see is peace. Yet the Soviet may be for war. In any case, my congratulations on joining the Revolutionary Army. After your struggle with the Russian language you ought to be in good training to fight the Germans."

Eying me with that inquisitive, discerning look, his eyes crinkling up in a smile, he said in an offhand manner: "One foreigner can't do much fighting. Maybe you can find others."

That is the way our International Legion came into being. I said I should like to try my hand at getting up a detachment. At once Lenin went into action.

Picking up a telephone, he tried to reach Krylenko, the Soviet commander in chief. Failing, he picked up a pen and scribbled a note to him. As I was to learn, this did not end Lenin's activity and characteristic attention to detail so far as the Legion and its formation went.

I started to get up. Lenin said, "Just a moment. Listen. We cannot fight them with bare hands; but we may have to. They may not accept an armistice. But we will do everything possible to avoid a fight—now. The peasants have had enough of war. And besides, you can't fight Germans with teakettles." There was a great dearth of guns and ammunition.

His eyes rested on mine briefly with that glint of warm kindliness which was a very real part of Lenin. Then he looked away, and dropped a few seemingly casual remarks about the inanity of war:

What a tragedy! What a paradox! Just think! Socialists engaging in war, planning to dynamite. A ruthless enemy blowing up bridges and houses—and in retreat we are doing just the same things. Unhappy Russia!

Again I started for the door, and stupidly dropped my hat on the floor as I arose. Lenin, moving quickly, retrieved it. He handed it to me, rather absently. I am sure it did not occur to either of us at the time that there was anything unusual in a correspondent's hat being picked up by a premier.

It was dark when I left Smolny. I could hear the siren shrieking the warning of the advance of the German troops, threatening the survival of the Red "Peter," the workers' beloved city.

I was cold and hungry, but now that the decision was over and acted on, I felt a strange sense of elation. I was now an integral part of the Revolution, of the defense of the capital against the oncoming Germans.

The next day was February 23, the day General Hoffmann finally replied with new and much harsher terms to the Russians' offer to accept the old terms. Yet with the new battles in the Central Committee and the Soviet Executive Council to occupy him, and with certainly even more difficult battles facing him in the coming week, Lenin still found time that day to make two telephone calls to the offices of *Pravda*: (1) to make sure that the Legion's call be printed, and (2) that it be printed in English as well as Russian. It appeared in *Pravda* February 23. And it was on Lenin's order that a briefer, snappier appeal to join was telegraphed throughout Russia later and translated into five languages.

Just as my memories of the International Legion are a mixture of the sublime and the ludicrous, the "Call" had a touch of both as it appeared in *Pravda*, peppered with blank spaces, for the font of English type in the composing room was woefully wanting.

It abounded in errors as well, and what is worse, it must have been written first in Russian and translated into English by the *Pravda* people, as nothing else can explain its tortured terminology. It was signed "Albert Williams. Samuel Agursky. F. Neibut." (Neibut's name was Arnold.) Headed "Call," it appeared below an item, also in English, headed "The First International Detachment of the Red Army." The latter story explained that we should be attached to the Grenadier Guard Regiment (Petrogradskaya Storona, Bolshoi Vufova Street), and that members would be volunteers, with "conditions of life . . . the same as those of the Red Army." Persons wishing to enroll should apply to the Maryinsky Palace. Signed "Members of College of the Section for the Formation an [sic] Drilling," it declared: "The Section gives herewith a translation of the Call of the initiators of the formation of the detachment Comrades American Socialiste Albert williams [sic] and Samuel Agusky [sic], who are at the head of the Bureau for the enrolling of volunteers."

The "Call," after the usual stilted phrases about the working classes and the imperialists, continued in part:

> The Soviet Power has made a heroic effort to end the war. . . . It sent its call out to all the workers of the world; so far the working classes in foreign lands have failed to come to the help of the Russian Revolution and now a terrible threat is being aimed at the heart of Soviet Power by the advancing army of the German Imperialists.

The eyes of the revolutionists in all foreign lands are turned to this revolutionary centre of the world hoping for its security. But we who are here can help directly to ensure that security. Our duty is to fight for the preservation of Petrograd."

The appeal later sent out from Moscow in five languages was more to the point than the "Call":

Russia is in prison. Even so, above the clangor of the world-war her voice cries out loudest for justice and humanity—for the poor and the oppressed.

Russia has enemies inner and outer, strong and cunning. And Russia needs not your words and pious wishes. She needs work, discipline, organization and

guns in the hands of fearless fighters.

Do you believe in the Revolution, in the International, in the Soviet Power? Then join the International Legion of the Red Army. It is formed for those speaking foreign languages and to it are coming the fighting revolutionists from around the world.

Are you a free man? Then enlist at once.

Are you working in shop or office? Then give your spare time to drill, rifle practice and the military courses.

Headquarters: 2 Nizhni Lesnoy Pereulok—near the Temple of the Saviour.

I have said that the Germans did not stop. They did not stop after they had received the message that the Russians would accept the old peace terms, nor did they stop after the Russians finally, just before the deadline given them to reply to the new terms, did agree to accept the new conditions. They did not stop until the German armies reached the Narva–Lake Peipus–Moghiliev line on the north front.

And even then Lenin's battle to get the comrades to agree to accepting the peace was not yet won.

The new terms were of course vastly worse than the old. It was just as Lenin had foreseen in his theses: unless the harsh peace terms laid down in January were signed, "grave defeats will compel Russia to conclude an even more disadvantageous separate peace." On the morning of February 23 the new German terms finally reached the Soviet government. Russia must renounce her rights to all of Riga and its environs, all of Kurland and Lithuania, and withdraw all Soviet forces from the Ukraine. Recognition of German occupation of Livonia and Estonia[3] was required, and the

3. Livonia was until 1918 one of the three Baltic provinces of Russia; now divided between Latvia and Estonia. In both Latvia and Estonia, Soviet regimes had been proclaimed at the time of the October Revolution but were wiped out by advancing German armies. After the surrender of Germany to the Allies in November 1918, bourgeois national governments

Soviets must make peace with the Ukrainian Rada. Russia would be de-
prived of her Polish, Baltic, and Belorussian (White Russian) provinces.
Payments to Germany were reduced in some instances over the terms of
the treaty proffered earlier, but this was offset by the clause that each party
would pay for the maintenance of its citizens who were prisoners of war,
signifying an enormous bill to be presented to the Soviets. Perhaps the
severest blow to Russia was the loss of the wheat and corn, the lumber and
cattle that the Germans could now plunder from both the Ukraine and the
fertile territories now ceded outright to the Kaiser.

The battle raged anew in the Central Committee. Only forty-eight
hours were allowed for a reply under the German ultimatum. Lenin faced
his greatest trial to date. Trotsky, whose position had been distinct all along
from that of the Bukharin group who wanted no compromises, no dealings
with any imperialists in any shape or fashion, now "leaned towards the war
faction," in the words of his biographer. He did not agree with Lenin that
at the moment they were helpless. They could give up Petrograd and Moscow. But Lenin had said that all along. Trotsky could not give up the role
in which he had become so immersed at Brest—not so quickly. Speaking
of the defense they could organize if they were united, he said, "We would
keep the whole world in tension." And "If we sign this German ultimatum
today, we . . . may gain peace but we shall lose the support of the advanced
elements of the proletariat."

Now as in October Lenin threatened to resign; Trotsky, sobered by
this, replied, "We cannot wage revolutionary war with a split in the party."
Lenin's ultimatum—he even spoke of it as such, he had been forced to it—
was that he would resign from both the government and the party's Central
Committee. "It is ridiculous for the members of our Central Committee to
speak of an international civil war. There is one in Russia, but not in Germany," Lenin said.

When Stalin suggested that the peace terms need not be signed, that
negotiations could be opened without that, Lenin said, "Stalin is wrong in
saying that we can afford not to sign. These terms must be accepted. Unless
you do that you will find yourselves signing the Soviet power's death war-
rant within three weeks."

Trotsky said he did not want to stand in the way of party unity, but

---

came to power in Riga, capital of Latvia, and Tallinn, capital of Estonia. They lasted only
until November 29, 1918, in Estonia, when the Estonian Soviet government was proclaimed
at Narva, and three weeks later in Latvia, when a Lettish Soviet Government was announced.
The Estonian Soviet Republic was recognized by Petrograd on December 8, 1918, and the
Latvian Soviet Republic on December 22, 1918. Early in January 1919, Soviet power extended to Riga. With the appearance of British naval forces in the Baltic later in January,
however, the Estonian Soviet Republic collapsed, and five months later the Latvian. Peace
treaties with the bourgeois governments were concluded by the Soviets in 1920. "The regime
thus established lasted for just twenty years." Carr, Bolshevik Revolution, I, 311–313.

could not continue as Foreign Affairs Commissar. On the final vote Trotsky and three leaders of the war faction abstained, and four (Bukharin, Lomov, Bubnov, and Uritsky) voted against Lenin. Lenin won seven votes (Lenin, Zinoviev, Sverdlov, Stalin, Sokolnikov, Smilga, Stasova). Abstaining, besides Trotsky, were Joffe, Dzerzhinsky, and Krestinsky. The latter three issued a statement saying they could not see a war fought against German imperialism, the Russian bourgeoisie, and "a section of the proletariat headed by Lenin." Bukharin, Uritsky, Lomov, Bubnov, Smirnov, and Piatakov denounced the decision as a minority opinion, and resigned from all offices in party and government. Lenin tried to prevent their taking this step, and the Central Committee urged Trotsky to stay in office. He agreed not to make his resignation public until the ratification was voted on.

This was the situation among only Lenin's own party leaders; an even more crucial test of his leadership abilities awaited him that night.

By now, February 23, I was up to my ears in efforts to organize the International Legion. Nevertheless, I stole away with the Professor, Charlie Kuntz,[4] to the Taurida Palace that night. If I could not remain for all of the meeting (the crucial vote was taken at four-thirty the next morning), I could at least get the flavor of it.

The spacious lobbies were crowded, the lights blazed. Little knots of people stood about, some quiet and stunned, others voluble with fury and anxiety. Apparently no one had suspected that the Germans would levy such terms as these.

By now, with Lenin's published articles, support for his point of view was growing. His theses, which would appear in print the next morning, were making the rounds and were hotly discussed. Never, before or since, have I seen people under such tension. And all of us shared it. The deputies talked freely if they talked at all. Some had a dazed appearance, and more than one friend looked at me unseeing. Madame Kollontai, usually affable and voluble, passed by as if in a trance. In general I could not see that the revolutionary-war advocates were subdued. On the contrary, I heard both Left SR's and anarchists declaring: Let the Germans come; the more land they swallow, the more indigestion they will have; the more the Revolution is forced to go underground, the more it will be kept intact, to wreak havoc in their rear. And there were Bolsheviks, too, who were still harping on that one note, that now above all principle must count, they must be an example; they would go to their deaths if they must, but only as "true revolutionaries." I did not question their sincerity. Many of them would go to their deaths. Many of these were the most staunch when the ravages of civil war plus intervention hit them. And Lenin would work with them,

---

4. Kuntz was employed in the Bureau of Propaganda of the Foreign Ministry as a translator.

need them, make full use of them for the Revolution, and two of them would be assassinated in the first wave of the White terror.

Among the Bolsheviks now, too, were those who for the first time expressed bitter criticism of Trotsky. Returned to Brest with wide powers confirmed by the Third Congress, they said, he might have accepted the terms when he found there was no chance of further delay. Then there were others of the Bukharin faction who criticized Trotsky just as bitterly for first switching to Lenin's support, and then in the end being neither for nor against. Trotsky was not to be seen.

Kuntz and I wandered away to a remote corridor and speculated on how the vote would go that night. Lenin would win, Kuntz said. I did not feel like arguing with him. At the time, either dismemberment by Germany or continued war seemed so horrible I could not envision it. In any event, I said, if President Wilson would not stand up to Britain and France and give Soviet Russia some support, she would wind up a bleeding carcass.

No, Kuntz persisted, the Revolution would live, it would even outlast imperialism. "Lenin has it all planned," he said cheerfully. "Haven't you heard? He has confounded all the leftists, Radek and Bukharin included, with his plan for a Urals-Kusnetsky Republic—particularly as most of the comrades don't know where the Kusnetsky basin is, and have only vaguely heard of Kusnetsky coal. Lenin's idea is the government will retreat first to Moscow, then to the Urals—there to found the UKR. The Petrograd and Moscow workers will follow, and with the Ural industries and Kusnetsky mine proletariat, the Revolution will survive. Or he'd go clear to Kamchatka! But wherever, they would stand, until the international situation changed. The U-K Republic would mean a breather and a chance to build a new Red Army. Then, Lenin says, they'd come back and take Moscow and Petrograd back."

"But are there peasants there? You can't eat coal," I said.

Then we saw Lenin. He was striding down the corridor toward us. We knew, of course, that he had no time for chitchat, and we had no valid reason to stop him. At the same time, we reacted simultaneously, and perhaps we could not help doing so. "Have you a minute, Tovarish Lenin?"

He pulled up short and bowed to us gravely. "Will you be so good as to let me go this time, comrades? I haven't even as much as a second. They are awaiting me inside the hall. I beg you to excuse me this time, please." He bowed again, shook our hands, and was on his way.

It was enough. We felt immensely cheered—or I did. Kuntz never needed cheering.

"How calm he is!" I said, astounded. Kuntz chuckled. "How polite!"

I continued. "He's the only man in the Taurida tonight, I'm certain, who has kept his poise."

"And his bite—which will be all the sharper because he will be dispassionate. You'll see."

I could not remain for the joint meeting of the delegates of both the Bolsheviks and the Left SR's which was decided on because in both of the parties as they met separately they were about evenly divided. The anarchists also joined in the larger meeting in the central hall. This was about midnight; the formal meeting that included Mensheviks and Right SR deputies began about three o'clock in the morning. My friend Philips Price, of the *Manchester Guardian,* was there through both meetings and has left a vivid account. He speaks of the "atmosphere of depression and tension," the few spectators like himself "suffering the same mental torture as the delegates."

Even though I myself had made my decision and taken my stand, I probably would have felt much as he did (except that I would never, as he did, have called Lenin's attitude one of opportunism) if I had been in my usual place in the press gallery and not reporting for military duty at the Maryinsky Palace. Following the first meeting from the gallery, he said:

"At one moment I found myself secretly hoping that Lenin's cautious, if opportunist, policy would prevail. At another moment I was almost about to cry out to the delegates in the hall to refuse to sign and declare a Holy War on Western Imperialism."

Price described the impression on the delegates left by the reports of Krylenko on the retreat of the remnants of the old army, and a Baltic Fleet sailor's reading of Marine Commissariat reports which showed defense of the Gulf of Finland impossible in view of the absence of Red Guard sailor detachments sent to fight Kaledin in the south.

The struggle was clearly hopeless. But this seemed only to rouse the heroic spirit in the breasts of some Bolsheviks and Left S. R. 's. Madame Kolontay, the Commissar for Social Welfare, was engaged at this moment in bitterly accusing Lenin, whom she had buttonholed behind the tribune, of treason to the Revolution in publishing his thesis. "Enough of this opportunism!" she cried; "you are advising us to do the same thing which you have been accusing the Mensheviks of doing all the summer—compromising with Imperialism." Lenin, calm and unmoved, was stroking his chin and looking on the ground. Meanwhile the stormy petrel, Radek, was walking nervously up and down behind the tribune, with pale face and bloodshot eyes. . . . He asked to speak, and in biting terms he exclaimed from the tribune that the signing of this peace would mean the moral bankruptcy of the Russian Revolution and the handing over of Eastern Europe to Prussian reaction. . . . After Radek came the trade union leader, Ryazanoff, who passionately denounced the idea of signing peace, and said that it was better for the Revolution to go down with honour than expire with disgrace. No one seemed to be ready to speak in favour of signing, and it looked as if the idealists would win.

Then up rose Lenin, calm and cool as ever. Never did such responsibility rest on the head of one man. Yet it would be a mistake to assume that his personality was the most important factor in this crisis. Lenin's strength at this time, as at every subsequent time, lay in his ability to interpret the psychology, both conscious and unconscious, of the Russian workmen and peasant masses. . . .

Lenin's speech took effect. "No one could summon up courage to reply, because everyone seemed to feel in his heart that Lenin was right." But when the sitting was adjourned at two A.M. to become the full sitting of the Central Soviet Executive by the addition of the Menshevik and Right SR factions, the Left SR's, whose spokesman was Kamkov, admitted the correctness in fact of Lenin's thesis but refused to go along with signing the peace, preferring to retire into the interior and defy the Germans to come on. If the final decision was otherwise, the Left SR's would not resist it, but would withdraw from the government. Price says it was five A.M., not four-thirty, as some historians put it, when it was decided to take a free vote, uninfluenced by party discipline. Hands were counted: 116 for signing peace, 84 opposed, 24 abstentions, according to Carr. Price's figure was 112 for, 84 opposed, 24 abstentions. At once a telegram was dispatched to the Germans.

Even after Chicherin and Sokolnikov, as members of the new peace delegation, signed the treaty on March 3—subject to ratification by the All-Russian Congress of Workers', Soldiers', and Peasants' Deputies—the Germans continued to march. We lived in hourly expectation of catastrophe. Lenin had sent wireless messages on the twenty-fourth to the provincial Soviets in every territory, explaining that while the Central Soviet Executive had accepted the drastic German ultimatum in order to halt the advance, they would vote on the treaty at an extraordinary congress to be called as soon as possible. In the meantime, what did they think—should it be ratified or not? We knew by this time what the workers in the giant factories thought. Bolsheviks opposing Lenin went to Viborg to canvass them the day after the Central Executive reached its decision. They came back admitting that the workers thought resistance impossible; why should they alone attempt it when the peasants were not with them? But as the

German advance continued, the workers began to mobilize into Red Guards, and once again they were to be seen with rifles over their shoulders, spades, hoes, knives, any convenient instrument in hand, trekking to the Baltic Station and preparing to dig trenches about Petrograd.

Within a week answers to Lenin's telegrams to the provinces were coming in in floods, and as printed in *Izvestia* confirmed Lenin's almost unerring knowledge of the thinking of the majority of peasants. Once again, the single voice had sounded against the voices of virtually all the members of the ruling groups, not to mention the Right Mensheviks and Right SR's who seemed to be longing to fight the Germans—or have others do so. But behind the single voice was a cold appraisal of that 85 percent of the Russian populace.

As the Germans continued, seemingly intent on devouring as much land as possible before their diplomats signed on the dotted line, a hurried evacuation of Petrograd began. When the German armies finally stopped, everyone breathed a sigh of relief. At least the workers' Red Peter was safe—for the time being; the moving went at a more leisurely pace.

• 14 • Legionnaire

While the German troops were getting closer and closer to Petrograd, I thought more than once of all that copy Jack Reed and I used to pound out, copy calculated to get the German troops out of the trenches. They were quitting the trenches, all right, all along the 1,200-mile front—not to raise the red flag of revolt, but to obey their masters and dismember the young socialist republic. Reed was still in Christiania, waiting for that ship. At any rate, I was saved the Homeric laughter that the sight of me in a legionnaire's outfit doubtless would have inspired.

Among the sixty-odd men who answered our call to serve as Red Army men in the International Legion, few, to my relief, cut any special military figure. One was an even less likely candidate than I.

When I first told Kuntz that I was a volunteer, I was a bit on the defensive. Without doubt the Professor would have gone through gunfire, prison, or torture for the Revolution, but to be ready to kill for it would have been asking a good deal of a forty-eight-year-old man who had come to Russia straight from a New Jersey chicken farm, where, wearing the Tolstoyan tunic, he had divided his time among his chickens, writing and studying, and tutoring nieces and nephews.

Rather truculently, I told Kuntz I could no longer remain a mere passive partisan. Like Gumberg, Kuntz was one of the Russian-Americans in Petrograd who had no affiliation with party or faction, but had known Trotsky on the *Novy Mir* in New York. I knew he was altogether on Lenin's side as to the necessity of peace. That did not mean he would be prepared to fight if the Germans actually attacked Petrograd, and at this time they were still coming.

"And so, Professor," I said, drawing myself up in what I fancied a stern military posture, "I am no longer armed with sympathy, goodwill, and friendly words, but with a gun. I've joined the Red Army."

The Professor was the pleasantest, the most urbane of men. To my knowledge, no aspect of the chaotic revolutionary scene, upon which he landed as if by some interplanetary accident on the precise eve of the October Revolution, ever evoked his surprise. Nor did my news.

"Good," he said serenely. "The poor frightened diplomats are fleeing, and the bourgeois ladies are getting ready their bouquets to toss at the conquerors when they goose-step into Petrograd. Anything but the Bolsheviks! Lenin, of course, is right, because he sees it from the class angle. The international working class deserves to have this revolution saved. As for German insurrection," he added with a twinkle in the benevolent eyes visible behind his pince-nez, "it's idealism, not Marxism, to count your chickens before they're hatched." As a sort of afterthought, he added that he, too, was "signing up for your International Legion."

"But you're a pacifist," I said unthinkingly. "You couldn't kill a bedbug."

My mind busy with other details—his age, his gentleness, his eyesight—I presume I looked my horror. He peered at me ever so benignly, but a bit mockingly, and laughed. I had forgotten that I too was a pacifist! Or had been.

So Kuntz and I found ourselves as enrolled volunteers under the authority of the Section for the Formation and Drilling of Troops at the All-Russian College for the Organization and Administration of the Red Army; and, as Internationals, trying to set an example in military discipline. We had not imagined ourselves in this role. But the Professor was unperturbed. "Once you say 'A,' you say 'B,'" he said gaily. In reply I clicked my heels and saluted—neither of which was done, of course, in the Red Army—and acknowledged his logic irrefutable.

Attached to the Grenadier Guards Regiment, our detachment was given a recruiting office on the third floor of the elegant Maryinsky Palace. English was decreed as the Legion's language, but we were of various nationalities, shapes, and sizes. If our International Legion was no great contribution to the Revolution, at least our motley crew was within weeks welded into some sort of military shape and thus testified to the creative organizing power of the Revolution.

Despite the law putting factories under workers' control, in point of fact many factories were not working; owners remained and sabotaged, or departed; engineers deserted, and many workers, figuring there would be at least bread and cabbage soup there, returned to their peasant families in the provinces. Everywhere we seemed to encounter sabotage, which grew more bold as the counterrevolution was buoyed up by the German advance.

In the chaos and mess we often despaired of getting any guns or ammunition, let alone anything resembling uniforms, despite the note I had seen Lenin writing to Commander in Chief Krylenko. But then, the Red Guards who were volunteering for the new Red Army at the rate of about 2,500 a day since February 25 were faring little better.

The solution, according to our Legion commander, a humorless Czech, was simple. We were just outside the Maryinsky, leaving for drill practice —without guns, of course. The commander pointed to the windows in the Maryinsky. "You want guns? You want end to sabotage? Throw all those bureaucrats out the window." A number voiced loud support. The commander failed to see they were joking. One said gravely, yes, of course, had not Marx said to smash the bourgeois state machinery? The Professor tactfully persuaded the commander not to try it; the Revolution would need the state machinery quite a while, and someone had to run it. Throwing the bourgeoisie out of the windows, even the saboteurs, was not specifically recommended in Marx's *Critique of the Gotha Program*.

Not long after my decision to volunteer, I made a point of telling Robins about it. At this time the Germans still were advancing on Petrograd, their planes flew over the city at night, every day there were fresh rumors, and the facts were ominous enough. Robins was not particularly pleased at my news. He seemed to think my chances of becoming a corpse were fairly good. "But after your exploits, I don't suppose you can do anything else," said the Colonel. Then, with a gleam in his dark eyes, "At any rate, you're showing up all the bourgeoisie who were yelling themselves hoarse that the Germans should be fought to a finish; now that the Germans are within killing distance, you're willing, while they're filling the railway stations, beating it out of Petrograd."

Ambassador Francis left all arrangements for his getaway to Robins, who went directly to Lenin to ensure the Ambassador and his entourage easy and safe departure. And when Francis and a large number of Americans, including the personnel of the National City Bank, departed for Vologda, a small provincial town some hundreds of miles distant, on the direct railroad line to Vladivostok, Robins, Gumberg, and others in the Red Cross set off with them. They were joined within a few weeks by other Allied delegations. The British, however, tried to exit by way of Finland and got through, leaving only Lockhart and a few others behind. Vologda became a busy little town filled with nervous diplomats, of whom droll stories were later told me by Gumberg. Lockhart quotes Romei of the Italian General Staff as saying, after their one brief visit to Vologda, "If we had put all the Allied representatives there in a cauldron and stirred them up, not one drop of common sense would have come out of the whole boiling."

I felt sure Robins would be on the scene again soon; I could not picture him cooling his heels in some safe haven. While I did not see him again that I recall until the government, and with it the Legion, moved to Moscow, actually his reappearance in Petrograd closely followed his dispatch to Lenin reporting the Ambassador's arrival in Vologda on February 28. (In the same message Robins asked for news of the German offensive, and if the peace had been signed. Lenin replied less than thirty minutes later: "Peace not signed. Situation without change. . . .")

I remember the bombs dropped on Petrograd the night of March 2–3. One hit the Warsaw Station, crowded with people trying to make their escape. We wondered if the peace treaty signed March 3 would mean anything to the Germans.

Robins phoned Lockhart from Vologda to say that in all probability the Ambassador would leave for home the following day by way of Siberia, but that if Lockhart received any encouragement from Lenin, Robins would remain, and would attempt to persuade Francis to stay. On March 1 Lockhart, in his first interview with Lenin, did receive encouragement— that they were prepared to "risk co-operation with the Allies." And by March 5, two days after the peace was signed, Robins was back, and both were interviewing Trotsky, separately. Both of them discussed some form of substantial collaboration with Trotsky. Lockhart's cable to his government of March 5 reflects this.[1] But it was Robins who got the Russian conditions for such collaboration down in black and white. Not only this, but after obtaining the note from Trotsky, he and Gumberg and Trotsky proceeded to see Lenin, and Lenin agreed on the terms. Actually the document sets forth that in case the congress refused to ratify the Brest-Litovsk peace, or if the Germans renewed their offensive, or if the Soviet government was forced by actions of Germany to renounce the peace

---

1. The cable, "Secret and Confidential," to the British Foreign Office, March 5, 1918 (Cumming and Pettit, *Russian-American Relations*, pp. 82–84), concluded: "The Congress meets on March 12th. Empower me to inform Lenin that the question of Japanese intervention has been shelved, that we will persuade the Chinese to remove the embargo on foodstuffs, that we are prepared to support the Bolsheviks in so far as they will oppose Germany, and that we invite his suggestions as to the best way in which this help can be given. In return for this, there is every chance that war will be declared (in fact, war between the Bolsheviks and Germany is in any case inevitable) and that it will arouse a certain amount of enthusiasm. . . .

"I cannot help feeling that this is our last chance. If we accept it, we stand to gain considerably, and in any case we can lose nothing more than we lost already.

"I leave in a few days for Moscow. Please telegraph your answer in duplicate both to Moscow and Petrograd.

"Please show my telegram to the Prime Minister and Lord Milner.
(Signed) "Lockhart."

treaty, it would be important to know the answers to a series of questions: Could they rely on the support of the U.S., England, and France? What kind of support would be furnished? What steps would be taken by the other powers should Japan seize Vladivostok and the Eastern Siberian Railway?

Lenin had told Lockhart, "In the event of German aggression, I am even willing to accept military support. At the same time I am convinced that your government will never see things in this light."

There is no doubt that Robins and Lockhart both were hopeful. Lockhart wired London urging that the offer be accepted. They approached Harold Williams, anti-Bolshevik correspondent for English papers and *The New York Times,* and described by Robins before the Overman subcommittee as an intelligence agent of Great Britain. Williams, as well as R. R. Stevens, leading National City Bank representative in Petrograd, and Charles Smith of the Associated Press, all appealed to Britain and the U.S. to seize the opportunity. Robins turned the message over to military-mission aides to be sent to Vologda over the military wire before departing himself for Vologda. Arriving late the night of March 8, he found that the two men who knew the cipher code had been dispatched by Francis to Petrograd to negotiate with Trotsky, after Francis had been appealed to by Sadoul at Trotsky's request, and sent assurances he would "recommend moral and material co-operation provided organized resistance is sincerely established." The fact that Francis' emissaries, Ruggles and Riggs, were busy promising aid in Petrograd reassured Robins, who gave the Ambassador the original document and turned around to proceed to Moscow in time for the Fourth Congress.

Ruggles, not questioning the integrity of the Ambassador, sent a strong wire to the Army War College recommending an immediate and positive answer when he learned of the questions formulated by Trotsky and Lenin. The Ambassador, meanwhile, was in no hurry to transmit the document to Washington; a leisurely paraphrase of sorts was made March 9. As Professor Williams notes, "Even then he did not note the need for speed; nor did he stress the importance of the inquiry." And when he finally advised Washington of the Soviet action, he added that "if the Department thinks above questions require reply in addition to President's message," he would transmit it to the Soviets through Robins. When an edited version of the Soviet note reached Washington on March 15,[2] the die was cast.

---

2. All of the mystery surrounding this Soviet note of inquiry to Washington has never been dissipated. For example, Harper (in *The Russia I Believe In: The Memoirs of Samuel N. Harper, 1902–1941,* ed. by Paul V. Harper with the assistance of Ronald Thompson, Chicago, 1945, pp. 112–113): "Ambassador Francis forwarded this proposal by cable, and in code, to

254 • JOURNEY INTO REVOLUTION

On the day following the signing of the peace treaty it was announced that a congress of all the Soviets would assemble in Moscow on March 12. At the same time the government set up a new Supreme War Council, with Trotsky as president, and issued an order for the arming of the entire people. Thus when Francis sent Ruggles and Riggs to negotiate with Trotsky, it seemed no idle gesture. Both French and American officers would help train the Red Army now in formation, it seemed. This was only how it *seemed* in those early March days—when, as a sort of fifth wheel of the new army, we in the International Legion were mercifully preoccupied with matters far removed from the politicking that went on at Vologda.

I always associate the International Legion's march along the Nevsky Prospekt, on our way to entrain for Moscow, with a flaming sky of purple. For all I know, the sky of Petrograd that raw March day may have been leaden-hued. Perhaps it was only a reflection of my exalted emotions at the time. Nevertheless, it stays in my mind's eye as purple and crimson, behind a few tattered racing stormclouds.

The spectacle of the Professor marching down the Nevsky with a rifle over his shoulder—we had at last got our guns, though no uniforms—was strangely moving and reassuring. If the Revolution could make a soldier out of Kuntz, it was capable of anything. Once when his beard got entangled with his gun as he shifted it, he patiently extricated it, and at my smile said, "The perversity of the inanimate—with the animate triumphant, you see."

We had come to expect sabotage as the order of the day. So it was with pleasant surprise that we found the boxcar of the Petrograd-Moscow train that had been promised us. It was dusk when we entrained. We stretched out on the bare floor of the dark box and fell asleep. Throughout the night we were shunted, battered, and bumped about. At least the heaving jars and grinding jolts assured us we were on the move, and finally we slept. About daybreak, waking as the motion of the train stopped, we rushed to the door, expecting to see the spires of Moscow. Instead, we saw in the distance the familiar outlines of the Petrograd skyline, except that now we

the State Department; and, as I happened to be in Washington when it was received, I was asked for an opinion. The cable contained three paragraphs, of which the third went over to a second page; and in this third paragraph the ambassador quite properly expressed his own view, which was distinctly skeptical as to any sincere resumption of war against Germany by the Bolsheviks in the light of their doctrinal views and their actions. No reply was made to this proposal.

"Later, during the Senate investigations in 1919, when Robins presented this basic document on the subject . . . the third paragraph did not appear in what he said was a copy of the cable given him by Francis himself. I tried to determine . . . whether Francis had suppressed his third paragraph . . . or whether Robins had suppressed it. . . ."

were on the other side of the capital. (The center of Petrograd is on the left, or "Moscow," bank of the Neva, where the river curves abruptly.) We had lost five miles in the night.

An Italian legionnaire grabbed his gun, muttered, "Sabotage and treason!" and, swearing he was going to shoot either the stationmaster or the train dispatcher, made his exit. We never saw him again. Although the rest of us did not take to direct action—nor was there any evidence that he did—we were loud in our fury and disgust. All but Kuntz, who shrugged and said that sabotage, even treason, were "phenomena of the crisis," that the Revolution would triumph all the same, and we might even get to Moscow. We did in time, and had a fine building allocated to us as headquarters for the Legion.

Actually life seemed tame in Moscow. I was living at ease in the National Hotel, only a few steps from Room 24, Lenin's room in the three-room suite he and Krupskaya occupied. I felt vaguely guilty that it was not a wind-swept barracks such as I had anticipated when I signed up as legionnaire. As we awaited the Germans and a call to action that did not come, it was easy to become restless, morose. Danger deferred can be like love deferred; the appetite for it may slacken. It was a period in which the Red Army was being built up; all the accent was on organizing.

Without bothering to wait for the Fourth Congress and final ratification of the Brest treaty, the Germans, invited into the south by the dispossessed Ukrainian Rada, were quickly overrunning the Ukraine, putting the Rada back into power while it readied its own German police and military authority. Red Guards were ordered to retreat. But if it was a time for Red organizing, it was the same for White. Having been chased out of the Ukraine by the Red forces before the Germans arrived, the Whites now lay licking their wounds in the Caucasian foothills, biding their time, reorganizing, and making deals with the Allies, who had been subsidizing them more or less openly since January. All were girding their loins for a more decisive battle to come.

It was in this period that they put me behind a desk in Legion headquarters in Moscow. They made a Legion organizer of me. It was not what I had had in mind. And it was in this period that I realized that for some reason—possibly he was restive, too—Lenin was taking a new interest in me. Whatever his reasons, Lenin proposed to Boris Reinstein, and later to me, that we get together a small Marxist study class, five or six.

"You seem to have learned something about our language and our people and our revolution," he said casually to me one day. "But how about the theory of the Revolution, the ideas back of it? Couldn't you gather a few together who could spend a couple of hours studying Marx two or three times a week?" Then he added: "And if you desired, I might drop in now and then to see how you were getting along."

It seemed incredible to me that he could seriously contemplate, in the midst of enough problems to overwhelm several heads of state, spending a few hours a week teaching a half-dozen students. But then a week or so later I learned he had made the proposal to Reinstein too, and that since mentioning it to me he had again asked Reinstein how his proposal for a study group was shaping up.

Years later, in 1924, I tried to explain to Lenin's sister Anna why I had failed to grasp the opportunity to study Marx under Lenin. His duties, I said, were enough to stagger any mortal man as it was; how could I in good conscience add one more duty? But she, like Reinstein, seemed to see nothing surprising in Lenin's proposal. "Not a duty, but a diversion," she replied. "You should have had no qualms on that score. The study group would have been a pleasant relief from cares and problems for Ilyich, for above all he had a passionate love of teaching."

Nevertheless, I put Reinstein off. Was it a basic American aversion to theory as such that made the whole idea of forming a Marxist study group in the midst of a revolution seem alien to me? It is just possible. I was baffled at this peculiarly Russian emphasis on the value of study while the great vital issues of the Revolution, even its survival, remained unsettled. Russia was prostrate, spent, hungry, with rumors again current of an imminent Japanese invasion of Siberia (which Robins had reason to believe he at least postponed, as a March 9 cable he persuaded the Ambassador to send suggests). Couldn't Lenin have waited, I asked Reinstein querulously once when he again brought up the subject of the class, at least until this crisis was past? "Don't you see," he replied, "that we will be in one crisis or another for a long time?"

Lenin must have cautioned Reinstein to be patient with me, for he kept all references to the class casual. There was a delicacy and sensitivity in Lenin which made allowances for the individual, for his diffidence or doubts or whatever misgivings he had so long as he was honest. And apparently this applied even to obscure American socialist journalists, even while he persisted in nudging Reinstein about getting me to make up my mind.

At another time when Reinstein spoke briefly to me about the class, I said I could understand that Lenin and Krupskaya had been elated about their small class of students in Longjumeau, fifteen kilometers outside Paris, but this was not the same. "He's not in exile now, and even if the government moves beyond the Urals and me with it before I get home, there are so many others who would benefit—why *me*?"

Boris looked down at his shoes, embarrassed and solemn. Then he glanced up, smiled, and said evenly, "Comrade Lenin thinks that you may lack perhaps a full understanding of the Bolshevik principles and concepts." Then, after a pause: "Even after the intellectual has identified himself with the working class, he is apt to weaken and vacillate unless grounded in theory."

That, he said hastily, was strictly his own offering. "It is just that Comrade Lenin in his talks with you thought he discerned that you were not altogether cognizant of . . ."

I laughed and slapped him on the back and assured him that Lenin could not be more right. "My knowledge of Marxist ideas is pretty pitiful. I probably know more than the average member of the American Socialist party about theory—I may even know more than the average member of the Socialist Labor party—but that's not saying much."

Still, I had not given Boris my answer. I never did.

In the several talks I had with Reinstein, and twice when Lenin referred to the hypothetical study class in our talks, I never heard any name mentioned but my own. Possibly Vladimir Ilyich initiated the idea of the class with me in mind; a few others would be invited if I agreed. At the time it would not have occurred to me that I was that important. To Lenin, incurably interested in America, I apparently was.

At any rate, it was in character. Lenin showed people in deeds that he cared about them and worried over them. In London in 1907 he felt the sheets in Gorky's hotel room to see if they were damp, knowing about his bout with tuberculosis. He had seen I was wanting in knowledge of the Russian language, and proceeded to encourage me and tell me how to acquire it. He had shown his interest in the work Reed and I were doing in the propaganda bureau. And now he felt I needed background in theory.

"Without correct theory, there can be no revolution, no socialism." This sentence of Lenin's has become an aphorism in socialist lands. It was not the formulas and theories of revolution that interested me as a writer, however, and it was as a writer that I saw my relation to the Revolution; although I had taken up a gun, the International Legion was more of a propaganda device than anything else, I was beginning to suspect. I had seen the Revolution, the stirring and shaking of the long-sleeping colossus, the people; the upsurge of the poor and downtrodden; the masses on the march. I wanted to write about the unconquerable spirit, above all, in the new burst of revolutionary zeal that followed, incredibly, the shame and agony of Brest-Litovsk as Trotsky organized the Red Army and Lenin was unsparing with its most militant fighters, the young Bolsheviks. Why learn the science that lay behind it when this was the story I wanted to write and tell to the people at home?

In later years when the story got around among my friends that I had turned down a chance to study Marx under Lenin, I had to defend myself against many stern and sharp criticisms. My critics, the most severe of them Marxists, probably were right. But Lenin dealt far more gently with me; he never sat in judgment on others in personal matters. He was the most thoroughly civilized and humane man I ever have known, and, if politeness is consideration of others, the most polite.

Of course, this interlude when I was becoming bored behind a desk and hankering to start on my way home to write (I would be a long time getting there) all happened after the Fourth Congress. We must have arrived about a day behind the government—on March 11, as I reconstruct it. (In shouldering a gun I had shuffled off my notebook and pencil.) The Congress, originally announced for March 12, had been postponed two days, and I have no reason to doubt, as Kennan does, Robins' statement that Lenin had it put off to give him a chance to hear from America. Lockhart was expecting to hear from his government daily, too.

When March 14 came around, I was in the gallery. It was a day I shall never forget. Kuntz kept repeating the three lines from Nekrasov that Lenin used as his "lead" in a remarkable article in the *Izvestia* of March 12. What other head of state ever began a principal statement in a national crisis with poetry? It was in character for Lenin, nonetheless. It is from a longer poem[3] that has many verses, of which I have seen many translations, but the official Soviet translation in English of the lines he chose are good enough:

> Thou art wretched, thou art abundant,
> Thou art mighty, thou art impotent—
> Mother Russia!

---

3. Nekrasov's "Who Can Be Happy and Free in Russia?" First published in Russia in 1879, a translation by Juliet M. Soskice appeared in *The World's Classics*, London, 1917. The verse is taken from Young Grisha's song.

· 15 · Peace and War

At both the First and the Third All-Russian Congresses of Soviets I had been more participant than reporter. At the Fourth Congress I was neither. It was just as well, for never did I feel less like a reporter. The Fourth Extraordinary All-Russian Congress of Soviets, opening in Moscow on March 14, two days after the government moved to the older of the two capitals, was convened for only one purpose. There was no time for greetings from the international proletariat, so I was saved the embarrassment of going through my usual act. I was not feeling supremely proud of that proletariat at the moment.

Now an International Legionnaire, I still sat with reporters in the gallery, looking down on the stately Hall of the Nobles with its famed crystal chandeliers, and saw played out the denouement of the Brest-Litovsk drama.

There were six separate opposition groups, each with a different solution and a separate resolution, and all their spokesmen found ratification impossible. Lenin was attacked in vitriolic terms, and perhaps none was more painful for him to hear than those of his old comrade at arms Martov; he and Martov had been arrested together, and for a time worked together on the original *Iskra* editorial board. Writing of the split of the Social Democratic party in 1903 that divided Bolsheviks (majority) from Mensheviks (minority), Krupskaya says, "His personal affections for people made these political ruptures incredibly painful. I remember how miserable Vladimir Ilyich felt at the time of the Second Congress when it became clear that a break with Axelrod, Zasulich and Martov was inevitable. He and I sat up a whole night shivering. Had he not been so passionate in his attachments, he would have lived longer." He never lost his feeling for Martov. "When Vladimir Ilyich was already seriously ill, he said to me somewhat dolefully, 'Martov is dying, too, so they say. . . .' " writes Krupskaya. "There was in his voice a note of tenderness."

And now at the Fourth Congress Martov, making the chief speech for the Menshevik resolution opposing the Brest peace, said in small part: "If this treaty is signed, the Russian proletariat will make war on the government that signed it. This treaty is the first partition of Russia; Japan is preparing for the second; and the third will not be long in coming. By this treaty we obligate ourselves not to carry on propaganda against the government of the Quadruple Alliance. I congratulate Lenin. From now on he is under the protection not only of the Red Guard but also of Kaiser Wilhelm. The Soviet of People's Commissars should resign in favor of a government capable of tearing up this document and carrying on the war against imperialism."

Boris Kamkov, again making the chief statement for the Left Social Revolutionaries, mimicked Lenin: " 'We must have a breathing spell,' says Lenin. Who is going to benefit by it? We or the Germans? . . . As long as we stand by the internationalist point of view, it matters little how much territory Germany grabs. Sooner or later the international proletariat is bound to come to our aid. By ratifying this robber treaty we admit that we are traitors to those parts of Russia that are being handed over to the Germans to save other parts."

From even the most distant provinces the delegates had come to decide whether they would accept the fate of being carved up by Germany or whether they would repudiate the treaty. The entire assemblage who would vote included 795 Bolsheviks, 284 Left SR's, 14 anarchists, 3 Ukrainian SR's, 24 Maximalists, 29 Center SR's, 11 Internationalist Mensheviks (Martov's group), 6 United Mensheviks, 21 plain Mensheviks, and 17 nonparty delegates.

The debate continued for three days. On March 17 the answer must be given to the Germans, and if it was not to ratify, they would renew hostilities. Trotsky, now Commissar of War, had stayed behind to organize the defense of Petrograd; the German advance had stopped short of the city.

Reversing the process under which old Russia, or Muscovy, expanded under the early tsars at the rate of fifty miles a day, Soviet Russia now was rapidly shrinking. In one sense, the shrinking had started a few days after the October Revolution, when the Declaration of the Rights of the Peoples of Russia recognized the equality of all nationalities and the right of secession; in December Sovnarkom recognized Finland's independence. Now the Germans under Mannerheim were butchering militant Finnish workers, and an anti-Bolshevik government with German aid was wiping out remaining pockets of Red Guards and Finnish resistance. With Finland gone, and the Brest treaty demanding recognition of the independence of

Georgia and the Ukraine as well, and further demanding that Poland, Lithuania, Latvia, and Estonia be left to the disposition of Germany and Austria-Hungary, Russia's territory was diminishing at a rate that made fifty miles a day insignificant. A final humiliation thrust on the reluctant peace delegates at Brest-Litovsk was the demand that they hand over to the Ottoman Empire all of Kars, Ardahan, and oil-rich Batum. Thus with ratification, Russia's territory would be reduced by 1,267,000 square miles, or 32 percent of her arable lands, and 75 percent of her coal and iron mines. In these lopped-off territories resided 62 million people. As has been pointed out since, "It was a sad end to Russia's participation in a war in which 2 million Russian soldiers had lost their lives, over 4 million had been wounded, and nearly 2.5 million had been taken prisoner."[1]

General Denikin, pointing out that in mid-January 1917 the Russian army was holding 187 enemy divisions, or 49 per cent of the enemy's forces operating on the European and Asiatic fronts, quoted French sources as estimating the losses of the various armies alone in those killed as (in millions): Russia, 2.5; Germany, 2; Austria, 1.5; France, 1.4; Great Britain, 0.8; Italy, 0.6. He concludes: "Russia's share of the martyrdom of all the Allied forces is 40 per cent."

At the Fourth Congress, Lenin used the same tone toward his opponents —although not the musical sentences—that characterized his latest article, the one beginning with lines from Nekrasov. On neither occasion did he have any unkind words for his comrades in leadership who had steadily fought against signing the treaty, and thus given Germany a chance to dictate far harsher terms.

The chief source of disagreement among the Soviet parties, he told the delegates, "is that some people too easily give way at times to a feeling of just and legitimate indignation over the defeat of the Soviet Republic by imperialism," give way to despair and wish to decide tactics of the revolution "on the basis of their immediate feelings."

Lenin spoke of how the German people, after the Tilsit peace forced on them by Napoleon, and at a time when they were weak and backward, "managed to learn from its bitter lessons and to raise itself up." Then I found one of his passages moving. "We are in a better position; we are not merely a weak and backward people, we are the people who have been able—not because of any special services or of historical predestination, but because of a definite conjunction of historical circumstances—who have

1. Sidney Harcave, *Russia: A History*, Philadelphia, 1959, 4th ed., p. 499.

In less than a fortnight after the signing of the treaty at Brest, "the Germans seized Kiev and vast parts of the Ukraine, the Austrians entered Odessa, and the Turks Trebizond. In the Ukraine the occupying powers crushed the Soviets and reinstalled the *Rada*, only to overpower shortly thereafter the *Rada*, too, and to place *Hetman* Skoropadsky at the head of their puppet administration." Isaac Deutscher, *The Prophet Armed*, I, New York, 1954, 394.

been able to accept the honor of raising the banner of the international socialist revolution."

Lenin wound up by saying that because the proletarian in the West was living in the underground, it was not easy for him to raise his voice. Soviet troops thus "will need much time and patience and will have to go through many trials before the time comes when he will aid us—we sha l use even the slightest chance of procrastination, for time is working on our side." And—they would see—they would be able to make "a heroic retreat," then "wait until the international socialist proletariat comes to our aid" and the revolution would be "worldwide in its scope."

For the first time it dawned on me: Lenin was not sure they would survive.

No one looked happy. For once, even the bourgeois reporters appeared depressed and concerned. After Lenin's remarks the debate began in earnest.

Restlessly pacing around or sitting close to the platform throughout the three days of the Congress was a familiar figure. Most of the Allied diplomats and their staffs were huddling together in distant Vologda; few foreigners were present, and Raymond Robins stood out like a sore thumb.

I knew nothing substantial at the time about the Soviet query addressed to Washington through Robins—presumably meant for Wilson himself— or of its delays and amputations in arriving, of which Robins himself was then unaware. I did know how he hoped even now that ratification would be voted down, although he was shrewd enough to have told me early in the Brest-Litovsk debate, in February, that peace was bound to be immensely popular with the peasants, and that it was only to the intellectuals that the issue was so complicated. That was when he also told me that one of Lenin's theses on the peace was that it would be impossible to get the old army to fight, and a revolutionary army must be mobilized and trained. This showed, he said, that Lenin still was concentrating on the peasant, and that in this he was far more realistic than Trotsky.

Robins was the one American providing actual information to his government from Russia during virtually the entire period after October, having by dint of hard work gained the confidence of Lenin, Trotsky, Radek, and others. All during this time, however, his country, and the other Allies, took the position that this government he dealt with so painstakingly was nonexistent.

Originally he had others with him aiding in this task, including Judson, his "first convert." Writing of the situation in Russia before he himself was recalled, Judson, in a letter to his old friend Postmaster General Albert S. Burleson on April 10, 1919, at a time when abuse was being heaped on

Robins by the press and his public speeches were attended by federal agents, said in part:

> When the Bolshevicks finally got in, in November 1917, we who alone, among all the Allied representatives and agents, had done anything of real moment to keep the Bolshevicks out, recognized that they were in fact firmly established for the vital period of the war; and we alone seemed to realize that if the peace negotiations, which were at once undertaken at Brest-Litovsk, were to be prevented or delayed, or otherwise affected in our interest, it would be necessary to deal quickly and wisely with the Bolshevick leaders. For this task Raymond Robins was rarely fitted, through possession of the very qualities, perhaps, that make him so many enemies here and now. He is a great idealist and a man of almost too broad human sympathies, if you can understand what I mean. Thus there lay in him some strong appeal to Lenin and Trotsky, fanatical idealists as they are, even although these leaders know, on his own confession, that Robins had worked hard, with Thompson's million dollars and the Breshkovskaya committee, to keep them out of power. . . . When I was ordered home he even made himself and the Russians think I was being sent for to explain to President Wilson how best he could help the Bolshevicks, if they refused to sign a peace with Germany.
>
> My own interview with Trotsky, which was greatly misrepresented in America . . . did its part in stiffening up Russian reluctance to sign the peace.

Judson was convinced that Robins, and for a time he himself, had been "effectively heartening the Bolshevicks there to resistance of German terms by near-promises which we hoped were not without proper justification," and thus contributed to delaying the "signing of a peace that was really scarcely a peace at all." But those who did this work, which he saw as weakening Germany in the West, "seem now, most unfairly, to be receiving only obloquy."

> I am naturally of a cheerful disposition, as you know, but if I do not live to see this injustice corrected, I shall believe, not only that Republics are indeed ungrateful, but also, with a certain cynical historian, that "History is a pack of lies agreed upon."

Unlike Lockhart, Robins could not even wire his government. He had to play upon Francis to get any cables sent to Washington. They were all signed by Francis, who, after setting forth Robins' reports, often added his own contradictory surmises. (Robins could cable only the Morgan official

Davison, his Red Cross chief, in New York, or send messages through Davison to William Boyce Thompson.)

The fate of Robins' reports once they finally reached Washington was another question. Some time later a Washington correspondent for a Philadelphia newspaper, Lincoln Colcord, sent Robins some extracts from his private journal of March 1918 to show that State Department and other officials who should have known knew nothing of the Lenin-Trotsky query.

Colcord added, "The first news we had of it was when you arrived in Washington in the early summer. From all this, I think it fair to assume that Polk [Frank Polk, Acting Secretary of State at the time Wilson sent the message to the Soviet Congress] knew nothing of this communication; and I shall always believe that the President did not see it. I think it went to [Secretary of State] Lansing and was pigeon-holed. As you know, Colonel House admitted to me on the 9th of August, a week after intervention had gone through, that he had never seen or heard of this communication before."[2]

---

2. The letter (Robins MSS) was in confidence, dated February 5, 1919. The March 9, 1918, extract said in part: "Had an hour with Colonel Thompson this afternoon; he called me up, saying Justice Brandies [sic] had suggested that I might do something. He is feeling very badly over the way our policy towards Russia has been drifting. Showed me . . . cables from Raymond Robins, who is staying on in Petrograd, and who reports that there is no cause as yet for us to change our views of the situation there. Sisson has shown the white feather— left Petrograd for Stockholm on the 4th of March. So it goes." In the morning he and Miles gave Bullitt ideas for a memo for the President on what should be sent to the Russian Congress.

The March 10, 1918, extract reported spending the forenoon at the Shoreham Hotel with Thompson, William Bullitt (a State Department aide who was then all for American-Russian cooperation) and two others. Thompson thought the All-Russian Congress ratification of the Brest-Litovsk treaty, which, unaware of the postponement, they believed would be taken up March 12, "is hanging in the balance." "He feels that the President *must* send a word to them, and follow it up by definite action and assistance. Yesterday afternoon . . . Norman Hapgood called up Colonel House for him and urged action by the President. Colonel House admitted . . . that the necessity was vital, and said that he would call up the President and urge him to send a message to the Soviet Congress. Bullitt told us that he had little hope that the President would act; his reasons . . . were based on information obtained early yesterday. He . . . had not sent his own memorandum to the President. . . . The President had not seen Colonel Thompson since his return from Russia. Neither will he see General Judson, who has now been in Washington three weeks."

The March 11, 1918, excerpt, besides saying that the President had sent the note to the All-Russian Congress [which House had praised in his diary as "one of the most cleverly worded, three-sentence messages extant"] and that it would be released to the press the following day, said: "M——— to dinner. He says that on Saturday Polk [Frank Polk, counselor of the State Department] got a letter from Thomas Lamont saying that if America didn't recognize the Soviets all hope of a democratic victory would be lost—that no matter what it cost us, we mustn't fail now to recognize the Soviets."

Colcord tells Robins "the above extracts cover accurately the Washington end of the incident." He adds that "in all our conversations at that time, there was no hint of the communication from Lenin and Trotsky which must already have reached Washington." "Bullitt, who saw pretty much everything that came into the Department, . . . had no knowledge of the communication."

Exactly how much knowledge Washington did obtain in advance of the Fourth Congress in regard to what was a serious query and, if not an offer, a clear implication that, depending on the reply, ratification would be reconsidered, even by Lenin, has never been entirely cleared up. The Robins papers, by no means fully exploited by historians, should help, however.

Aside from the fact that Robins believed that the query reached Washington, both England and the United States had plenty of opportunity to offer aid with or without that query. Some kind of cooperation had been envisioned even as early as December by Judson, and notes he made en route to America are vibrant with his feeling of urgency that the dreaded Brest-Litovsk treaty must find response from America, that it was its last chance to help Russia—and be helped by Russia in turn. He even noted in his diary that the United States should send over a different caliber of propagandist (obviously thinking of Sisson) who could understand the Revolution, and dryly he suggested that an honest approach might be in order.

Leaving Christiania on February 7, Judson wrote on February 12, "News by wireless that Russians have refused to sign peace treaty but declared peace exists on all fronts and army ordered demobilized. Is this true? Couldn't we have prevented it?" On February 17 he wrote, "Off Long Island—due in N.Y. tomorrow morning. Our propaganda in Russia is rotten. Vide [see] the patronizing film about Uncle Sam patronizing Ivan, which our Y.M.C.A. workers say disgusts [,] and the real Ivan, who is not so unsophisticated as people think—We need real radicals in Russia for propaganda work with the Bolshevicks against our Enemies—along lines when the said radicals' honest purposes would run parallel to the purposes of our government."

Most historians have presented Robins in a one-sided, oversimplified fashion, with the exception of Professor Williams. At times it is true he sounded like a partisan. Then would come doubts. Angry at the Revolution, angry at Lenin, when the Brest-Litovsk peace finally was approved by the Petrograd Soviet Executive Council for the first time, he berated me as if I were personally responsible. "You can draw the right deductions from this capitulation," he cried; his own deductions were clearly that the whole sorry thing could be attributed to their godlessness. Even so, he never held a grudge. (Except for Sisson, and with good reason.)

Not unlike others I was to know at home who became committed to the Revolution, when it made blunders, he took it personally. (Not that Robins was committed to revolution as such—and in future years, back in America, when he spoke from coast to coast on Russian recognition he avoided like the plague audiences under the auspices of persons or groups even suspected as radical.) He had a possessive feeling about the Soviets, and he felt it as almost a personal affront, a matter for indignation, when the Red Army fell back as Denikin was moving up on Moscow. I had run into Robins on Broadway in New York. He had staked his word that the Red Army would hold out, he told me. The Red Army was not so much failing Russia as failing him.

As a personality Robins always intrigued Radek. "Robins," I heard Radek say, "is like no one else. Here is a religious man who prays and reads his Bible every day, but numbers among the six triumphs of the Revolution the breaking of the power of the Orthodox Church."

Now Robins seemed withdrawn, brooding. I had some inkling of what was consuming him when I heard the public reading of the cable sent by President Wilson to the Congress, which Robins had handed to Lenin in advance.

It would have been difficult, of course, for any of the Allied governments to address the Soviet government and still maintain the fiction that it didn't exist, but up to this time President Wilson was the only one of the Allied heads of state who directed messages to the Russian people. The others talked to each other or to their own parliaments. Lord Balfour at his patronizing best had just delivered himself of an opinion to Parliament on March 14, the opening day of the Congress in Moscow, and nine days after Lockhart's lengthy cable to the British Foreign Office suggesting aid and cooperation after his interview with Trotsky. Lord Balfour painted in pitiful terms Russia's helplessness against German penetration. "The Allies —America, Britain, France, Italy, and Japan—should do what they can at this moment to help Russia." And what was that? To support Japan in its plan to intervene in the East, decrying any tendency to consider Japan as moved "by selfish and dishonorable motives." The implication was that all should intervene, for Russia's own good.

At least Balfour had the decency not to address these remarks to the All-Russian Congress. Wilson had the insensitivity that goes with some Messianic natures, and the temerity to address the Russian people themselves—through the extraordinary congress called by their government, the congress that was their highest council of government.

It was not a long message, but there was only one sentence in it that had any meaning to the delegates, and it took them no time at all to grasp that meaning: ". . . the government of the United States is, unhappily, not now in a position to render the direct and effective aid it would wish to render. . . ." All Wilson's phrases about eventually helping to restore Russia to "her great role" among nations and so on left them utterly cold.

Lenin had a draft reply ready, which was quickly read by President Sverdlov, who said he assumed the applause that followed (and it was considerable) meant they agreed on the reply to be sent from the Congress.

(The Congress ignored an insufferable greeting from Samuel Gompers made "in the name of world liberty.") The reply to President Wilson:

> The Congress expresses its gratitude to the American people, and primarily to the working and exploited classes of the United States of America, for their sympathy with the Russian people expressed by President Wilson through the Congress of Soviets in the days when the Soviet Socialist Republic of Russia is passing through severe trials.
>
> The Russian Soviet Republic, having become a neutral country, is taking advantage of the message sent it by President Wilson to express to all peoples, perishing and suffering from the horrors of the imperialist war, its profound sympathy and firm conviction that the happy time is not far away when the working people of all bourgeois countries will throw off the yoke of capital and establish the socialist system of society, the only system able to ensure a durable and just peace and culture and well-being for all working people.

With that business dispatched, the congress quickly got on with its reason for assembling—the debate over the peace treaty.

The vote came late the night of March 16. For "the brigands' peace," as Lenin so often described it, were 784; against, 261; abstaining, 115. Abstainers included Bukharin and his revolutionary-war following.

During the debate Lenin had seemed almost alone; the results were more than two to one, under the circumstances an overwhelming victory for Lenin and peace. The "breathing spell," whether little or long, was what the people wanted. Once more Lenin's genius for reading aright their aspirations was proven.

I heard no vituperative remarks made about Wilson or the United States by Lenin at the Fourth Congress. As a matter of fact, a search of Lenin's speeches of this period finds him omitting this country by name from his attacks.

There was a reason for this, and it was not solely his liking for Robins. It must be recalled that the United States was not the big brother at that time to the British Empire; it was the other way around. Compared to both France and Great Britain, the United States was the junior partner in imperialism. Moreover, the U.S. had reason to fear the power of Japan in the Pacific, and Lenin every reason to think it would be the last country of the Entente to agree to Japanese intervention—as it was.

And if some considered that the Congress' reply to President Wilson's note, drafted by Lenin, was impudent in that it was addressed first of all to the exploited classes in the United States, *Izvestia* was far from considering it a rebuke to Wilson. A long editorial the following day maintained that America, because of its own interests, might one day "give us money, arms, engines, machinery, instructors, engineers, etc., to help us to overcome economic disorder and create a new and strong army." It argued that Russia at the moment was faced by "two imperialisms, of which one has taken us by the throat (Japan), while the other . . . is ready to hold out to us a helping hand. . . . [The United States], in view of its rivalry with Germany and Japan, could not allow Russia to fall under the domination of either of these Powers." And, sounding much like Lenin, its conclusion was: "We are convinced that the most consistent socialist policy can be reconciled with the sternest realism and most levelheaded practicality."

Unfortunately, what the same editorial alluded to as "the state significance of the Russian revolution" was a subject for vacillation by President Wilson, if he ever even faintly grasped it. It was not that he was kept in ignorance; he deliberately excluded advice and information from all he considered to be on the side of recognition or even minimal cooperation with the Bolsheviks at this time.

Characteristically, once the Congress and ratification were over, Robins wasted no time in sulking or feeling useless. His papers reveal him day after day cabling Francis, encouraging him to do more in the way of opposing Japanese invasion of Siberia, meeting with Trotsky, and working out with Lenin another plan for economic help. On March 19 he began his diary notes optimistically: "Am[erican] Amb[assador] on wire and Siberian issue is pounding away. . . ." On April 3, two days before the Soviets made strong protests against the landing of Japanese and British troops at Vladivostok, Robins' entry reflects his pessimistic reaction to some unnamed news he has received: "There is no answer to failure of general cooperation except German control."

During all this time Robins patiently kept Francis informed of all events and did everything he could to stave off a decision for intervention by Washington—everything, of course, having to go through Francis' hands. On April 3 he confided to Wardwell:

Between the Ambassador and myself there is perfect good will and no little cooperation, but our relations are a Peace of Necessity similar to the German-Russian affair at Brest. I am still being used by him for all relations between the two governments and am in receipt daily of confidential communications. Still I know that if he held me over a cliff and could afford to let go he would do so with a sigh of genuine relief.

And on April 8 he gave vent to his weariness and disgust: "What a desperate hour in the world['s] need to have such a boob."

On April 18 he recognized that the Lenin-Robins plan for economic help would not materialize: "The plan of government for economic help America—not in program."

During this period, which must have been a deeply disturbing one for him personally, Robins nevertheless found time to worry about the lawless bands, anarchists, and criminal elements calling themselves anarchists who took over some of Moscow's finest homes, collected arsenals of machine guns and rifles, and robbed and stole and terrorized. He protested to Lenin, and to Trotsky too, and eventually Trotsky ordered simultaneous raids on known anarchist nests and the closing down of the illegal cabarets on the city's outskirts.

Robins was less concerned for his own safety than for Lenin's, and I unwittingly added to his worry when I told him of a simple incident that I witnessed in late March or early April. Having worked on my notes in my room in the National Hotel until around midnight, I left for a stroll and a breath of fresh air. The night was seasonably mild but the sky overcast. A few hundred yards from the hotel, in the dimly lit Moskvaya, I heard footsteps, and soon made out the forms of Lenin and Krupskaya, arm in arm, strolling along.

Lenin recognized me at the same time, and to my routine "How are you, Comrade Lenin?" he said, "A bit tired tonight, I must confess. Too long a meeting! Too many speakers!"

"And," added Krupskaya, "too much talking afterward and hand-shaking with comrades."

He was nonetheless in his customary genial frame of mind. I walked along with them to the hotel, while Lenin inquired about my health and welfare. Although I was a bit nervous until we reached the lights from the hotel, I managed to think of some funny incident to relate, at which Ilyich shook with laughter. He asked if I cared to come in, but I left them at their door and proceeded to my room down the corridor. For a few moments I pondered on just how it would feel to be Lenin's bodyguard, assuming the Bolsheviks ever got around to convincing him it was essential to have one. What a terrible responsibility it would place on a man!

Meeting Robins the next day or so, I told him of this midnight meeting on the street. Why, said Robins, all the foreigners he knew who were unfortunate enough to have to be abroad at night walked in the center of the street, and fast. Then he earnestly tried to get me to go to Lenin and protest his going about alone. I persuaded him I did not have that much influence on Lenin, and left him brooding over the situation. Later he took it up with Peters, who asked me if Robins was really "that sincere." I assured him he was.

Robins was a worldly man, he mixed with many elements, and he was in a position to know that many might be plotting an end to Lenin's life.

The Bolsheviks knew this in theory. But apparently none of them, including Peters, who was so needlessly wary of Robins, sought to convince Lenin that the safety of the Revolution demanded the safety of its leaders, and that his practice of going everywhere unprotected was unwise.

Lenin always lived dangerously. When he returned to Russia in April 1917 he expected no waiting enthusiastic throngs at the Finland Station; he thought he might be jailed on arrival. In this he was quite different from most of the revolutionists returning from exile. They saw the end of their troubles. They had had enough of the hard, unpleasant things of life, and they could not be blamed for wanting a little respite, to cash in on their revolutionary past. So they trimmed their sails, they would be satisfied with the revolution the people had made in February without them, and they made their party programs, unconsciously, one may suspect, to that end: not to run into trouble.

It was quite the contrary with Lenin. He knew that his program was not acceptable to the public at large in April, or to the other parties, or even to his own, and he knew full well the danger it threatened. He pursued it, but he was not foolhardy; there was no bravado about Lenin. When he was in danger in July, he went into hiding, albeit reluctantly (and he had been in hiding at times in 1905). Lenin could be serene in danger—and so he wrote *State and Revolution*, until he felt it was time to act.

But now there were so many things for all of them to do, more pressing than thinking of his safety, that the Bolsheviks had not got around to it. And they did not—a tragic oversight. As for Lenin, isolation from the people would have been painful to him. He wanted to know what people had to say, hear their complaints, receive their petitions.

He refused to absent himself from the workers waiting to hear him on August 30, although his sister Maria and Bukharin both pleaded with him at lunch not to go. They had just learned of the assassination that day of M. Uritsky, chief of the Petrograd Cheka; and Volodarsky had been assassinated on a Petrograd street June 21. Lenin had two engagements to speak that afternoon. The first went without incident. Then he spoke to workers at the Michelson factory. After his speech he paused outside the factory to answer questions from some of the workers who walked out with him. When he turned to enter his car, a girl ran out holding a paper, as if presenting a petition. As Lenin reached out for it, another girl, Fanny Kaplan, fired three bullets. Lenin was hit twice. He never entirely recovered from the effects of the bullet that entered his neck.

· 16 · I Say Farewell to Lenin

It was late in April, the spring thaws had set in, the air had a different
smell. For weeks I had longed to make another visit to the villages, but
was pinned behind a desk with the International Legion job in Moscow.
The German armies were occupying the Ukraine, the White armies re-
grouping in the Caucasus with new lures of Allied gold and promises of
intervention. The cities were hungry; the situation in the countryside was
tense and bitter. There were not enough tested Bolsheviks to go around. In
the north, English and French forces were in Murmansk and Archangel,
insisting they were there only to guard Allied supplies against the Germans. The center of danger, however, lay far to the east. And that was
where Kuntz and I were headed, on our way to Vladivostok and home.

I was getting the story of the treachery with which the Allies had operated to foment counterrevolution while enjoying diplomatic immunity in
Russia. It had begun even before Judson's recall. Only the sight now of
Robins' broad shoulders in his Red Cross uniform as he strode from the
Kremlin gave me some assurance that my country was no longer flirting
with the White generals. Or was it, behind his back? Or—since he had
known earlier about the conniving of Allied agents, as he was to reveal in
1919 in a Senate hearing[1]—did he know of any deals now with the Jap-

---

1. To underline the appeal made by the Lenin-Trotsky query to the U.S. government on
what aid could be expected if the Brest-Litovsk treaty were not ratified, Robins said he submitted it to Harold Williams, London *Daily Chronicle* correspondent, a "secret information
agent for the British Foreign Office," whose stories were carried by the *New York Times*
(usually conflicting with Ransome's London *Daily News* stories also appearing in the *Times*).
Robins' account of what he told Williams, which ended with Williams cabling both his paper
and the British Foreign Office in favor of support to the Soviets at this time, included the
following:

"You went down to Kief [Kiev] and worked with the Ukrainian rada. . . . You helped to
get American and French and English officers down there to cooperate with the Ukrainian

anese or the Cossack general Semenov and his bandit raiders in Siberia? All I knew was that he was still conferring with Lenin and Chicherin on the Japanese menace, and still bringing all the pressure he could on Wilson, by way of Ambassador Francis, to oppose intervention.

The coming of spring gave me itching feet, not for Vladivostok and America, but for the provinces. There lay the hidden heart of the crucial question: Would the Soviets survive? The need to do something at home to warn against intervention took precedence over all else, though. So I was giving up my equivalent of the Red Army soldier's pay—all fifty of the monthly rubles. The International Legion would have to struggle on without Kuntz and me. Meanwhile I tried to get others' thinking on how the wind was blowing on the land.

Even in Moscow there were visible signs of dislocation. Trains were crowded with refugees pouring into the city from regions taken over by the Germans. Others disgorged poor peasants and Red Guards who had joined forces to seek land farther east. And trains from Petrograd carried workers laid off by plants sabotaged by management or by shops where workers' control could not solve distribution problems or material shortages or where production simply creaked to a standstill. Other workers were quitting to return to the villages they had come from, where at least they could eat, they figured. The railroads were splitting at the seams with all these people on the move.

Meeting the *Manchester Guardian* correspondent Philips Price, who had been surveying conditions in the countryside for several weeks, I was given a vivid picture of the general confusion. Price was disturbed. A fine reporter, and one who generally shared my view, he was distressed about the gathering stormclouds of intervention.

He had been in several provinces and found conditions chaotic, a spirit of anarchy abroad in the land. Lenin insisted that one clause of the Brest-Litovsk pact (not all) be carried out: that there be no more attacks on German troops by bands of Red Guards. Ordered home, some wandered reluctantly and sullenly back to the cities. Others refused to disband, and having enlisted the sympathy of some peasants, continued raids and attacks on the Germans, who were in some cases now supplanting the Rada, which

rada. You helped to get the 130,000,000 francs that were paid to the Ukrainian rada about four days before it sold out, body, boots, and breeches, to the central powers, opened the front, and let in German rifles. I did not say . . . that you were an enemy of the allies or a German agent, or that you were being buncoed by the Ukrainian rada. I said you had made a bad guess, but that you were a perfectly sincere and patriotic man. Then, when you went down to Rostov on the Don, and worked with Kaledines [Kaledin] and Korniloff . . . you believed . . . that his Cossack soldiers would fight . . . , and then you came away, after we had gotten implicated in a counterrevolutionary move. . . . another bad guess." *Bolshevik Propaganda,* Hearings of the Overman Subcommittee of the Senate Judiciary Committee, Washington, D.C., 1919, pp. 803–804.

they had reinstated. Some of these bands included Bolsheviks who could not stand to retreat, having won back the power from the Rada in January and February. Other Red Guard bands turned outlaw in earnest, commandeered entire trains, dumped passengers unceremoniously, and forced the engineers to take them where they wanted to go.

The most noted of the bands of Red Guards was led by an old acquaintance, the dashing and fearless Dybenko, who presumably still held his post as head of the Navy and yet defied the Central Committee and continued guerrilla actions against the Germans in the western provinces. "He'll get away with it, too," I said, and Price agreed. We were right, incidentally; later arrested by less anarchistic Red Guards and brought before a revolutionary tribunal, Dybenko was merely reprimanded.

The new land law, effective on February 19, the fifty-seventh anniversary of Aleksandr II's decree emancipating the serfs, was spottily applied, but it was helpful already in some villages and counties where the poor peasants, acting on it, elected new land committees or transformed the old ones into units operating as part of local Soviets. Price said that committees in many places, however, remained under the control of the Right SR's. And the Left SR's, under the guise of a patriotic hatred of the Germans, were steaming up the peasants to oppose the Bolsheviks—in each case to protect their petty-bourgeois followers against the growing organization of the poor peasants by the Bolsheviks.

In other respects the law was no great advancement over the land decree of the Second Congress, except that the Bolshevik principle of large farms, instead of the "black partition" principle of the SR's, was set forth—on paper, at least. This article stipulated that collective-farm holdings were to be favored over individual holdings, and any peasants taking part in them were to be helped to practice horticulture, stock raising, market gardening, and dairying. As yet this was little more than a dream, but it was a dream put on record.

The time was ripe, Price said, for Lenin's "second revolution" to take place; nothing else could change the relation between city and town, and by no other means he could see would the needed grain and other farm products flow to the hungry city workers. By spring, in fact, the second or "October" revolution was beginning on the land. The landless peasants, or those who formerly eked out the marginal existence they got from tiny plots by working for richer peasants, in some sections were organizing.

The reason the actual land increases after October were so small in some communities was that most of the land grabbing had been accomplished prior to the Bolsheviks' seizure of power, and the most cunning had done the most grabbing. The main contingents of city workers on food detachments in the villages came later, but in April their advance guard arrived,

armed with clothing, spades, and other products of the factories to exchange
for grain. The peasants who had welcomed the Soviets for legalizing their
seizure of land and confirming them in their possession of it had attained
their objective, and now they had had enough of socialism. They greeted
the grain-requisitioning teams with hostility; the workers' tribute of clothing and so on was taken, and they were forced to return empty-handed.
"What price the land if the Soviets take what we grow on the land?" asked
the kulaks, and even the middle peasants. The ranks of the middle peasants
had swelled, thanks to their acquisitions when the red cock crowed in the
summer of '17. However, even in April there were instances, reported in
the press, in which the poor peasants were numerous and well organized
enough to dominate, to force a reorganization of the land committees and a
redivision of the land. The middle peasants gave up their new status and
newly acquired land to the poorer in these cases. The kulak was a harder
nut to crack. And the organization of the semiproletarians was just getting
under way. There was a beginning of violence; the country would later be
stippled over by peasant uprisings—open revolt against the Soviets.

Price and I agreed that things looked dark indeed. In his *Reminiscences
of the Russian Revolution*, Price's chapter on this period reads in part:

> Everywhere it could be seen that the spirit of rebellion still stalked
> the land. There were no more landlords or Cadet bankers to rebel
> against now, but there were invading Germans, for whom their own
> treaties were "scraps of paper," and there were Soviet Commissars in
> Petrograd and Moscow. The latter represented authority, and all au-
> thority was anathema in those days. Cyclopean fires, smouldering for
> centuries beneath the surface, were burning themselves out. The
> primitive instinct for revenge on age-long class oppressors was strong,
> and did not shrink from theft, murder, rape and outrages on the now
> defenseless bourgeoisie. In memorable lines a Left S.R. writer de-
> picted the spirit of these days [Aleksandr Blok in the poem "The
> Twelve"]. With amazing candour and honesty, the revolutionary
> poetry produced in Russia during the end of the winter 1917–18
> describes these types, and Blok half deifies them. It is most impor-
> tant, however, to understand that these symbols of rebellion were also
> the symbols of that very lack of discipline against which the Bolshe-
> viks had to commence now a relentless struggle.

What a lot of complications this first dictatorship of the proletariat had
to face! Lenin still consistently stood on one of the two planks that he had
laid down as long ago as 1905 as necessary for a successful revolution: the
proletariat and peasant alliance. It had passed its first stage when the city
workers joined with the peasantry as a whole to oppose the landlords; now

its second stage, when the city workers and poor peasants would struggle against the kulaks, was beginning.

What of the other plank? That was the support of the international proletariat. Did Lenin mention that these days? Oh, yes, he was still mentioning it the following August in the "Letter to American Workers," when he said, he knew that help would come from the advanced workers in other countries. "In a word, we are invincible, for the world proletarian revolution is invincible."

I must say I felt a long way from the American proletariat as I was turning homeward and beginning to think of the audiences I would be addressing. (As it turned out, I spoke to all groups, church organizations, businessmen, laboring men, intellectuals, but certainly the two million who bought copies of my little pamphlet[2] were not intellectuals.)

This, then, was the situation in the last week of April as Kuntz and I made our farewells. After the October Revolution their antagonists said in derision the Soviets would collapse within a few days; then they made it a few weeks. Now most of the Bolsheviks I spoke to harbored the suspicion that their tenure of power would be brief. They did not admit, however, that if it collapsed, they had failed. If it were a failure, it would be a highly successful failure. Like the Paris Commune, it would stand as a reservoir of lessons to be drawn upon in mankind's next effort to build a socialist society.

Some of them adopted a mood of almost ghoulish humor. Peters, with that Cockney accent of his, said, "We'll meet again, old man—that is, if we aren't all hanging on lampposts within a few days." He said it cheerfully.

Lunacharsky, more grim than I had ever seen him, said, "We may have to abandon Moscow. But if we slam the door and get out, we shall be back again!"

Robins (who was to follow me out within days, in May) still was doggedly cabling Francis in the hope that Washington might reverse the approval of Japanese intervention, warning that hatred of the Japanese would unite all presently warring factions and pointing out that recognition of the Soviets might be preferable. To me he indicated that he felt that without U.S. support, the Bolsheviks were doomed. "They made a good try. It will be your job to set them right before history. And mine."

"That hasn't the slightest appeal for me, Colonel. I want to see them go on making history. I'm not interested in any autopsy of the corpse and a

---

2. Albert Rhys Williams, *76 Questions and Answers on THE SOVIETS*, Chicago, n.d. In the same year, 1919, it appeared as *76 Questions and Answers on the Bolsheviks and the Soviets*, New York, n.d. Others printed it, too, I think, here and in England. It was sold at meetings on Russia, generally for ten cents.

precise fixing of the cause of death. I only want to help prevent it. How venal can those men in London and Paris be? They refuse to recognize the government here on the ground that it's temporary, unstable. Then when it looks most stable, they decide it must be crushed. Who else could stay in power six months?"

I did not know at the time, of course, that Wilson's decision was made. The man famed for insisting on self-determination is said to have let his adviser Colonel House make it for him, to spare his own squeamishness; he acceded to it in any case. And the Russian people, who did not want any kind of war, and followed the Bolsheviks in October because all other parties had failed to deliver peace, must keep on bleeding and dying and killing. Bukharin, Radek, and the so-called left lost out in their desire for a holy war against all imperialists; it was the Allies who were to wage a holy war on the workmen's and peasants' government of Russia. The Germans had carved off a huge slice of the sprawling giant. Presently Muscovy would shrink to little more than its small area of 300 years earlier, as the Far East came under White counterrevolutionary rule and Admiral Kolchak briefly sported the title of Supreme Ruler of Russia.

Charlie Kuntz and I left Moscow about April 24, 1918. My memory for dates and figures is wretched, and my notes and diaries from the date I helped organize the International Legion onward were missing when my materials were returned to me by the U.S. government the second time (the first was in Vladivostok) from Washington. Kuntz and I were going to Petrograd first, spend a day there, and take the weekly Trans-Siberian Express from the Nikolai Station the next night at eight P.M.

I recall telling Kuntz a couple of evenings before we left Moscow what I found to be the mood of some of the comrades to whom I was saying "so long." I was tired, discouraged, and feeling a little guilty, as if I were deserting the ship. Kuntz reacted with unusual sharpness when I gave him a sampling of their forebodings. He reminded me that after October too many of them had expected to attain socialism in short order. "There was one who did not, and we will be seeing him before we pull out," the professor said, and now he smiled at me.

"Lenin?" I asked incredulously. I thought I had persuaded Kuntz it would be presumptuous to take his time to say farewell.

Yes, he said, it was all arranged. He had phoned the Kremlin and talked to Lenin's secretary. The reply came shortly: "He has only five minutes to spare." We were to see him the morning of our departure and get the evening train to Petrograd.

It was about ten A.M. when we began our conversation with Lenin. It was noon when we were ushered out.

We arrived at his office much earlier. His secretary, in the anteroom, told us he was engaged. As time went on we grew curious as to who could be holding the Premier in conversation so long. The two visitors who emerged were two peasants such as one met by the million all over Russia, dressed in shaggy sheepskin coats, one wearing shoes made of strips of bark and the other wearing high felt boots.

Lenin was still smiling as he received us. Apparently the peasants had left him in an indulgent mood. He begged our pardon for keeping us waiting. "But we were having a lively conversation on some important matters." He strode up and down the room, hands behind him, a short stocky figure with a shining bald head, which Gorky aptly described as a Socratic skull. He radiated good humor. The peasants were from Tambov; one was an exceedingly shrewd old man, he said, and the other was also worth listening to.

Quite obviously there was plenty to discuss with peasants at that time. Lenin switched from English to Russian and occasionally to German as he spoke to us frankly of the serious problem of hunger, and of unemployment in the cities. Hunger the poor of Russia had always known, but that it should be with them now, when there was plenty in the bins of the rich peasants, was intolerable. Using a phrase he often employed, he said that "life itself" would force the Bolsheviks now to do what should have been done earlier in the Revolution—the organizing of committees of poor peasants. A start had been made in January, but the work was interrupted by the critical events around Brest-Litovsk.

Now, however, he said calmly, the initiative of the proletariat would be forced to assert itself. The result would be more "iron detachments" of workers to go to the villages. Such detachments fought and defeated the volunteer army of the old tsarist officer class; a much larger number of the working class would be needed to vanquish the kulaks, and in the process to establish self-discipline and vanquish their own vices. I have always remembered that; it showed that Lenin did not glorify workers, while at the same time he insisted they must take a more active part in the work of administration. What were these vices? Grown out of their sudden acquisition of power, they were petty-bourgeois concepts, resulting in efforts to get grain or bread only for their own, or for their friends. The Revolution did not produce pure souls overnight, greed was not limited to the bourgeoisie, to the grain hoarders or bagmen. To enforce the great socialist principle "He who does not work, neither shall he eat," those who enforced it—the people themselves—must acquire the idea of producing for the community.

Then Lenin glanced at us appraisingly and asked if we had been studying up on Siberia, and if we were ready for our "long hard journey." Indeed, he seemed greatly concerned about our trip, excited, almost as if he himself were going to America—which doubtless he would have liked to do if he had not been otherwise occupied. He turned to a map of Siberia to show us just where we would be going. He envied us, he said. Of course, we should be ready for every contingency, but his warnings were made with the impersonality of someone suggesting alternate routes for a friend bound on a long holiday; and in his enthusiasm over Siberia he was more like a travel agent proposing a ticket for the most distant spot within reach of our pocketbooks.

Did we have everything we needed for the trip? he asked. Was I taking many mementoes back with me?

I told him that I had a trunkful of diaries, notes, documents, newspapers, broadsides, copies of *Die Fackel*—material I hoped to base a book on. And described a motion-picture reel showing the creative and artistic side of the Revolution which the artists of the Moscow Arts Theater cooperated in producing. I was expansive about how I would show it all over the country. Lenin stroked his bald head, looked up at the ceiling, then said, "I'm afraid they won't allow all your literature and films to get into America. It must be pretty bad stuff, really."

He walked to the window, looked out, then turned and said cheerfully, "It is a beautiful country, you know, and the people—well, you will see the comrades in the Soviet at Vladivostok." Then, looking directly at me, he said, "But you are heading into the first point of the Allied invasion, too, remember. The Japanese and the British are there to greet you already. It would be unfortunate if you did not get there ahead of the American forces. I suggest you make all haste possible."

"But surely you cannot be serious," I blurted out. "Why, when I told Colonel Robins good-by he still seemed fairly hopeful of United States recognition, or some sort of support."

"Yes," Lenin said, "but Robins represents the liberal bourgeoisie of America. The liberal bourgeoisie does not decide the policy of America. Finance capital does. And finance capital wants control of Siberia."

To be altogether fair to Robins, although we later became close friends and I visited him on his Florida estate more than once, in the spring of 1918 he was not likely to confide in me, and while he spoke of hopes, formally, I felt that he was whistling in the dark. Being Robins, and tenacious, however, he would work until the last. I had no inkling that the last would come so soon. On April 25 he wrote a farewell letter to Lenin, correct in all particulars, and Lenin wrote a short reply which, also correct for the record, bristled; but significantly, the Lenin-Robins proposal for economic cooperation that they had been working on for Robins'

submission to Washington was sent Robins in May![3] Lenin must have
shared Robins' chief hope, then: that enough hardheaded industrialists and
those same finance capitalists would be interested in doing business with
Russia to bring some influence to bear on the "idealist" Wilson. Logically
they might well be, and as Carr points out, the document was virtually a
replica of agreements that later became standard Soviet practice in granting
concessions to foreign capital.

"And now about that trunkful of literature and diaries and so on,"
Lenin said briskly. "It would be a shame if something happened to that.
They may not welcome it in your country, but *we* shall give it a safe
exit insofar as it lies in our power." (He was quite right as to the papers'
reception in my country. Eventually the trunk, with some parts of my
diary containing entries of the last two months and a partially completed
first draft of my book on the Revolution missing, reached me, via Naval
Intelligence via the Department of Justice. The film was gone, too. There
was an addition that partly consoled me, however: my dossier, which
someone had been nice enough or careless enough—I prefer to think the
former—to place on top of everything else.)

Without more ado Lenin reached for a pen and wrote out a note,
signing it with the name that was to prove such powerful magic throughout our six-thousand-mile journey: *Lenin*. He directed the note to railway
personnel, asking that they extend every courtesy and care to see that our
trunks and luggage were undisturbed, and handed it to me. (It is ironical
that, with all the vicissitudes accompanying my trunk of notes and documents, most of them did find their way to my Greenwich Village apartment, whereas this note to the railway personnel and another that Lenin
wrote to me I lost entirely, by entrusting the two precious documents to
a comrade in Vladivostok for safekeeping.)

I made some mention to Lenin of the hopes I had for carrying out the
plan Chicherin had discussed with me, that on arrival home I should
head a Russian Bureau of Public Information, and assured him that it
had the approval of Arthur Bullard, since Sisson's departure the head of
the American Bureau of Public Information in Russia, and of Colonel
Robins.

For some reason Lenin did not comment on our plan, of which he
obviously knew. Perhaps there, too, he was more astute and less hopeful

3. More importantly, it is difficult to see Lenin indulging in any "curt reprimand" (as
Louis Fischer interpreted Lenin's letter), and a fortnight later forwarding to Robins, on May
14, a preliminary plan for Soviet-American economic cooperation on which they had had discussions, saying in a covering letter, "This preliminary plan was deliberated in the council of
export trade in our Highest Council of National Economy. I hope this preliminary [plan] can
be useful for you in your conversation with the American Foreign Office and American Export
Specialist." (Robins MSS)

than Robins and I, and realized Bullard could do little but approve so long as he and Ambassador Francis were on Russian soil. If so, he was right. The State Department decided the Soviets could have no information bureau in the United States, as their existence was not recognized.

Lenin spoke with the utmost confidence of what the socialist future would hold. Seemingly forgetting that Russia was beleaguered, her cities hungry, the solution to the food problem nowhere near settled, Lenin pictured what Siberia would become under socialism. He spoke of Siberia's great wealth in mines, from platinum to coal, its wide expanses, forests of virgin timber, and above all its long powerful rivers. Harnessed, dammed, they could be used in electrification; he saw great blast furnaces for steel mills, and cities arising in the wilderness.

In this vision not only the industries of Petrograd were electrified, but the unbuilt cities of Siberia too, and the mines of the Urals were developed along the most up-to-date lines. He grew so graphic that for years afterward, when certain canals were built, or dams or hydroelectric stations, I would think, How strange! I could have sworn that was built years ago! and then I would remember Lenin's pointing out on a map just where these projects should go. His faith in his people would not allow him to believe that Russia's plight was hopeless.

He laughed when I said he did not seem dejected by the prospect of being cooped up in the Urals. Oh, he said, the Urals are a sizable area. And they breathe freedom.

The odds confronting them were heavy. Lenin was now unsmiling, but neither was he mournful. He repeated more or less what I had heard him say before, that the Soviets faced a situation unlike anything Marx had foreseen. Nevertheless, there would would be resistance to intervention, not only within the Socialist Republic, but within the capitalist countries by the working classes, depending on their development.

That, I said, was why we were going home—to try to strengthen protest against such policies, hopefully before they were adopted.

Lenin began hitching his chair toward mine. He wanted to get across the full impact of his ideas, I thought, so that none should get lost in the intervening space. But it was my ideas he wanted to capture. He had a way of turning those inquiring, half-ironic, and altogether penetrating Tatar eyes on one, and then putting questions, pumping facts from the interviewer. As Bob Minor once said, Lenin "made the other person wag his tongue while he himself used his ears." (Hostile at the time, an anarchist, Minor had tried to put Lenin on the spot in an interview, but this proved the first step in Bob's being won to communism, and shortly he was to lay aside his brush and charcoal and become a Communist party policy maker, and the country thereby lost one of its best cartoonists.) Other correspondents I compared notes with had had similar experiences. We might be the reporters, but Lenin was the master reporter of all time.

And so it was that I found myself being questioned about American engineers and scientists ("We need thousands of them") and telling Lenin more than I had suspected I knew about engineers and scientists—facts I had picked up and forgotten, but now pulled out of my subconscious (a word not yet in fashion) by this human magnet. Then, with another question, as he edged his chair even closer, he exuded such warmth that I wanted badly to share his enthusiasm.

If Lenin was an insatiable questioner, he was also an insatiable listener —so long as one was saying anything worth listening to. He accorded others the same respectful attention he wanted for himself. When the person talking to Lenin ran out of ideas, that was another story. Then it was Lenin's turn. He was ready to discuss the situation in America, the development of socialism, and what factors in American society would affect relations between the classes. Alas, I had no brilliant ideas on the subject. In fact, from the theoretical viewpoint I had no ideas at all. So, as usual, when Lenin saw I had no ideas or information worth listening to, he took over.

At one point Lenin and Kuntz were talking philosophy in rapid Russian and German, and I let my mind wander. I was recalling what Robins told me. Lenin, he said, was addicted to two subjects, the Arctic and electrification. When Robins had satisfied Lenin with tales of his experiences while gold prospecting in the Klondike, he then felt he could slip in some talk on his own special enthusiasms—such as religion. When Lenin became restive, Robins would throw out a fact or two on electrification and recapture his interest. When I mentioned this to Gumberg, he said with some visible glee, "Yes, but the last time Robins began sounding off about the Nazarene and so on, Lenin confounded him by listening intently and then saying, 'It is easy to understand why these beliefs had such appeal for the oppressed. Marx had a profound understanding of it when he wrote, 'Religion is the sigh of the hard-pressed creature, the heart of a heartless world, as it is the soul of soulless circumstances.' Robins knew only the last line of the quote, 'It is the opium of the people,' and had thought it was made in scorn. He was a bit subdued."

Nevertheless, I decided to use Robins' gambit now, and see how long I could hold Lenin's interest. So when I had a chance, I interrupted the flow of philosophical talk to mention that I had heard he had written a book based on his studies of U.S. government statistics on agriculture. So of course, I said, he was aware of our own marginal lands, our tenant farmers, as well as our great farm holdings with their big yields. I threw in a bit about the readers of socialist periodicals in some poor areas. And here

I slipped in my experiences in the Russian hinterland with Yanishev, and the time I had lost face with the peasants by admitting I owned no land. While Lenin was still laughing I got in my question.

I meant to return to Russia, I said, as soon as it was feasible (I did not foresee that intervention would last until 1920, and much longer in Vladivostok) after telling my countrymen what I could of the Revolution. By the time I returned, would the middle peasant, whom Lenin had described as a man who had a pair of horses but barely made ends meet, have the socialist understanding not to despise me for owning "not a single dessiatine" of land?

This opened up a wide vista of controversial questions, and apparently Lenin sensed that that was just what I intended, for he eyed me with a sort of delight, as if saying, So you can be a shrewd muzhik, too! He said in effect that until "October" came to the land (the rampaging of the red cock had been the peasants' "February Revolution"), this consciousness could not be widespread. There was a beginning of it, even now, however, as evidenced by the Tambov peasants. No wonder he had taken such pleasure in their visit!

His talk about the coming war between the classes on the land, in which he saw the city workers as partners with the poor peasantry, led quite naturally to another subject. Socialism could not survive long in only one land, and a complete triumph of October—i.e., a classless society, or communism—was a long time away. It depended on the revolution of the international proletariat, and Lenin put no time limit on that.

He admitted without any hesitation that so long as the dictatorship of the proletariat was needed, it would be like any other dictatorship. He promised that the intransigent minority, who had been top dogs in tsarist times, would be repressed as ruthlessly as their resistance demanded. More than once I had heard Lenin point out that the Paris Commune failed because it did not crush the bourgeois resistance at once. And if I did not know it then, I since have found his epigrammatical formulation of what Engels said: "So long as the state exists there is no freedom; when freedom exists there will be no state."[4]

When would that freedom or classless society come about? It was, he said, not dependent on Russia alone. Russia was at present the lone state where the dictatorship of the proletariat was practiced; and despite her weakness and present impotence, it looked as if all the powerful capitalist

4. In *The State and Revolution*, in which he adds: "Only then can we speak of freedom. Then people will become accustomed to the observance of these elementary rules of social life, known for centuries, repeated for thousands of years in all sermons. They will observe them without force, without constraint, without the special apparatus of compulsion called the state, which will wither away and die. In the words of Engels, 'the government over persons will be replaced by an administration of things.' "

states were quaking at the idea, and determined to wipe out this power.

At times he spoke of how the October Revolution would triumph "soon." At other moments he indicated there would be "a period of wars and revolutions lasting from fifty to seventy-five years" in various lands, and then the "soon" became simply a matter of ultimate triumph. It was a matter of *when* it would triumph most of the time, and not *whether*.

Far sooner than that, however, and in the process of being accomplished now, was the abolition of man's exploitation of man and the ownership of private property. Under present circumstances the work of destruction of the old state apparatus had gone almost too swiftly; the more radical Communists were impatient even at the new land law, declaring that the plan for state farms would mean that men worked for others, a return to wage slavery. This was said dryly by Lenin, who had been urging the workers not to take over plants until they knew how to run them.

"We will triumph—if we survive meantime; but this means we will have to make a few concessions *for the moment* to get the productive machine going enough to survive. And, if we triumph, or even if we do not, our example will be the inspiration of revolutions in far-off Asian, South American, and African countries."

It should not be long before the European proletariat joined them. No, he said, he would not say when. Others had made that mistake. "But I will tell you this much. The Kaiser's downfall will come within the year. That is absolutely certain." It was a more definite prediction than I had ever heard Lenin make before, and he was right. Seven months later, on November 10, Kaiser Wilhelm abandoned his army and fled to Holland, after he had been asked to renounce his throne by his own appointed imperial chancellor, Prince Max of Baden. In Holland Wilhelm was given a castle, and there he spent his remaining years, aloof from the world's events.

"In the end," said Lenin, with the same assurance, "countries will coalesce into a great socialist federation or commonwealth—in seventy-five or one hundred years."

The fact that Lenin specifically mentioned the Asian and even the African peoples without saying anything about when the American revolution would occur interested me far less at the moment than what he had said earlier about American intervention. Realizing we had stayed far longer than he had intended us to stay, I put one last question.

"But all you say about the future—if intervention is a reality, if my country puts no brake on it but aids it, what then?"

"Then," said Lenin, "it means all-out defense on our part. We are going on that assumption now. It will take priority over all else. In that event," he went on, "the Revolution might be slowed or even temporarily distorted

284 • JOURNEY INTO REVOLUTION

in form; its purpose, its goals would remain the same, their achievement only postponed. Under foreign invasion our war-weary people will find a new stimulus to fight, and the peasants to defend their land. They will learn that, just as it did with the Germans, the coming in of Japanese, British, French, *or* Americans will mean the return of the landlords. For any invader must have a base, and the only one he can find among the people will be the White officer class. So who knows? The revolution may be hastened by your imperialistic government. If so, it will be a great mistake—for your country, your people, and for mine.

"For we will triumph in the end," he said, "make no mistake about that."

Then he turned to me and, much as if remarking on a concert we had missed or the.outcome of a game of chess, said he was sorry to be losing me as a prospective member of the Marxist class. His eyes were kind as he said he understood, I was very American, but I would learn; times of crisis were especially good times for learning something of theory.

I remember walking back down the corridors of the Kremlin with Kuntz. Neither of us had much to say. It did not occur to us to feel flattered that the Chairman of Sovnarkom had talked with us for two hours. I doubt if the two peasants from Tambov thought about it, either. We were simply engrossed in the incredible difficulties ahead; such were his simplicity and his power of concentration that his words burned into his hearers and caught fire, even when their expression seemed casual.

Lenin's voice saying, "We will triumph in the end"—a voice rather high-pitched and harsh and inexpressibly dear and familiar—in the rather bare, workmanlike room he had picked for his office in the Kremlin, is part of the picture I retain.

Later on it struck me: So he had never quite reconciled himself to abandoning the idea of that Marxist class! Nor was there any hint of chiding in his mention of it. It was just one more affirmation of the correctness of the estimate I reached long before I knew Lenin himself, based on everything my Russian-American friends had told me. In respecting another's convictions Lenin did not urge one to go beyond where, on his own initiative, that person was willing to go, and that is part of the art of being a nice human being. Lenin was as nice a one as ever I knew, in addition to being a great man.

· 17 · Destination Vladivostok

Petrograd-bound, Kuntz and I recalled that it was less than two months since we had entrained with our band of International Legionnaires for Moscow, our beloved Red Peter in peril from the Germans. We were going north now instead of south, in a train no less dilapidated but less crowded, for again the exodus from Petrograd was the heaviest, because the hunger there was the worst. The next night we would head west.

"Before we were worried about the Boches; now it's the Japanese and the tricky French and English," said Kuntz, as the train lurched and banged and rattled away. "And it won't be long before the American doughboys arrive to help restore 'order' under the Whites."

I still did not agree. "I'm not sure Lenin does either, really. Or why would he be talking about attracting American engineers and scientists? A thousand, no less! By the way, what was it Lenin said to you in German this morning? My German is getting rusty. Something about dreaming."

"Oh, yes," the Professor said. "Lenin said, in effect, we are not utopians, but one must have the courage to dream, or socialist planning would be useless."

"I hoped that was what he said!" I could have crowed. "Now if I could only see Yanishev and Voskov! And they call *me* romantic! Now I could answer smugly, 'But Vladimir Ilyich has nothing against dreaming.' And why should he? Every revolution began with a dream of a fairer world to come."

Suddenly it hit me with sickening finality. Possibly there would be no "next time" for banter with Voskov or Yanishev. There were rumors that Yanishev was in the north, being groomed as a Red Army political commissar by Trotsky; at any rate, he had vanished from sight. There was a chance we might see Voskov in Petrograd; or was there? We would arrive late in the morning (at least this time we were not in a boxcar, and so we were in less danger of being shunted to some siding) if our luck held. I had not seen Voskov since before he was sent to Finland. Only by the barest chance had he survived. Robins recently gave me news of him: he was in Petrograd, commanding Red forces protecting the city—in other words, resting, as the city was not threatened. But this was three weeks ago that Robins had checked and learned he was there.

By tomorrow, I grumbled, Voskov might be sent to some other danger spot, if he hadn't been already. This was of course before full-scale intervention whipped up the civil war, but it was not long after this that Trotsky issued an order for disciplined Communists "ready to die" to be sent to the Volga, where the White volunteer army was attacking; that communication of Trotsky's added characteristically, "Lightweight agitators are not needed here."

When we pulled out of Petrograd on the weekly Trans-Siberian Express at eight the next evening, standing on the platform for one last look at Petrograd, we had failed to locate Voskov.

In a sense, I was relieved at not seeing him after the heartbreaking experience of Finland, where he had seen a workers' and peasants' government erased by the Germans under Mannerheim. Would that blithe spirit I had come to love be finally altered, would the spring have gone out of what I perversely considered the true Russian soul, so different from that mystical Dostoyevskian soul? Maybe it never changed; I prefer to think so. Anyway, I never saw him again. Nor Yanishev.

As for Lenin's "dreaming," proof of how it was coupled with the most down-to-earth practicality was contained in a copy of *Pravda* of April 28, which we did not see until we got to Vladivostok. And long afterward I saw the editorial it inspired in the *New Republic*, which termed it "a remarkable statement . . . difficult . . . for a revolutionary leader to make," adding, "It is blunt, courageous, intelligent, based on a deep knowledge of history and economics and infused with a flaming revolutionary spirit, and at the same time it is as cautious, concrete and prosaic as though written by an American business organizer."

More sharply than he had stressed before, Lenin in that speech said, "Keep accurate and conscientious accounts, conduct business economically, do not load, do not steal, maintain strict discipline at work." In other revolutions the proletariat and toiling peasants did the work of destruction and the propertied class followed with the work of construction, but in a socialist revolution the main job of the proletariat and poorest peasants was to build "an extremely complex and delicate net of newly organized relationships covering the systematic production and distribution of products which are necessary for the existence of tens of millions of people."

Possibly he had been trying out his ideas on us, for in the speech made so soon after our departure he also spoke of buying the services of "a thousand first-class scientists and specialists," adding that even if they paid these capitalist experts "twenty-five, fifty or even a hundred thousand rubles a year, they will be cheap at the price."

For some reason, neither the Professor nor I doubted that we would see Lenin again. Both of us were to return to Russia and spend a good many years there.[1] It is possible Kuntz did see him again and neglected to say so; it is possible out of negligence I did not think to ask him.[2]

The journey from Petrograd to Vladivostok was lightened for me by the fact that I journeyed with the Professor. In a sense it was one long, though interrupted, commentary on Lenin and the Revolution by the Professor and me. When there was no avoiding the White émigrés who were our fellow passengers, it became a sort of traveling forum. Kuntz regarded them with detached decorum. Their pose of offended persons mangled by an ungrateful peasantry was irresistible to me; I had to tangle with them. An old aristocrat insisted on quoting Herzen on revolution to me. When I pointed out that it was the results of the 1848 revolution in Paris that sickened Herzen, the old boy replied in French, "Revolution is revolution, wherever and whenever; and peasants are peasants." So I took pleasure in replying that according to Herzen, the gentry were the gentry, and that it was on Herzen's authority that I learned, as a seminary student, that half of the landowners murdered in Russia by their serfs had perished in consequence of their misdeeds.

Most Russians like to talk as much as I do, so although I affronted some of them, they would leave in a huff only to return later with some new argument. Kuntz was a wonderful audience, and I suppose I enjoyed showing off; later at home he would repeat my sallies with delight and improve on them.

A pleasant feeling of timelessness set in. The steppe country recalled Chekhov and Tolstoi, and seemed mysterious and beckoning, much as the Dakota lands must have seemed to the Norwegian immigrants in America. A sense of the vastness of the country through which we moved took possession of us.

1. ARW was in Soviet Russia again from 1922 until December 1927, most of which time I was with him. He returned for another period, that of 1930–31, and again in 1937 for a stay of about six months. See the Epilogue.—ED.

2. As for myself, when I first returned Lenin had suffered his first stroke. Because he was not then seriously ill, it would have been possible to visit him, but some overscrupulous diffidence prevented my requesting permission—my only real regret of a lifetime.

(From an associate of Kuntz in Icor, one of the *Freiheit* editors, I learned that a rumor persisted for years that when Lenin was seriously ill, Kuntz was one of the few persons allowed to see him. Had the editor asked Kuntz about this? Never, he replied testily; Kuntz's reticence forbade it. His relatives doubted the truth of the rumor.—ED.)

I had arrived in Petrograd in June 1917, and now it was May 1918. We had lived so intensely, our senses and minds and hearts so taken up with the moment that there had been little chance to sit back and reminisce, or even to get a perspective. I thought now with real nostalgia of those September and October days, roaming through Viborg with John Reed, the lights blazing in the Smolny many a night through, and I regretted these clattering wheels taking us far away. I had a sudden desire to talk about Jack to the Professor, who had a special feeling for him.

Kuntz made me tell him what I knew of Jack's background, and that was little—only that he had been born and brought up in a big house in Portland, Oregon, surrounded by respectability. Being a Westerner at Harvard and making lots of clubs, but not the best ones, may have helped turn him into a rebel. Kuntz had me repeat some of Jack's anecdotes, and I found one he did not know.

This was one of a series of skits called "The Morning After," in which Jack alternated in the roles of a good bourgeois citizen and of the prosecutor before a revolutionary court. To the charge of antirevolutionary activities, the culprit entered a firm "Not guilty." Then the prosecutor took over.

"But were you not seen entering the Union League Club?"

"Never. I have always voted a straight Democratic ticket."

"That is no alibi these days, comrade. And weren't you a subscriber to *The New York Times?*"

There were better Reed stories, but Kuntz laughed enormously. I told him how Reed envisioned returning to the Harvard Club in New York (which he did, many times; a note he wrote to Mrs. Raymond Robins, enclosing something for her husband and explaining casually that he [Reed] was out on bail awaiting trial, was written on cheap paper but from the Harvard Club). In this skit a classmate who was a stockbroker or a lawyer with the Department of Justice would approach Reed, slap him on the back, and ask indulgently what chicanery he was up to now.

"Nothing much. Just drawing up this list of people to be hanged after the revolution," and glancing at the paper, Reed would add: "Like Abou Ben Adhem, your name leads all the rest."

Kuntz had heard that one, but remembering how Reed laughed, he himself laughed immoderately, then fell silent.

Day after day the great ribbons of steel unwound endlessly. One could lament over the hardships of the journey, as the White émigrés did, or point out that throughout the breadth of continent in the turmoil of a colossal revolution we traveled with few privations. The steady click of the wheels had a hypnotic influence. After three weeks of it I found it hard to sleep in Vladivostok; I was train-tipsy.

Along this very route in tsarist times the exiles had dragged themselves, and the clank of their leg chains and their mournful songs sound forever in the great Russian literature of the nineteenth century. This was a highway of sorrow and tears, of "the unfortunates," as they used to be termed by sympathetic peasants.

Early in the journey I managed to learn more about Kuntz. He had studied philosophy in Vienna University, in Paris, and elsewhere in Europe, and after coming to America in the mid-nineties he spent some four years at Columbia in New York studying anthropology, sociology, and philosophy, becoming a close associate of Professor Franz Boas. Returning to Europe, he divided his time between the Bibliothèque in Paris and the British Museum in London for two years, studying anthropology. He never sought degrees or formal teaching jobs. He returned to America to take up chicken farming plus writing ventures, including a vast socio-logical-philosophical work he never brought to a conclusion. (When he died penniless in 1953, having given away a fortune, he left a mountain of manuscripts in the one-room shack where he spent his last days.)

I reminded Kuntz, as we stood endlessly in line to fill our teakettle with hot water at a boiler, a feature of railroad stations throughout Russia, of the many times I listened to his syllogisms proving the inevitability of the triumph of the Revolution. "Yet if it was inevitable, why did you bother to shoulder a gun for the Revolution?" Finally we held our kettle under the faucet until it was full and barely made our way on board when the bell sounded.

Kuntz laughed delightedly. "This occupied men's minds in the seventeenth century, at least in England, when materialism was declared inconsistent with a belief in free will. This was nicely answered, long before Marx and Engels worked out dialectical materialism, but it arose again, and it was argued anew that this doctrine would lead to quietism. Plekhanov settled all this long ago, but it will be argued again, tiresomely, by those with dusty souls. Among other things, old Plekhanov pointed to the religious sects that were necessitarians—the Puritans for instance, who even believed in fatalism—as being the most energetic souls imaginable. In the same work[3] Plekhanov shows the importance of individuals in history. But to answer you, no, for me to take up a gun involved no violation of the dialectic, my dear Albert."

That eased my mind considerably. What he said about individuals

---

3. George Plekhanov, *The Role of the Individual in History*, New York, 1940. Some subjectivists, in stressing the individual, refused to recognize the historical progress of mankind, and "some of their later opponents, striving to bring out more sharply the coherent character of this progress, were evidently prepared to forget that *men make history, and, therefore, the activities of individuals cannot help being important in history*. They have declared the individual to be *quantité négligeable*. In theory, this extreme is as impermissible as the one reached by the more ardent subjectivists" (23). Plekhanov's essay was first published in 1898.

reminded me of Professor E. A. Ross, one of the many Americans who wandered over to Petrograd in 1917. A sociologist at the University of Wisconsin, he journeyed widely and observed much in Russia. I took issue with him on one of his favorite themes: that without Lenin and Trotsky the same revolution would have occurred. He argued that it was solely a product of the people, the implication being that their leaders were reduced in political significance to something like that of Democratic ward heelers in New York City. Until I met Ross I had felt that my special mission was to show the people as the real force in the Revolution. "But he annoyed me," I told Kuntz. "He was too sweeping. I would admit that the Revolution might have occurred without either Lenin or Trotsky; but he wouldn't admit that it might have foundered without them."

Plekhanov, Kuntz said, quoted Carlyle on heroes, calling them "beginners," and he agreed with Carlyle because "a great man is precisely a beginner [who] sees *further* than others and desires things *more strongly* than others."

"How that fits Ilyich, yes?" said the Professor.

"Yes, and by the way, without a Lenin, Marxism might have sunk to an arid science that little sects fought about," I said, without thinking. I saw Kuntz's color rise. I had hurt him, unintentionally, and knowing it would be effrontery to apologize, I quickly turned to something else that might challenge him without wounding. (Years later when I read an insufferable but interesting obituary on Lenin in the *Times* of London, which indicated that without the Revolution, Lenin would have remained an obscure member of an obscure sect splitting hairs about what Marx really meant, I recalled this painful moment with Kuntz.)

"But what about Lenin's remarks?" I began with a show of truculence.

"What remarks, Albert?" the Professor said politely, polishing his glasses.

"Why, this time differential. It bothers me. The Revolution will survive, and as he said at the Third Congress, socialism in one state cannot survive. Now he tells us he foresees twenty-five, fifty, seventy-five years of wars and revolutions. Is it all the same if the Revolution triumphs in seventy-five years as if it triumphs in ten? For there was a time when he said Russia would have socialism in ten years, right?"[4]

---

4. In *The State and Revolution* he briefly took issue with the anarchists for indicating the state could be done away with "overnight"; the transition would occupy "a whole historical period."

In 1917 most of the Bolsheviks I knew were more optimistic than Lenin as to the final victory of worldwide socialism. Still, I do not think this wishful thinking is confined to the Slavs. Bernard Shaw confessed that when, in 1888, he became imbued with the vision of socialism and was asked how long it would be before it was established, he replied, "In from three to four years."

Kuntz laughed gently. "What do you want, a seer? Lenin has no crystal ball."

"Agreed. But I'm saying that if Marxism is the science it's supposed to be, Lenin wouldn't have to change his estimate of when world revolution will be here or when a classless society is achieved. So why don't all of you quit using this word 'inevitability'? I'm not talking about free will versus necessity now—you won that one."

"But Lenin does not play with Marxism like words in a puzzle. As for the classless society, it was an indulgence to speak of it at this time, or any time—but he is not altering in any essential way anything he said earlier."

"All right," I conceded grudgingly. "Still, mistakes are made. Lenin keeps saying so." I listed a whole series of problems whose solutions seemed far from guaranteed. It was said that Lenin was uncertain about Trotsky's policy (eventually Lenin backed Trotsky in it strongly) of wooing tsarist officers to join the Red Army, giving them positions of command. The Left Communists and Left SR's were complaining bitterly about it. Would Kuntz say with certainty that Trotsky's policy of iron discipline in a revolutionary army would work? The memory of discipline as it existed in the tsarist army, companies of peasants forced to go into hopeless action without guns or shoes when they would be mown down like grass, was all too much alive.

Because of this insistence on authority, Trotsky was threatening with severe punishment commanders or political commissars if they incorporated partisan guerrilla bands of the Red Guards. This was a far cry from the people's militia that Lenin envisioned in his pamphlet, written in hiding, *Can the Bolsheviks Retain State Power?*[5]

That was just one problem. Then, the peasants who had the grain had enough land and enough revolution. There was not enough arable land to go around without that third revolution. Three revolutions. Three times and out. But who could wait for the third? And where would Trotsky get the troops, without further dislocations in the factories?

"So, what are you proving?" the Professor asked benignly.

"Why, that trial and error are all that's possible in the first revolution of its kind in all the nineteen hundred years of Judeo-Christian civilization."

---

5. Written in late September 1917, it poses a workers' militia using *"revolutionary democratism"* and operating in town and country alike to "heal the frightful wounds the war has inflicted on the people," distributing provisions, clothing, footwear, the land, and so on. The entire people would be mobilized, led by the class-conscious workers, who would enlist the oppressed for the "work of administration." Here Lenin puts forth the idea of universal labor service. With the grain monopoly, bread rationing, and universal labor service in the hands of the proletarian state, the sovereign Soviets would have "the most powerful means of accounting and control."

"Quite true. Or the thousands of years of Chinese history, with countless peasant revolutions, and we might as well throw in Greek and Roman periods, too."

"Professor," I said, "maybe I'm scared. I want the October Revolution to win out, and I believe it will. But just because I want it, I can't say it will. And I worry. And Lenin is shouldering too much."

This was a theme more real than our academic jousting over abstractions. How much could a man do and not burn himself up? But the thought carried with it no foreboding; that Lenin would live such a short time, die at fifty-three, was inconceivable to any of us, barring the ever present threat of assassination.

Lenin held in his hands the reins of command issuing from the Kremlin to the Far East and to every trouble spot on every front, checking up here, there, everywhere, on the telephone, by telegram, by notes sharp and impatient, holding out no mercy for the lazy or shiftless or unthinking or bureaucratic.

And all the while he was coping with all the other giant problems—how to get production going, how to manage distribution with the railroads falling apart, how to get grain from the sullen kulak population. Yet he made time to confer with Chicherin and Robins (the poor and valiant Colonel, he never really gave up until he was ordered home) on the ominous situation in the Far East.

It must be remembered that intervention was just beginning. At a later date it held both advantages and disadvantages for the stricken Russian Federation of Socialist Republics. Resentment against foreign interference mounted with the Allies' invasions and turned resentment against the German occupation in the Ukraine and other parts of the south into hatred of the Allies, now openly supporting the White Guard. The nationalist sentiments of a portion of the officer class and the middle-class elements were aroused, and these elements, however reluctantly, rallied to the defense of the Soviets.

In May, however, this had not happened. It was only later that the peasants were swung over to the side of the Red Army. It was only later that the corruption of elements in the White officers' volunteer army (they were taking money from the Germans and large sums from the Allies as well) became so flagrant that those who really wanted to act from patriotic motives were weaned away by the Bolsheviks.

I never understood Kuntz's philosophy entirely, or how much of it was determinism and how much was Marxism. Whatever it was, he got a vast degree of comfort out of it. I am not saying Kuntz always saw the reality. I am saying that he always seemed to hold to his philosophy and to maintain the most imperturbable belief in mankind, and to remain sunny and kind in the face of many trials, meeting all rebuffs and irritations with great equanimity.

As we moved up through the low winding passes of the Urals, I said scornfully, "Do you call these mountains? Why, they're only hills—they're not much higher than the plain. I thought of something grand, like the Rockies." I remember a stone that marked the senseless dividing line between two continents. We read the word "Asia" as we approached; looking back, we saw it read "Europe" on the other side. It was hard to believe it was all Russia, at that. We began to speculate on how long it would take us, going east, to reach our own west coast.

From forests of larch and silver birch and occasional blue, blue lakes seen through the budding trees, we entered the green tunnels of the taiga, the evergreens close on either side of the track. Lenin's map and his vision of great blast furnaces bore little relation to the wilderness around us. I tried to visualize what Gary, Indiana, would look like in this forest primeval, belching forth its smoke, its open-hearth furnaces visible for miles, but even the sparks from our wood-burning locomotive seemed anomalous here.

We traveled peacefully, except for a few exciting moments when the train was held up because of a rumor that the Tsar and his family[6] were in flight and on board. That was somewhere near Omsk. While the miners and Red Guards searched the train, by producing my letter from Lenin I eventually persuaded one of the railwaymen to tell me what the holdup was about. A telegram from Omsk had warned that Nikolai had made his escape and with a staff of former officers was on the Trans-Siberian Express. Before the heavily armed hunters departed, and the burzhuy in our car began tearfully thanking God they were alive, Kuntz and I, as virtual emissaries of Lenin, were embraced on the platform outside and sent off with cheers. But at the next crossroads the brakes ground again, the car was invaded, the search repeated.

"At this rate," I complained to Kuntz, "our luxurious fast express will be as slow as the old Erie."

At Marinsk, where we again showed our credentials and tried to convince the invaders that the Little Father was nowhere around, and again overrode suspicions that our documents were forged, a commissar took action. He sent a telegram to other stations along the line. It failed to stop

6. Later, on the night of July 16–17, 1918, the former Tsar and his family were shot in Ekaterinburg by order of the Ural regional Soviet. The Czechs captured the town ten days later. Concern that he would become the symbol around which a counterrevolutionary movement could gain adherents had been growing as the Czechs advanced, seizing the key point of Samara on the Volga on June 8, then Ufa and Simbirsk before Ekaterinburg. Carr, *Bolshevik Revolution*, I, 166, 351.

the holdups of the train, but turned the would-be lynching parties into receptions for two Americans:

> To all Soviets:
> Kuntz and Williams, General Organizers of the Red Army, are on Train Two. I ask that representatives of the Soviets meet with them for consultation.
>
> SADOVNIKOV

So we substituted for Nikolai II, and the crowds gathered at each station heard the message read aloud—which called for a lightning switch of mood. Probably we lost some of the audience Nikolai would have had, but in each case, those who remained upheld the honor of the Revolution and gave us a gala welcome. Kuntz was discomfited, and even I, with all my platform artifices, was at a loss when, after following their stories of how their Soviet or their new school was functioning, I was approached by newly organized Red Army groups and solemnly asked for military counsel. The entire business made us more suspect than ever to our émigré fellow passengers, but it was a wonderful chance to see how even in those faraway places the Revolution was in force; not uniformly, it is true, and with great variations, but the workers were in power, and in some cases the peasants were joining with them.

By the time we got to Cherm (Chermkhovo), notorious as the most brutal of the tsars' inland penal colonies, our fellow passengers were weak with fear. When the two miner commissars of Cherm summoned Kuntz and me outside, we were greeted with red banners welcoming "the miners in all lands" and "our comrades throughout the world," and joined with them in singing the Internationale. Kuntz was so moved he could not make his speech of reply to their delegate's fervent welcome and their expressed hope that workers of other lands would soon own their mines, too. My Russian fled. So we sang again, and climbed on the train. Leaning out, we waved as long as we thought they could see us, and until their great red banner was no longer visible to us.

As we returned to hostile looks and sarcastic comments of "jailbirds turned politicians," I for once had no heart for civil rejoinders.

"Now do you see why we are leaving? Imagine Russia being directed by unkempt beasts like that!" hissed one faded woman to me. She had poked her head into our compartment and held her face close to mine and her breath was bad.

I told her she was doing the right thing, gathering up her jewels and valuables and fleeing her homeland altogether, as she meant to do. "It is all your peasants want of you." And I pulled up the window.

Kuntz spoke at one point of the temperate character of the Revolution as we had seen it. He had seen exactly one man killed. During the seizure of the Winter Palace and in the telephone building I heard shots aplenty, but few were killed. What he said was pertinent and true—up to now.

Presently all this was to be completely altered. The Revolution was to turn bloody. With the introduction of a new factor, violence was to become open and naked. The new element, of course, was intervention. Now limited, it would soon plunge the entire country from the Pacific to the western border into the tornado of civil war. Almost no section would fail to be involved. The very rail route over which we traveled in such a generally amiable mood would be drenched in blood, as "trains of death" with their tragic convoys would shuttle back and forth, filled with ill, dying, and dead Bolshevik and other Soviet prisoners, and with more dying as cities under White domination refused to allow them to stop.

With so much of our journey behind us—and, hopefully, all the unscheduled interruptions—we began thinking of what lay ahead. It was strange to think that we would penetrate much farther into Siberia than Lenin or Martov or any of the revolutionaries we had left in Moscow.

When Lenin went to Siberia in 1897, after a year in jail, he paid his own way and took the Trans-Siberian railway, then traveled by horseback, fording the river Ob, and went on by train to Krasnoyarsk, where he remained while the authorities picked out his exact place of banishment. When he went to Shushenskoye on the great rolling Yenisei River, he was within sight of the foothills of the Sayan Mountains. All these details I learned later from reading Krupskaya's memoirs; in all his talk of Siberia, Lenin had not mentioned them.

"Both Lenin and Krupskaya looked on their stay in Siberia as a sort of holiday," Kuntz said when we tried to figure how far from Shushenskoye in the Minussinsk region lay our destination, Vladivostok. This was surprising to me, but I assumed he was right. The always modest Kuntz knew both Lenin and his wife, I suspected, better than I, although I was not sure; if he relayed any personal anecdote about them, which was rare, he told it as if it were common knowledge. Lenin loved skating on the Yenisei when it was frozen over, and hunting. Having studied law, he gave advice on its mysteries to peasants, and after winning a case for a man who had worked in the Lena gold fields he was consulted by many. Legally he was not allowed to do this, and conceivably the kulaks whose workers he advised of their rights might have got Lenin sent to a penal colony. Actually political prisoners, once they landed at their place of Siberian exile, enjoyed a surprising amount of freedom. Of course, they were also free to contract tuberculosis, as old Martov, Chernishevsky, and any number of others did.

Lenin was starting on his second year of exile when Krupskaya, banished to Ufa, obtained permission to join him as his fiancée. Taking her mother with her, she arrived in May 1898 with orders to return to Ufa at once if they did not marry. Since Lenin's identification papers had not arrived, the district police official refused to issue a marriage certificate. But finally the red tape was untangled, the certificate was issued, and they were married July 10, 1898. Krupskaya writes, "After the winter frosts, Nature burst forth tempestuously into the spring. Her power became mighty. Sunset. In the great spring-time pools in the fields wild swans were swimming. Or we stood at the edge of a wood and listened to a rivulet burbling, or wood-cocks clucking." Lenin's exile came to an end in February 1900.

Krupskaya, her mother, and Ilyich rode horseback 300 versts along the Yenisei, changing horses frequently and riding day and night, "thanks to the moonlight, which lit up everything." Lenin wrapped both women in their elkskin coats at every stopping place. Then at Ufa he left them, as Krupskaya had yet to complete her term of exile in Siberia. Lenin went on, meeting Martov and entering Petersburg, where they were promptly arrested.

If the gendarmes who were following them had been clever, and held up to the light a piece of paper Lenin carelessly had with him, they might have noticed it was doctored. And that might have been disastrous, as on it were names of all the contacts he meant to visit in regard to starting a newspaper. As it was, he and Martov both received only a nominal ten-day sentence—a close shave, and really impermissible for a revolutionary, as it was routine for the Tsar's secret police to tail all returned politicals and if possible obtain their convictions on charges more serious than loitering, vagrancy, or whatever it was that Lenin and Martov were charged with.

I had heard the details of the arrest described by comrades in Petrograd, with different reactions. Peters, who so disliked his secret-agent role in the Cheka, felt proud that Ilyich by nature was such a miserable conspirator. I think it was Yanishev who seemed distressed when I asked him about it, as he said it showed Lenin "had no instinct for self-protection whatsoever." At any rate, I brought it up with the Professor for another reason.

"How odd," I said, "that Lenin, who made such a point of being vigilant, taking precautions, was so careless himself."

Kuntz seemed to agree, but said that Lenin learned through several early instances of his own carelessness. "By nature he is impetuous and open. So was his brother, which is why he was caught. Ah, what a family! It is fortunate, though, that he had Krupskaya to check his impetuousness and to go about for him in 1905, and again in 1917, and be his ears and eyes when he had to go into hiding. And how fortunate, too, that she could follow him to Siberia; in solitude, the spring might not have been so alluring." Having no wife, Kuntz had given no hostages to the future, and there was a certain wistfulness about these words. Years later I heard he had fallen in love with a girl in old Russia; her family frowned on the marriage, probably because he was only a penniless Jewish tutor, and he never loved again.

Musing pleasantly on spring in Siberia, Kuntz and I were unaware that serious trouble was brewing in connection with the Czechoslovak Legion, which must have been close on our heels and soon would be strung out all along the route of the Trans-Siberian. Here was a mixup that would turn Bolshevik generosity (like their humane promptings in turning loose General Krasnov and the Kadets after the October insurrection) into a disaster they would not soon forget.

The Czech divisions were made up of former deserters from the Austrian armies. They were excellently armed, disciplined troops. They found a refuge in Russia, and by an arrangement among the governments had been allowed to remain there, under the charge of French officers, in Kerensky's day. Early in 1918 the Bolsheviks agreed with French and British representatives to permit the Czechs to travel through Russia to ports from which French ships were to take them to fight against the Austrians and Germans on the French front. Months passed, however, and France did nothing about providing any ships. In February, when an Austrian-picked detachment of Galicians, led by the Rada, advanced on Kiev, Czech volunteers joined some Red Guard troops to fight the oncoming forces. They did not get on well, the Red Guards and Czechs, but no open break developed.

Under the Brest peace treaty, however, the Soviets were obliged to disarm the Czechoslovak Legion. At the same time, the Red Guards were ordered to retire. The result was that the Legion, which had originated among prisoners of war and had been all along generously dealt with by the Russians, became, especially the officers, easy prey to anti-Bolshevik propaganda by French agents. When they were asked to surrender their arms, they declined. The Soviets were reluctant to force the issue. Trotsky guaranteed the Legion full security, and offered its members the opportunity to work and settle in Russia if they wished. With their arms, they began moving toward ports—Vladivostok, Murmansk, Archangel. And just at this time, when they were stretched from the Urals to Siberia and in the north, the rumor factory operating through the Allied embassies in Vologda (as the Robins papers show) sent out alarms: the Bolsheviks were deploying German soldiers in Siberia; they were about to extradite the Legion to the Germans; and so on.

And the Legion, through the ignorance of most of the soldiers and their naïveté as to Allied promises (which never matured; after doing the Allies' dirty work the Czechs were treated miserably by them), took up arms. Throughout Asian Russia the Czech divisions occupied city after city. As I had a personal encounter with the Czechs and the White Guards under Semenov in Vladivostok, I can say with some knowledge that the historians are correct: the Legion and Cossack Ataman Semenov (and his successor, Admiral Kolchak) made common cause.

Even so, there were contradictions. Fortunately, I am a living testimonial to that. Being fought over as to whose prisoner I should be, the Czechs' or the Whites', was not the most comfortable of experiences.

· 18 · Under Fire

In retrospect I suspect that Jack Reed and I, despite all we had learned, were still naïve when we made our respective getaways from the Russian capitals, he from Petrograd, I three months later from Moscow. We still expected our own country to be markedly different from the corrupt old societies of Europe. It took Jack's eight-week detention in Christiania and my baptism of fire in the erupting intervention at Vladivostok to fully sober us.

I was kept waiting seven weeks in Vladivostok. My awakening did not come all at once. I was still not convinced that Lenin's warning had been made in dead earnest, or that he was correct if it was. Kuntz obtained a visa and a ship within a few days, and Kuntz too had been with the International Legion. As for me, the American consul was waiting to hear from Washington before he could visa my passport, but he was most affable. He offered to visit the Japanese consul on my behalf, and did, when a Japanese ship made its appearance. The Japanese consul was most courteous, and did nothing.

Actually, I settled down rather happily to the idea of a lengthy delay, for the book I had been planning all these months was beginning to take shape in my mind, and I felt like writing.

The only trouble was that I found a group of Russian-American Bolsheviks in Vladivostok just as perceptive and warm as those in Petrograd, and here too they were in the thick of things. Through them I met other men and women, returned exiles or natives of Vladivostok. Writing is a painful business at best, and doubly so for one as gregarious as I am.

From the consulate I went to the local Soviet, and the next day to the office of one of two local papers established since Vladivostok's October insurrection, *Krestianin i Rabochy* (*Peasant and Worker*). Here I hoped to locate Arnold Neibut. After the Call for the International Legion, Neibut had run out on us. Where was he? I demanded. As a commander in the new Red Army, Arnold was training new recruits somewhere in the interior, I was told by Jerome Lifshitz, Russian-American who edited the newspaper's "English section."

"Oh, we know you," sang out a young woman, who turned out to be Zoya Ivanovna Sekretaryeva. "The izvoschik laughed and thought your Russian was Chinese when you told him where to take you."

Lifshitz grinned. "Our papers are on the serious side, but since Arnold was fool enough to write the story up, we let it ride. Zoya here had her doubts—it was a little flighty for us—but I see you've disarmed her."

"I don't say that my joke was the funniest in the world; its main virtue was that it was told in Russian. But I'm on your side. I'm quite aware that the average Russian workingman in Petrograd and Moscow reads more serious stuff in the newspapers every day than the average American businessman reads in a month, and I suppose it's the same here. They need a break once in a while. The *Pravda* editors are unconscionably solemn."

I told them how Russian artists talked Bob Minor, the most powerful cartoonist in America before he quit to raise money for the Tom Mooney defense fund, into drawing a cartoon for *Pravda* when he arrived in the spring of 1918. It was a fine cartoon, but the very idea of a cartoon seemed too light for the editors, who stuck it in the most inconspicuous corner they could find.

It is mainly of these and the other comrades with whom I shared so much joy and tragedy before I finally set sail in an old Chinese tub that I want to write in my remaining pages. My own exploits in Siberia, in some ways the most dramatic of my personal experiences in the Revolution, I have explored fully in other writings. Bumping over cobblestoned streets in a car with a revolver stuck in each side of my ribs makes good copy when it's all over with, but once it has been told, there is nothing more to say except that I survived. Most of my Vladivostok comrades, like most of my friends in Petrograd, did not. That is the difference.

I stayed on Russian Island, near Vladivostok, with the family of the newspaper's editor, Pyotr Vasilyevich Utkin, a Russian who learned English as an émigré in Australia, long enough to get a good start on my book. I had with me my little trunk full of notebooks, newspapers, decrees, broadsides, cartoons, photos, and documents. The words poured out without effort on my part. Pyotr, Jerome, and Zoya, who was called Zoya Bolshaya (Big Zoya) to distinguish her from Zoya Stankova, who was called Zoya Malenkaya, or Little Zoya, dragged me out from my lair nevertheless. An eight-hour day was not only on the books, it was *enforced* in Vladivostok, they said proudly—and they made it apply to stranded Americans.

The girls made a party for me at their "commune" at 99 Svetlanka Street. Little Zoya was a member of the city Communist party committee, and the other member of their trio, Tania Tsivileva, was secretary of the financial department of the local Soviet. Jerome Lifshitz and Pyotr were there. We sang revolutionary songs, and before the evening was over I was enlisted as a visiting correspondent. This was Jerome's idea. "But why do you have an English section to the paper anyway?" I asked. And he explained.

As a port of exit, Vladivostok drew all manner of bourgeois citizens hoping to escape Bolshevik rule; many had their bank accounts in other countries. Many of the intelligentsia, Social Revolutionaries especially, were drawn there in hopes of helping the Allies, who would need them if they were counting on overturning the Soviets and establishing any "democratic" government. Otherwise, Russians of *all* classes would resist naked foreign rule. Vladivostok also was a port of entry, to which were flocking even then business entrepreneurs of many lands, Japan, the United States, Britain—anyone who hoped to get a foot in the door leading to the great Eldorado of Siberia with its mines, profitable forests, and other riches in natural resources. Some came hopefully as future shipbuilders, or agents of exporters and importers. Some had come as railway experts during Kerensky's time, like the Stevens Commission, and remained, doing little, and torn by disagreements. And now there were British and Japanese marines camped within the city limits. Yes, I added bitterly, and a U.S. ship now was riding in the harbor of the Golden Horn.[1]

Vladivostok was waiting. The bourgeoisie were coming out from behind their shutters, hopeful now that the foreign forces were there. The workers were wary and the Soviet was vigilant, but they were assured by the Allies, especially the British diplomats, that they were there only to cooperate and to prevent a forcible take-over by the Japanese. Meanwhile it would be useful if I wrote a series of articles on intervention, said Jerome. Most of these visiting firemen read English. Yes, I added, and if Lenin was right, my own countrymen would be there in force before long to add their readership. I would think it over.

Within a few days I met young Konstantin Sukhanov, chairman of the Soviet Executive Committee, a most impressive young man. At twenty-four years of age he had all the coolness and the contained fire of a veteran.

Had I received too glowing a report of how well workers' control was

---

1. Actually the ship, the *USS Brooklyn*, a cruiser, had entered the harbor much earlier. It "was ordered north on January 3, 1918." Williams, *American-Russian Relations*, p. 127. A Japanese cruiser also entered the bay at Vladivostok in January. Christopher Hill, *Lenin and the Russian Revolution*, London, 1949, p. 249. English and Japanese landed forces at Vladivostok April 5, and the Allies landed small forces at Murmansk March 5.

working in their mills and plants? I asked. How did it happen that they seemed to have solved problems that still were serious in Moscow and Petrograd? By now I had mastered enough Russian to be able to get my questions across to him, as well as my congratulations on their adult classes for workers, their strides in setting up a program to eliminate illiteracy, and the functioning of two newspapers, a people's university, and three workers' theaters.

Sukhanov and I were standing on one of the numerous hills on which the city of Vladivostok is situated. We could see a number of the factories, which, with the old workers' homes, were located in the valleys, as in any typical American industrial town. Some of the homes of the rich on the hilltops would gradually be acquired by the government and their extensive lands used for workers' homes and rest homes, he indicated; not everything could be done at once. He pointed out that when they seized power not a drop of blood was shed, but they still faced organized opposition by SR's and Mensheviks in the Soviet. Not all was clear sailing. Yes, it was true they were finally getting ahead with production in the shops, he said.

They followed closely every decree issued by the Executive Committee of the Soviet, every speech of Lenin's. His April 28 article emphasizing the need of introducing cost accounting was not his first on the subject. He first spoke of it in January, and the Vladivostok plants under workers' control (five had been nationalized when management balked at any cooperation; others had partial worker control, with management being retained on a limited basis) already were operating on a strict accounting system. Its introduction, said Sukhanov, had shown that a plant producing plows and rakes was turning out articles that cost more than the same articles had when imported from abroad. Naturally they wanted to correct that—otherwise why make rakes and plows?—so they had put into effect changes necessary to reduce costs. "Even speedup," Sukhanov added with a grimace.

Principally he laid their limited success to the large number of longshoremen, miners, railroad shop repair workers, shipbuilding repair workers, both skilled and unskilled laborers in the basic industries in the city who had taken an active part in the Soviet—a leading part, one might say, backed and encouraged by the Bolsheviks. Of course, the old SR's and Mensheviks, largely intellectuals, were exceedingly vocal in the Soviet, and had opposed the Bolsheviks at every turn. The Bolsheviks had strong allies in the Miners' Union. In all the shops and unions, he said, the workers' class consciousness was sharpened by the presence of returned political émigrés, many of whom were on shop committees.

"Fortunately for the Revolution," he said, "even the intellectuals who escaped from tsarist prison or exile and went to your homeland were forced to make their living as workers, I believe. They returned excellent workers, impatient with our easygoing ways, and they have the respect of the men. We even have a former English professor who was so educated by your homeland that he is now chairman of our Trade Union Council. The Siberian workers are thoroughly Russian in that they are not anti-intellectual. So, you see, America unwittingly helped us. The exiles are able to convince the men that they are the bosses now, and that means they have to practice discipline, streamline production."

As young Sukhanov talked, his seasoned air, his balance and thoughtfulness helped explain how at the age of twenty-four years he was not only president of the Vladivostok Soviet, but a member of the Far Eastern territorial bureau of the Communist party. He was not deliberate—that one associates with age; rather, one felt in him a bold creativeness held in check by caution, which he had consciously acquired. At times his youthful face seemed lined and taut, but the movements of his rather small, well-knit body were never tense, but remarkably swift, lithe, and well coordinated. At rare intervals his laughter burst forth, and with it gaiety and daring lit up his eyes. For all his youth, there was an unmistakable air of command about Sukhanov. He was more solemn than Jerome, who for all his sad eyes loved quips, and liked to feed me exaggerated stories. Jerome insisted, for instance, that after October all the unemployed who roamed the streets at the end of the Kerensky regime were organized by the Miners' Union into councils of fifty or a hundred, given prospectors' equipment, and sent to the gold-rich Amur River. There each man panned gold enough to bring in fifty to a hundred rubles a day. When one of the men brought forth the old Socialist dictum "To each the full product of his labor," it caught on wonderfully. Fought out on the floor of the Soviet, however, they listened to the voice of the majority and settled for fifteen rubles a day.

I asked Sukhanov to tell me about his own and other leaders' backgrounds. A bit defiantly, he admitted that he was from a bourgeois background, as were the others who were students when the February Revolution took place—the three girls and his chief deputy, Vsevolod Sebertsev, whom I also knew by now. Sukhanov's father was more than petty bourgeois; he had represented Nikolai II, sitting as a magistrate when both his son Konstantin and his daughter were found plotting against the Tsar. I am not certain what punishment was meted out by the father, but at the time of the February Revolution, Konstantin had been in prison twice, and was a student in the University of Petrograd, and a Menshevik. He hurried home, and after the Kornilov fiasco became a dedicated Bolshevik.

After October the roles were reversed; the father was accused of plotting against the Soviet, and Konstantin was his judge. Konstantin demurred at imprisoning his father, and I heard no criticism of him for this fact.

Konstantin assured me earnestly that he and Sebertsev and the three girls all had undergone criticism and self-criticism, purged themselves of bourgeois ways of life, and found it surprisingly easy once their income was reduced to that of a proletarian. Indeed, I found them living as austerely as Lenin did. The "commune" held only army cots with straw pallets and a few plain tables and chairs.

All my reservations fled. All my determination to get more than an outline for my book—to complete an entire first draft—went by the board for the time being. I told myself, of course, that there were reassuring details. Had I not found the head of the YMCA to be Fred Goodsell, an old friend? Had not the consul, John K. Caldwell, seemed most obliging? Above all, was it not true that while Lenin's prophecy already was proved in part by the U.S. Navy craft riding at anchor in the harbor, the *Brooklyn*, Admiral Austin M. Knight (commanding the Asiatic fleet, no less) had invited me to dinner on board and plied me with questions about the situation in Russia? All these men took pains to make it clear they disapproved of my ideas, but all assured me they wanted to hear facts; and to show the Admiral's open mind, a copy of Thomas Kirkup's *A History of Socialism* was lying ostentatiously on his desk during our interview.

The truth is I was an internationalist, and for the life of me I could not don and doff the trappings of an internationalist at will. When I asked Sukhanov to tell me frankly what lay in store for Soviet power in the near future in this port more than six thousand miles from the scene where Trotsky was organizing the intensive training and disciplining of the Red Army, he answered:

"What can we do? We have a fine record. Our Red Guards drop their tools and march into the mountains and chase back the most vicious of the several Cossack atamans raiding from Manchuria. They are fine guerrilla fighters. But can we threaten the British, Japanese, and Americans with the rifles of our Red Guards? Can we say to the Czechoslovakian divisions pouring in here—there are about fifteen thousand now and they are still arriving—'Give us the guns you refused to lay down for Trotsky?'"

On May 28 the Czechs, acting concertedly, had overthrown the Bolshevik power in city after city in Siberia. It was quite obvious that Vladivostok's turn was coming.

"All I can say is we are in constant communication with Comrade Lenin." He reminded me Lenin had said in May that "the question of war and peace hangs on a hair both in the West and in the Far East." But, he said, his face gone taut, "Neither do we forget that Lenin said the imperialist rivalry of America and Japan to date has restrained the imperialists from an all-out effort to strangle Soviet power."

I told Jerome I would write a piece on intervention. Jerome said he would print it in two installments, to run on consecutive days. He placed it in a prominent position, but under a pedantic headline, "Some Observations on the Present Stage of the Russian Revolution." I told him he would never make a Hearst headline writer. He laughed. "That's to throw them off. The bigwigs will settle down to read it as if it were a release from Creel's U.S. Information Agency."

By a curious coincidence, the first of the two installments appeared on June 6, the day Robins, Gumberg, and an American newsman, Louis F. Brown of the *Chicago Daily News*, sailed from Vladivostok.

I saw them off at the pier. Robins mentioned my article in the paper. "Look, Williams, don't you *want* to get away from Vladivostok?" he asked, looking stern.

On his way to Vladivostok Robins had received a message, actually from Lansing but cabled by way of Davison, saying his recall was being reconsidered and to remain in Russia for three weeks. It had been sent on May 26; Robins had departed from Moscow May 14. Ambassador Francis forwarded it, then cabled the State Department that Robins' return to Moscow would be interpreted as "American support of the Soviet government, if not . . . recognition thereof." Thus a ship was waiting for him, and while I was unaware of Francis' maneuvering, it was apparent that Robins was being hustled away. Actually in Vladivostok he not only was informed that the State Department wanted him to continue homeward, but was ordered to make no comment for publication until further notice.

Little was said at the pier in regard to U.S. involvement in the intervention, and none as to his plans, but there was no mistaking his gloom as he told me, off the record, that there was small chance the Siberian Soviets could make a comeback alone. Was he still hoping for American rejection of intervention? I could not tell. By the end of May the Czech troops were occupying Cheliabinsk, Penza, Syzran, and Kazan, and in the intervening week the seizure of power in Asian cities was continuing. Robins said only that it was ironic he had been blamed for acting unofficially when everything he did was with the full knowledge of Francis, and now he was being rushed away "because certain Americans are aching to act fast, *before* authorization—in case it does not come." Then he added: "I cannot help you to get a ship, Williams. But people at the consulate inform me your life is in danger from both factions, the Whites and the Czechs—and, they infer, it would be very embarrassing to the United States in the existing delicate situation if you were to be, shall we say, noticeably done in."

I said I would try to save them that embarrassment.

Gumberg eyed me with what was, for him, a not unaffectionate gaze, and contented himself with a mild parting shot. "The trouble with you writing fellows is that it's not enough for you to record history; you insist on making it, too."

He reminded the Colonel that the *Kamo Maru*, on which they were shipping to Seattle, would sail shortly, and that Sukhanov, whom he was careful to identify, and two aides were approaching. As Robins turned away to greet them, Alex lingered for a moment.

"Not everyone can be so modest as you, Alex, or have your talent for making history—but always in the background." I said it in a bantering way, but nevertheless it was true, and I meant it admiringly, too. And his record for doing just this continued until his death. I saw something else was on his mind, however.

"I thought you'd want to know about Reed," he said now with elaborate carelessness.

"Yes, what about Reed?"

"He sailed from Christiania on April eleventh. So he'll beat you home. Thought you'd like to know," he said gruffly.

We shook hands. The Colonel needed him as translator with Sukhanov. As usual, Gumberg became the soul of tact when it was required. The conversation went about like this:

Robins: "If no help comes from the Allies, how long can the Soviet last?"

Sukhanov shook his head and remained tight-lipped.

Robins: "Six weeks?"

Sukhanov: "Not much longer." Then he flushed and looked Robins in the eyes with the frankness that in the young can be so easily mistaken for innocence. Fortunately Robins would not make that mistake. "I assume you mean how long it will be until we are attacked by the Allies, using the Czechoslovaks as their dupes. If it were not for the Allies, and the Czechoslovaks they maneuvered here, we could hold out forever against our own bandit gang, the Whites. Semenov!" he said with contempt. "Where would Semenov be today if he were not being paid by the Japanese? No, we want nothing from the Allies but to be left alone." Then, reverting to the manners taught by his father, he bowed formally. "As for America, we do not yet know, but we do not count her as the other Allies."

I saw Robins' face as he climbed the gangplank, sad, set, his jaw thrust out grimly. For as long as we could see him he stood at the rail looking back at the city that was so many thousands of miles distant from the "iron battalions" of the new Red Army.

Jerome became my almost constant companion whenever I left off writing. I met other Russian-Americans, too, including Aleksandr Krasnoschekov, who, without being named, figures in Major General William S. Graves's remarkable book, *America's Siberian Adventure*. In digging into the records of what Colonel George H. Emerson of the Stevens Russian Railway Commission unwittingly stumbled onto in his efforts to get Allied diplomats to persuade the Czechs to proceed to Vladivostok peacefully, so that Emerson's carful of visiting railway personnel could get through to Vologda, Graves made more than one discovery. One of the first Soviet commissars Colonel Emerson met on this journey in late May is described by Graves as follows:

> When Colonel Emerson arrived at the office of the Commissar [in Khabarovsk, or as he spells it, Habarovsk, on May 20, 1918] he discovered this official spoke English with very little accent, and expressed his surprise at finding a Russian Soviet official in the interior of Siberia with such a thorough knowledge of the English language. The Commissar replied: "It is going some to change from a bum lawyer in Chicago to a Commissar of the Soviets in Eastern Siberia in two months."

After reading the official reports of Colonel Emerson and his powwows with Allied officials and diplomats and Czech officers, who freely spoke of the "new Government" which would come to power, General Graves concluded:

> I am clearly of the opinion that as early as May 28, 1918, there was no intention of sending the Czechs to the Western front. I am unable to say exactly when this decision was made, but it was at least two months and six days before I received my instructions [August 3, 1918, orders written July 17, 1918] in which appeared the sentence, "For helping the Czecho-Slovaks, there is immediate necessity and justification."

The general who led the expeditionary forces to Siberia found this of special interest, as the main reason advanced by those interested in military intervention in Siberia, was the immediate and urgent need for protection of the Czechs who were supposed to be trying to get through Siberia to Vladivostok and then to the Western front where they could join the Allies.

Robins also had met and talked with Krasnoschekov at Khabarovsk, Konstantin Sukhanov said, and asked if I wanted to meet him. Krasnoschekov, who now was no less than chairman of the Council of People's Commissars of the Far East (Dalsovnarkom), with headquarters at Vladivostok, moved around a lot and happened then to be in Vladivostok. By now I had heard many stories of Krasnoschekov, and felt certain of only one thing: he must be an operator of talents that were largely wasted when he was a mere Socialist party organizer in Chicago.

"So how does it feel to be a worker?" I kidded Krasnoschekov when we were alone. I would not have said it in front of the idealistic young Sukhanov. Krasnoschekov had been telling me how he had been most distressed for a time that production was at low ebb, but that now everything was different, shops and factories were doing fine since they offered the *foremen* bonuses when the workers stayed overtime to get out an order.

He laughed easily at my jibe, knowing that I knew he had never been near a shop in Chicago. Unusually tall and slender, and handsome and youthful-looking even years later when my wife and I were on friendly terms with him and his brother Jim in Moscow, he was an impressive man after a fashion. But how different his talk of the workers sounded from that of Sukhanov! He set about telling me earnestly what I already knew—that the party officials there limited their pay to 300 rubles, 200 rubles less than that decreed by Sovnarkom in European Russia, on the grounds that living costs were lower. What he failed to say was that it was the Vladivostok Soviet that put through the cut. If the party regional bureau followed suit, I had a hunch it was not Krasnoschekov's fault.

Like a cat, Krasnoschekov always landed on his feet. Knowing a good thing when he saw it, he had promptly joined the Bolsheviks as soon as he arrived in Vladivostok in July 1917. The party sent him to Nikolsk-Ussurisk, where he made a good record. His star rose rapidly. During the still lenient twenties, when we knew him and his brother in Moscow, they got into some sort of trouble and were "detained" somewhere outside the city limits, but roamed around freely on weekends. We often met them on the streets, and they seemed as buoyant as ever. In the end, like so many, he was a victim of the Stalin purge.

Although I had not met him before my visit to Vladivostok, I had heard the story of "*Nash! Nash!*" and I assured him I would not tell on him if he still passed as a worker. Since he was one of the intelligentsia, as well as a worker, I was careful to add, maybe he could tell me what was going to happen. Were my new young friends, this wonderful Sukhanov lad and the others, going to receive aid in time? They were in an exceedingly ticklish position, it seemed, and invested with great responsibility. Still, might it not be prudent for the leaders to go underground now? He answered in generalities, using the type of jargon that always befuddled me. The relationship of forces was such that the immediate tactics called for a stance of self-confidence and a show of cooperation to meet the formal cooperation being extended by the British, and so on; I could make neither head nor tail of it.

In parting, Krasnoschekov (or Tobinson, as he was called in Chicago) laid a friendly hand on my arm and said, "In times such as these, my dear fellow, there is much solace to be gained by reading Lenin. As soon as it comes out in an English translation, you should read a very early work of his, *What Is to Be Done?*"

As in Petrograd, many of the political émigrés, without ever attaining the heights of a Krasnoschekov, went into the shops and took an active role in the unions. These included Olia Levich, a milliner, Raev Artyshchuk, the Rabizo brothers and Kraizelman, all from the United States, all my friends. Whether the émigrés had been in America, Australia, Italy, or France, exile sharpened them and increased their technical skills and revolutionary techniques. Peter Nikiforov, who later wrote a book on Vladivostok, Yakov Kokushkin, who still corresponds with me, and Dmitri Melnikov, a worker, were political exiles and prisoners together. They had studied mathematics and French, and now the math was useful in setting up accounting systems in shops run altogether or in part by the workers. Melnikov was not a Bolshevik, but when his two pals went into the Soviet, he did too, becoming Commissar of Posts and Telegraph.

A professor of English, Lev Vaks, unlike Krasnoschekov, never hid his intellectual past, but just the same he went into the shops, became a factor in the vanguard, and was chairman of the important Trade Union Council. With his wife, Elizaveta Mikhailovna Dymzen, he had spent some years in America. I liked visiting them, and Lifshitz, Lev, Elizaveta, and I had marvelous talks over tea lasting till midnight. All these people gave me a sense of being surrounded by cultured, warm, sensitive individuals, just the opposite of what one expects to find in Siberia after reading the nineteenth-century Russian masters. When I mentioned this to Lev, he said, "But this is a different Siberia—and a different Russia. The masters were right, and don't forget that a vast amount of the old remains. Chekhov hated passionately the vulgarity, vacuity, and mean pretentiousness of the petty bourgeoisie, in the provinces or in Moscow; he hated passionately the bureaucracy and corruption and shiftlessness; he saw the peasants as corrupted by the church, the bureaucrats, and drink, and the talented people idle and indifferent. Doesn't Lenin hate passionately the same things? He likes both Chekhov and Tolstoi, and he sees the same vision Chekhov puts in the mouths of many of his characters—that someday another generation will know life as it could be, beautiful and good."

I asked Vaks, "Why did Krasnoschekov suggest I read Lenin's *What Is to Be Done?* It must have been written—when? Fifteen years ago?"

Something like that, he said. I told him I had been twitting Krasnoschekov about rising so fast once he decided to become a Bolshevik. Vaks flushed. I could see there was something he took exception to, and thought it was my poking fun. "I'm sure he's able," I said. "It's just that by virtue of having a big party position, he thinks he knows all about shop workers and can tell them what to do. Or peasants. I'm sure he would have had all the answers for them, too."

Vaks was not at all concerned with my explanations; he was, I gathered as he talked, displeased rather with what he guessed was Krasnoschekov's misinterpretation of *What Is to Be Done?* It stuck in my mind all these years because it became the fashion for critics of Lenin to seize on that book. Vaks may have been wrong in attributing to Krasnoschekov any attitude or interpretation; but it fitted in.

Only a superficial reading of the book, Vaks said, could be interpreted as meaning that Lenin intended a small group of leading cadres to make all the decisions and hand them down ready-made to the workers. Lenin insisted on—and this was what divided the Mensheviks from the Bolsheviks—a party organization of professional revolutionaries. Only in this way, in despotic tsarist Russia, could the party work underground without endangering both it and others. Trade unions and other organizations should be as open as conditions would allow. But from the outset—and the book makes the point again and again—more workers rather than more intellectuals should be brought into the leadership, and in no wise should the underground professionals do the thinking for the workers. He himself seized on every letter that came from a worker, studied it, learned from it, was delighted and encouraged at every sign that workers were becoming active in the movement. He constantly warred against the self-satisfaction that certain exiles developed remote from the actual class struggles taking place.

Vaks abhorred any injustice, however, and pointed out it was just possible that Krasnoschekov thoroughly understood Lenin's meaning. In that case, he would think of himself as having been advanced to a position of leadership in an emergency, in order to help train and develop less advanced cadres. "It is true," Vaks said, "he is not a man noticeable for his humility, but then, neither is Lenin. The party does not need at this time men primarily of my own kind, who were teachers, and lacked the boldness—"

But here I interrupted. "Yes, that's all very well, though I must remind you, first, Lenin is a great teacher—and Vladimir Ilyich *always listens*." And I told him of the long wait Kuntz and I had had while Lenin drew out information he found valuable from the two earthy peasants. "I may be wrong. I've only talked to Krasnoschekov twice. But I can't picture him listening to the workers. Why, a fellow like Melnikov, who is thoughtful, not glib, who gets around and listens to the shopworkers, and thinks up ways to save needless duplication of orders and paperwork—he could teach Krasnoschekov a thing or two."

"Still, Albert, we do not know, it may just be that Krasnoschekov wanted *you* to get a true idea of how the party operates, and Lenin's underlying plan as adopted by the Second Congress in London, and set forth in that early book."

"Or how it *should* operate—although all that was for its operation during illegal conditions. It's now the party in power, a big difference," I put in. "But mainly I wanted to say that I've heard Lenin say too many times how slowly the party moves—scolding the comrades, getting them to move, saying the masses are ahead of them, that they are underestimating the revolutionary mood of the masses, and so on."

"At times that is so," said Vaks thoughtfully. "And sometimes that is good, and at other times not so good; it is then our job to hold them back. I am worried now as to what will happen here. The initiative of our workers is so great, the militants on the waterfront are so fearless. They have their government now, free of bosses, and they mean to keep it, and—well, you have seen that American flag on that battleship, and the Japanese guns and the British. And the French are busy with the Czechoslovaks. Will there be a stalemate, each holding the other? Or will they get together and stab us in the back, and if so, will there be a blood bath? I get very worked up inside, and then tell myself I am getting old, I am too fearful. And you, my friend," he said, "you too are like our longshoremen, you take too many chances."

Yet when the time came when I was in trouble—when the Whites had arrested and released me, but I was still subject to momentary arrest or worse—this gentle, modest teacher and his wife hid me from time to time, and it was in their home I spent my last night in Vladivostok.

Riding with Sukhanov and a small group to the Grodskovsky front gave me some idea of how difficult it was for these young activists of the Vladivostok Soviet to come to any real decision on the burning question "What Is to Be Done?" in regard to the immense issue of Allied intervention. Psychologically as well as practically, it was in a different realm from the immediate issue: beating back another invasion of Cossack Ataman Semenov.

Logic might tell us that the two were not separate, that Semenov, in the pay of the Japanese, might also be amenable to the French, that even this action of his might be part of a plan cleared with them, the English, and possibly some of the Americans. The common knowledge Reed and I had of Allied backing of Generals Denikin, Alekseyev, and Kaledin eventually was documented; Consul Poole had recommended that the United States follow suit as long ago as December. It was logical to assume that Semenov also had backing. Semenov repeatedly had been turned back by the Red Guards since January, but always retired into Manchuria to regroup his Hun-Huz bandit and monarchist and Cossack fighters. Next to Denikin, Cossack Ataman General Kaledin of the Don had been the Allies' favored man on horseback to "restore order" in Russia and eliminate the Bolsheviks. Semenov grew more ambitious, more ruthless, and better armed after the events of February 12, however. On that date General Kaledin at Novocherkassk summoned the ruling local Cossack government and listened to Field Ataman A. M. Nazarov report that the Bolsheviks were advancing and were only a few miles from Novocherkassk, and that "the Cossacks do not wish to fight." Kaledin then said in a low voice, "The struggle is hopeless," and resigned as ataman. When the assemblage returned for the afternoon session, they found he had destroyed some papers in an anteroom and put a bullet in his heart.

Now Semenov was making a real grandstand play for the Allies' approval. For two or three days I trailed Sukhanov around the rather extensive front. I was impressed with the large units of Red Guards—mostly mechanics, longshoremen, workers from the railroad yards and factories who had downed tools and started the march up the mountains. *Krestianin i Rabochy* described our visit in formal terms, in its issue of June 20, 1918. I was there as a correspondent, and for once I had a decent camera and was given free reign to take photographs. I talked to peasants and to workers, for most of whom it was not the first time they had met the Semenov bands; usually they made contact in the Manchurian mountains and drove them back. Semenov had skilled guerrilla forces, I said to Sukhanov. "But many are mercenaries," he replied. "How can they compete with our men, who have neither uniforms nor officers, but have a reason to fight, know why they are fighting, and have before them the sacred red flag?" I had made the remark as a reporter does, to bring a response. But before those clear young eyes and the passion in his voice I retreated. It was my last attempt to be an "impartial" observer with Sukhanov.

At the Grodskovsky front I heard men singing revolutionary hymns as they went into battle. There was nothing mournful about the songs. They were sung with defiance and a wholesome righteous hatred and contempt for these Hun-Huz bandits and Japanese mercenaries who dared this impudent invasion. Hearing them, I felt a searing shame for the stupidity of my country. I was convinced now that Robins' recall meant but one thing: that we were joining with the British and French and Japanese to help destroy the Soviets.

"Don't they know that this force is invincible?" I demanded furiously of Sukhanov, forgetting to speak in Russian. The words were incomprehensible to him, but he saw the anger in my face and I saw the surprise in his, but could not stop the outburst. "Oh, they can win for a time. We may be wiped out here, it is possible. But no force in the world can prevail against us in the end if we stick together." I was using the "we" involuntarily, as it was what I felt: if my country went against these workers, these poor peasants like the old man I had talked with over a campfire an hour ago, then I was on their side.

Sukhanov, alarmed that I might be objecting to some point of battle strategy—I, the great organizer of the International Legion—had summoned the translator who rode with us. "I am just saying that if the Western powers intervene, it means the return of the landlords and the capitalists, and then no powerful artillery, no planes or bombs could help them. They would lose in the end. The poor will inherit the earth, and first of all the land of the Soviets. Not because justice always wins, but because they are more numerous and Lenin is giving them the key—the knowledge of their power, their pride in the human condition. And in every land they will learn from you."

Most of the Red Guards were young, so I had taken pains to talk to the old peasant, after photographing him. I asked him what made him come out to the hills to fight. He said, "You see, brother, life in Siberia is not easy. For nine months you battle cold and try to keep the landlord's cattle dry and warm, and never take off your own boots. Then for three months you break your back to plant and cultivate and get the harvest in. I am a hard worker. I had ten children, the game and fish are plentiful, and they ate. But a Siberian landlord will kick and beat you for nothing. It was a dog's life. I asked God why I had these children to grow up to live as I did. Now for the first time I see some sense in it. I feel like things don't have to just happen to me, if you grasp what I mean, brother. I've got some say-so in it. I think my children will have a better life."

In my two days at the front I witnessed a fascinating demonstration of the sagacity of the Vladivostok Soviet. Inasmuch as the Allied consuls, except for the Japanese, were playing a cat-and-mouse game with the Soviet (the British excelled in this duplicity), the Soviet turned to China with special warmth. For a time the Chinese, having been so abominably treated by all tsarist governments, were wary, but the Soviet gave Chinese citizens equal rights with other foreigners, not as inferiors to exploit, but as human beings. Thus a Chinese delegation made contact with Red Army men and declared themselves opposed to the practice of allowing

Semenov to mobilize and regroup his forces in Manchuria and opposed Allied efforts to force China to place an embargo on any supplies for Siberia. "We want our food and produce to go to Russian workmen and peasants," they said.

What I witnessed was a formal (as formal as the battlefront permitted) conference attended by delegates of the two nationalities representing one-third of the world's population. The Chinese were addressed in their own tongue by the brilliant twenty-one-year-old Tunganogi, like Sukhanov the embodiment of young revolutionary Russia. Leading the Soviet delegation was Krasnoschekov, who wound up the extremely practical arrangements for increased cooperation, in which Sukhanov had a hand, with a speech in which he eulogized this brotherly meeting under the open sky, and said, "The Chinese and Russian masses are true children of nature, uncorrupted by the vices of Western civilization, unversed in diplomatic deceit and intrigue."

Beside the Red Guards on our tour of the front we saw the rising units of the new Red Army. Here at least it was an international army, including, importantly enough, Czechs who resisted their officers and went with the Red Army. In all, here and at another front where other Semenov detachments were being driven back, there were some four hundred of these Czechs in solidarity with the Bolsheviks. There were also Koreans, and around the campfires they were reported as saying, "We will fight for your liberty now; someday you will fight with us against Japan for ours."

Semenov was not the only contender for the honors of a Napoleon of Siberia; he was simply the brashest and brassiest to date, announcing his intention of pushing on to the Urals and from there to Moscow and the Kremlin.

No matter how often the Red Guards had to leave their factory benches and their farmwork (as it was June, the sun scarcely set at all, and every minute of daylight had to be utilized on the land), they were fussed over on their return and welcomed as heroes.

I commented to Lifshitz that they must lose a lot of time at work this way, and it all got to be pretty repetitious.

"Maybe so," Lifshitz said. "But each time they come back, we know it will not be long before they have to return to fight. And they know it. So a man can stand being told he's a hero. And words, even words from the heart, are one thing we have in abundant supply," he said a little shyly. "I only wish we had modern guns and bullets and grenades in such amounts."

Their shops were busy making guns, of course, but the really big guns on the fortresses overlooking the harbor, the Golden Horn, had been shipped off to Petrograd much earlier, I believe during the Kornilov adventure in which Kerensky himself was compromised.

There was a certain logic in what Lifshitz said. Something in Jerome reminded me of Voskov. He did not have Voskov's fey humor, but there was a certain tough fiber that was alike in each. I suspected, too, that, like Voskov, Lifshitz was at his best in crises and drooped only when things went well, but I could not prove it as the whole seven weeks I was there the crisis never abated, it only worsened. With Jerome I always felt relatively cheerful, just the same. Although he was seriously handicapped with a wizened body and a back he could not straighten, his gift for looking at facts straight (which he attributed to his Marxism, of course) was such that in his presence I never thought of him as handicapped.

When I was to make a speech before the Soviet on June 9, I asked Jerome, "Isn't it a bit anticlimactic to speak of the need of beating Semenov, when I have just said in two articles printed by your estimable paper that he was completely routed?"

"Of course not. Why do you bother about such trifles? You artists— you want life to reflect your words, rather than vice versa. We may have to rout him once a week from now on. Well, are we going to play it down on that account, and only regard it as news if Semenov wins—in which case we wouldn't have a paper to print the lament? So give 'em hell. Besides, your articles were in English to impress the foreigners, and we hope Woodrow Wilson is reading them now. But your speech will be heard by the men from the docks and the mills."

So I spoke. That was on a Saturday, June 9. And on June 11 in *Peasant and Worker* the speech appeared in full under what even I felt to be a rather provocative headline:

A CALL TO ARMS

They [Semenov's forces] have officers and money; but on our side are both the elemental and the moral forces. They are fighting for the restoration of the old, cruel, despotic order; we are fighting for a new, free, just order. Getting out fom under the lies and slanders with which the Russian Revolution has been covered, the world is beginning to understand what it is striving for: a society without warring classes, where the beaten, despised and oppressed of the earth shall come into their own and by basing things upon the right economics, mankind shall find something besides pretty sentiments in the assertions of human brotherhood.

After saying the workmen's and peasants' revolution of October saved the Revolution from the chasm into which it was heading, I added:

With the most generous cooperation from every side the task of reconstructing Russia would have been staggering. But instead of receiving help, the workers received from every quarter blows and insults. They were sabotaged by the former officials, deserted by the intellectuals, boycotted by the Allies, almost guillotined by the Germans, while almost every so-called liberty-loving citizen from the democracies of the West lent his moral support and sometimes physical aid to their traducers and their stranglers.

But there are no forces that can in the long run crush the Russian Revolution and today the Soviet Government strikes its roots deeper down into the soil of Russia than ever before.

And I wound up:

Your president has just said: "Whoever moves across the frontier line of Siberia threatening the Workmen's Government must die upon the spot!" So say we all of us! He must die or else we must die!

Life is sweet to us: to live in the sunshine; to watch the light play across the waters; to know the love of dear ones—that is all precious. But dearer and more precious still is the brotherhood of humanity; the fate of democracy and the triumph of the International. For these we do not dare refuse to die!

Long live the Soviet Power! Long live the Red Army! Long live the International!

The day after I gave my speech, on June 10, there was a large meeting at Station Square to welcome home other Red Guards. These were a part of detachments from both the Vladivostok and Suchan areas, who with garrison soldiers and sailors of the Siberian fleet had taken part in important actions along the Trans-Baikal area front.

As it happened, this *was* a final routing of Semenov, but unfortunately, other factors than his decisive defeat were involved.

Leading the entire force was a young military strategist, Sergei Lazo, known throughout this part of Siberia for his exploits with a Red Army detachment. Returning for the welcoming celebration were many weary local Red Guards, and among the speeches celebrating their triumph was one by the visiting American correspondent. *Peasant and Worker* was content this time, in its June 12 issue, simply to mention that I also spoke; even Jerome was getting a little tired of my speeches.

The take-over, when it came, was not by Semenov. The Czechs had continued to arrive by the Trans-Siberian until now there were 17,000 in Vladivostok. On June 29, aided more or less openly by the French, the British, and the Japanese, they occupied the city, arrested all the Bolshevik leaders they could lay hands on, hauled down the red flag, and ran up the hated tsarist flag. The Americans too played a part: a cordon from

the cruiser *Brooklyn* surrounded the United States consulate for protection—just in case, I suspected, some members of the Soviet might seek
refuge there.

I felt sick through and through. Was intervention, then, all decided,
even on the part of my country?

As Vaks had feared, the militant dock workers refused to accept this
state of siege, despite the cannons pointing at the city from the harbor
and the rifles in the hands of the Czechs. Charging into the empty Red
staff building where Sukhanov, seated at his desk, had been surprised and
arrested early that morning, these workers held the building for forty-eight
hours, armed only with a few rifles. They shouted defiance fom the windows, sang the English transport workers' song that Vaks had taught them
("Hold the fort, for we are coming! Union men, be strong!"), and were
driven out only when at night a Czech slipped in close to the building and
threw an incendiary bomb through an open window.

The blood bath Vaks had feared ensued. Many were shot as they
stumbled, blinded by the smoke, from the building.

On July 4 we held a Red funeral for them. I say "we" with some pride,
although my part in it was small—merely attendance at an underground
meeting of those comrades who were not in jail, to plan the funeral. Vaks
felt it dangerous for me to go. As chairman of the Trade Union Council,
he was being sought by the Czechs or White Guards or both, and the
party, or what was left of it, had decided he should stay away. I told him I
had been arrested a couple of times, the Czechs had broken into my room
and seized my papers and my book manuscript, and I was tired of hiding;
I was going. He told me I was being "irresponsible," and I flared up and
said that I had the advantage over him, that I did not have to submit to
any party decisions, I made my own.

I thoroughly enjoyed the drama of being led down dark streets and
alleys and into a room little more than a cave, lighted by a single candle.
For all that, once the meeting got under way it was singularly prosaic. No
words were wasted on sentiment. The few there knew time was precious,
and each came with specific proposals.

The funeral itself was so public, with thousands of working men and
women on the hillside silently opening ranks for the red-flag-draped cof-
fins of their comrades, that no attempt was made to break it up. Lifshitz was
in the First Little River concentration camp, as was Pyotr, and the paper
did not come out, so for all I know my chapter "The Red Funeral" in my
book on the Russian Revolution is the only record of it.

Of course, Vaks and I made it up later, and I had to admit it had not
even occurred to me that if I were being followed, I might have caused the
arrest of others.

The last few days I was in Vladivostok, after the funeral, are hazy in my memory. It was at about this time that I learned of Volodarsky's assassination on a Petrograd street on June 21. This news, on top of the events in Vladivostok, and news of the first 150 American marines landing at Murmansk on June 11, left me utterly depressed. How could I go home now to be snug and safe, and leave Sukhanov, Utkin, Sebertsev, Lifshitz, and all the others to God knew what tortures under the White Guards, who would doubtless take over from the Czechs?

My Chinese visa had proved worthless, as it seemed only the British really controlled Chinese shipping; eventually a British visa had come through, but the money I expected from America had not. Should I let the old Chinese liner sail without me? In my low spirits I did not greatly care; why go home if intervention was as certain as doomsday? I asked Vaks. He took me to task. The degree of American intervention was all-important, he said. Public protest would be a big factor, since the Wilson administration all along pretended to believe in self-determination.

A few days before I was to sail, word came to me to meet Big Zoya in the longshoremen's restaurant at Egersheld, the outermost part of Vladivostok. She was beaming; the workers had raised two thousand rubles for my passage home. I explained I could not take it. How could I be sure the money I would send to repay them would ever reach them? I took it in the end. Only in later years did I have proof the money I sent in return reached Little Zoya in roundabout fashion.

By July 9, judging from a newspaper I saved, I must have been in Shanghai, where I spent another month before casting off for the United States. By September 16, when I arrived in San Francisco on the SS Nanking, the entire Far East was occupied by the interventionists, including the Americans, who had landed in Vladivostok in August, as well as in Archangel, and with augmented forces in Murmansk. It is not my purpose to describe the American venture in the Far East or in the north of Russia. That has been done by others who took part. Major General Graves in his book wrote:

"I was commander of the U.S. troops sent to Siberia and I must admit that I do not know what the U.S. was trying to accomplish by this military intervention."[2]

---

2. Even more frank is General Graves's indictment in a personal letter to Colonel A. J. Galen, Helena, Montana, written from Fort McKinley, Rezol, Philippine Islands, August 20, 1920. A copy of the letter was sent to Robins in confidence by Senator Hiram W. Johnson of California. Johnson said, "Of course this letter comes to me confidentially, and you and I cannot at present say anything about it. . . . When Congress meets, I plan to have an investigation of this whole Siberian business—that is, if an investigation will be permitted, by our masters." Graves reveals that when he came to the Philippines "I received a cable

Most of my Vladivostok comrades (not the Vakses or the girls) were killed in the civil war. Their deaths were particularly brutal, incredibly savage, in many cases. I listed a few in *Through the Russian Revolution*, along with those of my Petrograd friends. Over the years I have learned more details from survivors. In bare outline, the roster is:

• Konstantin Sukhanov and Dmitri Melnikov, taken from the First Little River concentration camp, November 1918, supposedly for transportation to prison, marched into nearby woods, and murdered. "I saw the spot where they were killed, and their still warm bodies. They were shot point-blank in the face."

• Vsevolod Sebertsev (as well as Sergei Lazo and one Lutsky, unknown to me), burned alive in the firebox of a locomotive in May 1920, by White Guards, at a railroad station between Vladivostok and Khabarovsk. The Japanese had turned them over to the White Guards.

from the Secretary of War . . . suggesting, not ordering, that I refrain from discussing Siberian matters with anyone."

"The Japanese, I am sure, and the English and French, I believe, became convinced in September 1919, that the sentiment in the United States was such that I must use American troops to fight for the reactionary Kolchak crowd, which included Siminoff, Kalmikoff, Roganoff, etc., or they would have me relieved. In the first place the President, in the latter part of June agreed to give support to Kolchak. This support, of course, did not include military support, because it could not without going to Congress. . . . The Japanese paid Kalmikoff 30,000 yen Sept. 1st, 1919. Sept. 4th Kalmikoff arrested and had beaten severely a corporal of troops on Spasskoe hill. I demanded names of men who arrested this corporal, punishment of men who beat him, the corporal's immediate release, and an apology.

". . . I began plans to arrest Kalmikoff, who was in Vladivostok, but he . . . ordered the corporal released. They said the American corporal was arrested because he had no passport. Rozanoff [in command, at instigation of British Gen. Knox] never apologized, never gave me the names of the men I demanded, but the Secretary of War gave out the statement to the public that Bukmekoff had made suitable apologies. . . . they never were made."

A Vladivostok paper controlled by the Japanese began a "most violent anti-American press campaign," mostly along the lines of reporting "another innocent Russian girl raped by American." When demands that it cease availed nothing, Graves arrested the editor and closed the paper, on advice from other military that it was a Japanese scheme. "If I took no action . . . the prestige of Americans would be injured in the East. If I took action it would help them bring pressure in the U.S. to have me relieved. The State Department stated in U.S. that I was trying to stop the paper because it criticized me, and that I had been ordered to attend to my own business.

"The first was not a fact, and I never got the order. . . .

"The English, Japanese, and Kolchak crowd began pressure in Washington to have me relieved because they could not get along with me. . . . The reactionary State Dept. representatives did not want their own policy carried out but they wanted the Commander to be the goat.

". . . It is unfortunate people of the U.S. do not know the facts. . . . The State Dept. did not seem to have any interest in letting our people have the facts. . . . I cannot see where Germany committed any act any more indefensible than is the act of Japan in Siberia. . . . We have here an excellent opportunity to practice our professed principles, justice, fair dealing, and humanity, because we were instrumental in getting the Japanese into Siberia. . . ."
(Robins MSS)

• Pyotr Utkin, the editor, one of three escaping from First Little River concentration camp January 13, 1920, the following summer was sent to the Japanese command with two comrades as truce envoys. Successful negotiations ended, they were on their way home, on a Japanese train, when White Guards were allowed to seize them and murder them.

I learned little new about the execution of Neibut by the Whites in Omsk in 1919, except that Neibut had continued work there in the underground after Omsk became the seat of the Kolchak government.

Along with all these and with Yanishev and Voskov and Volodarsky, I think of John Reed. Only Reed is well known around the world. Of all the others, only Volodarsky is mentioned in Western histories. Only Yanishev and Reed are buried by the Kremlin's massive wall in Red Square. Heroism was so ordinary in those days and the Bolsheviks were used so unsparingly in the key areas of fighting that most Russian histories, so far as I know, say nothing of Yanishev or Voskov. Several Vladivostok writers have done better by the Maritime Province heroes.

It has often seemed strange to me that I should live so long while these men I loved died so many years ago. If a life is purposeful, death has meaning, so I did not grieve for them, but each death hardened me in my resolve never to betray these men I held dear, or the cause for which they died.

Even now, I cannot help thinking what books Reed could have written. Even now, I cannot look at the photographs of Reed taken in that Finnish prison where he lived on frozen fish for more than two months without wanting to fight his traducers. I look at that face, gaunt and defiant, and feel anger at all those who have tried to show Reed as disillusioned when he died. I was not there, nor were they, but Louise Bryant was—and it was only after her death that the legend of the disillusioned Reed was blown up by those who were themselves disillusioned.

Even now I grieve when I think of the way some of my Vladivostok comrades died. Full-scale intervention struck first at Vladivostok, and lasted longest there. Long after the Kolchak government was overthrown and the British, French, and Americans had largely withdrawn from the Far East, large Japanese forces remained. Not until October 25, 1922, did the Soviet, again victorious, run up the red flag in Vladivostok.

So if I never ceased to feel shame for the role my country played in this joint effort to strangle bolshevism in its cradle and socialism for good and all, and if I helped in some small way to mitigate the guilt of being an American, I am satisfied.

It is quite obvious why critics and historians have invented humane reasons for America's role in the inhumane intervention and boycott of the new and still untried socialist government. For the nub of American foreign policy from 1918 onward has reflected continuing opposition to communism and the aspirations of people for social change. This governed our policy in the Spanish civil war, in the Cuban, and in all true liberation movements in Asia and Africa up to now, the winter of 1961.

The sacrifice of the men I admired and loved in European Russia and in Vladivostok only stimulated me to write and fight against that policy.

Only the death of one comrade, learned of in recent years, served to disorient and paralyze me for a time. I had heard from little Lifshitz in 1920—a cheerful letter despite Japanese occupation and an extra prison term of a few months he had to serve in Vladivostok due to a stupid White slander. Years later, on my last trip to the Soviet Union in 1959, I learned his fate. It seems he moved to Moscow after the liberation of the Maritime Province, and died there in 1937, a victim of the Stalin purges.

I can only say, with Lenin, that it is more interesting to live through a revolution than to write of it.[3] I have been neither a prophet nor a seer; but at that, I came closer than the Americans who at each critical turn of history lost faith in internationalism and socialism itself, and in the Russian people's ability finally to create, as I believe they will do, the socialism Lenin envisioned.

---

3. Lenin's famous Afterword in his unfinished *The State and Revolution:* "It is more pleasant and profitable to go through the experience of revolution than to write about it." (As quoted by Hill, *Lenin and the Russian Revolution,* p. 111.) He stopped in the middle of a sentence to take part in the October Revolution, and never completed the pamphlet, first published in early 1918.

Epilogue

What of the years since? What has happened since Reed and I moved from the periphery of the Revolution to its raging center, and fell in behind red banners whipped in a cold wind, with men marching sublimely out of step, eyes ablaze with a dream of true internationalism?

Not all of the years were as lighthearted for me as when, some nine months after I lost my manuscript in Vladivostok, I began writing it over again in John Reed's little cottage up in the wooded hills over the Hudson River. True, I was suffering from acute sciatic pains, and Jack, with professional flourishes, from time to time would run a flatiron up and down my ailing spine and leg. Our hopes were high and spring was in the air; sciatica was unimportant.

We both had been speaking a lot on Russia, though Jack had begun to turn down invitations in order to do his revolutionary organizing and to write. When I argued that it seemed more important to me to speak than to write, before the country got deeper into intervention and while there was still a chance to influence the government, he demurred. No, I should write more, he would not let me off the hook; there were too few who had been there, I could reach a wider audience in print than by speaking, and besides, Robins now was speaking against intervention.[1] That was why he made me come out to Croton, to see that I sat down and wrote.

1. After Robins testified before the Overman subcommittee of the Senate Judiciary Committee, General Judson not only wrote Robins joyfully congratulating him, but began writing others. Among them was his classmate, General Peyton C. March, Chief of Staff, U.S. Army, at Washington. A copy of a lengthy letter to him marked *"Personal"* was dated May 21, 1919. Speaking of Robins' and Thompson's quick and correct appraisal of the Bolsheviks as the party that would remain in power during the critical period when the Allies hoped to ward off a separate peace, Judson continued:

"Fortunate it now was for America and the allies that Robins was in Petrograd and that

Each of us was making a choice at the time. Mine was to promote U.S. understanding of our embattled comrades and the cause of socialism by trying to reach those not yet won over, primarily the middle class. Reed's was to organize a vanguard movement to make a revolution here. For us both, once we had seen the Revolution, everything else was of secondary importance. Thereafter, for us both, and for the world if it only knew it, all would be changed:

> ... changed utterly;
> A terrible beauty is born.[2]

Each time I returned to Soviet Russia the changes there were startling, and with them came dizzying turns in policy. I first returned in 1922, remaining until December 1927. During those years I was mostly in the villages, teamed up with Lucita Squier, who had gone to Russia in 1922 to do a reconstruction film for the Quakers. We had met and married. Together we covered a good bit of the countryside, often visiting villages separately and then coming together again to pool our findings. Lucita had been trained in films; in fact, she was Hollywood's first "script girl." Now, when the coffers ran low, she would dash over to London and write scenarios to refill them.

When I arrived in 1922, the famine was petering out, but in the Volga villages survivors told tales of stark horror. These I reported without mitigation, and some of the stories are in my *Russian Land*. NEP (the New Economic Policy) had been instituted in 1921; speculation, experimentation, and new ventures were the rule of the day. There was a story in every village street, and I sold all I could write to periodicals like *Harper's, Atlantic Monthly, Yale Review*, the *New Republic*, and *Asia*, a slick-paper monthly that went in for illustrations on a lavish scale.

I felt more at home among the peasants than in the cities. I loved the Russian land itself, and this feeling of kinship with the peasants persisted wherever I went. I ranged from the Karpovo district forest far north of Archangel, traveling six days and nights by boat just as a starter to get there, to villages on the Black Sea and Kahetia in Georgia. But with all due respect to Louis Fischer, who in his 1941 autobiography *Men and Politics* kindly alludes to me as one "who understands what was Tolstoyan

---

he was just exactly the kind of a man he is. His enemies say he is a socialist. I believe him where he says he is not, but I do not give a tinker's dam whether he is a socialist or not. He is certainly a man of very broad human sympathies and very tolerant of people whose theories he can not agree with." In "almost daily intercourse" with "Lenine and Trotsky," and "in perfect sincerity, so far as concerned his own convictions," he "convinced the Bolshevick leaders that the Germans were asking too much; that the Bolshevicks could get better terms the longer they waited; and that the United States would probably assist the Bolshevicks if they came to a final falling out with the Germans. . . ." Judson MSS, Newberry Library.

2. W. B. Yeats, "Easter, 1916."

in the soul of the Russian peasant," practical considerations and logic were involved in my choice. I was less interested in the news of political events, whose sources were in Moscow or Leningrad, than in their effects; and Russia was largely a peasant country. If the great program to achieve socialism begun by Lenin were to succeed, the Revolution would have to be carried to the countryside.

Some of the correspondents, Walter Duranty of the *New York Times* in particular, were enthusiastic over NEP, even to the point of completely misunderstanding it. They were not alone: some of the Bolsheviks had fantasies of endless plenty. Bukharin told the peasants, "Enrich yourselves," and those that could did just that. And more than one old revolutionary seeing the socialist state resort to operations of the market and private initiative, committed suicide rather than acquiesce to NEP.

I had no trouble in seeing the reason for all these early changes. Lenin resorted to War Communism only as a dire necessity, and when he no longer needed it, he abandoned it. With it went, for all time, everyone agreed, the labor battalions about which Jack Reed had interviewed Trotsky; the unfinished piece appeared after his death. The concept that anything other than minimal production in mine or mill could be obtained under force had misfired. Now NEP was used to try to get bread into the cities. Lenin said the danger that capitalism would take over was less serious than the danger that the Revolution would alienate the middle peasant. So this concession to the unsocial, to the primitive acquisitive instincts, was a stopgap, for without foodstuffs the factories would only creep along.

NEP was all right, up to a point. I wanted to see in particular how the inefficient (poor) peasants fared under it. I figured the efficient (middle) peasants would survive; they did, they grew more prosperous, especially when regulations forbidding the sale or leasing of land were modified and the poor leased theirs to the better off. Even the provision denying the peasant the right to hire labor was done away with. As under the Stolypin decrees, the rich grew richer and the poor got children.

In the midst of all the too wild enthusiasm over NEP, Lenin said wryly, when he returned to work in October 1922: ". . . if we work hard enough, we can have socialism instead of NEP." The countryside was burgeoning with little capitalists. The opposition howled. After 1924, the pressure grew to end restrictions protecting the poor peasants, so important a part of the Revolution's first legislation in 1917. Industry's prewar rate of production was regained in 1925. Despite all the inducements of the "free market," under NEP the increase in productivity in agriculture lagged dangerously behind that of factories.

The problems were huge, there were no blueprints, and the debate raged back and forth, shrilly, bitterly. Everyone knew a better means of farming had to be found. Everyone knew the classic Marxist formula for large-scale collectives was the only economic method, but how to achieve it? Trotsky demanded tougher measures for the kulaks. No one precisely defined the kulak, but everyone agreed it was a bad thing to be. Lenin, as early as 1919, had pointed out that some of the measures aimed at kulaks fell as a heavy burden on the middle peasant. Now NEP was turning some of the middle producers into something close to kulaks.

Although Trotsky had been expelled, the opposition—right and left— still was vocal up to the time I left Soviet Russia in December 1927. Some wanted more emphasis on heavy industry, some on consumer goods. And all had ideas of one kind or another about the peasants. When the harvest was good, almost as good as the bumper 1926 yield, and still grain collections that fall were abysmally low, the opposition taunted Stalin, accused him of coddling the kulaks.

A coming change could be felt in the air. Still, at the time I left the atmosphere was quite relaxed. Leniency was curiously mixed but notice- able. Personal freedom involved exemption from reprisal for differing with the majority, even *after* a decision was made. But Lenin's marked tolerance in the arts (even when a work was personally distasteful to him) was beginning to be diluted. As to what should take first priority, differing voices still were heard. Stalin had not consolidated his power.

I next returned to Soviet Russia in 1930. The party, with Stalin over- ruling all attempts at moderation, had made the drastic decision in Decem- ber 1929 to smash through with collectivization of agriculture on a vast scale. At the party congress two years earlier Stalin had expelled the opposition. And now in one fell swoop he was adopting its central feature, and on a massive and ruthless scale that was all the more staggering con- sidering that the first tractors did not issue from the new Stalingrad tractor plant until 1930. (Throughout the twenties tractors were imported from the United States.)

The concept of efficient, large-scale collective farming was familiar to the socialist world, as it had been advanced from the time of Marx, but after Marx's death Engels gave the specifications for converting small peasants: "not . . . by forcible means, but by example and by offering social aid for this purpose." And Lenin in March 1919 drafted a resolution passed by the party that in encouraging agricultural communes of middle peasants, representatives of Soviet power "should not permit the slightest com- pulsion"; those who did, even indirectly, should be "removed from work in the countryside."

I have written in *The Soviets* of the collectivization and described the novel ways in which the kulaks, with the reactionary priests, spread rumors and fears about the collectives. In Tolvin, it was said, the *kolkhoz* president was killed by a cross falling from the skies. Women roused to furious resistance paraded before local Soviets chanting: "Cut off our hands, chop off our nose, but you can't make us join your damn *kolkhoz!*" I recited how the kulaks paid for all this:

The chief offenders and wreckers were denounced by their neighbors. New lists were drawn by the poor and middle peasants. In thousands the kulaks were marched to the stations, under Ogpu guards they were deported to the lumber-camps in the North and new settlements in the far-away steppes and tundras. This in turn brought those who remained up in arms with ax and knife and sawed-off shotguns. In scores the Communist officials perished—waylaid in ambush, clubbed to death, or hacked to pieces. And, throughout the land, the "red cock was set to crowing." . . . two whole intransigent Cossack villages in the Kuban were exiled to Siberia. In some cases ordinary peasants for fighting against the collectives were branded by their neighbors as kulaks and suffered their fate. In many regions opposition took the form of passive resistance. The fields went unsown or unweeded, crops were ungathered or left to rot on the ground to be eaten by mice or gophers. In the wake of this followed what has been controversially called the "acute food shortage" and the "famine" of 1932. In any case undoubtedly many perished of hunger and disease.

And still, when I accompanied three United States Senators into the rolling plains of Vladimir in 1931, the contrast of the pitifully narrow strips and tiny plots of the individual peasant holdings to the unbroken expanses of the *kolkhozes,* and even more, the sight of the women bending double as they reaped rye with sickles, while in the *kolkhoz* a mower sliced it down in wide swaths, left no doubt as to which way would win out. Thus I wrote: "Victory for the collectives, in the last analysis, was due not to the fact that they were backed by the coercive powers and propaganda of the State, formidable as they were. It was because on their side vastly more formidably were arrayed the machines, the forces of science and technique."

Just the same, I could never reconcile myself to the use of force to accomplish this revolution in agriculture. In the Stalin-approved, if not Stalin-written, *History of the Communist Party of the Soviet Union* (1939), it is said on the elimination of kulaks as a class: "The distinguishing feature of this revolution is that it was accomplished *from above,* on the initiative of the state." Of course, it added that millions wanting to throw off "kulak bondage" supported it from below.

It was a far cry from Lenin's constant call for "initiative from below," in the much darker days of 1918. Coercion had failed in the labor battalions. What would be the long-range effect on the countryside? It was another blunder, born out of the exigency of the moment. Lenin himself had often followed a pragmatic course, he had made many compromises, but he had always labeled them compromises and insisted there be no illusions about them. He admonished party organizers in the NEP period not to be complacent and to remember that "among the people we are as a drop in the ocean, and we shall be able to administer only when we properly express what the people realize."

So I was not unused to swift changes of policy in the U.S.S.R. When I returned in July 1937, expecting to stay a year or more, I reminded myself of this. History is not like a buffet, permitting one to pick and choose the dishes that please him. It was too much to expect that all would be good and beautiful. I remained no later than mid-March, however. This was a time unlike any other for me in Soviet Russia. Always before, I had seen the reasoning behind developments—even when I regretted the methods, as in 1930–31. Now I felt baffled.

In *The Soviets,* published that same year, I had written, rather lightly, I now felt: "Like a republic, a revolution is ungrateful. It devours its own children. It has to." This saying now struck me as something other than an aphorism. I had written that factionalism, "which, in the eyes of the party, is the seven deadly sins rolled into one," had brought the downfall of "Trotsky and his Left Opposition with its demand for more 'democracy,' more drastic measures against the kulaks, and its insistence on 'world revolution.'" And I had inserted a few lines on the two trials of Zinoviev, Kamenev, and the others (there were sixteen in all) who in 1936 were condemned to be shot after "their own confessions that they had 'planned and directed the murder of Kirov as well as assaults on other Soviet leaders.'" Briefly I mentioned the 1937 trial in which Radek, Piatakov, and Sokolnikov (and thirteen others) confessed to terrorism and sabotage in a Trotskyist plot to seize state power with Nazi agents.

The purges were continuing, however, and I could no longer be so detached as I had been when I was writing of them at a distance. It was not only leaders who were being accused and tried. For two months after I arrived I roamed through the provinces. Even in the villages I saw mention in the press almost continuously of trials against local defendants.

In Moscow I saw the splendid Red Square celebration of the Revolution's twentieth anniversary on Sunday, November 7. Too soon, however, the glow of the demonstration and the three-day festivities was over, and I was again reading reports of more trials.

Of course, there was a struggle for power going on, but it was much more complicated than that. Great questions were at stake on which might depend the socialist state's survival. As in the days of Brest, there were those who felt that the kind of socialism that survived was more important than survival itself. Always before, when the wind shifted and the ship foundered, it eventually was brought back to a socialist course. A man was at the helm now, however, to whom the heavy outlines of the channel were clear, and he meant to move in a straight line, as fast as possible. He had put in effect collectivized agriculture; now he would drive ahead just as ruthlessly to speed up industry.

In Lenin's thoughtful "Last Will and Testament," addressed to the Central Committee, given to Krupskaya in December 1922, not to be opened until after his death, he warned of the weaknesses of both Trotsky, overaddicted to the administrative end of things, and Stalin, who as general secretary of the party had "concentrated tremendous power in his hands, and I am not sure he always knows how to use that power with sufficient caution." Then, after Krupskaya had an unpleasant experience with Stalin, Lenin added a postscript on January 4, 1923:

> Stalin is too rude, and this fault . . . becomes insupportable in the office of General Secretary. Therefore I propose to the comrades to find a way to remove Stalin from that position and appoint to it another man . . . more patient, more loyal, more polite, and more attentive to comrades, less capricious, et cetera. This circumstance may seem an insignificant trifle, but I think from the point of view of preventing a split and from the point of view of the relation between Stalin and Trotsky . . . it is not a trifle, or it is such a trifle as may acquire a decisive significance.

After Lenin's death, Krupskaya was outmaneuvered by the "triumvirate," Stalin, Kamenev, and Zinoviev, and prevented from carrying out Lenin's wish that the letter be read to the next party congress. The letter was published in the Soviet Union in 1961, some eight years after Stalin's death; Max Eastman had revealed the fact of the letter here in 1926.

On the surface all of Moscow went about its business as usual. On the streets nothing hinted at concern on the part of the people: no gathering crowds, no unusual traffic. Certainly the government was at the peak of its powers. It was to be expected that there was great fear of Nazi Germany and the imminence of war. Were all the plots and counterplots charged against the imprisoned or executed men real, was there actual danger that the Soviet government might be overthrown?

Certainly from the economic viewpoint all looked well for once. The success of the Five-Year Plans was writ large. On all sides one heard admissions of Stalin's triumphs on that score.

I decided to look up old Reinstein. I could speak frankly with him, and surely he would trust his old protégé of 1917. What about all these confessions? I asked. "Why would they confess unless they were guilty?" he replied.

Not all had confessed, however. Old M. P. Tomsky, who headed the Trade Union Central Committee from October 1917 until 1929, had been charged as a member of the "Trotskyite-Zinovievite center" in 1936, and committed suicide rather than face arrest and disgrace. But Reinstein was a true believer.

To whom else could I go? I still wanted to unearth what lay behind the stated reasons, if anything. I was not willing to throw in the sponge and attribute everything to an inscrutable, Kafka-like system that stood above rational questioning. It was too contradictory, when one knew that by the very success of its central planning, the superiority of a socialist economy over capitalism was impressing itself on many who were shaken by the depression years. Nor was I willing to shrug my shoulders and say, "Well, power corrupts." Lenin had not been corrupted.

Lucita and I had known Commissar for Foreign Affairs Maxim Litvinov and his wife rather well. Litvinov was in Geneva, though, except for a very few days in November when he rushed into Moscow and out, headed for a Brussels conference. Aleksandra Kollontai was in Sweden as ambassador. Chicherin was dead, and so were Lenin's sisters.

Better to see someone high in authority, Andrei Zhdanov or Abel S. Yenukidze. In the end I went to see Abel. A hearty, big blond Bolshevik from Georgia, Yenukidze was Commissar for Heavy Industry and Secretary of VTsIK (Central Executive Committee). It was good to see him again, but again I had the disturbing feeling that here was a man who was unable to grasp all that was going on. Of course I had no inkling, and I doubt very much that he did, that he would be seized and executed, reportedly in prison, before the end of the year. Later, Zhdanov also was liquidated.

Before I left Moscow, I spent a day roaming through art galleries, trying to get my bearings. I spent the day alone, staring unseeing at the crowds. I felt I had to resolve in my own mind my relation to the Revolution, and I found myself thinking insistently of Lenin, of Reed, of those long-ago days of certainty and soaring hope.

If I had taken Lenin up on that offer of a study class in Marxism, would I be better prepared to understand the reason for the enormous power of the secret police and the use of official violence against Communists in a socialist state now without question a world power? Was there a Marxist explanation? Or was it a distortion and violation of what Marx

330 • JOURNEY INTO REVOLUTION

and Lenin taught? The thought of the study class recalled Lenin's sensitiveness and consideration of others. How anxious he had been that I should feel under no pressure! Not then nor at any time since on Russian soil had any Bolshevik ever asked me if I were or were not a party member. They trusted me.

Lenin had written, in a preface to Reed's *Ten Days,* that Reed understood and explained the dictatorship of the proletariat. Remarkable, it seemed to me now in 1937, thinking back twenty years, that we both had grasped it, unread in Marxism as we were.

I expect to be judged by my time, which stretches into other decades. Why after 1937–38 did I never write critically of what was happening in the Soviet Union? There are two main reasons. In 1938 the foreign policy being pursued by Stalin was a principled one, and so far as I could see far more so than that of America, England, or France. We had failed to lift the embargo on arms to Spain, and Russia was giving help to the Loyalists. The Spanish war and the crushing of the Republican government by the elite troops of Hitler and the planes of the Nazis and Mussolini virtually ensured World War II. And at the time the Soviet Union was helping China with arms and matériel in its fight against Japanese aggression. It had supported Czechoslovakia when France welshed on its pact with the Czechs. Then came the days of the Soviet-Nazi pact, and I would not have added to the hysteria that swept this country against everything communist. I have only to remember the equating of "communist" and "fascist" and the word "totalitarian" to be sure I was right. And then the U.S.S.R. was attacked and I spoke gladly and widely for Russian War Relief, and the war eclipsed all else in importance for me.

In 1959 I returned to Moscow with Lucita, as guests of the Writers' Union. I spent several months in the Kremlin Hospital under the care of Russian specialists for lukemia, and credit them with prolonging my life by at least two years. During our visit we found that many people, especially among the armed forces, had returned from exile when Hitler attacked Russia. But I didn't go around asking about the purges or about who had been rehabilitated. The key word everywhere was *peace,* and let's forget about the hard times brought on by the war.

As to my own inconclusiveness in assigning reasons for what happened, anything more searching must depend on a deeper analysis than the Khrushchev report, and it can be undertaken only by the Russians themselves.

Finally, if I have remained true to the Revolution and still look forward to the final triumph of socialism in the world, it is because, like Lenin, I do believe in the essential goodness of man. It is not capitalism that holds the key to the future. And if the socialism produced in the short term of forty-odd years is not foolproof, we bear a large responsibility for the past, for if bolshevism was not strangled in the cradle, it was not the fault of the democracies. The most talented young Bolsheviks ended in unknown graves on the many fronts during intervention, and, left with too few Bolsheviks to do the work of administration, Lenin worked himself to death. And the evils of our foreign policy during those years have continued as a dark shadow over both America and Russia.

Since the October Revolution the world has never been the same. Despite all the mistakes and all the fear and all the ruthlessness, the Revolution by its mere existence hastened the stirring of the Asian peoples and inspired the Cuban revolution and the awakening of the colonial peoples of Africa and Latin America. The center of twentieth-century civilization has slowly been shifting from the West and will do so increasingly.

Neither Jack Reed nor I saw the final development of the Revolution's grandiose aim, the total transformation of man. The important thing was that, imperfectly realized, the goal remained as the perdurable concept of an end to man's inhumanity to man. It was what had made socialism alluring to me in the first place.

Philips Price and I, when exchanging books, like to inscribe them with Lunacharsky's lines:

> Out of the tears and blood of generations
> Mankind shall yet blossom—innocent and wise—
> And thou, my Planet, freed from abominations,
> A green-jade star in the moon-silvered skies.

I feel sure that Price, like me, would not claim that our planet is yet freed from abominations. But the goal is there, illumined, illuminating, matchless in its radiant portent.

Index